Ideologies in Action

Walter de Gruyter
1749
250
1999
Berlin · New York

Language, Power and Social Process 3

Editors

Monica Heller
Richard J. Watts

Mouton de Gruyter
Berlin · New York

Ideologies in Action

Language Politics on Corsica

by

Alexandra Jaffe

Mouton de Gruyter
Berlin · New York 1999

Mouton de Gruyter (formerly Mouton, The Hague)
is a Division of Walter de Gruyter GmbH & Co. KG, Berlin.

Library of Congress Cataloging-in-Publication Data

Jaffe, Alexandra M. (Alexandra Mystra), 1960—
   Ideologies in action : language politics on Corsica / by Alexandra
Jaffe.
      p.   cm. — (Language, power, and social process ; 3)
   Includes bibliographical references and indexes.
   ISBN 3-11-016445-0 (cloth : alk. paper). — ISBN 3-11-016444-2
(pbk. : alk. paper)
      1. Sociolinguistics — France — Corsica.   2. Corsica (France) —
Languages — Political aspects.   3. Language planning — France —
Corsica.   I. Title.   II. Series.
P40.45.F8J34   1999
306.44′0944′945—dc21
                                                        99-32850
                                                        CIP

Die Deutsche Bibliothek — Cataloging-in-Publication Data

Jaffe, Alexandra:
Ideologies in action : language politics on Corsica / by Alexandra
Jaffe. — Berlin ; New York : Mouton de Gruyter, 1999
   (Language, power and social process ; 3)
   ISBN 3-11-016444-2 pbk.
   ISBN 3-11-016445-0 cloth

Printing: Werner Hildebrand, Berlin.
Binding: Lüderitz & Bauer GmbH, Berlin.
Printed in Germany.

Acknowledgements

The writing of this book has spanned many years. I want to thank Bill Graves and Bonnie Kendall for encouraging me in the early stages of writing about Corsica. In the last year, Shana Walton has been an invaluable critic: generous in her support, incisive in her commentary and relentless in her editing (all misplaced commas, however, are my own). Research for this book has been carried out with support from the French Government *Bourse Chateaubriand*, the National Endowment for the Humanities, and summer research stipends from Cortland College.

En Corse, je tiens à remercier beaucoup de gens, certains qui ne sont plus avec nous, sans lesquels ce livre n'aurai jamais vu jour. Je ne prétends pas pouvoir les nommer tous, et j'espère que ceux qui ne figure pas sur cette liste me pardonnent. D'abord, je remercie tous les habitants de Riventosa pour l'acceuil et l'amitié qu'ils nous ont offerts et en particulier, César et Francescha Pieri, Michel Ristori et famille, Julie et Dominique Pasqualetti, Pascal Alberti (et famille), Gaston et Cathy Murraciole, la famille Perfettini, les Ordioni, Jacqueline Luiggi, et Martine et Jean Casanova. Je remercie les Franceschini de Listinchellu, Noëlle Vincensini, et la famille Vincensini de Pietrosu, et Maria et Charles Sansonetti de Venaco. Je remercie tous ceux qui m'ont accordé des entretiens et qui m'ont aidé à distribuer mes sondages sociolingustiques. Beaucoup de gens m'ont aidée dans mes recherches de maintes façons, parmi lesquelles Jacques Thiers, Jean Chiorboli, Jacques Fusina, Jean-Joseph Franchi, Francette Orsoni, Georges Ravis-Giordani Petru Casanova, Lisandru Bassani, Jean-Marie Arrighi, Toni Casalonga, Nicou Maraninchi, Paul Simonpoli du PNRC, Christian Peri et Jackie Emmanuelli (merci pour les corrections). Je remercie l'Université de Corse pour son soutien et son acceuil depuis 1988; en particulier l' Institut d'Etudes Corses; l'IDIM, tous ceux qui travaillent à la Bibliotheque di U Palazzu, , et tout le personnel de la Bibliothèque Universitaire. Egalement, je veux reconnaître le soutien de l'Assemblée de Corse, du CCECV, de FR3 Corse, de RCFM, de Scola Corsa di Corti (et M. J-B. Stromboni), de Scola Corsa di Bastia (et M. F. Perfettini), et de l'ADECEC.

Finally, a thanks to my husband Jeff Pachuilo, for being there.

Contents

Acknowledgments   v

1 Introduction 1
   1.   Introduction 1
   2.   The ethnographic process: methods and relationships 2
   2.1. Village life 2
   2.2. Language planners   3
   3.   Language in Corsican society: central, complex and contested 6
   3.1. Vignette 1: In two language classes 7
   3.2. Vignette 2: The politics of orthographic identity 9
   3.3. Vignette 3: One nationalist's struggle: language in the politics of
        identity vs. language in everyday life 11
   4.   Metadiscourse, language and political economy 14
   4.1. Language and political economy 16
   5.   Diglossia 18
   6.   Resistance 20
   6.1. A typology of different kinds of resistance 23
   7.   Radical models of resistance: challenging dominant assumptions 29

2 Social space and place: models of identity 33
   1.   Geography: social and linguistic space 35
   2.   The village 37
   2.1. Vignette 1. Pierrette 37
   2.2. Vignette 2: Paul 38
   2.3. Vignette 3: Jean 39
   2.4. Vignette 4: Michel Mallory 39
   2.5. Vignette 5: Henri, and others 41
   2.6. Summary: language and the village 43
   3.   History, social relations and identity 43
   3.1. Outside rule 44
   3.2. Kinship and "the clan" 46
   4.   The diaspora 52
   4.1. The "unbroken cord": inalienable identity 53
   4.2. Ambiguous status and ambivalent reactions 59
   5.   Corsican nationalism 66
   6.   Conclusions 69

3 Language shift and diglossia: ideology, history and contemporary practice . 71
   1.   Corsican and Italian: a classic diglossic relationship 71
   1.2. Corsican and Italian verbs 74
   1.3. Articles and endings 74
   1.4. Vocabulary 75
   1.5. Pronunciation 75

1.6. Summary 76
1.7. Diglossia with Italian vs. diglossia with French 76
2.   French linguistic politics 77
2.1. Language and nation 78
2.2. The role of the schools 80
2.3. Language and cultural integration 83
2.4. The military: national service and the mother tongue 84
3.   Sociolinguistic effects of French language domination 86
3.1. Prestige and insecurity 86
3.2. Language shift: compartmentalization of language use by age 87
3.3. Domains of practice: inner and outer sphere 92
3.4. Gender 103
4.   Codeswitching and language mixing 108
4.1. Conscious language choices and an "alternative market" 110
4.2. Heterogenous practices 110
5.   Contact-induced varieties 112
5.1. *Le Français régionale de Corse* 112
5.2. *Francorse* 114
5.3. Gallicized Corsican 115
6.   Conclusion 117

4 Language Activism Part I 119
1.   Introduction 119
2.   Language and nation: biological versus strategic essentialism 122
3.   Overview of language activism and language legislation 126
3.1. The seventies 126
3.2. The eighties 128
3.3. The nineties 130
4.   Major themes and debates in Corsican language activism 131
4.1. Differentiation from Italian: pragmatics and ideology 132
4.2. Language unity: the drive for elaboration 144
4.3. The boundary with French: the "purists" vs. the "sociolinguists" 146
4.4. Critical grammar as synthesis 156
5.   Conclusions 157

5 Language Activism Part 2 160
1.   Introduction 160
1.1. Background for the debates: the early eighties 161
1.2. Sources of data and survey results 162
2.   Support for mandatory Corsican 163
2.1. The primordial link 163
2.2. Acknowledging language shift: a sense of urgency 165
2.3. The pragmatic effects of symbolic action: legitimacy and language
      attitudes 167

2.4.   Summary 169
3.   The argument against mandatory Corsican: "choice" and oppositional
        value 170
3.1.   "Choice" and language hierarchy 172
3.2.   "Choice" as the cornerstone of language value 172
3.3.   The discourse of "choice": Corsican identity and the rejection of that
        which is imposed 174
3.4.   Choice and the mother tongue 176
4.   Lingua Matria 177
5.   Coofficiality 179
6.   From diglossia to polynomy 185
7.   Conclusions 189

Chapter 6   Language learning: its social evaluation and meaning 191
1.   Reactions to a foreign learner: boundaries and community 192
1.1.   The underestimation of competence 193
1.2.   The exaggeration of competence 195
2.   Social drama: learners as performers 196
3.   Myths of acquisition: more boundary maintenance 198
4.   The Corsican learner: problems of identity 200
4.1.   The problem of the "prise de parole": inauthenticating error 201
4.2.   Learner's Corsican 205
5.   Pedagogical strategies 206
5.1.   A sociolinguistic approach to variation and authenticity 207
5.2.   Sociolinguistic choices 208
5.3.   Limits to "choice": linguistic judgments in the classroom 209
6.   A return to the problems of linguistic and cultural boundaries 210
7.   Conclusions 212

7   Cracks in the public performance of Corsican literacy: the Second
Annual Corsican Spelling Contest 214
1.   The meaning of orthography 215
1.1.   The role of writing in minority language promotion 215
1.2.   Internal coherence: Corsican as an autonomous code 219
2.   The symbolic meanings of the Spelling Contest 221
2.1.   The cracks in the mirror 222
2.2.   The role of writing 223
2.3.   Language and social hierarchy: the question of elitism 227
2.4.   "They" have an academy: the question of linguistic authority 229
2.5.   Language standards and linguistic alienation 233
2.6.   Regional diversity vs. a standard orthography 238
3.   Conclusions 245

8   Moving language off center stage: media and performance 247
    1.   Radio: *Radio Corse Frequenza Mora* 248
    1.1.   Contests and standards: *A Ghjustra Paesana* and *l'Accademia
           di i Stralampati* 249
    1.2.   Language alternation and language mixing on the radio 253
    2.   Corsican reimagined: reference to Italian and other languages 258
    2.1.   Italy on the radio 260
    3.   Theater and storytelling 261
    4.   The newspaper 263
    5.   Some persistent "old" politics of representation at play in the media . 264
    5.1.   Sociolinguistic responsibility vs. professional ideals 265
    5.2.   Popular purism: reactions to codeswitching and neologisms 267
    4.   Conclusions 270

9   Conclusion 271
    1.   Responding to dominance: stances and consequences 271
    2.   Applying dominant models of language to minority contexts 272
    3.   Lived experience and the persuasive power of dominant discourses . 275
    4.   Problems of legitimation 276
    4.1.   The absence of an Academy 277
    4.2.   A short literary history 277
    4.3.   Linguistic value and identity as local and oppositional 278
    4.4.   Lack of a strong base of oral practice 279
    4.5.   The politicization of language and language choices 280
    4.6.   No social or economic coercion 281
    5.   The production of authoritative discourses 282
    6.   The role of ethnography in the comparative project 284

Notes 286

References 294

Name index 313

Subject index 317

Chapter 1
Introduction

1. Introduction

This is a book about language practices and language ideology in Corsica. Its specific focus is on language planning: the efforts made by Corsican cultural activists to reverse the process of language shift from Corsican (the minority language) to French (the dominant language). I look at the ideological under-pinnings of the strategies of language planners and explore how these ideologies of language are historically rooted in European and French political economies. Here, there is ample debate, since Corsican cultural activists do not agree about the best way to resist language domination. I emphasize that the divergent positions that they take are all equally coherent responses to dominant language ideologies and their effects on people's lives. This book does not, however, just focus on language planning from the perspective of a small group of activists; it also looks at the effects of dominant language policy and minority language activism on popular practices and attitudes. Of particular interest is the fact that there has been a good deal of popular resistance to fairly conventional minority language planning strategies. I make the claim that these negative popular responses are related in complex ways to the ideologies of language that contributed both to language shift and to language planners' efforts to reverse that shift.

The ethnographic focus of this book is on the lived experience of language ideologies and linguistic policies. That is, it looks at the way that political economies of language are translated into explicit policies and implicit assumptions that shape individual experiences at the local level. It is an ethnography of the concrete ways in which ambient ideological structures shape language attitudes and language practices, with a particular emphasis on enactments of linguistic and social identity. The Corsican political economy of language is in large part defined by the language ideologies and linguistic policies of the French state that are embedded in social institutions like the school. It is also defined by local reactions to language domination. These reactions include a variety of forms of accommodation and resistance. In the last thirty years, Corsican nationalists have made language issues a central part of their political platform. Their emphasis on language to justify claims on cultural identity and political autonomy has become part of Corsican popular consciousness. Since the mid-eighties, the emerging insti-tutionalization of Corsican in literary and educational domains has also shaped the political economy of Corsican. This economy is also, of course,

intimately connected to extralinguistic political, economic and social structures and forces which I evoke in my ethnography of language choices and
attitudes.

At the same time as the data in this book illuminate the particularities of
the Corsican situation, they also raise a much broader question: under what
conditions can dominant ideologies of language and identity be resisted or
transformed? I propose an analytical typology in which I distinguish between
a "resistance of separation," a "resistance of reversal"and a "radical resistance". These different strategies are described in detail below; here let me
just point out that what distinguishes them is the extent to which they accept
or challenge dominant language ideologies. Case studies in the book illustrate
the limitations of resistances of separation or reversal and explore the difficulties of putting into practice forms of resistance that *do* challenge deeply
rooted monocultural/monolingual models of identity. Here it should be clear
that I view language use and discourse about language as fundamental forms
of social agency. It is in discursive space that social identities are proposed
and negotiated in interaction, and where moral and political orders are established and contested (see Cameron 1995; Fairclough 1989; Hymes 1996;
Poche 1987: 73).

2. The ethnographic process: methods and relationships

In my fieldwork, I engaged with two kinds of linguistic practices: everyday,
largely unconscious patterns of speaking and relatively self-conscious
discourses about language. My learning and observation took place in a
variety of contexts, but the two most important social milieux I belonged to
were the village where I lived and Corsican academic/cultural circles.

2.1. Village life

During the fourteen months I spent on Corsica, I lived in a small village called
Riventosa (with a population of about 100 permanent residents) that was 11
kilometers from Corté, a town of about 5000 permanent residents where the
University of Corsica is located. Because of patterns of residence on the
island, it can be argued that the Corsican village is a microcosm of the larger
society. On the weekends, the villages are populated by their native sons and
daughters who live and work in the two major cities on the island during the
week. In the summer, the population swells (in Riventosa's case, to over 200)
with Corsicans who live "on the continent" (the French mainland) the rest of

the year. Between these two groups and the permanent, working-age residents, a wide variety of professions were represented in Riventosa: nurse, school-teacher, road crew, plumber, university administrator, shepherd, herb farmer, hotelier, mechanic, builder, delivery driver. Like other villages, the majority of the population was retired, many from various branches of civil service. By 1988, Riventosa also had a fair number of young couples with children–enough to warrant the reopening of the village school several years earlier. Living in a village gave me the opportunity to make more than a casual observation of how much Corsican was spoken by what categories of people, and to find out what an average cross-section of the population thought about some of the public, political issues surrounding Corsican language use. It was also in Riventosa that my husband and I developed a small number of close, sustained relationships and friendships with people. Being with and observing the same people over time, in a wide number of situations, provided an image of Corsican language practice that was a critical backdrop to my observations of linguistic practices in a variety of social circumstances and to my collection of metalinguistic commentaries in questionnaires and interviews of relative strangers.

Village life was important both as a kind of Corsican experience and as a locus of meaning for Corsicans themselves. Living in a village was a signi-ficant point of reference for understanding and being able to talk to Corsicans about Corsican social and linguistic experience. Some of this significance is geographical. Many of the villages of the mountainous interior are remote; separated from the coastal cities by miles of winding roads. In the past, many Corsicans never traveled far beyond their own small canton. While this is less true today, many people in Riventosa were unfamiliar with other parts of the island. In a general way, these limits on experience have contributed to the way that very local attachments to place have characterized Corsicans' experiences of and ideas about being and speaking Corsican. For many Corsicans I spoke to, the village experience was in the common idiom that they used to talk to each other about identity and belonging.

2.2. Language planners

Another very large part of my fieldwork was devoted to the ethnographic study of Corsican linguistic and cultural activism, a domain of practice as "real" and compelling as the village context. The University, especially the Corsican Studies Institute, was a prime location for studying Corsican activism from the inside, since many militants were also students and teachers. It was also a place where I could maintain contact with Corsican researchers studying language and culture. I took Corsican classes offered in both the Corsican Studies Center and the School of Social Sciences and Humanities, and I went to student meetings and other University events. While the students in the Corsican Studies Institute were often highly politicized about Corsican language and identity, this was not the case for the rest of the students at the University. Taking part in the life of the University as a whole gave me a chance to observe the language practices and attitudes of a wide cross-section of Corsican youth.

Riventosa's central location proved to be a great advantage: I was a little over an hour by car from either Bastia or Ajaccio (the two major cities). This put me within reach of most of the political, cultural and linguistic events that took place on the island. I went to meetings of linguistic associations and attended private language classes they offered. I took part in some of the meetings of the Language group of the CCECV(*Conseil de la Culture, de l'Education et du Cadre de Vie* [Council of Culture, Education and Quality of Life]) at the Corsican Regional Assembly and did some translating work for them. I attended public sessions of that Assembly; went to film festivals, book fairs; literary gatherings; political meetings and festivals; public debates and colloquia; conferences; musical; dramatic and humorous performances; visited Corsican language classes in elementary schools; and observed and interviewed radio and television professionals. I was fortunate to arrive in the summer, when political and cultural activity peaks, for the abundance of public events provided me with an easy initial access to various aspects of the culture before I really got to know anyone. My attendance at this broad spectrum of events allowed me to observe the core members of the *culturels* 'culturals' (as they often called themselves) over time and in a variety of circumstances. This small (50–100 people) dedicated group of teachers, authors, artists, performers, amateur linguists, film makers and broadcasters involved in the promotion of Corsican culture was my other "village," and it came complete with all the constraints on individual action that the intense familiarity and interdependence of social relations in a village imply. Despite a few people who quite understandably resented my presence, my faithful involvement in the cultural life of the island was more often interpreted as a sign of commitment, and many of these people became acquaintances and friends and confided in me. This experience gave me an opportunity to observe the internal dynamics of the group, and to situate some of the debates that divided its members in the context of personal, political and professional relationships among its members. I also got a good sense of the often frustrating relations the group had with the rest of Corsican society–from the passive resistance of ordinary people to any measures or policies that challenged their sharply compartmentalized images of the value of Corsican versus French, to the active opposition or inactivity of local, regional and national politicians on legal/institutional matters.

2.2.1. Language politics and fieldwork practice

Here, I should say something about the nature of my involvement with this group, for the ethnographic study of academics/intellectuals by another academic/intellectual falls somewhere between an "exotic" and a "native" anthropology (as Rogers, 1991, points out in regard to all American anthropology in France). First of all, there is an ideological dimension built into my decision to study Corsican, in that I came to Corsica with a bias in favor of cultural and linguistic diversity. This meant that I was (and am) a proponent of the Corsican language; I would like to see it survive even though I believe that Corsican cultural particularity does not depend on its survival. Given the political nature of the issue of language, my proponency had social consequences. I did not feel, for example, that I had an unlimited warrant to poke my nose into some of the affairs which I became a part of without making some sort of contribution, without revealing myself in the way I was asking (forcing?) Corsicans to reveal themselves to me. I do not mean to say that I abandoned all efforts to be neutral; in fact, I carefully guarded every opportunity for neutrality so as not to close any avenues of discussion. But, in many cases, conversation itself was predicated on some demonstration of sympathy on my part. That sympathy had to be, and was genuine. As time went on (and I suspect this will increasingly be the case in the future), my access to certain people became limited based on what they believed I thought. As a result, I spoke to more people who support Corsican language education than to those who do not. With time, it also became more difficult for me to suppress my own viewpoint. I was not a passive collector of opinions; I had them, shared them, argued them. The intellectuals I studied were not exotic creatures, they were who I would be if I were Corsican.

Despite the involvement and identification that this kind of identification implies, I was of course *not* Corsican. My role in this group was ambiguous, and this ambiguity sometimes caused tension. Like many people doing fieldwork, there was a moment in my fieldwork when I wanted to be fully accepted as an insider; I wanted to identify completely and be completely identified with this group. This led me, at one point, to naively underestimate the political implications of the sociolinguistic survey project I conducted (see Jaffe 1993c on the difficulties of doing survey work about language in a place where language and identity are heavily charged with personal and political value).With the advantage of hindsight, my experiences trying to do survey work allowed me to experience, first-hand, the extent to which cultural politics infuse all academic pursuits on Corsica. In the end, some of the problems I had with my survey project led me to a more measured and fruitful form of identification in which I recognized that, like Corsican *culturels*, I was constrained by the economic and ideological contours of my own academic society. But I also had to recognize important differences of degree. The fact remained that my sensitivities to the political and social implications of my research are more often a matter of personal choice than they are for Corsicans. These sensitivities are not forced upon me in a myriad of ways in my professional and personal life, because the topic that I study is not charged with significance in American cultural or political life. This difference cannot help but have implications for the way that my Corsican colleagues and I write about the Corsican language. My work, for example, owes a considerable debt to the excellent research of the Corsican sociolinguist Jacques Thiers. But even in the many instances in which we share a particular analysis or a general theoretical perspective, the vantage points of our written work are quite different. Everything that Thiers writes is, by definition, a political act, for which he is accountable not just as an academic but as a Corsican. I do not mean to imply by this that I can be objective where he cannot. Rather, our subjective assessments of what it is important or necessary to say differ because of who we are.

3. Language in Corsican society: central, complex and contested

Since the seventies on Corsica, issues of language and identity have been constantly in the foreground in the public domain. This was particularly true in the summer of 1982, when I did my first, preliminary fieldwork on the island in the midst of the electoral campaign for the first Corsican Regional Assembly. The hope and passion of that campaign charged the summer atmosphere during the two months (July and August) when most of the Corsicans living on the continent returned to the island, and when cultural activity peaked. By 1988, when I returned to spend fourteen months doing my dissertation research, the atmosphere was considerably more sober; the Assembly had not lived up to its promise as an agent of change, and the cultural/linguistic militants of the "seventies generation" seemed slightly wearied of the sometimes painfully slow rate at which language practices and attitudes changed. Nevertheless, there was no mistaking the central role that the issue of language played in the constant debate in Corsican public life over what it meant to be Corsican. In newspapers, political campaign materials and debates, television programs and casual conversations in cafes and on the streets, people talked and wrote about the institutional status and the cultural value of Corsican, about linguistic authenticity, purity, authority, variation, standardization, personal and political responsibility in regard to its promotion and salvation.

The following brief vignettes illustrate the kinds of contradictory data that I had to make sense out of; they also illustrate the some of the tensions between models of identity and authenticity that characterize Corsican discussions of language. They show that language planning/revitalization is an immensely complex process; that there are no neutral or purely linguistic choices or policies. Language choices and language form are heavily invested, in Corsica, with social and political significance.

3.1. Vignette 1: In two language classes

It is the first day of the first-year Corsican language class at the Corsican Studies Institute in 1989. The teacher asks what seems like a very ordinary question: why had these students chosen to enroll in Corsican Studies? There is little response, the students are waiting and watching. One by one, the professor calls on them. A handful speak with ease in Corsican but many seem both uncomfortable speaking Corsican and unable (or unwilling) to say why they might want to speak it or study it. They are, of course, reticent because it is the first day, and they do not know one another. Some of this reticence, however, continues over the course of the semester even as students get to know the professor and one another. The wide disparities in Corsican fluency among the students only becomes more evident; the limited number of them who speak Corsican with fluency and confidence are singled out and deferred to by the others. Sometime in November, students start giving presentations in Corsican on a topic of their choice. Few are at ease with the requirements of extended discourse about a serious topic. They grope for words, they correct verb endings in midstream, shuffle their feet, cough and laugh nervously, and hesitate over syllable stress in midword. When they express this nervousness linguistically, it is most often with the French discourse markers *enfin* 'so' and *bon* 'good". One day, we are forced to move classrooms, and I notice that almost all of the light chatter ("Where are we going?" "Is it this room?") that accompanies the move is in French. The physical movement out of the classroom into the hallway seems to be a shift of symbolic space: in these marginal areas they are relieved of the "requirement" to speak in Corsican. Later in the semester, we engage in a very interesting exercise: we translate "modern" French terminology into Corsican and discuss the criteria by which one translation might be considered superior to another.

In some cases, it seems as though we can all agree, but in many other cases, the exercise makes "right" answers seem slippery and elusive.

In a different classroom across campus in the school of law, students file in to a required Corsican course. They dutifully copy into their notebooks the information that the professor puts on the board. She lectures on the beginnings of the language movement. Dates go up on the board: the first publication of *Rigiru*, the first all-Corsican literary review; the year that the Deixonne law was expanded to allow Corsican to be taught in the schools; the founding of *Scola Corsa* and the ADECEC[1] (organizations promoting Corsican). I know that this teacher had participated in the Corsican renaissance, but I do not hear any hint of her personal involvement as she speaks. She presents the events dispassionately and without much editorializing. We move on to some vocabulary, grammar and spelling exercises from a novice-level primer. A lot of good-natured (French) conversation circulates in the classroom about the errors students discover on their papers. Some of them raise their hands to offer regional variants on vocabulary words. In this class, my status as a foreign learner of Corsican seems quite normal, because it resembles a foreign language class more than anything else. It is true that the students know more about this language than they know about English or German but they do not in any way command Corsican or seem to mind that they do not.

In the first class, I came to realize that the students' silence went beyond the normal fear of error; they were paralyzed by the judgments of cultural authenticity attached to linguistic production in Corsican (see Chapter 5 for further discussion). By declaring a Corsican Studies major, students had expressed their will to connect with their Corsicanness, and had made a claim on cultural authenticity. Their struggles with the language in the first year class, however, reminded them that they had to learn the mother tongue that they "ought" to know naturally. The errors that were a natural part of the learning process risked being culturally *inauthenticating* ones. Students with limited knowledge of Corsican also knew that "pure" and "authentic" Corsican was socially defined as a recognizably local variant, uncontaminated by French; thus they were justifiably anxious that the standardized Corsican they did know would be disparaged as too frenchified, not locally authentic.

In the second class, the political and cultural meaning of Corsican was more or less vacuumed out. At the time that I was doing fieldwork, I was struck by the dissonance between the role that the representation of Corsican in this classroom and the language demonstrably played in public life. Moreover, I passed judgment: treating Corsican as just like any other foreign language was risky, I thought, because one could not argue that Corsican had the pragmatic value of studying English, German, Italian or Spanish. I reasoned, like some Corsicans, that since the value of Corsican was cultural rather than practical, a successful promotion of Corsican language education had to focus on the cultural. At the same time, I recognized that the fact that Corsican was not overloaded with cultural and political meanings in the second class was one of the reasons that there were none of the tortured, politically charged silences I had witnessed before.

These two types of classrooms are a useful springboard for a larger issue that reappears throughout this book. The two pedagogical strategies I observed represented two different ways of taking a stance towards dominant language ideologies and the fact of language domination. The "sociolinguistic" classroom in the Corsican Studies Institute exposed the arbitrariness of linguistic boundary making, and the politically motivated nature of sociolinguistic categories and judgments. As we will see in the fuller discussion in Chapter 5, it located linguistic identity and authority in collective social action, rather than in linguistic form; it defined Corsican (and by extension, Corsicanness) as "becoming" rather than "being". The other class, in its matter-of-fact presentation of Corsican as a subject like any other, represented Corsican as a language with a legitimacy and authority that could be taken for granted, in the same way that the legitimacy and authority of French could be taken for granted. Rather than expose the contingent and arbitrary nature of linguistic domination, the teacher in this classroom deployed dominant modes of discourse in the service of the minority language, tapping into the power of practices to authenticate embedded language ideologies. She assumed the right, for Corsican, to "prescribe, while seeming only to describe". This class prescribed legitimacy in the description of Corsican as a linguistic system which existed independent of society. The students in this classroom were addressed as linguistic apprentices rather, as in the other class, as sociolinguistic agents. Despite these significant differences, however, both one of these pedagogical strategies proposed a model of linguistic authenticity that excluded and stigmatized certain ways of speaking or thinking about language.

3.2. *Vignette 2: The politics of orthographic identity*

The Regional Assembly voted unanimously in 1989 to promote research on Corsican place names, with the goal of generalizing their use on road signs. In the years that followed, questionnaires were sent out to all municipal councils asking them how they would like their town or village's name to be written in official documents and on road signs: in Corsican, in French, or in both. The Region also supported academic research on Corsican toponyms.

The survey had mixed and perplexing results. Half of those surveyed failed to respond. Many of those who responded said they did *not* want to corsican-ize their names. Some of these places (Bastia, Castirla) could not possibly change their names to be "more Corsican": they were already written exactly as they were pronounced. Others objected on the grounds that written Corsican would be misunderstood or mispronounced by non-Corsicans. Some villages with equally unchangeable names (like Meria) wrote back saying they wanted new, Corsican road signs. Personal contact with some of the municipal councils by members of a research team revealed that few had even debated whether or not to have the bilingual signs, and some were pleasantly surprised to see that it was an option. Some municipalities that failed to respond (or responded that they did not want the Corsican or bilingual signs that were being financially subsidized by the Assembly), subsequently went out and purchased signs with their own budgets. Other villages proposed changes that did not reflect their own Corsican pronunciation: residents of Speloncato (current spelling) wanted to mark the place-name as Corsican by replacing the final *"u"* with *"o"* (to create the spelling *Speluncatu*), but did not wish to adopt a spelling that reflected the way they pronounced it, which was [spʊnkadu]. In Venaco (pronounced by all residents as [bɛnaku]), the mayor vehemently opposed putting *Venacu* on the street signs, arguing that Francophone readers of such a spelling would deform the pronunciation as [bɛnakü], whose last syllable sounded too much like the French word *cul* 'butt'. Five years later, the bilingual signs that had been so long a subject of debate were a fait accompli, ubiquitous, hardly noticed and seldom com-mented on.

Here we see a vivid illustration of the way that identity politics are projected onto orthography, the epitome of arbitrariness in the representation of linguistic form. On the surface, what is striking about this example is the inconsistency with which people responded. However, there are several frameworks within which their choices become more understandable. First of all, they were operating in a social context in which all matters of language representation were politicized in every sense of the term. Mayors and municipal councils knew that any choice they made would be interpreted as an ideological or political position. Once the issue of bilingual place names was put into public debate, it became a definitional moment in which social actors could take a stance on the meaning and value of written Corsican in public life, or make claims on orthographic representation as a site for the assertion of identity. No matter what they did–even if they failed to respond–others would see them as having made a choice. This explains why some of them felt compelled to take positions on the issue even when there was no linguistic or orthographic variable to choose.

We can also see, in this example, people taking different kinds of positions on the relationship of orthography to identity. In the Speluncatu example, the villagers accepted a gap between spelling and pronunciation. They did not expect to see the intimacy of oral language in the graphic depiction of their village name. For them, the substitution of *"u"* for *"o"* was doing representational work for outsiders: it distinguished the graphic representation of the village name from both Italian and French. The Speluncatu town council was engaging with spelling at a pan-Corsican, rather than a local level, using orthographic difference from French and Italian to emphasize the autonomy of Corsican as a language. In Venaco, the mayor was also looking at spelling through an outside lens. In contrast to the villagers of Spelunacatu, however, the mayor of Venaco did not see local pronunciation as an inviolate arena of intimacy, disconnected from the public domain. It is for this reason that he rejected Corsican toponyms as a way of preserving the integrity and intimacy of oral usage. His fears of Francophone contamination of the pronunciation of the village belied a lack of faith in Corsican's ability to propose itself as a discrete and autonomous written code. He did not believe that the *"u"* would be read as proof of Corsican difference and language status; he did not believe the *"u"* would escape being read with a French voice. Rather than let this French voice into the circle of intimacy and identity, he advocated Corsican retreat from a public, written arena in which was bound to be dominated by French. This is an example of what I am calling the resistance of separation.

The variety and inconsistency of the village councils' reactions also illustrate a resistance to what is imposed: the communes that bought their own signs distanced themselves from the Regional Assembly and cast their choices as "personal" and independent ones. This small example offers a glimpse into the way that language policies are interpreted, and the difficulties faced by Corsican language planners in achieving any social consensus about any linguistic policy on Corsica. These difficulties emerge in greater detail in Chapters 4 through 7.

3.3. Vignette 3: One nationalist's struggle: language in the politics of identity vs. language in everyday life

The setting is rue César Campinchi, one of the two commercial streets in the town of Bastia that parallel the huge Place Saint Nicolas that overlooks the port, neatly ringed by palm trees and flanked by cafes and their busy terraces where the Bastiais sit, see and are seen by those who stroll by. In the midday calm, while all the stores are closed, I visit *U Carminu* 'The Fireplace,' a tiny shop that specializes in traditional Corsican products–*figatellu* (fresh sausage), *lonzu, prisuttu, coppa* (all cuts of cured pork), chestnut flour, regional wines and white rounds of goat cheese from all over the island in different stages of succulent ripeness. Philippe, the owner, had not gone home for lunch in order to talk to me. Philippe and I kissed cheeks and asked each other about our mutual friend, Pierrette. I congratulated him on his third place prize in the recent Corsican language short story contest. Whenever we met, we always spoke as much Corsican as my abilities allowed; he never hesitated to correct me, and liked to teach me new phrases. He had filled out my long (five page) questionnaire with evident gusto and in abundant detail; his written comments were eloquent illustrations of his nationalist politics. For example, he wrote,

> Corsican is a vernacular which is deeply rooted in the Corsican people. It is not the language of a few academicians but the language of a hard working people that possess a communitarian social structure. It has been orally transmitted from the depths of history. It has its own unique sounds, a structure, a distinct syntax, and thus it is unique [my translation].

On the questionnaire he stated that "I never feel obliged to speak Corsican because it comes to me completely naturally," and that "In the presence of people who are very close to me, speaking another language than Corsican would be equivalent to "speaking Chinese".

Philippe viewed my questionnaire as just one more place in which he had an obligation to manage the public representation of Corsican. He had been imprisoned for nationalist activity and his current business partner had been recently released from five years in jail without trial, under charges of conspiracy and possession of arms. Faced with competing models of identity, Philippe had made a choice: his self-definition as Corsican excluded French and Frenchness. In his two years of university studies at Nice, his sense of cultural difference was intensified by his experience of "racism" against Corsicans. In his formulation of "authentic" Corsicanness, French and France are "orientalized" in the comment, above, about speaking French and in his characterization of Corsican culture as far more "oriental" than western.

Philippe was committed, furthermore, to expressing this separation of cultures in his use of language. Partly tongue-in-cheek, he asked his customers for "*centu franchi francese*" ['one hundred French francs']. He smiled, and so did most customers, at his exoticization of the standard currency, but the intent was serious. He told me that his brother-in-law was French (he refuses to call him "continental," for the term implies that Corsica is only geographically distinct from France) and that he did try to speak French around him but said he invariably lapsed into Corsican, the language in which he and his sister passed their childhoods. This linguistic exclusion was not a question of rudeness or lack of respect: "After all, this is Corsica, it should be natural for them to speak it." Up to the age of four or five, he never spoke French, and even after he learned it, he spoke Corsican out of preference. He reported that when adults said to him, *"Parlami francese"* ['Speak French to me'], he would answer, *"francese"* ['French']. He only learned about language hierarchy when he left his village school to go to High School in Bastia. There, he was called *paisanò* 'hick,' and discovered that villagers in town made special efforts to learn and speak French in order not to be considered backward.

Despite Philippe's experience and competence in Corsican, and his careful coordination of his public political, cultural and linguistic stances, his interview revealed the difficulty of bringing one's private life in line with public ideals. Philippe's wife was of Corsican origin, but she was born in Tunisia. Although she understood Corsican, she did not speak it, and did not seem to share his radical nationalism. Their children were called Béatrice and Chantal because she had not been receptive to the idea of giving them Corsican names like their cousins. Philippe was quick to point out that Béatrice was almost the same in both languages. His wife, he said, had too many other concerns to set about learning Corsican, which he described as a *sacré effort* 'huge effort'. His children took Corsican language classes in school, but it was taught, he said, as if it were just another foreign language. He tried to do what he could in the home to give them an "ear" for the language, but he admitted that it was not enough. The girls had, he believed, "a certain [nationalist] sensibility"; they knew that he had been in jail for his beliefs, and he noted that they had absorbed his sense of oppositional identity–he had heard them say to other children, "I'm Corsican, he's French." Despite his aggressive pro-Corsican politics, his habit of speaking Corsican in the shop and in public and his involvement in the elaboration of Corsican literacy, Philippe's private life escaped his ideological influence. His wife was a product of her upbringing and did not feel as Corsican as he did; his children were growing up in a French-dominated urban environment, and a home setting in which French also predominated. The language of his relationships with his siblings and parents may have been Corsican, but Philippe had to live out his relationship with his wife and children in "Chinese". In his family life, he was forced to integrate the two languages and cultures he kept so separate in his public discourse and personal sense of identity.

Philippe's interview, like many others I conducted with Corsicans who were actively involved in nationalist politics and the promotion of Corsican, was rich with tensions, contradictions, strong sentiments and self-conscious representational strategies and stances. Circulating in his discourse about the language is an extremely powerful image of a pure and unproblematic link between speaking and feeling/being Corsican that he experienced as a young child, and which is congruent with the model of language and national identity that drives his adult politics. This model of what an authentic Corsican should be is the only one that either his French education or his Corsican nationalist politics legitimated, but it conflicted with his lived experience. This conflict remained unresolved insofar as Philippe had no alternative model of linguistic and cultural identity which might recognize the hybrid nature of Corsican linguistic practice and cultural identity.

4. Metadiscourse, language and political economy

These brief vignettes point to the ideological, political and pragmatic difficulties faced by activists trying to raise the status and promote the use of Corsican. The vignettes also illustrate the central focus, in this book, on the way that representations of language are interpreted, experienced and circulated as political and social capital. Cameron has argued convincingly that reflexive critical judgments on language use make up a significant part of communication in any society (1995). In places like Corsica, where there are multiple, stratified and/or contested identities, this sort of metadiscourse plays an even more strikingly ubiquitous role.[2] Urban makes the important point that metadiscursive reflections constitute part of the publicly accessible, historical collection of instances of language from which meanings are culled; they are part of the sociolinguistic resources which make shared meanings possible. Instances of metadiscourse contribute to the politicization of meanings in a given society, with particular relevance to social understandings and constructions of authority and continuity (1991: 9–12).

Are we saying anything about metadiscourse that we cannot say about discourse? On an analytical level, the answer is no. As Quéré (1987: 73) writes, *"l'usage n'est pas seulment la mise en oeuvre...du répertoire linguistique: il constitue un acte social en soi...produit avec une revendication de 'normalité' ou d'appropriation normative, et dont sont partie intégrante des opérations d'évaluation, de reconnaissance, de catégorisation ou éventuellement de contestation, de demande de justification etc."* [usage is not just the putting-into-practice...of a linguistic repertoire: it is in and of itself a social act...whose production involves claims on "normalness" which are founded on {social}operations of recognition, categorization and even contestation and demands for justification etc.]. In other words, just as metadiscourse is social action, linguistic practice is also always metadiscursive at some level.

This does not mean that we cannot examine the differences between metadiscourse (explicit language ideologies) and language practices. For example, in the brief vignettes above, we get a glimpse of some of the disjunctures and inconsistencies between everyday communicative practices and explicit linguistic ideologies in militant circles. The same disjuncture can be seen in nonmilitant contexts, where many people will stigmatize the Corsican–French language mixtures that they use all the time, and which neither they, nor others, sanction in everyday practice. And there is often a gap between the image of language practice that militants promote and popular conceptions and practices of Corsican.[3] There is no temptation, from my perspective, to consider spontaneous linguistic practice as more "real" than ideological statements about language. Rather, the point is to explore the social forces that shape discourse and metadiscourse, as well as "the dialectal tension between discourse and metadiscourse [that] may well be central to the processes of culture" (Urban 1991: 7). It is possible, as Urban writes, that "if there is bound to be a slippage between metadiscourse and discourse–between the ideology of language use and its empirical characteristics–there is also bound to be a pressure on the two to align" (Urban 1991: 19). In this study, I emphasize both the way in linguistic structure is subject to idealization[4] and the way that metalinguistic discourses are themselves both social facts and agents in the exercise of social power. I also look at the effect that the gap between militant discourse and social practice has had on popular responses to language planning and how these responses have caused changes in the discourse of language planners.

As the opening vignettes illustrate, language in Corsica has become one of the key symbolic sites in which issues of identity are articulated. Corsican metalinguistic discourse is political in two senses of the term. First, there is the sense in which all representations of identity are inherently political, since control over representations of self and collectivity is relational and oppositional. Thus in constituting the self, you are always also constituting "others". Corsicans (and other minority populations) have a heightened consciousness of the negative repercussions of being defined by more powerful outsiders (see Chapter 2); this makes their struggle for representational control all the more significant. The experience of linguistic and cultural domination by France (see Chapter 3) is thus a constant point of reference (sometimes silent, sometimes explicit–as with Philippe). Second, the fact that language has been one of the cornerstones of the Corsican nationalist movement insures that discourses about language are also acts of political alliance and affiliation–they are constitutive of social relations at every possible level.

4.1. Language and political economy

The approach I develop above owes its basic insights to the theoretical framework of "language and political economy". As Irvine (1989: 263) writes,

> linguistic forms have relevance to the social scientist not only as part of a world of ideas, but also as part of a world of objects, economic transactions and political interests. The verbal sign relates to a political economy in many ways: by denoting it, by indexing parts of it, by depicting it...and by taking part in it as an object of exchange.

Quéré underscores the importance of such an approach in the study of language revitalization, writing that it must take into account the way in which power is conceptualized, structured, distributed and enacted among social, cultural and economic institutions in a society, as well as how it is connected to knowledge and concepts of social accountability (1987: 65).[5] This implies a focus on the interrelationship of local and supra local linguistic and political economies.[6] The study of the political economy of language is thus by definition concerned with (a) the process of domination: how, precisely, language is associated with the processes that generate a particular distribution of authority and enable certain groups to exercise domination/hegemony, and the relationship between language and power (Grillo 1989: 5); (b) how "deeply held conceptions that mediate between identity and speech" are a "part of political struggles," and finally; (c) how and whether dominant discourses may be challenged or resisted.[7] These "deeply held conceptions" are language ideologies; they are, as Woolard puts it, "a mediating link between social structures and forms of talk" (Woolard 1992: 235).

Chapters 2 through 5 survey the various economies (ideological, linguistic, material, local, supra local) that frame contemporary linguistic practices and ideas about language, power and identity. As both Heller (1994) and Rampton (1995) demonstrate, differences in the power and images of languages or linguistic codes outside the local context have a profound effect on their meaning in local interactions. In the Corsican case, I examine the way in which in which dominant language ideology and policy affects both militant/academic (Chapters 4 and 5) and popular linguistic ideology and practice (Chapter 3). I also explore the mutual influences of militant and popular practices and ideas about language.

Chapter 2 describes the social and physical spaces to which Corsican identity is linked. Significant local political and social structures include a segmentary, egalitarian kinship system with a strong emphasis on individual autonomy, and the "clan": a kin-based political class that mediated Corsicans' relationship with the French government (see Chapter 2). I argue that both of these lead people to define their identities and interests and allegiances in extremely local terms which are viewed as being inherently in competition or conflict with the supra local. The value of the local is also illustrated in the central symbolic role played by the Corsican village in the articulation of social and linguistic identity. Chapter 2 explores some of the imagery of the village in popular discourse and looks at the way that Corsican "otherness" is intensified by both the physical boundedness of islands and by Corsicans' experiences living in France and in the French colonies. Corsican discourse about the diaspora reveals a tension, however, between the ideal model of a completely separate, inalienable Corsicanness and the "blended" identity of minority populations. Chapter 3 takes a close look at the history of Corsican's relationship with two dominant languages: first Italian, and then French. The very different sociolinguistic outcomes of the Italian–Corsican versus the French–Corsican hierarchy point to the tremendous impact of the institutional-ization of linguistic hierarchy. This was absent under Italy and extraordinarily well-developed under France. Chapter 3 describes in some detail the political economy of language and identity embedded in Corsicans' experiences of the French educational system. Corsicans did not just learn to speak French in the schools, they learned a language hierarchy in which their own language was dismissed as a worthless patois. They learned that French was the zenith of formal elegance, and that linguistic form embodied all the virtues of reason, civilization and citizenship. They learned the link between language unity and national identity.

Chapters 4 and 5 survey over two decades of Corsican language activism, at once documenting language planning milestones and accomplishments and tracing major themes, ideological currents and debates. Chapter 4 explores the ideological bases for debates in activist circles over the importance of the boundaries between Corsican and Italian and Corsican and French. For many Corsican language proponents, Italian played a key symbolic role in the articulation of an independent and authentic Corsican linguistic identity as an external language from which Corsican could be differentiated. Another cornerstone of Corsican language legitimation is the representation of the language as internally unified. This concern gave rise to debates over both the meaning of regional linguistic variation and the significance of Corsican linguistic forms that are the result of contact with French. Corsican language activists have been divided over whether or not these forms should be accepted as "authentic" Corsican. These positions are explored through in this chapter's description of the debate of the mid-eighties between the (self-styled) "sociolinguists" versus the "purists".

Chapter 5 examines the ideological underpinnings of the failure of numerous motions for officialization of Corsican and mandatory Corsican language education that were debated in the Corsican Regional Assembly. Analysis of published Assembly deliberations and survey data reveals that the authority of language legislation runs counter to powerful Corsican discourses about the voluntary and affective value of the mother tongue. The rest of the chapter looks at language planners' efforts to create a new public discourse about language that challenges a monolingual, essentialist view of language. Under the banners of "coofficiality," "*Lingua Matria*" and "polynomy" and locates language value and identity in plural communities of practice, where minority language competence is not the sole gauge of Corsican identity.

5. Diglossia

The combination of French language ideology with the opportunity for economic and social advancement offered by speaking French were powerful catalysts for language shift towards French. As the name implies, language shift is a process; in Corsica, this process has been (and is still being) drawn out over several generations, which means that it has resulted in various kinds of bilingualism. The particular bilingualism generated by language shift is called "diglossia". I will be using this term to describe a complex of language practices and attitudes. Because there is still considerable disagreement about the scope of this term in the sociolinguistic literature (see Tollefson 1983 and Hudson's preface to his 1992 bibliography on diglossia), let me explain my position.

In Ferguson's original (1950) formulation, diglossia referred to situations in which a speech community had two distinct varieties of the same language, distinguished by status ("high" and "low") and function. His clear cut examples of this sort of relation included Greek (*katharevusa* and *demotic*) and Arabic (classical and modern) and excluded relationships between a standard variety and its dialects. Fishman's 1968 elaboration of the concept of diglossia explicitly included the latter type of sociolinguistic relations (in Tollefson 1983: 3). Later, Fishman and others would expand the concept of diglossia to include compartmentalized, hierarchical relationships between different languages. This expanded definition of diglossia has been widely used to refer to all dominant--minority language relations in western Europe. In French sociolinguistics of minority languages, diglossia has been applied specifically to situations in which there is linguistic conflict as a result of language domination/hierarchy (Boyer 1991: 18–23; Couderc 1974: 3; Gardy and Lafont 1981: 75; Giordan 1982; Marcellesi and Gardin 1974; Thiers

1987, 1989a). This broader use of the term is the one that I am adopting in writing about the Corsican situation.

This broad use of diglossia has not been without its detractors. One vein of criticism is that the expansion of the situations to which diglossia is applied has made it a sort of catch-all phrase with little explanatory value (Prudent, in Boyer 1991: 16). Berruto (1989) argues that diglossia should be treated as a subcategory of "types of linguistic repertoires with status and function differences," and advocates a classificatory system which differentiates between the relative status and elaboration of the two languages or language varieties; how sharply they are differentiated linguistically and by their speakers; how clearly their functions and domains of use in a speech community are separated, and whether or not there are intermediate varieties.

In this study, I do use diglossia as a shorthand for status and function differences between Corsican and French. This use in no way implies that diglossic situations are homogenous. In fact, my analysis of the Corsican case is conceived of as a case study of language use and ideology in the context of language domination and conflict that can be compared with other specific cases. My use of diglossia is thus not intended as an explanation, but as a starting point for the exploration of the nature and causes of differences in diglossic situations. I also retain the term as a useful shorthand for what I see as the key ideological factor influencing language practices and attitudes: the existence of an oppositional model of linguistic and cultural identities.

Another line of criticism of the use of diglossia is that it reduces the dynamics of language conflict to a set of static relations. That is, it does not take into account the circulation in the minority speech community of multiple linguistic codes, of hybrid or intermediate forms of language. This is incontestable at the level of description, and is illustrated quite clearly in several of the chapters in this book (in particular, Chapters 3 and 8). Far from ignoring the hybrid nature of language practice, my study is explicitly concerned with explaining both the social evaluation of such practice (and its relationship to a diglossic ideology) and the extent to which such practice contributes to or is based on resistance to dominant ideologies of language.

There are several common features of all diglossic situations that are relevant to the Corsican case. First, the minority/dominated language is stigmatized by the dominant culture and ultimately becomes devalued by its speakers, who assign greater prestige and value to the dominant language. Second, dominant language policy excludes the minority language from the public/official domain, and it eventually becomes confined to the domain of sentiment and affect. Finally, the minority language (Corsican) is perceived to be the language of the heart and of the hearth, of the warm and informal context of social relations in the village (the symbolic core of Corsican culture), while French commands the domain of the formal, the authoritative, the instrumental and intellectual.

This restriction of domains of use and value clearly works to the disadvantage of the minority language, particularly when the dominant language is the means to economic success and social prestige. Not only does this restriction encourage language shift away from the minority language, but it also has linguistic effects (the reduction of the lexicon and grammatical integrity of the minority language) that may contribute to its speakers' judgment of its inadequacy (Sasse 1992: 14). That is, language domination stigmatizes the minority language, which results in restrictions of its social use, which leads to linguistic changes that the dominant ideology of linguistic value also stigmatizes.

6. Resistance

As Terdiman writes, "no dominant discourse is ever fully protected from contestation" (1985: 56–57). Beginning in Chapter 4, I use detailed case studies of language planning strategies and their social reception to address the issue of how language dominance (in both its material and ideological forms) can be resisted. In doing so, I make a fundamental distinction between forms of resistance that are rooted in/structured by a dominant, diglossic model of language value and identity and those that in one way or another challenge some of the fundamental premises of that model. Here, I should make it clear what I am labeling as "resistance" (see Gal 1995: 445).

First of all, I take as axiomatic that the relationship between linguistic form and social meanings, stances, roles and identities is complex, inconsistent and local (Eckert and McConnell-Ginet 1992). Recalling the vignette about the orthography of place-names, we can see that it is impossible to tell, without a deep understanding of specific contexts, collective and individual understandings, motivations and intentions, whether a using or advocating a particular linguistic variable "means" compliance or resistance.

This general approach to the relationship between linguistic form and social meanings emerges in several themes in current scholarship on resistance. First, it is possible for behaviors that appear to comply with mainstream or dominant values to have a subversive meaning for social actors. As Mertz puts it in her description of language shift in Cape Breton Gaelic, "In apparent yielding to hegemonic values, there may also be resistance and creativity" (1989: 113). An example of such resistance can be found in Reed-Danahay's description of peasant ideologies of *débrouillardise* 'getting by' in the Auvergne. There, peasants behave in ways that do *not* overtly challenge middle-class values. Their emphasis on "getting by" causes them to embrace dominant forms of interaction but, Reed-Danahay points out, it does not mean that they necessarily internalize dominant values or grant them any intrinsic merit (1993: 221). In a similar vein, Rampton describes the social connotations of "Stylized Asian English" (SAE) in British society. Despite the fact that SAE is linked with negative images from the dominant culture of compliant, subservient and incompetent Asian immigrants, Rampton shows that it can be used by Asian adolescents in interactions with white adults to index minority–majority relations and thereby, show resistance to white domination (1995: 52–53). In her work on Bedouin women, Abu-Lughod shows how adherence to one of the structures through which male domination is exercised and perpetuated (separation of domains, restriction of women) can be employed in a certain kind of resistance. She describes Bedouin women who "fiercely protect the inviolability of their private sphere," where they enact minor defiances of male power through their poetry (1990: 43).

Secondly, it is equally the case that acts which appear to resist dominant structures may not be intended or read as resistant. For example, Shuman points out that while adolescent collaborative writing is a potential site for the subversion of notions of authorship, authority and voice, that subversive quality is not given in the *form* of the text. Some collaborative texts make subversive claims about the nature of representation; others do not (1993: 265). Rampton's work on language "crossing" (where people adopt a code not normally considered "theirs") among British adolescents shows that what appears to be a very heterodox, subversive practice may or may not make radical representational claims. On some occasions, it may even reinforce conservative notions of group boundaries. This can also be seen in Bucholz's study of crossing into African American Vernacular English by White high school students. While some White students' crossing indexed membership in mixed-race social networks, others used it to discursively distance themselves from Black culture (1996).

Resistance, in other words, is related to speakers' understandings and intentions rather than given in the form of their utterances. This is not to say that differences in form do not play a central role in the production and interpretation of meaning. In order to send, or interpret a message of "resistance" or "compliance," social actors (and ethnographers) have to understand what Irvine calls "the topology of linguistic differentiation": culturally specific ideologies that link social identities, role relations, ideological and political stances with choices between linguistic alternants (1989: 252). Such a topology delimits, but by no means fixes the range of meanings that a particular linguistic form may have in a particular context. Take for example an individual's choice to speak in Corsican. Given the diglossic situation in Corsica, that choice will be interpreted in reference to norms of French versus Corsican domains of use. Such norms establish French as "un-marked" in public, official spheres. This makes it possible for a speaker to use Corsican in such a context as a contestatory act, as a claim for parity between the two languages that challenges French language dominance. But to determine that a particular person's use of Corsican in public is in fact inten-ded as such a form of resistance, we have to engage in a far more fine-grained analysis of the speech event. An elected official who gives his entire annual report in Corsican is sending a far more oppositional message than the person who uses Corsican only for off-the-record comments or asides. In the latter case, the content of speech in Corsican is consistent with a diglossic system in which the minority language is associated with solidarity and intimacy and the dominant language, with power and distance. We could use the "topology" to read the use of Corsican in "asides" as an index of (or claim on) intimacy or solidarity in a formal context. But even this could be jumping to con-clusions without corroborating data. Such corroboration could be drawn from systematic observations that establish patterns of language choice and topic (French for "serious" and central themes; Corsican for less formal and more peripheral talk). Knowledge of a particular speaker's habitual patterns of language use is another potentially crucial kind of data. In the case of some habitual codeswitchers, it would be a mistake to attribute any intentionality to discrete instances of language "choice".[8]

These examples point to another complicating factor in the formal identification of "resistance" and compliance. That is, while the "topology" postulates more or less fixed contexts and social identities, we know that language choices can be used to frame events and establish identities. Language use is an integral part of the negotiation by which the nature of the situation is socially defined (Hanks 1996).

This means that we have to go beyond talking about resistance as a function of formal choices, and look for the possibility of resistance in the structures of discourse, in the presuppositions and premises that are embedded in linguistic representations and arguments. From this perspective, an act which is intended and perhaps even read as "resistant" may or may not be a "radical" resistance; it may or may not challenge the fundamental structures and ideologies through which domination is enacted.

6.1. A typology of different kinds of resistance

6.1.1. A resistance of reversal

Chapter 4 shows how the first phase of Corsican language activism resisted the outcomes of French language domination but did not resist its structures of value. The basic strategy of activists trying to revitalize Corsican was to reverse diglossic language hierarchies by propelling Corsican into the social, linguistic and conceptual domains previously occupied only by French. Literacy was a key component in this struggle, for it was through writing that activists sought to codify Corsican spelling and grammar and display that code as proof its unity, autonomy and legitimacy. Writing was also important for corpus planning–building up a body of written evidence that Corsican was capable of formal, literary expression; it was also a tool for creating the pedagogical materials needed to develop a school curriculum that might slow the process of language shift. Other forms of normalization involved using Corsican in the print and broadcast media and other public domains, and pushing for language legislation that would make Corsican an official language and/or a mandatory school subject. This kind of language activism is clearly derived from dominant language ideology; it does not disturb the diglossic schema and its hierarchy of values, but rather, attempts to improve the standing of Corsican within the existing framework. As Terdiman writes, "the counter-discourses which exploit [the vulnerability of dominant discourses] implicitly invoke a principle of order just as systematic as that which sustains the discourses they seek to subvert" (1985: 57).

I interpret this kind of language planning strategy as both an outcome of Corsican language activists' internalization of the French language ideology transmitted in the schools and a pragmatic response to the "diglossic mentality" they could observe among their compatriots. If Corsican was devalued because it was "not a language," then proving that it *was* a language was an important act of validation in their effort to change language attitudes and through them, language practices. This strategy is also an outcome of the political economy of language in the nationalist/autonomist political agenda, in which Corsican had been a key building block. The Corsican Nationalist program was profoundly influenced (as were other ethnoregional movements) by the following tenets of Western European thought about language and political identity: first, that there is (or ought to be) perfect congruence between linguistic, cultural and political boundaries (one language, one people, one nation); second, that those boundaries are "natural" and impermeable, and enclose internally homogenous systems (Balibar 1991; Gal 1992; Handler 1988; Hobsbawm 1990). It is no surprise that in their quest for national recognition and greater political autonomy, Corsican nationalists tapped into a preexisting dominant metalinguistic discourse.

6.1.2. Unintended consequences

In Chapters 4 through 7, I explore some of the unintended social conse-quences of a resistance of reversal. First of all, not challenging dominant criteria of value invites people to judge Corsican on French terms (the "monoglot standard" in Silverstein's 1987 formulation). When this compari-son is invited during the process of minority language standardization and normalization (that is, *before these processes are completed*) the minority language inevitably suffers in the comparison with the dominant one. This comes out clearly in Eckert's observations of Occitan; she describes how any variability in the minority language "is invoked as evidence of a process of decay, and the comparative homogeneity of French is taken as proof of that language's superiority"(1983: 294). There is also a disjuncture between the representation of the nature and value of Corsican and popular experience of its value. Because of language shift and diglossia, that experience is, for most Corsicans, linked to local ways of speaking and voluntary identification and practice which stand in explicit contrast to all that is standardized and imposed (see Chapter 5). An emphasis on literacy when practice is limited can also result in linguistic insecurity: people become aware of standards of correctness without having easy access to literacy training. We see this at work in popular images of Corsican language acquisition (Chapter 6) and in the representational risks run by the Spelling Contest (Chapter 7).

6.1.2.1. The impact of the monolingual norm

There are a host of further problems in the social acceptance and implementa-tion of language planning that go beyond the rejection of authority or images of authority with respect to Corsican. These problems can be traced to various facets of the promotion of a model of language as a closed, bounded, autonomous code that is embedded in the political agenda underpinning language activism in Corsica. First of all, it places an inordinate amount of symbolic/political weight on linguistic form. We see this in the vignettes, above, and in Chapters 4 through 7. This leads to both academic and popular minority language purism, which have the potential to create new forms of linguistic alienation and insecurity among Corsican speakers and "semi-speakers" (for parallels see Hill 1985: 735; Roseman 1995; Urla 1993: 113).

The political salience of language purism also symbolically "overloads" formal choices in the act of speaking. In Chapters 4 and 5 (and in the vignettes, above) we can see that the dramatization and politicization of language choices subordinates communicative to symbolic functions of language and in the process, sometimes silences would-be speakers.

Another problem in the adoption of a unitary model of language, culture and identity is that minority activists ignore the complexity of minority identity. Linguistic and cultural contact inevitably produces new, hybrid forms–mixed ways of thinking, speaking and doing. Corsicans are both French and "not French". From a purist perspective, all language variation is a problem. The regional dialectal diversity that is so central to Corsican experiences of linguistic identity is viewed both as a practical obstacle to the process of standardization and a theoretical impediment to an image of language unity based on homogeneity. This emerges quite forcefully in the discourse of several contestants in the spelling contest described in Chapter 7. Purism also de-legitimizes mixed forms of language (codeswitching of all kinds as well as French-influenced forms of Corsican and Corsican-influenced forms of French) that, as I argue in Chapter 3 and 8, are distinguishing features of Corsican sociolinguistic space and key sociolinguistic tools in the Corsican interactional repertoire.

6.1.3. The alternative linguistic marketplace: a resistance of separation

One of the most interesting unintended consequences of Corsican language planning strategies that fail to challenge dominant models/criteria of identity and value is the popular counter resistance they have provoked. On Corsica, the Regional Assembly has on several occasions rejected motions that would establish "obligatory bilingualism" (and compulsory Corsican language teaching in the schools), and as late as 1990 voted down a motion that called for a more diplomatic "coofficiality" of Corsican and French (these arguments are described in Chapter 5). There has never been strong grass-roots support for Corsican language teaching in the state schools, and in contrast to such places as Wales, Brittany and the Basque Country, there has also never been widespread public support for Corsican-language schools established outside the state system. This is not to say that there has been unqualified public support or enthusiasm for language planning in some of these other western European minority language contexts. But in most cases, public opposition and/or apathy has not prevented comparable language legislation from being enacted.[9]

The popular counter resistance I have alluded to above is as firmly anchored in the diglossic model as the language planning measures it opposes. The difference is that language planners attempt to penetrate the boundaries that exclude the minority language from domains of power. The "counter resistants" view those boundaries as essential tools for preserving an authentic, autonomous identity. The local language ideologies that provide the basis for this kind of "resistance of separation" have been addressed in a number of recent works that emphasize the existence of an "alternative" linguistic market from which the dominant language is excluded. Even if speakers undervalue the goods in this marketplace (intimacy and solidarity) in relation to the those in the dominant market (power, status, economic wealth) they are linked to a set of persisting social relations with everyday value. Here, let us return to the mayor of Venaco's rejection of a Corsican place name. His behavior exploits the diglossic model's stark opposition between French and Corsican worlds of use and value to draw protective boundaries. The mayor locks Corsican in a fortress (of intimacy and orality) where it may be scorned, but where it cannot be touched by the dominant culture.

Woolard also reminds us that the use of standard or dominant forms can be negatively sanctioned within the minority community; that it can be as important to produce "correct" forms of the vernacular in local contexts as it is to produce "correct" standard forms in the wider linguistic market.[10] Moreover, the practice and/or celebration of denigrated forms embodies alternative models of the social world than those proposed by dominant cultural and linguistic ideology.[11] We can see this principle in action when we look at the use of metaphorical codeswitching on Corsica and in other diglossic contexts. For codeswitching to have recognizable social meanings, conversational partners must associate different languages or varieties of language with two exclusive or opposing systems of value/models of relationships. Both codes have value: the meaning of a switch depends on their copresence.[12] Many of the documented uses of codeswitching also show the extent to which the code of intimacy and solidarity is a valued resource in interaction. In some instances, the interactional meaning of codeswitching can also transcend the opposition it makes use of. That is, codeswitching is a practice in which linguistic boundaries may be blurred (Woolard 1990). As an inherently plural, local use of language, codeswitching also indexes a (minority) community of use (see Chapters 3 and 8) defined by its ability to manipulate more than one language. As Herzfeld (1987) points out, the very diversity of this kind of local discourse challenges the idea of a monolithic, unitary, dominant language.

To the extent that claims to political autonomy are built on assertions of cultural difference, we can see that a binary model is empowering; it gives strength to minority identity. McDonald has described a parallel situation in Brittany, where she writes that the "Breton–French language difference lies at the heart of a very general system of oppositions through which militants define a 'Breton' world in contradistinction to all things French" (1989: 74). Woolard (1989a: 43) reports the same phenomenon in Catalonia, where Castilian versus Catalan "is used as an exhaustive contrast set" of social values and attributes (see also Dorian 1981: 84).

The point is, that in diglossic situations, the oppositional nature of the two codes becomes the symbolic vehicle through which any number of different cultural contrasts and values can be articulated. Some of these are disempowering, some are not.

In this light, it becomes clear that paradoxically, the very rigidity of a diglossic model that devalued Corsican and contributed to its decline was also a significant factor in the survival of the language. Diglossia permitted Corsicans to resist total assimilation: insofar as Corsican was defined as everything that French was not, its value, albeit derivative and socially undervalued, was not compromised by the French system (see Heller 1994 on the status of French in Canada). This connects us to the discourses of the diaspora and social identity in Chapter 2, where retired Corsicans of the diaspora represent their French lives as parentheses that in no way compromise their "true" Corsican identity and language. In one sense, the compartmentalization of domains of language and value created by French linguistic and social domination made it possible for Corsicans to retain some sense of detachment from the dominant system, to constitute it as "outside" (see for example the lyrics to "*U mo figliolu*" in Chapter 2).

6.1.4. The limits of a resistance of separation

But–and this is a large "but"–the same mechanisms of passive resistance that kept Corsicans from a total linguistic assimilation to French also work against language planning measures. This is because these forms of resistance do not challenge the authority of the dominant language, but rather protect the value of the nonauthoritative, "alternative" linguistic market associated with the minority language. Lack of popular support for Corsican language planning can thus be understood as a consequence of the deep-rootedness of the diglossic system of value and identity; it is a tenacious adherence to a logic of total opposition. Following the logic in which Corsican is defined as everything that French is not, the efforts of language planners to insert

Corsican into public, official, authoritative social space previously occupied by French alone are often seen as a "deformation" of the essential character of Corsican. This emerges particularly clearly in the debate over compulsory education (Chapter 5), in the social meaning attributed to learning Corsican (Chapter 6), as well as in the social contestation of linguistic authority in regard to Corsican that is expressed in resistance to linguistic standardization and normalization (Chapters 4–7).

This dimension of popular resistance to language planning highlights another unintended consequence of *successful* remaking of a minority language in a dominant image, which is that "the authoritative becomes authoritarian" (Joseph 1985; see also Pratt in Grillo 1989: 222). In a pattern deeply embedded in social forms like kinship and in the history of Corsican relations with outside powers (Chapter 2), the authoritarian is often rejected outright. "How can you force me," said one of my friends, "to learn *my* language?" One of the points that can be made here is that forms of language activism that reproduce a dominant language ideology also reproduce the structures of domination. The linguistic standards set by writing distinguish good from bad usage, and thus establish a social hierarchy which confers authority and prestige on those who write, and "speak properly" (see, among others, Bourdieu 1991; Cameron 1995; Crowley 1996; Luedi 1992; Urciuoli 1996). The resistance to the idea of linguistic authority associated with Corsican, in addition to being a form of passive resistance/adherence to a diglossic separation of value, is thus also a form of active resistance to the exercise of power. As Chapter 7 in particular illustrates, the invocation of authority in the abstract (in this case, in reference to orthographic standards) is almost invariably personalized; it is read as an attempt by a person or group to dominate another. This is in part an expression of an egalitarian ideal contrasted with the social hierarchy of the dominant polity (see Hill and Hill 1980), but is also evidence of a fundamental lack of faith in that ideal. It is a recognition of the strategies by which those with power naturalize and legitimize relations of social and linguistic inequality (Bourdieu 1991; Grillo 1989).

Another point that can be made in regard to Corsican reactions to the "imposition" of Corsican or of academic linguistic standards is that the values of Corsican and French "spill over" the diglossic model. Even though people talk about the opposition between Corsican and French as an "exhaustive contrast set" of social values, neither the value of the dominant language nor the devaluation of the minority language does in fact exhaust the ways in which these languages are judged by the community. As Moore (1977: 49) writes, "the negotiable part of many real situations lies not only in the imperfect fit between the symbolic or formal level and the level of content, but also in the multiplicity of alternatives and meaning within each, which may accommodate a range of manipulation, interpretation, and choice."

The diglossic schema has this built-in indeterminacy, because it comprises multiple and conflicting values attached to both Corsican and French that are in simultaneous operation in Corsica. The coexistence of these competing discourses means that in actual practice, dominant and alternative linguistic marketplaces are not always clearly delineated. Put another way, there are moments in everyday experience where Corsicans do not experience Corsicanness and Frenchness (and French and Corsican) as being in conflict and opposition. These moments of integration of plural identities, however, are seldom articulated in the public discussion of language and identity.

7.   Radical models of resistance: challenging dominant assumptions

Crowley writes: "The question is this: if the dominant forces can adopt monoglossic, polyglossic and heteroglossic forms and representations to their own purposes...then why cannot the forces which oppose them do likewise?" (1996: 96). This question is taken up in several chapters. Chapters 4 and 5 describe the emergence of currents in Corsican language activism in which language identity is identified more closely with political action and collective choice than it is with "pure" linguistic forms. This can be seen in the last language bill put before the Regional Assembly, which abandoned the quest for Corsican as the sole official language in favor of "coofficiality" for Corsican and French. Corsican academics also backed away, in the late eighties, from a rigid insistence on linguistic differentiation from Italian; in 1989 over one hundred people signed a manifesto advocating a renewed cultural and linguistic link with Italy, and encouraging teaching Italian in the schools. It can also be seen in the sociolinguistic concept of Corsican as a *langue polynomique* 'polynomic language' which asserts "unity in diversity" and promotes the a democratic definition of Corsican in which linguistic unity is based on social consensus rather than linguistic homogeneity. A similar philosophy is embedded in another document, *Lingua Matria*, in which the president of the Regional Assembly's consultative council on culture attempted to replace the idea of the "natural" link of language and people (the mother tongue) with a more social-constructionist view of shared identity as an act of collective choice. Another illustration is found in the second half of Chapter 6, which is a detailed exploration of the first university classroom evoked in the vignette above, where the professor emphasizes the political and social nature of judgments about language standards and language boundaries.

But what Chapters 6 and 7 demonstrate is that the political economy of language in Corsica makes it difficult for language planners to persuade the public (and one another) of the validity, authority and authenticity of plural forms of language practice and of complex creative strategies in the representation of Corsican. One of the costs of a radical form of resistance is the loss of a persuasive idiom with which to make claims of linguistic and cultural identity. This is because a (diglossic) logic of oppositional identity has shaped how many Corsicans have thought about and experienced being Corsican.

This oppositional logic sometimes means that complex and subtle positions are simply not heard; it is just very difficult to unseat the unspoken assumptions of dominant ideologies. We see, for example, that even though there is considerable internal debate among language activists, and significant differences in their representational strategies vis-à-vis Corsican, most popular reactions to language planning measures show that people take them to be fundamentally all the same, and interpret them from within the dominant model.

Yet we should not construe the public simply as an unsophisticated consumer of language policy. On the contrary, I believe that public reactions to language planning also illustrate something we have gotten a glimpse of in the vignette about the spelling of place names: that the Corsican public views linguistic action as inherently ideological and political. Embedded in its distrust of language planners is an implicit understanding that there is no such thing as a neutral linguistic position. At some level, this public recognizes that all linguistic descriptions–even sociolinguistically sophisticated ones which oppose standard prescriptivist stances–are definitional, ideologically motivated choices about what counts as (good/authentic) Corsican. Inevitably, such descriptions validate particular models of identity and linguistic practices over others, and this hierarchy of values inevitably gets translated into institutional practices (textbooks, exams etc.) over which specialists and academics have control–a control the public does not unhesitatingly sanction. Thus, popular resistance to language planning is not always directed at the content of particular policies, but rather, at a social process from which many people feel disenfranchised.

To summarize, despite the fact that resistance does not inhere in particular forms of language or action, and observable linguistic practice always "spills over" the confines of the diglossic model, this model nevertheless exerts a strong influence on both action and interpretation. It is part of the social history of language use that establishes conventional links between form and intention/meaning. Thus while some local discourses are intentionally subversive and others unintentionally illustrate the permeability of official "unitary" language, a great deal of explicit local discourse about language and values tends to reproduce the poles and values of the binary model. So, for example, language use on Corsica may reveal a large number of intermediate or hybrid linguistic forms, proof that the boundaries of the dominant language are not inviolate. However, we find that in discourse about language, the separateness of French and Corsican is often fiercely maintained; ultimately, the authority of French and the ideology in which Corsican is kept separate and unequal not questioned. In other words, explicit linguistic ideology seems to bolster the simple, exclusionary nature of the binary model, even though people express contradictory opinions and behave in complicated ways.

This is of course one of the reasons that literary and academic justifications of a plural model of language identity fall on deaf ears: they keep the focus at the metadiscursive level where the hold of dominant language ideology seems to be difficult to avoid. They are also embedded in literate domains and practices which, as I have suggested above, are far removed from the everyday communicative practices through which most Corsicans constitute their social selves and appreciate language(s).

Chapter 8 examines the application of radical models of resistance outside the academic and written domains by looking at aspects of media practice that have the potential to challenge dominant ideologies of language. The thesis of this chapter is that popular, creative, performative contexts like radio, television, plays, comedy shows etc. constitute a popular, socially validated and widely shared domain of *practice* that may have the power to validate new concepts of language identity without drawing excessive attention to language. That is, unlike anything to do with writing, the use of Corsican in the media can "embed" and "naturalize" plural language ideologies in practices that are for the most part eagerly and uncritically consumed. The bulk of the data in Chapter 8 is drawn from radio broadcasting, since it is this medium that is the most developed and has the widest dissemination. The chapter analyses the language ideologies embedded both in the format and production philosophies of different broadcasts and in the character of listener reactions to those broadcasts. One feature of these broadcasts is their heavy use of "mixed" forms of language. While these forms are still stigmatized by listeners and radio professionals when judgments of "correctness" are elicited in a sociolinguistic interview, they are far rarer in unstructured responses to programming. While radio practice includes a great deal of Corsican and highlights its social and interactional importance, radio policies and practices also acknowledge and *de-dramatize* the fact of French language dominance in the life of the island. Overall, the data suggest that media practice may eventually promote a general, unreflexive acceptance of both hybrid forms as "normal" and as "Corsican". I suggest, following Woolard (1989b: 361), that speakers' willingness to label hybrid forms acceptable may contribute to the survival of Corsican, by shifting the definition of what language is from its formal functions to its social use and communicative properties.

In the conclusion (Chapter 9), I reflect on the difficulty of reconciling a pluralistic model of language and identity with a powerful social and linguistic ideology in which diversity is conceived of as a threat to unity, authority and authenticity. Following Quéré (1987: 75), I suggest that language is a powerful metaphor for identity because it can be seen as an autonomous code, but that the Corsican case illustrates that this image of linguistic and cultural autonomy does violence to the complex and heterogenous experience of life in two languages and cultures. Secondly, the analysis of the successes and failures of the Corsican linguistic, cultural and political movement invites a consideration of the nature and possibility of resistance. In situations like the Corsican one, I make the claim that for a model of resistance to be successful over time involves recognizing and legitimating the long-term effects of an investment in dominant discourses. This is extremely difficult, for it means that minority activists must simultaneously recognize a binary, oppositional model of values and promote some kind of synthesis and balance between dual identities. It is here that we become most acutely aware of the sense in which linguistic and cultural minorities are constrained by dominant discourses.

Chapter 2
Social space and place: models of identity

This chapter explores aspects of Corsican geography and social organization that have influenced the way that Corsican identity is conceptualized and articulated. First, it considers the impact of "islandness,"and makes the claim that the tangible, physical separation of Corsica from the mainland intensifies and reinforces the experience of "otherness" Until recently, the rugged relief of the island and poor roadways also separated Corsican micro regions from one another, heightening Corsicans' identification with local varieties of language and lessening consciousness of pan-Corsican linguistic identity. The following section explores Corsican discourses about the village: the epitome of the intense experience of local identity. The Corsican experience of otherness has also been shaped by political, economic and cultural dimensions of Corsica's relationship with continental France. This chapter describes some of the political and economic effects of French policies, and explores the cultural reverberations of the demographic shifts prompted by economic underdevelopment on the island. Members of the Corsican "diaspora" living on the continent or in the French colonies were confronted with the differences between French and Corsican culture; this confrontation simultaneously contributed to a strong sense of cultural uniqueness and solidarity and was a powerful catalyst for assimilation. One of the focuses of this chapter is on the way that contemporary discourses about the diaspora reveals tensions in the definition of Corsican identity. Is it an inalienable cultural essence, or is it the sum total of collective experiences, including absorption of French values and practices?

The chapter also takes up patterns of Corsican social and political organization, looking at the way that traditional Corsican kinship systems as models for social and political behavior shape contemporary Corsican collective mobilization. The argument is that these patterns foster localized, highly personal modes of identification and allegiance and short circuit pan-Corsican political unity. This serves as an important backdrop for the discussion of collective mobilization around the issue of language officialization taken up in Chapter 5. Finally, the chapter considers the Corsican nationalist movement, which has been the practical and ideological springboard for the language activism with which this book is concerned.

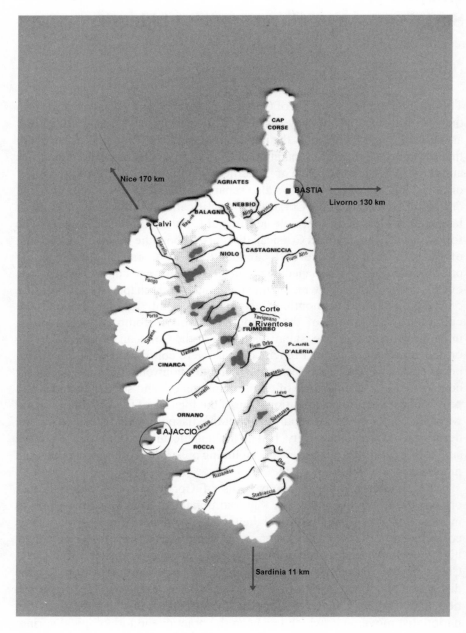

Figure 1. Map of Corsica

1. Geography: social and linguistic space

Corsica is a Mediterranean island in the gulf of Genoa. It is 173 kilometers long, and 85 kilometers wide. There is no doubt that insularity has consequences for the way that islanders perceive their identity and their relationships with the outside world (see Codaccione-Meistersheim 1988: 105). On the one hand, the fact of islandness can serve as a powerful material reinforcement of what are otherwise socially constructed boundaries. In the Corsican literature, getting to and from the island, crossing over the frontier of the sea, intensifies the perception of distance and difference. In his analysis of the causes of the relative vigor of Corsican regionalism compared to other French regional movements, Dottelonde gives partial credit to the fact that *"La Corse constitue, de facto, une entité avec des frontières immutables. La Corse, on pourrait dire, a toujours existé"* [Corsica constitutes de facto an entity with immutable frontiers. Corsica, one could say, has existed forever] (1989: 108). Corsicans are *"unifiés par la mer qui définit nos frontières"* [unified by the sea which defines our boundaries], writes Desanti; Corsican soil becomes a "place of refuge"(1984: 17–18). It is the locus for *"une vie intense et intime"* [an intense intimate life] (Codaccione-Meistersheim 1987: 106). Similarly, Franzini writes: *"Les contours de l'île donnent une frontière réele à l'irréel du sol natal, de la terre sacrée. Cette collision entre réel et irréel est elle une des causes de l'attachement particulier des insulaires à leur terre?"*[The contours of the island provide a real frontier to the imaginary natal soil, sacred ground. This collision between the real and the unreal–is it one of the causes of the unique attachment of islanders to their land?] (1991: 35). The idea of safety and refuge is linked to other potent images of motherhood: hence the recurrent theme of the island as the *"terre-mère"* [mother earth] (Giudicelli 1984: 190; Codaccione-Meistersheim 1989: 110).

But the separation imposed by the sea also brings with it an intensified consciousness of the world beyond its limits; the perception of one's own otherness also gives the "other" a perpetual presence. *"Le dehors nous attache au dedans et le dedans nous pousse au dehors"* [The outside attaches us to the inside, and the inside pushes us towards the outside], writes Desanti, for whom being an islander is *"le tourment de l'ailleurs, l'angoisse d'avoir affaire à l'Autre"* [the torment of elsewhere, the anguish of having to deal with the Other] (1984: 19). Both Desanti and Codaccione-Meistersheim write about the simultaneous push and pull of island identity; in Codaccione-Meistersheim's words, there is *"la tension permanente dans laquelle vivent tous les insulaires: le désir de partir de l'île et le désir d'y retourner quand ils l'ont quittée"* [a permanent tension that all islanders live: the desire to leave the island and the desire to return] (1988: 110). This tension permeates the large Corsican literature of "exile" and return to which I will refer below.

While the sea unifies, the interior geography of Corsica does not. Desanti writes, "*la terre nous a divisés, singularisés à l'extrême. Ce petit monde si bien dessiné, qu'une vue aérienne nous livre aujourd'hui en son entier, a été formé de mondes multiples et séparés. Au milieu du siècle dernier encore la Balagna était un autre monde pour un habitant du Sartenais*"[the earth has divided us, distinguished us to an extreme. This little world, drawn out so well, that is presented to us in its entirety today by an aerial view, has been made up of multiple and separate worlds. In the middle of the last century, the Balagne [a region in the North] was still another world for an inhabitant of the Sartenais [a region in the South]] (1984: 18).

As the map (Figure 1) illustrates, the island is extremely mountainous. The central spine of granite mountains angles from the northwest to the southeast, cutting the island into two regions, *U Cismonte* (the east side of the central mountain ridge) and *U Pumonte* (the west side of the ridge). These two regions roughly correspond with the current two French departments, *la Haute Corse* and *la Corse du Sud*. The two major dialectal varieties of Corsican are defined by this relief. From the central spine, ridges and valleys stretch to the coast, further dividing Corsican social and linguistic space into discrete micro regions.

Even up until the 1950s, it was not uncommon for Corsicans other than traveling salesmen and shepherds to never leave their own small regions. Corsican geography has thus led to strong forms of internal insularity, which, as I have suggested in Chapter 1, have complicated contemporary debates about language.

Insularity can also be experienced as a form of suffocation, as suggested by the title of Corsican author Marie Susini's book *La Renfermée, La Corse* [*The Closed-In, Corsica*]. Acquaviva and Canarelli also write about "*l'espace cloisonné, fermé par les montagnes...encerclé par la mer*" [enclosed space, closed in by the mountains...encircled by the sea] (1981: 41).

The experience of insularity also dramatizes the experience of dependence on the "center". On Corsica, transportation links with the mainland are critical to its economy because of its heavy dependence on tourism. Almost 90% of the island's food and 100% of its fuel are imported. In recent years there have been several strikes that have cut off plane and maritime traffic, the longest (in 1989) lasting almost three months. Not only do these strikes hurt business, but almost immediately impact every person on the island. Moreover, it is almost always the case that the strikes are about the "handicap" of insularity, with Corsican strikers demanding compensation in customs, tax or salary policy.

2. The village

In Chapter 1, I made reference to the importance of my life in the village as a way of entering into a widely shared discourse of identity. The village is used as a metaphor for general aspects of island identity; in particular, an intense attachment to a place which is remote and particular. In effect, the village constitutes an island within an island. The pervasiveness of the village as an idiom of identity is interesting when you consider the fact that over a third of the population of the island (about 100,000 residents) is concentrated in the two cities of Ajaccio and Bastia. It is interesting that, for the most part, there is little distinction drawn between villages and much larger towns in everyday discourses of social identification. That is, people may be described as *Bastiacci* (from Bastia, a town of 50,000 inhabitants) or as *Venachesi* (from Venaco, a village of 300 residents): discursively, there is no particular distinction drawn relative to population size: the city is treated as a large village. Corsicans do identify strongly with microregions: people who describe themselves as *Venachesi* may be from the area around Venaco, and not the village proper. *Fiumorbacci* come from the valley of the Fiumorbu river and *Niolinchi* from the mountainous Niolu region. But these microregional identities are seldom articulated in isolation: in discourse, people situate themselves in reference to the microregion *from the vantage point* of a particular village. The following vignettes are adapted from some of my fieldnotes. Taken together, they represent the kinds of experiences and conversations from which I developed my understanding of the symbolic importance of the village.

2.1. Vignette 1. Pierrette

When she was a little girl, the factory where her father worked closed and he was obliged to accept a job in Algeria. She cried and cried before they left. Every year, in the early summer, she wound herself up to a high pitch of excitement weeks before they left to return to the island. The anticipation was almost unbearable. Years later, after she had moved back to Corsica as an adult, she was visited in her village by an old friend (of Corsican origin) from Algeria, on his honeymoon trip. He had to see her village, he said, because she had described it in such abundant and tender detail that it had become engraved in his childhood memories; this village had lived all these years in his imagination, fleshing out his images of the island.

Now, she cannot bear to live anywhere else. Coming back is a need. She has an apartment in Ajaccio, where she works, but it is about the village that she talks. She goes there every chance she gets, she goes there to vote; she ran for mayor under the nationalist ticket. Nor could she be happy, she thinks, married to a non-Corsican, even though her separation from her first husband was painful. He was an "authentic, real Corsican male: strong, egotistical". When she first married, he represented an ideal, tied up with the yearning for the island that had brought her back. The day he told her that "they did not share the same culture," she packed her bags and left. It was "the biggest slap in the face of my whole life".

For Pierrette, the village represents "authentic" Corsican culture; its image took on an almost mythical dimension during her childhood. The city where she works is somewhere in between "away" and "home". Listening to her, we hear someone who works very hard to connect with her Corsicanness and worries that she will be judged (by people like her ex-husband) as culturally deficient. For her, the village is the place where her membership is unconditional.

2.2. Vignette 2: Paul

Our conversation began in the crowded dais where the public could stand in some discomfort during sessions of the Regional Assembly. We were both there for the debate which would culminate in what is now called the "historic" vote in recognition of the Corsican people. The interminable intermissions provided plenty of chances to chat with one's neighbors. We started by talking about language; we ended up on the topic of village identity. Pierrette, who had introduced us, spoke glowingly of my ability to speak Corsican. Paul refused to be unduly impressed: "Oh well, when you're bilingual, it is easier to pick up another language." I said I did not consider myself bilingual, that I was not able to think or express myself equally well in English and in French. Did he, I asked, think in Corsican as well as he did in French? Quick as a flash, almost before I had finished my sentence, he said "better," and claimed that he thought mostly in Corsican, except when he was working as a computer programmer. It was in Corsican, he said, that his most ingrained habits of speech existed. In the village, he told me, all his Corsican conceptual and linguistic reflexes kicked in automatically. He could not imagine...it did not occur to him to speak French there.

Statements like Paul's do reflect certain aspects of the sociolinguistic reality explored in greater detail in the next chapter. My emphasis here, however, is the discursive status of "speaking Corsican in the village". It figured largely in responses to my sociolinguistic survey question "Where do you speak Corsican the most?" In Chapter 6, "speaking Corsican in the village" emerges as an explanation of how I came to learn Corsican. The village symbolizes the spaces and social relationships Corsicans associate with speaking the language.

2.3. Vignette 3: Jean

"The village," he says, "is paradise." He lived in Paris and Toulouse for 23 years (he is 35 or so), but he says that "when you have spent the first ten years of your life in the village, you just cannot do without village life." The village is where people really care about what you do, where people help one another. In the week, he teaches at the University of Corté, and lives in a house which belongs to an acquaintance who only returns in the summer. You get the impression that he is only really camping out there, amongst other people's things, but that it does not matter. On most weekends, he flees, to paradise, to his own home, his own village.

He sees this paradise, however, as ephemeral. He cites figures. The interior of the island used to have over 100 people per square kilometer, now it is below 30. Some villages are reduced to 10 residents in the winter; the summer only provides the illusion of health; when all the visiting relatives leave, the shutters close and the chill sets in to the old stone houses.

"A language needs to be spoken to survive." On one hand, Jean views the village as the only remaining locus of linguistic vitality and authenticity. The Corsican spoken in the Corsican Studies classes is "unintelligible". His criteria for intelligibility turn out to be related to authenticity, measured by whether or not an old villager would understand. He does not think he could use Corsican to teach his subject (a scientific one). Implicitly, Jean adheres to and contributes to a sociolinguistic situation he explicitly condemns: "a language needs to be spoken in all domains of life," he tells me, "and this is no longer the case for Corsican. It is limited, confined to the village." So for Jean, the village (and Corsican) is a paradise that is by definition disconnected from "real life" and the demands of everyday existence.

2.4. Vignette 4: Michel Mallory

This is a French stage name that the singer has not bothered to change with his entry into the Corsican market. His repertoire is highly sentimental. The lyrics, below, are taken from an album with the following song titles: *"Mamma"* ['Mama'], *"Canta"* ['Sing'], *"Amicizia"*['Friendship'] *"Nostalgia"*

['Nostalgia'] and "*Corsu*" [Corsican]. The following lyrics are from a song called "*Munticellu*," which is the name of his natal village.

Zitellettu di u paese
[Little boy of the village]
Ma mi guardanu cum'è un sgiò
[But they look at me as if I were a lord]
Un mi cunnosci micca?
[You don't recognize me?]
T'aghju à di di u quale so:
[Then I have to tell you who I am:]
Sò un zitellu
[I am a son]
Di Munticellu
[Of Munticellu]
Paese amatu
[Beloved village]
Ind'è eu so natu
[Where I was born]
Francatu l'estate
[Once the summer comes]
Cum'è un acellu
[Like a bird]
Rivengu quì,
[I return here]
In Munticellu.
[To Munticellu.]
Aghju lasciatu u mo core
[I left my heart]
E una parte di me
[And a part of myself]
Per sta piazza per ste loche
[On this plaza, in all these places]
Ch'eu cunnoscu quant'è te
[That I know as well as you.]

It is interesting to read these lyrics in light of Pierrette's comments. Mallory, like Pierrette, has lived elsewhere, and returns to a village where he claims an inalienable belonging: he is a "son" of the village. In some senses, he represents himself as never having left (since his heart always remained there). At the same time, he evokes the possibility of alienation, giving voice to the fact that people may look at him as an outsider (with high social status) which he works hard to deflect by reminding other villagers that he has the same intimate knowledge of place that they do (see the last line). These tensions of identity and belonging do not diminish the symbolic role played by the village in the assertion of an authentic identity.

2.5. Vignette 5: Henri, and others

For the second year in a row, I go to the fair at Francardo for a musical event that is delayed, and quite possibly postponed indefinitely or forever. No one knows. Wandering around the predictable array of booths, *buvettes* (makeshift café/bars) and carnival games and rides not yet glamorized by nightfall, I meet Henri, a University librarian. He is equally bored. Could he offer me a drink? Even a man, a Corsican man does not feel comfortable going to a *buvette* alone-- "This shows that there is something wrong, there is a malaise there." On the way, we stop to look at some nicely carved lamp bases, and Henri immediately asks the craftsman, "*D'induve state?*" ['Where are you from?'] "*Je ne suis pas corse*" ['I'm not Corsican'], the man replies, "*si vous me parlez corse...*" ['if you speak Corsican to me...{understood: it's no use}'].

The *buvette* is manned by a pleasant couple, and we are the only customers. After having chatted with them, Henri introduces me as the American who has been here two or three years (fourteen months, I correct him) and speaks Corsican so well. He has in fact been speaking to them, and me, in Corsican, something he has never done in the University setting, where we only meet at the circulation desk and say hello in the halls. The *buvette* couple is surprised but we do not linger on the topic of my competence long.

They are more impressed that I have heard of their village, Aïti. "*Sa tuttu, megliu chè noï*" [She knows everything, better than we do] says Henri. "A week does not pass," says the man, "that I do not go up to Aïti. I can't do without the village, it is my youth, all my memories are there." Henri is also on his way to his village, Noceta; like the buvette owner and many Corsicans, he talks about it as "going up," to **the** village ("*monter au village*"). Like Jean and Pierrette, he attaches little affective importance to his weekday life at work.

It is Friday night, and Henri is not the only one to leave Corté and the University. By Saturday morning, the University parking lot will be dramatically empty; the few remaining cars belong to the unfortunate law students who have Saturday classes. The dorms are deserted, the library and the cafeteria are closed. The dozen or so foreign (mostly North African) students are left to fend for themselves.

This does not just happen at the University. In a satire about an oriental anthropologist who comes to study Corsica, the protagonist, Malikha, arrives in Bastia:

La ville lui parut jolie, mais il fut étonné de la voir aussi déserte...Après avoir parcouru à pied le centre de la ville...il s'avisa de trouver un restaurant. Peut-être allait-il pouvoir apprendre ou étaient passés les Bastiais? Le restaurant dans lequel il entra était pratiquement vide, et la serveuse semblait s'ennuyer mortellement. Comprenant qu'elle avait affaire à un étranger, elle fut ravie, après avoir pris sa commande, de venir bavarder avec lui...Malikha put enfin lui poser la question qui brûlait les lèvres. "Mais où sont donc les Français?....Elle lui repondait qu'en Corse les villes étaient désertées durant le week-end, chacun s'en retournant à son village dans son maison de famille. Ainsi elle-même, si elle n'avait pas été à service au restaurant, aurait passé son dimanche à Pino, petit village du cap Corse, avec le reste de sa famille (Granarolo, 1984: 61–62).

[He found the town beautiful, but was surprised to see it so deserted...After having visited the center on foot...he decided to find a restaurant. Perhaps he could find out where the Bastiais had gone? The one he went into was almost empty, and the waitress seemed to suffering from terminal boredom. When she learned he was foreign, she was more than happy to sit down and chat with him...Malikha finally asked the question that had been burning on his lips: "Where are all the French people?"...she said that in Corsica, the cities were deserted on the weekend, that everyone returned to their villages and family homes. If she did not have to work, she too would be in Pino, a small village on the peninsula, with the rest of her family.]

It is interesting that Henri, meeting me on his way to his village, treated the fair we were attending as though it were a village, and treated Corsican as an unmarked code of social interactions with the vendor and with me. It is impossible to judge whether his use of Corsican with the vendor was a self-conscious strategy meant to assert that Corsican should be an unmarked, or normal code, or whether he was unselfconsciously framing the context as a Corsican speaking one in which he could assume the vendor's competence. His use of Corsican with me was somewhat more remarkable. I found that it was extremely rare for any Corsican to use Corsican *with* me unselfconsciously (though people often spoke it unselfconsciously *around* me). So I think it is fair to narrow our interpretation of Henri's linguistic practice to two possibilities: 1) having left work, he was already, conceptually, in his village, where he spoke almost exclusively in Corsican. In effect, he had already switched over to Corsican as an unmarked linguistic choice, 2) it was very important for him to display a village identity to me since I was a foreigner, and since I had only ever interacted with him in a professional context. In this case, we can link his motivations to the pervasive association of village identity with authentic Corsicanness.

2.6. Summary: language and the village

Corsican discourse about the village is a romantic one. It has not, however, impeded villages from becoming depopulated. In the contemporary economy, it is impossible for many people to live all year in their villages; they are forced to live where they work, and work is concentrated in the larger cities and towns. It would also be a mistake to imagine that all the Corsicans who talk so passionately about their villages would actually want to live there all year even if they could. The value of the village is in some measure the value of contrast. The village is a refuge from the city, but the city can also be a refuge from the village, and many people fully appreciate the conveniences and advantages of city life. But the fact remains that the image of the village is still a very powerful one in the Corsican popular imagination. Later in the book, we will see that it is this very localized kind of experience of identity that people refer to when they talk about linguistic identity and authenticity. They talk more about what is unique to the language used in their village than they talk about their experiences of accommodating linguistically to people from other villages or regions. In other words, the village–local identity linked to one place on the ground–is an important part of Corsican metadiscourse. Movement between various places, and movement between different social identities does not have the same role in Corsican discourses of cultural and linguistic identity.

3. History, social relations and identity

In this section, I discuss features of Corsican history and social organization that are important for the understanding of contemporary Corsican culture and the formulation of Corsican identity. First, there are Corsica's relationships with outside powers. Second, there are traditional forms of Corsican social organization and how they articulate with external authority. Third, there is the Corsican diaspora, which captures the ambiguity of Corsican experience and identification with France. Finally, I discuss the nationalist movement which is the immediate backdrop for Corsican language activism.

3.1. Outside rule

Corsica has had a turbulent history of foreign occupation because of its strategically useful location in the Mediterranean. Going back to ancient history, the Phoceans occupied the flatlands of the eastern plain from 565 to 260 BC, when they were ousted by the Romans. Between the fifth and the tenth centuries, Corsica was invaded by the Barbarians and the Saracens and had a Byzantine occupation. For about two hundred years, in the eleventh and twelfth centuries, ownership of the island alternated between Genoa and Pisa until Pope Boniface VIII gave Corsica and Sardinia to the King of Aragon. The Genoans regained control of the island in 1347, but had to battle a Corsican revolt led by Sambuccio d'Alando (in 1358), numerous attempts by Aragon to reconquer the island and another French-backed Corsican revolt in 1553. In the mid-eighteenth century, France stepped up its efforts to acquire control of the island, backing a Corsican revolt led by Gaffori. Gaffori was killed, and his successor Pascal Paoli took over and proclaimed independence from Genoa. During his rule from 1755 to 1769, Paoli implemented a democratic Constitution which is sometimes credited with being the precursor to both the French and the American documents drawn up later in the century. Ultimately, Paoli was defeated by the French in the battle of Ponte Novu. He returned from exile in England, and with British backing, regained control of the island from 1794 until 1796, when the British withdrew from the island and Corsica became French.

The periodic uprisings against external rule in Corsica's history, and in particular, the period of independence under Paoli, serve as important symbolic resources in the contemporary articulation of Corsican identity. They are the basis, especially in nationalist discourse, of a self-image of Corsicans as fierce, proud, independent people, unwilling to submit to domination. Franceschi and Geronimi (1991: 24) claim that Corsicans' "family system" nourishes a rejection of any external authority, and discourages people from recognizing any central authoritative state structure as legitimate. This image is also supported by the modern representation of banditry; the "bandit of honor" embodies *"l'idéologie commune, l'honneur, la fidélité, le mépris de la mort...[et] lutte pour maintenir son identité, contre le pouvoir extérieur et centralisateur"* [communal ideology, honor, fidelity, scorn of death...[and] fights to maintain his identity, against the external, centralizing power] (Ravis-Giordani 1979: 84).

In more recent history, the extremely successful Corsican Resistance Movement during World War II has also contributed to the same collective image; it is no accident, as Ravis, above points out, that Choury's (1958) book on the Corsican Resistance is entitled *Tous Bandits d'Honneur* [*Bandits of*

Honor All]. There are also valued images of resistance to internal authority in Corsican oral culture: in one story, situated in the last century, a shepherd went into the town of Porto-Vecchio wearing a tie. A *Sgiò* 'Nobleman' threatened him, saying he didn't have the right to enter the city with a tie. The next week, the shepherd returned: his dog was wearing a tie and he was carrying a gun.

The image of otherness of Corsicans is not only generated from within, but imposed from without. As Culioli points out, continental French discourse always describes Corsicans in extreme terms: "*Héro ou vaurien, esprit fénéant ou aristocratique, bandit ou homme droit, le Corse n'a jamais su trouver sa juste place sur le continent–celle d'un individu comme tout autre, avec sa propre culture, bon ou mauvais comme tous les habitants de la terre*" [Heroic or good-for-nothing, with a slothful or aristocratic soul, bandit or man of law, the Corsican has never succeeded in finding his just place on the continent, that of a person like any other, with his specific culture, and good or bad like all the inhabitants of the earth] (Culioli 1990: 16).

The negative stereotypes about Corsicans usually outweigh the positive in the view from the center. Mezzadri (1991: 57) writes that "*Nos voisins des metropoles..rient..de l'archaïsme indécrottable qu'ils décèlent en nous*" [Our metropolitan neighbors...laugh...at the archaisms they see in us, sticking to us permanently like manure]. During the three month strike of 1989, in which Corsican civil servants protested the lack of compensation for the high cost of living on the island, some of the intensity and duration and extent of popular support for the strike among Corsicans was a response to reactions from the French government and press that Corsicans identified as part of a history of prejudice. The Corsican monthly *Kyrn* (1989, 248: 17) compiled a list of quotes from the national press entitled "Common Racism". A few of these illustrate the dominant tone: "*Si la vie est plus chère dans l'Île de Beauté, c'est parce que les petits malins rackettent les circuits de distribution*" [If the cost of living is higher on the Island of Beauty, it is because the little thugs racketeer distributors] (*Minute*, 30 March 1989). "*La Corse nous aura vraiment couté la peau des fesses...Moi je ne vois qu'un truc, lui accorder son indépendance*" [Corsica will have cost us the skin off our butts...As for me, I think the only thing is to give it its independence...] (*Le Monde*, 30 March 1989). "*C'est une île insupportable–on l'oublie quelques mois, on n'est plus 55 millions à son chevet: elle fait une poussée de fièvre*" [It's an intolerable island–you forget it for a few months, 55 million people are not by its bedside, and it spikes a fever] (*Le Monde*, 19 March 1989).

3.2. Kinship and "the clan"

3.2.1. Kinship

The image of Corsican independence and resistance to authority I have evoked above is an idealized one. It is necessarily selective, highlighting certain aspects of Corsican history and culture and obscuring others. In this section, I explore some dimensions of traditional Corsican social organization and structure. I draw on the analysis of anthropologists who have focused on Corsican kinship and political structures, for they offer important insights on the mechanisms through which Corsicans have both accommodated to and remained separate from French structures of authority. I also use these ethnological sources to sketch out prototypical models of Corsican person-hood and social relations, showing how such models make the very notion of a collective good problematic. This necessarily necessarily brief overview should not be taken as a static, homogenizing picture of Corsican culture; rather, it is meant to be backdrop for the ethnographically based discussions of reactions to language planning measures.

José Gil's classic analysis of Corsican culture shows that on the one hand, Corsican kinship organized people in egalitarian, segmentary networks of relations in which conflict and power were balanced in a continuous cycle of reciprocity and the public display of the fearlessness and autonomy of the individual. The ideology of independence and resistance was thus a critical part of the social performance of personhood (in particular, manhood: see Blok 1981, Gilmore 1987 and Herzfeld 1985 for parallels). On the other hand, Gil also shows that social equality, in this system, was not a function of individualism. The individual's public display of autonomy dramatized the social person, the network of kinship ties that sustained each Corsican. That is, Corsican social life continuously emphasized that individual affairs were always collective affairs (Gil 1984).

In this model, kin solidarity is expected and valued as the basis of collective behavior; Corsicans expect other Corsicans to unconditionally support "their own". One of the most extreme expressions of this was the vendetta, where families could engage in an endless cycle of violence and vengeance. In contemporary Corsican culture, this ethos still plays a role in almost all aspects of public life. Dottelonde's (1989: 112) analysis of the nationalist vote between 1982 and 1984 shows that the places that registered a significantly higher percentage than the norm of nationalist votes were those where the nationalist candidates were locals. He suggests, in concert with other Corsican political analysts, that Corsican voting patterns reflect the power of social and kin networks more accurately than they index political or ideological positions. It is also assumed that getting ahead, or getting things done in a bureaucratic or institutional context depends on social solidarity. A Corsican comic, *Teatru Mascone*, tells the story of when the Americans and Russians were racing to get to the moon first. When the first American finally arrived, he got out of the capsule to find two Corsicans already there. "But how did you get here?" he asked incredulously. The Corsican astronauts replied: "*Le piston*": literally, "with a push/piston action"; figuratively, through social connections.

The egalitarian, segmentary model is based on social competition. It has, therefore, a built in potential for conflict. Since this conflict could happen at any level of the segmentary system, every other person is both a potential ally and a potential enemy. Ravis-Giordani describes Corsican society as "*un univers dans lequel l'indifférence est impensable: l'amitié et l'inimitié y remplissent tout l'espace*" [a universe in which indifference is unthinkable, completely filled with friendship and enmity] (1979: 75). This means that trust and information must be carefully managed. Elsewhere, Ravis-Giordani writes that Corsican children used to be taught that the correct response to the question "What did you have for supper?" (a sign of social differentiation in a poor and frugal society) was "*Pane è pernice, affari di casa un si ne dice*" [Bread and partridge; one doesn't speak about family affairs] (1984: 33). The wider lesson of this rote response were that information was social capital, that people outside the immediate family should not necessarily be trusted, and information restricted to the smallest possible social unit. And, relations were to be carefully managed in interaction. One acquaintance recalled how this operated in a village. As a child, he would visit his aunt during his school holidays. As soon as he got off the bus, she would take him back to her house and give him instructions: "You say hello to person "x"; you give him a kiss. You only shake hands with person "y"; you don't speak at all to person "z".

Egalitarian relations are seen as being maintained, precariously, by a balance of forces that is constantly threatened by people's natural tendencies to dominate others. This has a number of social repercussions. In Corsican relations with other Corsicans, individual behavior is always interpreted as motivated by self or group interest that is automatically at the expense of others. In a pattern found in other small communities, this leads to a profound distrust of all Corsicans in positions of power (see Parman 1990; Messenger 1983; Wylie 1974). In a recent interview, Lisandru Bassani, current President of the Cultural, Economic and Social Council of the Corsican Assembly, described how these ideas translate into everyday comportment. When a man goes into a small bar in a village where he isn't known, he told me, he should not make the mistake of swaggering up to the bar and ordering a round for everyone. He should sit quietly at the bar, order a drink, chat a bit with the barman/owner and let himself be observed. Then, he should try to enter into light conversation (about the weather, for example) with the oldest person there. He should end up asking this elder for permission to buy him a drink. Only then should he try to turn to the rest of the clients and ask if they would allow him to buy a round. This careful social management is aimed to mitigate the suspicion that the outsider is there to dominate others (in this case, by "winning" by being the giver of gifts). As we will see, this sort of suspicion can have repercussions for the way that Corsicans respond to language planning efforts.

The Corsican kinship system is also a model of social behavior and justice that conflicted and still conflicts with French jural principles. Not only are competition and conflict deep rooted motors of Corsican social life, but there is also the law of silence that drops like an iron wall whenever a government investigation is attempted. This is particularly marked when the "crime" is a socially motivated one, because it is often assumed that one cannot defend oneself against crimes against one's honor using French law (Bassani, personal interview). The autonomist leader Max Simeoni gave me an example of this rejection of external authority and values in a 1988 interview. He reminded me of Corsican reactions to a 1985 incident in which Corsican nationalist commandos broke into a prison in Ajaccio and killed two prisoners being detained for suspected murder of a nationalist. In the press, and in private conversation, almost no Corsicans (nationalist or antinationalist) expressed concern that (French) principles of justice had been perverted by a few people taking justice into their own hands. Rather, they commented on how scandalous it was that security was so lax as to have allowed the event to happen.

In recent years, Corsicans have begun to question the ethos of social solidarity that is often glossed as "kinship" in Corsican discourse. A 1990 White Paper of the Corsican Regional Assembly comments that "*le réseau étroit de relations sociales qui caractérise les cultures insulaires risque d'empêcher l'innovation*" [the tight network of social relations that character-izes insular cultures risks being an impediment to innovation" (Préfecture de la Région de Corse 1990: 11). Jacques-Henri Balbi, President of the University and member of the group that formulated the White Paper said that he had to concede that within an externally imposed bureaucracy, strong ties of kinship on Corsica perpetuate "*le piston*": nepotism and patronage (Personal interview 1991). As Biggi writes, "*il est extrêmement difficile d'avoir des relations strictement professionnelles, strictement d'efficacité économique, dans un ensemble où la plupart des gens sont tenus par des liens de parenté*" [it is very difficult to have strictly professional, economically

efficient relations in a society in which most people are bound by kinship]
(1989: 14).

3.2.2. The clan

3.2.2.1. The clan as mediator with a distant state

The Corsican *partitu* 'clan' is "*la superstructure politique d'une infrastructure culturelle dont l'articulation repose sur la famille et les valeurs
traditionelles*"[the political superstructure of a cultural infrastructure
articulated on a base of family and traditional values"] (Olivesi 1983: 6) and
"*divisait chaque entité locale...et la société corse toute entière en deux
fractions ou factions homologues et antagonique à base de parentés et
d'alliances...*"[divided each local unit...the whole of Corsica into two
homologous and antagonistic factions or fractions based on kinship and kin
alliances" (Orsoni 1990: 192).

The *partitu* emerged in the context of the growth of the role of the state in
education and employment after the late 1800s, (Gil 1984: 69) in a pattern
common to Sicily (Blok 1974) and other parts of Italy (Holmes 1989). It
served as a mediator between the centralized French state and a dependent,
underdeveloped, largely agropastoral community, funneling and distributing
government money on the island and serving as a relay for the placement of
Corsicans in government posts on the French continent and in the colonies.
Merler writes that "*Da una parte, dunque, il "partitu" si sottomette e applica
leggi e mezzi degli occupanti (sia in termini politici che economici e
culturali), dall'altra parte le gira, le contorna, le adatta al suo profitto,
operando come una sorta di filtro*" [On one hand, therefore, the 'partitu'
submits itself to, and applies the laws and practices of the occupiers (be it in
political, economic or cultural terms), on the other hand, it twists them, goes
around them, adapts them to its own profit, operating like a sort of filter]
(1988: 80).

There was, then, a symbiotic relationship between the clan and the central
government. The central government needed the clan in order to effectively
govern the island, and was prepared to turn a blind eye to its abuses. This was
in part a reflection of the difficulties posed by Corsican social organization
and social violence discussed above. It was also, in part, a symptom of a
policy of disengagement: Corsica did not have enough votes or resources to
make it worth the bother.

For the clan, manipulation of the vote was the ticket to political office and government funds. A *partitu* was made up of kin and local alliances, and revolved around one strong leader whose mandate was usually inherited. All of the members of the group were to vote in the best interest of the group, which translated purely and simply into getting the leader into office, where he could distribute favors. This meant that the clan system worked towards "*il mantenimento, consolidamento e rinnovamento dei rapporti della dipendenza*" [the maintenance, consolidation and reproduction of dependent relations] between the island and the government (Merler 1988: 78). Ultimately, this contributed to Corsica's economic underdevelopment, because the clan's strongest hand was the control of external resources. Entrepreneurship—the creation of new markets or economic activities—actually threatened the status of the clan by multiplying the numbers of people outside of its domain of control.

3.2.2.2. Economic consequences

As Orsoni notes, the clan "protected" Corsica from outside influences that could have had a vitalizing effect on the economy (1990: 194). It can thus be seen as one ingredient of the weak Corsican economy. By the early part of this century, all Corsica's exportable agricultural products (chestnuts, grains, grapes, citrons) had either been decimated by disease or driven off the market by foreign competition. Large scale agricultural ventures were also discouraged by partible inheritance laws that parceled out tiny plots of land in such a way that it was extremely difficult for any one individual to amass acreage suitable for anything more than subsistence farming. The most farmable land, on the eastern plain, was infested with malaria until World War II, when the American Army sprayed it with DDT. Limited economic opportunities on the island drove many Corsicans to the continent and the colonies. In turn, the Corsican diaspora, discussed below, further weakened the island's economy. By 1960, 25% of the active population was engaged in agriculture or pastoralism, but these sectors provided only 7% of the island's revenues. The last tannery closed in 1963, the only mine in 1964; all other industrial ventures had folded long before. Today, the largest part of the economy is in the tertiary sector, followed by government service. By 1979, 36% of Corsican annual revenues consisted of pensions and other governmental assistance.

3.2.2.3. Cultural consequences

The strength of the clan system has had a number of cultural consequences. In its mediating role, *"il a contribué au maintien de la culture et de l'identité corses, en atténuant les effets et les répercussions de la loi, de la justice de l'administration étatiques"*[it contributed to the maintenance of Corsican culture and identity by attenuating the effects and repercussions of state law, justice and administration] (Orsoni 1990: 193). That is, the cultural brokerage of the clan fueled the Corsican perception of the French system as a distant entity with no moral authority and reinforced the authority of local models of justice. As Giudicelli remarks, *"la loi localisée du clan a toujours prévalu, d'où cette propension à ignorer la loi des autres, à être sa propre loi, à se faire justice"* [the localized law of the clan has always prevailed, which is the source of this propensity to ignore the law of others, to be one's own law, to render one's own justice] (1984: 196). Here we see a cultural basis for the linguistic resistance of separation I have alluded to in Chapter 1.

Despite its complicity with the state, the clan was still able to pass itself off as an *"istituzione di difesa comunitaria nei confronti di quello stesso Stato"* [institution of communal defense in the confrontation with that same State] (Merler 1988: 80). Part of the clan's strength and persistence stems from its use of the culturally valued idiom of kinship to disguise the fact that it does not act on behalf of the collectivity, and undermines the already limited potential for collective, solidary behavior built into the segmentary model. This has made the Corsican critique of the clan problematic, because the shared language of kinship makes it difficult to disentangle "genuine" and valued dimensions of Corsican kinship from their "perversion" in the clan system. As a consequence, *"il clan rimane ancora una forma essenziale di identificazione con i valori più profondi e sani della 'corsicità': l'onore, la solidarità, la giustizia, la fedeltà, l'importanza della comunità, la fratellanza etc."* [the clan still remains an essential form of identification with the most profound and healthy values of Corsicanness: honor, solidarity, justice, faithfulness, the importance of the community, brotherhood etc.] (Merler 1988: 78). For this reason, Olivesi asserts that the clan *"est donc conforme, non pas à la société corse, mais à la représentation qu'il s'en fait dans le corps social. Qui conteste le clan, conteste sa légitimité culturelle et le contestataire devient le fossoyeur de la société corse"* [thus conforms, not to Corsican society, but to the representation that it makes and diffuses in the social body of that society. To contest the clan is to contest its cultural legitimacy and the person contesting that becomes the grave digger of Corsican society] (1983: 23).

Paradoxically, the way the clan functioned short circuited the experience of pan-Corsican unity. This is because the oppositional logic that reinforced Corsican singularity through a contrast with France was also applied internally. The political success, and related economic benefits of one *partitu* was obtained at the expense of the other *partitu* at every level, from the village to the canton, to the island as a whole. Competition for resources within this system created cleavages in every social unit (Gil 1984: 58; Ravis-Giordani 1979: 82). People thus had no experience or concept of the idea of the common good (Gil 1984: 223). On the contrary, they accepted the fraud, violence and corruption in the political and social system as a customary, normal mode of operation. Gil writes that the way the clan functioned thus *"contribue à figer la société corse dans sa situation de dépendance à l'égard de l'état français...a diffusé et entretenue les modèles d'une réussite dépendante...la réussite fonctionnaire, du représentant de l'état...ou les professions libérales..."*[contributes...to the miring of Corsican culture in its situation of dependence on the French state...[it] diffused and sustained dependent models of social success...the success of the civil servant, the state representative...or the professions...] (Gil 1984: 165–166). While *le piston* is extremely gratifying when it benefits the individual, its pervasiveness undermines people's faith in the possibility of social planning and change at the collective level. As Urla (1988) has pointed out, local enthusiasm for language planning is related to ideas about the possibility of social engineering. On Corsica, there seems to be little faith in orchestrated social or linguistic change: few people seem to believe that laws or policies will ever be applied impartially, or based on coherent social principles.

4. The diaspora[13]

Incentives to leave the island for education and employment have been - extremely strong ever since the end of the 19th century. As opportunities closed on the island, many young Corsicans who wished to escape the rigors of pastoralism and subsistence farming chose to emigrate to the continent or the Americas. By the turn of the century, the Corsican peasant's goal was for his child to get an education and a civil service job, an ideal which many Corsicans met. Few of those jobs were on the island, which meant that Corsicans had to emigrate to the French continent or colonies. By 1968, there were more Corsicans on the continent than on the island, a pattern that has continued today. In the 1981 census, there were over 150,000 Corsicans in the Parisian region alone. In the first half of the century, the colonial services attracted very large numbers of Corsicans. It is estimated that there were

200,000 Corsicans living outside of continental France by 1950. Of these, almost 150,000 lived in North Africa. Some of them were involved in business, but a large proportion was in the civil service. By 1930, it is estimated that 20 to 30% of people in the colonial services (military and civilian) were Corsican; in some colonies, this figure rose to 50%. This emigration involved both men and women and whole families. One significant dimension of Corsican involvement in colonial service was that they were given month long vacations during which they returned to the island. These extended stays helped to maintain social ties and identities.

Corsicans living on the French continent and overseas had an extensive and well organized *amicale* structure. *Amicales* were social associations which organized activities that brought together expatriate Corsicans. They served as important social and cultural networks, helping newly emigrated Corsicans with housing, employment and so forth, and acting as a forum for the expression and maintenance of cultural and linguistic practices. In 1912, the *Union Generale des Corses et des Amis de la Corse* [General Union of Corsicans and Friends of Corsica] headquartered in Paris, counted in its membership 120 sections with 40,000 people.

In addition to its demographic and economic effects, the Corsican diaspora has also had cultural consequences. The following section will look at contemporary Corsican discourse about the meaning of the diaspora from two perspectives: that of the individual experience of those who left the island, and the collective meaning of this group to those who stayed.

4.1. The "unbroken cord": inalienable identity

As the section above on the village indicates, Corsicans who live elsewhere have always returned faithfully to their native villages and family homes in the summer and at retirement. In a 1991 survey of 556 Corsicans living in the Parisian region, 83% reported returning to the island at least once a year; 77% of the returnees went back to their village of origin (Forum Paris–Corse 1991: 40–45). Many vote on the island (by correspondence or proxy); as a group, they represent between a quarter and a third of the Corsican electorate. "*On ne part jamais de la Corse,*" goes a popular saying, "*on s'absente*" [one never leaves Corsica, one is only [temporarily] absent].

Departure is never separated from return, and in much Corsican discourse about the meaning of the diaspora, a claim is made for a simple, clear, inalienable Corsicanness. Those who live elsewhere often represent their attachment to the island in visceral terms; they talk about "the umbilical cord," "having the island under their skins," and "not being able to breathe" until they return, the "thirst for the island" that immediately bursts out in conversation when two Corsicans meet elsewhere. Writing in response to a call from the weekly magazine *Kyrn* during the 1991 debate over the vote of the diaspora, one man wrote the following poem (Raymond 1991: 23):

> *Êtres,*
> [Beings,]
> *cordon omblical insécable*
> [Umbilical cord that cannot wither]
> *vies d'une époque si lointaine dans l'espace et le temps*
> [lives from an epoque so far away in time and space,]
> *Ne pas oublier,*
> [Not forgetting,]
> *Ne pas perdre cette richesse qui m'a irrigué*
> [Not losing this richness that has flowed through me]
> *(comme d'autres, ailleurs)*
> [(as it has through others, elsewhere)]
> *cette sémence et cet engrais*
> [the grains sowed and fertilized]
> *Vivants et morts se ressemblent,*
> [The living and the dead come together]
> *malgré quelques errances*
> [despite having strayed somewhat]
>> *Mon lien avec la Corse à travers une activité?*
>> [My link to Corsica through an activity?]
>> *L'activité distraît de l'essentiel, le plus souvent.*
>> [Activity distracts from the essential, most of the time.]

The essential, in this poem, is returning *"pour simplement être là...revenir...s'impose comme une nécessité incontournable...le lien au lieu est la pure expression de la tradition"*[simply to be there...coming back is seen as an unavoidable necessity...the link to place is the pure expression of tradition] (Desideri 1991: 30). One Corsican who was asked the question by a newspaper reporter, "What is it that you come back for each summer?" said, *"Y répondre, c'est prendre en quelque sorte ses distances avec la Corse. Ce que je refuse de faire. Je reviens en Corse parce que je suis Corse"* [To respond to such a question is to distance oneself in a certain sense from Corsica, which I refuse to do. I come to Corsica because I am Corsican] (*Le Corse* 15 July 1991). In a newspaper interview, a Corsican who was the political desk editor of the national newspaper *Le Monde* said,

> *ne pas être autre chose que Corse. C'est une notion aussi naturelle que celle d'exister...Le fait de travailler à Paris n'y change rien....Je vote dans mon*

village, parce que c'est chez moi. Je suis concerné par l'élection de mon maire, du conseiller général et du député de la Haute-Corse. En tant qu'individu, la vie politiqe du 17ième arrondissement de Paris, où j'habite, ne m'intéresse pas (Colombani 1990).

[I am nothing but Corsican. It is a notion as natural as existence itself...The fact that I work in Paris doesn't change anything...I vote in my village, because it's my home. I am concerned by the election of my mayor, my general councillor and the deputy of the *Haute Corse*. Personally, the political life of the 17th arrondissement, where I live, does not interest me at all]

The inevitability of return is echoed time and time again. A newspaper headline about the diaspora described it as *"Un pélérinage doré pour retrouver ses racines"* ['A golden pilgrimage to rediscover one's roots'] (*Le Corse* 31 July 1991). In Riventosa, Charles is almost 70, but looks about 55. Sweating and muscular, he labors in his large gardens all summer long. He spent thirty years in Toulon in a civil service job, living an apparently idyllic life with a girlfriend and a poodle. To her surprise, but to no one's in the village, when he reached retirement, he packed his bags and in no time, had left both dog and woman to move back to Riventosa to live with his family. The girlfriend was left behind, I was told by others of his generation, because he was not about to get married and because his relatives would not tolerate him "living in sin" in the family house. Continental ways were left on the continent. But the return was equally inevitable for those who, like the retired General Alberti, loudly proclaimed their Frenchness, disparaged the call of the early seventies to *"vivre et travailler au pays"* [live and work in the region/land], and were critical of the "insular" mentality in its provincial aspects. He too returned without question when he retired. So did Madame Constantini, first woman ambassador in the French foreign service, born on the continent to educated parents, after a long and prosperous career.

Often, these years spent elsewhere are referred to as a parenthesis between the authentic Corsican experiences of childhood, periodic summer holidays, and the eventual return to the island at retirement.[14] I was particularly struck by this when I went to interview the owners of the hotel where my husband worked, Félice and Aurélien Albertini. I asked if they had ever lived anywhere else. Aurélien said, no, he had lived in the village of St. Pierre all his life. "Don't be silly," his wife snapped, reminding him of his 20 years of military service on the continent. He protested—it was just military service. "I did not consider it a *habit*." Thiers (1988a: 525) notes the same phenomenon in his conversations and interviews, citing a woman who downplayed her travels over five continents, emphasizing her life in Corté since her return. And Orsoni writes that the space of the exterior *"reste anonyme, tous ses lieux s'équivalent et les occupations que les Corses y déploient ou y ont déployés avant le retour au pays ne présentent pas d'intérêt véritable et sont à peine mentionnés: seuls comptent le titre ou le statut qu'elles permettent de faire valoir dans l'île même"*[stays anonymous, all of the places are the same, and the occupations that Corsicans engage in or engaged in there before coming back to the *pays* do not have any real interest and are hardly mentioned: the only thing that counts is the claim to title or status that they permit on the island itself] (1990:195).

The return at retirement is not only "as inevitable as death," but on occasion, motivated by the thought of death: *"Mêmes si nous vivons et mourons sur le continent, comment imaginer que nous puissions reposer en une autre terre que notre* terra materna?*"* [Even if we live and die on the continent, it would be impossible to imagine that we could go to our rest in other than our *mother earth*] (Castelli 1986: 64). As the Corsican proverb says: *"Aux enterrements et aux mariages, on reconnait les siens"* [At funerals and marriages, one recognizes one's own]. In the 1991 Forum Paris–Corse survey mentioned above, 78% of the respondents identified funerals as a family rite that was important to conduct on the island (Forum Paris–Corse 1991: 35). Death demands that people be returned to their "original" and "authentic" cultural and social space.

One of the cornerstones of the discourse of cultural continuity that is held by both those who left and those who stayed is the idea of "exile," a term that crops up incessantly in written and oral accounts. Graziani, for example, describes his autobiography as *"un chronique détaillé du temps passé (perdu?) hors de la Corse...l'itinéraire d'un enfant insulaire exilé de son village, arraché à l'environnement naturel..."* [a detailed chronicle of time spent (lost?) outside of Corsica...the itinerary of a child of the island, exiled from his village, ripped from his natural environment...] (1986: xiii). In letters to the papers, Corsicans of the diaspora arguing for their continued right to vote on the island wrote that they were "obliged to exile themselves" because they could not find work on Corsica, or "in order to bring up their children properly"; that people should know that they maintained their desire to return to Corsica despite being "prevented for economic reasons". A Monsieur Santoni who had spent thirty years as a postal employee addressed permanent residents in a letter to the paper with these words: *"Il ne faut pas oublier que notre génération est celle des sacrifices...qui a dû s'expatrier faute de développement et d'emploi..."* [You must not forget that our generation was the sacrificed one...which was forced to expatriate itself in the absence of development and employment...]. He emphasized the sacrifices they had made out of fidelity to their home, writing about *"tant de dures périodes passées à faire des heures supplémentaires pour pouvoir rentrer en Corse l'été..."* [so many difficult periods spent working overtime in order to be able to go back to Corsica in the summer] (*Le Corse* July 30, 1990).

The significance of the notion of exile is that it places responsibility for the decision to leave the island outside the control of those who leave. This bolsters both the individual's claim to cultural authenticity, and the collectivity's claim for cultural continuity. In the political arena, Corsican nationalists refer to exile as one of the ways that France has victimized Corsicans through their policy of "internal colonialism," which siphons resources and people from the peripheries to the center. This means that they are not responsible, either individually or collectively, for the decision to leave Corsica or for the negative economic and social consequences caused by the island's demographic frailty.

The experience of deserted villages, lack of economic vitality and the perception that Corsican culture and language are threatened make it all the more important for Corsicans to find evidence of cultural continuity in the diaspora. *"Diaspora?"* wrote one journalist, *"Non au sens étymologique. Les Corses ne se sont jamais sentis dispersés car ils se sont toujours rassemblés en communauté à l'extérieur"* [Diaspora? Not in the etymological sense of the term. Corsicans have never felt dispersed since they have always grouped together in communities abroad] (*Corse Matin*, June 16, 1991). Many Corsicans talk about the strong communities of Corsican *amicales*, which are often the subject of Corsican newspaper reports. A typical article about a Puerto Rican group said that it was *"faisant d'énormes efforts pour que nos compatriotes, venus ici depuis des générations, ne perdent point leurs racines, leur identité"* [making an enormous effort to insure that our compatriots who arrived there several generations back, do not lose one bit of their roots, their identity] (*Corse Matin* June 5, 1991). In newspaper and other accounts of faraway Corsicans who return after a prolonged absence, or who visit the island for the first time in their lives, there is often an emphasis on the instant cultural empathy these people feel. I was told, for example, about a Corsican of Puerto Rican birth who had never been to Corsica, but was nurtured on the image of his grandfather on his deathbed, clutching a bottle of water from his native village of Macinaggio. As a young scholar, he returned one summer to the island, was enchanted, and came back to teach at the University for two years. For several years, there was also a very popular radio program called *Décalage Horaire* 'Time Change'. It was a live broadcast of parts of conversations between Corsicans living in faraway places and their relations on the island. The accent, once again, was always on the continued Corsicanness of faraway kin.

If islandness on its own intensifies the awareness of otherness, the existence of a large population living on the French continent and returning regularly provokes a perpetual consciousness of contrast between Frenchness and Corsicanness. For those who left, living with continental stereotypes about Corsicans, and taking part in the close knit circle of fellow Corsicans in the *amicales* reinforced their sense of cultural distinctiveness. In Corsicans' accounts of their life abroad, there is always the theme of Corsican difference from the French: they are different in their solidarity, in their loyalty to each other, in their unswerving fidelity to the island and to the ideal of return.

Corsicans who worked in the former French colonies also talk about difference in their relations with non-French foreigners. Hélène R., a woman of about forty who had returned to live permanently on the island, told me that Corsicans were not hated like the French in the colonies because they did not mistreat the natives, and made the effort to learn their languages. Laurent, who had retired from a life spent working in oil fields around the world, recounted a story that had happened years ago in New Guinea. He was stopped by the police. They told him his passport was out of order and took him to the station for what was clearly about to become a lengthy exercise of bureaucratic harassment. "So," one of them eventually said, "you were born in Casabianca," misreading the name of his native village of "Casalabriva" on his passport. "Oh, no," he corrected, "it's Casalabriva, just a tiny Corsican village." "You're Corsican?" said the policeman, "why didn't you say so?" And, according to Laurent, the matter was closed. Another encounter was related to me by Madame Constantini, the diplomat. She was in Washington D.C. many years ago, as assistant ambassador. One day when she was in charge, an irate sailor came in, and she accepted an audience. He began to splutter emotionally about the mutiny he and his shipmates were planning. "Excuse me," she said to him, "but your accent sounds familiar. Can you tell me where you are from?" When he said he was Corsican they embarked (in Corsican) on a classic Corsican encounter ritual, exchanging the names and village names of relatives and friends until they found at least one person that they both knew or knew of. This ritual linked them to specific people and to specific points on the Corsican map. It was, of course, a particularly satisfying activity far from home. After this, the sailor told Madame Constantini that he realized how much trouble it would be for her if they were to mutiny in Washington, and promised to go back to the ship and convince them to do it somewhere else.

In much of the discourse of identity that I have evoked, above, being French and being Corsican are represented as mutually exclusive, obscuring the fact that these two identities exist in tandem, albeit not always in harmony. But the experience and value of Corsican identity in the colonies and on the continent was far from uncomplicated. As Culioli remarks, *"la Corse résista à l'intégration en même temps qu'elle chercha à tout prix à devenir française*" [Corsica resisted integration at the same time as it tried at any price to become French] (1990: 216). Ravis-Giordani enumerates several powerful sources of motivation for Corsicans to "be French". Corsicans were anchored to France, he writes, by the fact that they were called up in record numbers for service in the two World Wars, by Corsican involvement in the Resistance, and by the high rate of employment of Corsicans in government service. He writes:

> *Est-il besoin d'ajouter que ces hommes qui, durant toute leur carrière, incarnèrent, souvent dans des conditions difficiles et périlleuses, "une certaine idée de la France", ont intériorisé les valeurs de la République et de l'Etat, sans pour autant négliger le jardin secret de leur culture corse, l'expérience vécue de leur enfance paysanne et, en particulier, la langue maternelle qu'ils continuaient de parler en famille et dans les amicales corses, d'autant plus vivantes qu'elles étaient plus éloignées de "la petite Patrie"* (1979: 114).

> [Need we add that these men, who incarnated "a certain idea of France" during their entire career, often in perilous circumstances, internalized the values of the Republic and of the state, without, for all that neglecting the secret garden of their Corsican culture, the lived experience of their peasant childhoods, and in particular, their maternal language which they continued to speak in the family and in Corsican amicales [associations], that were all the more lively the further they were from 'the little Fatherland']

In the stories told to me above, we can see how the "secret garden" of Corsican culture allowed Corsicans to enjoy a certain distance from "being French," and to reap social benefits from their Corsicanness. But Ravis and Culioli remind us that this did not prevent the "internalization" of French notions of identity and value; Corsicans of the diaspora were both "French" and "not-French". In Culioli's words, cultural difference *"est ressentie contradictoirement par les Corses. Sont-ils différents des Français? Nous sommes Français, répondront une majorité d'entre eux. Alors, vous êtes comme les Français? Pas du tout, nous sommes corses et fiers de l'être"* [is experienced in contradictory ways by Corsicans. Are they different from the French? A majority will respond We are French! So, you are the same as the French? Oh no, not at all, we're Corsican and proud of it] (Culioli 1990: 255).[15]

4.2. Ambiguous status and ambivalent reactions

The dual cultural influences and allegiances of Corsicans of the diaspora created tensions, both for the individual and his/her experience of ambiguous identity, and for the permanent residents who received their returning relatives and friends. This tension is expressed in some Corsican accounts of life spent on the continent as a permanently unsettling sense of otherness and displacement. Mezzadri writes that even Corsicans who have been in Paris "forever" are "*ad eternam étrangers. Du moins nous sentant tels. Ni d'ici, ne de là-bas, ni d'ailleurs*"[strangers for eternity. At least, feeling like strangers. Neither from here, nor from there or elsewhere] (1991: 57). For Acquaviva, growing up on mainland France "*me faisait mentir, corse parmi les français, français parmi les corses, et toujours étranger*" [made me lie, Corsican among the French, French among the Corsicans, and always a stranger] (Acquaviva and Canarelli 1984: 40). In effect, Acquaviva's "lie" is that he cannot ever unequivocally hold just one cultural perspective. He betrays the ideal of a single, unproblematic identity.

The other "betrayal" is to the collective image of "exile": that all departures are "forced" and all Corsicans living elsewhere would prefer to live on the island. Corsican accounts of return after a long absence always evoke the intense pleasure of being reinserted into Corsican social space. But they also sometimes evoke the double edge to this social membership; because "one is first and foremost a member of a group" it is "difficult to be oneself" on Corsica (Olivesi 1983: 23). As Codaccione writes, "*Dans l'île...l'insulaire n'est jamais tout-à fait étranger car il n'est pas anonyme: s'il voyage à l'intérieure de l'île il doit se nommer, être identifié comme appartenant à telle ou telle famille, tel ou tel village...l'espace insulaire est toujours approprié*" [On the island...the islander is never a complete stranger, because he isn't anonymous: if he travels around the island he has to name himself, to be identified as belonging to such and such a family, such and such a village...space on an island is always appropriated] (1988: 113). In Marie Susini's novel *La Renfermée, La Corse*, the continent is a place of escape from the life in the village under constant surveillance, in the *on dit* 'one says' and the "*non-dit*" 'unsaid' (1981: 76). The sense of community is also tempered by one of the social consequences of intense social intimacy: because everyone knows everyone, it becomes necessary to develop avoidance behaviors of self protection—masks to protect from constant surveillance.[16] The discourse of exile can act as a sort of protective screen, which makes it possible for Corsicans whose lives elsewhere have made them ambivalent about what they have left behind to refrain from articulating their sentiments. They, and permanent residents, can collaborate in maintaining an image of Corsican cultural identity as completely distinct from French, immutable, constant, unaltered by the experience of life elsewhere.

But the discourse of exile is not maintained with perfect consistency. On the island, there is another voice, which recognizes how individuals and entire

cultures are changed by immigration; that years spent elsewhere *do* change
people. A popular song from the middle of this century illustrates that those
who stayed were well aware of the fact that those who left acquired French
language and values at the expense of their esteem for Corsica and Corsican.
The song also shows that there was far from a humorless, blanket acceptance
of all that was French:[17]

"*U mo figliolu*"
["My son"]
U mo figliolu hè ghjuntu da Francia
[My son is returned from France]
É li linzoli li chjama les draps
[And he calls linen *les draps*]
É le calzette li chjama les bas
[And socks, he calls them *les bas*]
U mo figliolu quant'ellu ne sà!
[My son, how much he knows!]
Per ellu ùn ci hè ne filetta ne scopa
[For him, there is neither fern nor brush]
Nè sbarca in Corsica più baccalà,
[No longer is salt cod {poor people's food} sent to Corsica]
Fougère, bruyère, morue et voilà
[*Ferns, brush,*[18] *cod and that's all*]
U mo figliolu quant'ellu ne sa!
[My son, how much he knows!]
S'omu ùn capisce issi nomi à la prima
[If you don't at first understand these words]
Vi dice "voyons!" *Vi face* " O la la!"
[He'll say, '*let us see,*' he'll go '*O la la!*']
É centu volte ripete "n'est-ce pas?"
[And he'll repeat a hundred times, '*isn't it so?*')
U mo figliolu quant'ellu ne sa!
[My son, how much he knows!
U mo figliolu cum'ellu hè struitu
[My son, how educated he is]
É v'addiletta à sente sfrancisà
[And he'll charm you, with his French talk]
Gendarmi nè merri ùn ci ponu luttà
[Neither policemen nor mayors can top him]
U mo figliolu quant'ellu ne sa!
[My son, how much he knows!]

In this song, the returning son's use of French is used to index his social
pretensions, which are satirized by his own parent. Today, permanent

residents are still sensitive to the fact that in the summer, returning Corsicans transform the village into *"un théatre où se joue la représentation de leur réussite"* [a theater in which their success is staged] (Simonpoli 1981: 314). In Riventosa, Hervé Sciacci told me that "some of them, people I went to school with, come back and hold out their arms, extended, like this, to shake hands with the tips of their fingers, almost as if they don't want to touch too much." Someone else told me the story of a man who told everyone in the village that he worked for the Ministry of Culture when he was a janitor in the Louvre; I have also been told about people who scrimped all year in order to be able to buy new clothes for their summer return.

The cracks in the collective collaboration in the myth of exile and cultural immutability are not invisible to the returning Corsicans. Mezzadri (1991: 57) writes that *"Nos cousins des villages... nous gratifient d'un silence de reproche de ne pas être là, avec eux, dans l'île. Leur mutisme est douleur qui s'étrangle parce que trop forte, faute de mots...C'est vrai, nous désertons"* [Our village cousins...gratify us with a silence of reproach for not being there with them on the island. Their muteness is a pain that strangles the words in its force...It is true, we are deserters]. The lyrics to Michel Mallory's song *Munticellu* (Vignette 4 above) implicitly recognize the silent rebuke of the permanent residents: the returning son sings that they "look at him like a lord" and hastens to reassure them that he is a villager just like them and does not have any airs or pretensions.

And sometimes the villagers are not silent. One day, on the village square in Riventosa, Martin, who had lived abroad only as a prisoner of war, teased his cousin Charles. *"Trent'anni in Pariggi,"* he intoned, on the public square, in front of a few of us, *"Hà cambiatu"* ['30 years in Paris–he's changed']. *"Innò"* 'No' protested Charles, *"Sò sempre listessu"* ['I'm still the same']. Martin brushed this aside, and continued his teasing with the choice information that Charles had engaged in activities at odds with Corsican definitions of manhood: *"Quallà, hà puru fattu a cucina, u ménage!"* ['Up there, he even did cooking and *housework*!'].

On another occasion, Laurence and her sister Marlène talked about a friend of theirs who was going to have to sell the new house she had built near the sea, as her retirement return was not working out. Laurence said that she had seen it coming several years before, when the friend was renting a house in a village. One day, she looked out of her door to find a group of people butchering a wild boar in the road, and using her steps to sit on. Appalled, she pushed past them huffily, without saying a word. "If she had only talked to them," said Laurence, "they probably would have given her some." She and Marlène saw this incident as proof that she really wasn't able to adapt to Corsican culture. She had been away too long.

Another time, I was sitting with Hervé, his son's "companion" and her girlfriend. It was a night in August, near the end of the summer holidays. The girlfriend said she was leaving the island soon. Hervé said "good riddance," in a joking tone, to which the friend immediately replied "*Sò curtinese, eiu, ùn sò micca pinzuta*" [Me, I'm from Corté, I'm no *pinzuta* (pejorative Corsican word for French continental)]. Her haste to distinguish herself from continental "tourists" belied the social insecurity that, in the eyes of permanent residents, Corsicans visiting in the summer were not seen as full members of the community or culture.

This insecurity was not unfounded. For even though many returning Corsicans are judged to "fit right back in," to "still speak Corsican just like us," what remains is the fact that Corsicans of the diaspora's Corsicanness *is judged*. This was particularly clear in the public debates that took place in 1990–1991 over the right of Corsicans living on the continent to vote in local elections, in which votes by proxy and correspondence have been notorious sources of electoral fraud and influence peddling that have kept the clan in power over the years. Although many Corsicans defended this vote as a cultural birthright, equal numbers effectively said that the Corsicanness that Corsicans of the diaspora were entitled to assert did *not* make them eligible for full rights of Corsican citizenship. Some Corsicans who favored the elimination of their right to vote on Corsica were very blunt on this score. One young man who wrote to the paper referred to the Corsicans of the diaspora as "Corsican *pinzuti*," and went on to say, "*La seule chose qui les intéresse c'est de profiter de la mer et du soleil. C'est vrai qu'ils on dû partir pour des raisons économiques. Mais ce qui se passe en Corse ne leur intéresse pas vraiment. Que font-ils pour l'économie de la Corse? J'ai choisi de vivre et de travailler ici. Je sais que cela sera dur. Mais il faut vouloir*"[the only thing that interests them is profiting from the sun and sea. It's true that they had to leave for economic reasons. But they are not really interested in what goes on on Corsica. What do they do for the Corsican economy? I have chosen to live and work here. I know it will be hard. But you have to want it] (*La Corse* May 15, 1991).

But comments and stories about Corsicans of the diaspora are seldom this critical; like the parents in the song about the "*figliolu ghjuntu da Francia*," Corsicans cannot afford to shut out a scarce and precious resource: family and friends. The existence and return of Corsicans of the diaspora is equally important for the collective definition of the Corsican community on the island. There are few Corsicans who do not have family members on the continent, and the yearly cycle of their departure and return has been part of village life for most of this century. The impact of these returns on the social life of the villages is dramatic, because of the diminished and aging population of the villages. The village where I lived was relatively prosperous, for it was near a midsized town, and easily accessible by a major road, and it went from 80 residents in winter to over 300 in the month of August. In some villages, a winter population of almost nothing (ten to thirty people) swells to several hundred. Without this yearly influx, the villages are dead. There is a sense in which no one can do without this period of reunion and vitality, even if it is only temporary.

The permanent residents also have an investment in the representation of the success of their own. There is another song of roughly the same era as "*U Mo Figliolu*" that is still played on the radio. Called "*O, Signora cosa ci hè?*" [Oh, Madam, what's the matter?], it is the mother who sings the praises of her son who is coming back from his military service. Although the song mocks her assertion that her son's "elevated" rank of Corporal has raised his social station so high that none of the girls in the village are appropriate marriage partners, it also reveals that making it in the French system, acquiring French language and culture, was a source of prestige. The successes of family and friends on the continent are important topics of conversation in the Corsican village; this success is measured in diplomas from the best schools, in prestigious government postings, in doctors, lawyers, authors, politicians. As Franzini suggests, the display of success is partially mandated from home; that it was perhaps "*pour compenser cette perte que le départ a été survalorisé que celui qui partait était celui qui réussissait, celui qui devait réussir?*" [in order to compensate this loss that the departure was overvalued, that he who left was he who succeeded, he who had to succeed?] (Franzini 1991: 35). So despite his comments about the condescending attitudes of the returning Corsicans, Hervé is out on the square, dressed up in his white shirt and pressed jeans (his party clothes) every day and every night in the summer, shaking the fingertips offered to him, chatting, sitting on the low wall and jumping up to greet the summer people in cars who drive through their region to roll down the window and say hello.

The general discourse of return–the myth of the perfect satisfaction of personal rediscovery of ethnic roots–masks the fact that for some, who knows how many, the catalyst for departure was not just economic, but also, social, and the result has been that Corsican culture has irrevocably changed. Back in the village setting, no matter what people say about the summer people, as September winds down, the days shorten imperceptibly and the initial relish of the permanent residents at the parking spaces liberated by departures turns to melancholy. The square is like an empty theater at night, the few players left hear their voices echo too lonely in the evening sky, catch a few scraps of conversation and go inside, early. There is no denying the sadness of the winter. And, some of the "permanent" residents are only a bit more permanent than those from the continent; many leave to go to Corté, or Bastia, or Ajaccio in late October. *"Qu'est-ce que vous voulez que je fasse ici en hiver?"* [What would you have me do here in winter?] said Francette, a widow in her late fifties, almost apologetically. *"Je ne suis pas trop télé...mon frère visite une fois par jour...il n'y a personne"* [I'm not much on T.V., my brother visits once a day--there is no one]. The cities, once summer conviviality is over, are a refuge from the isolation of winter life in the villages. By November of my stay on Corsica, people would ask me, "You are still here? We assumed you would have already left." Albertini, a Corsican who returns to live in Corsica from the continent, writes that "it takes a lot of courage to live through the Corsican winter" (1984: 50). She describes a depressing, rainy, cold day in her village:

> *On frappe. Des amis sont à ma porte, chargés de victuailles, de rires, de chaleur. On s'embrasse. Le feu prend et monte haut dans la cheminée, ensemble nous préparons le repas. Ça sent bon. Il y a du bruit et des chansons. C'est faux. Il n'y a personne. Le village est désert. Plus de jeunesse, plus d'école, plus d'enfant. Les vieux ne sortent pas. Une voiture passe...sans s'arrêter. La route est grise et solitaire. Le vent se lève. Je vais aller fermer le poulailler.*

> [There is a knock at the door. Friends are at my door, loaded with food, laughter, warmth. We embrace. The fire lights and rises up high in the chimney, together we prepare the meal. It smells good. There is noise, and songs. It is false. There is nobody. The village is deserted. No more young people, no more school, no more children. The old people don't go out. A car passes...without stopping. The road is gray and solitary. The wind comes up. I am going to go and close the henhouse.]

The intensity of the contrast between summer and winter social life on Corsica dramatizes the sense of social loss felt by permanent residents; unlike those who return for a month of sociability, they cannot forget the irreversible changes that have worked on Corsican society in the last fifty years. But no Corsican identifies winter residence in a deserted village as an ideal. The nostalgia for the social relations of the past is not coupled with any faith that they can be recreated. And the social and economic motives for leaving the village, or the island, are not fundamentally questioned. Neither the value of leaving nor the value of staying is unqualified; both are part of the Corsican experience.

These stories of Corsicanness, full of tensions and ambivalence, the reluctant, but resigned accommodation to the historical cycle of departure of working age Corsicans and return of retirees, are a necessary backdrop for any discussion of both the state of the language, and the state of attempts to revive it. They are, on the one hand, an antidote to the concept of total assimilation, linguistic or cultural. On the other, they are living proof of the extent of the grip of France and Frenchness. There is a profound sense in which being Corsican is powerful and real and unchallengeable. But this strength has been articulated in its ability to survive; this survival has involved compromises and adaptations. The language has been one of these compromises. That is, just as a strong sense of independent and separate identity prevented Corsican from disappearing completely, it also prevented, for years, the perception of the decline of the language as a threat to that identity. For many Corsicans, they not only could, but had to be Corsican without it for a substantial portion of their lifetimes.

5. Corsican nationalism

Corsican ethnonationalism emerged in the late sixties and early seventies, at the same time as other similar movements in western Europe in Brittany, the Basque Country, Wales, Ireland and so on. A comparative analysis of the nature of these movements is beyond the scope of this section. We can note in passing, however, that these minority nationalist movements often drew inspiration (as well as specific arguments and strategies) from one another. In this sense, they all contributed to the wide political and cultural climate context that favored their separate development.

In this section I look at the way how a combination of economic, political and cultural factors set the stage for Corsican nationalism. First, there is the issue of economic development. As Giard and Schiebling show, both the industrial revolution and the technological revolution that began in the twenties created huge disparities in French regional economies. Capital, industry and populations became increasingly concentrated in the industrial North and in large port and textile cities (1981: 39–40). It wasn't until after World War II, however, that these disparities became the object of government attention. Once reconstruction was accomplished, the government set in place regional development plans designed to correct the economic imbalances between different parts of the country. The first government commission on Corsica was founded in 1952. Barral points out that government policy in the late fifties and early sixties was still centralist in nature, but it was a centralism that attempted to take into account regional differences. In 1955, twenty-one regions of France were identified, and in 1960, additional policies and programs linked the newly defined "region" with existing departmental structures. In effect, these structures gave body to the idea of the region. In the case of Corsica (as well as Brittany, Alsace and Provence), the designated economic region was already connected with strong images of cultural and linguistic distinctiveness.

In 1957, a Program of Regional Action in Corsica was developed. The report of the Program left no doubt that Corsica was one of the regions that was significantly "behind". It addressed demographic weakness: by 1955, the population on the island slumped to a low of 170,000 residents, compared to 280,000 in the 1982 census[19]. This demographic low reflected a very real lack of educational and economic opportunity on the island; in effect, the few industries that had animated the island economy had long since folded. Neither the traditional pastoralism nor the small scale farming practiced on Corsican was competitive in the European market or attractive to young Corsicans, and tourism was not yet developed enough to create the expansion of the tertiary sector that can be seen today. There was no University; the only institution of higher education was the *École Normale* 'Teachers College'. Even teachers, according to Murati, arranged to be posted elsewhere (1983: 28). The fifties were characterized by both a lack of opportunity and a lack of faith in the island. Acquaviva and Canarelli write that in the classic myth of departure that they and their generation were nourished on, the island, despite all of its virtues, "*ne pouvait nourrir ses enfants...Elle ne pouvait être que le lieu de repos, estival ou ultime*"[could not nourish its children...it could only be a place of summertime or eternal repose] (1984: 43). Gifted students of parents who could afford it were sent to the continent for High School, it being understood that a diploma from a Corsican *lycée* (High School) would never get them into one of the *Grandes Écoles* 'Big [prestigious] Schools' of Paris. The 1957 report made reference to the inefficient methods of Corsican agriculture, documented the way that transportation costs drove the cost of living up on the island and showed that the standard of living on Corsica was below the national average. This program report identified the development of tourism and agricultures as two high priority government objects, and the SOMIVAC (*Société pour la Mise en Valeur de la Corse* [Society for Advancement of Corsica]) was formed that same year to organize those development efforts (Pomponi et. al. 1982, 5: 72).

The late sixties also provided a social context in which this distinctiveness took on increasing cultural and political significance. The 1968 student movement, in contesting established social and cultural structures and hierarchies, placed a value on the cultural roots from which people felt alienated. With the slogan *vivre et travailler au pays* [live and work in the land], the French were exhorted to combat the centrifugal and homogenizing forces of the French capitalist system by leaving the "centers" for the "peripheries" and all their local particularity and authenticity.

Corsicans studying in Paris, Aix-en-Provence and other mainland universities during these heady years were thus given a language to talk about linguistic and cultural "alienation"; in particular, the lack of popular appreciation for Corsican cultural and linguistic heritage. Carlu Rocchi, a singer of traditional Corsican ballads who began his career in this era, noted that when he first started to sing in Corsican, "everyone else was ashamed of it" (Mollard 1982: 44). Thus for Corsican students in Paris, the reawakening of ethnic consciousness of the late sixties and early seventies was a confrontation with the marginalization of the island–its language, its culture, its economic development–by both the French state and their fellow Corsicans.

At the same time as the notion of "region" was structurally acknowledged by the French government, the end of the Algerian war of liberation (and the end of the French colonial era) gave people a new idiom to talk about the cultural, political and economic relationships between the French "center" and the less developed regions. In 1962, the term "internal colonialism" was propelled into use by Robert Lafont, the Occitan intellectual. His argument was that the underdeveloped regions of France had been exploited for their natural and human resources by "France" (the "center") in the same ways as France and other colonial powers exploited their colonies. The analogy with colonialism both emphasized the cultural distinctiveness and rights to political sovereignty of the exploited groups. The answer was "decolonization". The central role of language in this process is crystal clear: "*Il s'agit de reconquerir la langue propre, fondement de la nation, ce qui permettra de legitimer l'autonomie politique et economique*" [We need to reconquer the language itself, which is the foundation of the nation and the thing that will legitimate political and economic autonomy] (Lafont 1975, cited in Giard and Schiebling 1981: 54).

The Corsican autonomist movement began to take shape in the Corsican student population on the mainland in the late sixties. The first extended public manifesto of this movement, *Main basse sur une île*, was published in 1971. Written by the FRC *(Front Régionaliste Corse* [Corsican Regionalist Front]) this document declared Corsica a victim of "internal colonialism". 1971 was also the year of the first incident which commanded public attention and mobilized Corsicans against the French government. This was the "*affaire des boues rouges*" the dumping of toxic wastes by an Italian company into the sea only forty kilometers from the Corsican coast. Popular protest met with little action from the French government; in 1973, thousands of demonstrators stormed the Prefecture in Bastia, hurling documents from the windows and roughing up the Prefect. Later that year, clandestine militants blew up one of the ships of the Italian company, which had failed to follow through on its promise to stop the dumping.

By 1973, the Corsican political resistance had already gone through several internal fissions. A new manifesto *A Chjama di u Castellare* ' The Castellare Call' proclaimed a common goal of internal autonomy, to be pursued legally, in order to do away with the negative effects of "French imperialism" on linguistic, economic and social progress on the island. Between 1973 and 1975, the movement expanded its popular base, notably, with the involvement of agricultural unions. Another semiviolent demonstration and confrontation with local representatives of the Ministry of Agriculture took place; tensions mounted. Finally, the autonomists' protest of the strategies of French developmental intervention was dramatized in the explosive events of Aleria in 1975. Autonomists led by Edmond Simeoni occupied the cellar of a *pied-noir*[20] owner of a large vineyard in order to protest the government policies that had secured him his enviable financial position and the blind eye that had been turned to his illegal activities of "cheptelization" (adding sugar to wine). This armed occupation, in which hostages were taken, was met with military action: the government flew in a thousand National Guard to surround the building. Tear gas was thrown, shots were fired, two men were left dead, and Simeoni gave himself up and was sent to jail. This event mobilized the public, as did his national trial, in which he eloquently defended the island. Aleria also marked the beginning of the separation of the autonomists into those who supported violence and those who did not, an issue which still divides the nationalist political "family," as does the question of the degree of autonomy sought from France. Beginning in 1976, the clandestine *Front de Libération Nationale Corse* [Corsican National Liberation Front, or FLNC] stepped up its program of bombings.[21] From that point on, the fact of nationalism was an inevitable reference point for issues of Corsican identity, to include the question of the language; the linguistic and cultural activism of the seventies cannot be understood outside of this political context. The cultural influence of Corsican nationalism goes well beyond its raw political presence (the highest pronationalist vote in the early 90s reached 20%; typically it hovers around 10%). Nationalists have consistently kept the issue of the Corsican language at the forefront of political discourse, and have been the catalysts for all of the early language related legislation in the Corsican Regional Assembly.

6. Conclusions

This chapter has identified some of the oppositions through which Corsican identity is experienced and articulated. These oppositions are internal and external. Within Corsican society, both geography and intense local forms of identification and alliance make it difficult for Corsicans to see social action as anything other than the promotion of sectorial interests in a zero-sum competition for resources. This aspect of Corsican society tempers the Corsican sense of unity and solidarity that is engendered by oppositional relations with France, where Corsica and Corsicans are not highly regarded. The Corsican diaspora has played a large role in bringing the French--Corsican cultural contrast into focus, both for those who left the island and those who have stayed. At the same time, the diaspora has also created "mixed" identities that blur the boundaries between Frenchness and Corsicanness. This blurring, however, is the source of considerable ambivalence, both at the individual and the collective level, since it violates ideologies of "essential" and immutable identities. This fundamental tension–between homogenous ideologies and heterogenous practices–can be seen in nationalist and popular linguistic ideologies described in the following chapters.

Chapter 3
Language shift and diglossia: ideology, history and contemporary practice

This chapter focuses on the way French linguistic ideology and language policies, in concert with the profound social and economic changes of the last century, have affected everyday patterns of linguistic behavior and ideas about language on Corsica. A brief discussion of Corsican linguistic relations with Italy and Italian both provides historical background and shows that all forms of language domination are not alike. The difference between the Italian--Corsican relationship and the French–Corsican relationship dramatizes the way that different social and economic conditions led to rapid language shift under France. The second part of the chapter examines the specific consequences of language shift and diglossia on contemporary Corsican patterns of language use, and uses a combination of ethnographic and survey data to describe sociolinguistic patterns of code choice, code switching, and the use of contact-induced mixed codes.

1. Corsican and Italian: a classic diglossic relationship

Despite the fact that France acquired the island in 1767, the penetration of French into all aspects of everyday life on Corsica was a fairly recent event. It coincided with the gradual spread of literacy in the provinces since 1882, when the Jules Ferry law made primary education compulsory, secular and free. Effectively, before 1900, the use of French was restricted to necessary administrative acts and communication with the state. Even this limited gallicization came after a long delay; local civil registers were written in Italian until about 1855. The transition from Italian to French was not fully accomplished until the early 1900s, and was accelerated by military service in the First World War. By the end of World War I, although Corsican was still the mother tongue of most Corsicans and was widely spoken, French had gained a significant role in the life of the community.

Until this point, Italian had been the language of education, literature, religion and administration. Rich young men like Napoleon went to Italy to study; in 1830, Corsicans represented a fourth of the student body at Pisa (Beretti, cited in Marchetti 1989: 77). Italian was a register of poetry and sophistication; it was also the language of formality and solemnity, spoken in the church and in the courts. The urban elite spoke Italian, which was referred to as speaking *in crusca*, after the *Accademia della Crusca*, the Italian language academy founded in the 16th century.

The Italian–Corsican relationship was a classic case of diglossia. As Ettori writes, *"Pendant des siècles, toscan et corse ont formé un couple perçu par les locuteurs comme deux niveaux de la même langue"*[For centuries, Tuscan and Corsican formed a pair that was perceived by speakers as two levels of the same language] (Ettori and Fusina 1980: 81). When Pascal Paoli was in exile in London, Samuel Johnson asked him about the existence of a "rustic language," very different from Italian and Latin. Paoli claimed that such a language only existed in Sardinia (Boswell 1768). This response might have been based on a diglossic consciousness of language hierarchy: Paoli may have been avoiding the inferior connotation of "rustic difference" from Italian. Paoli's response might also have reflected the normalness of a gap between the written and the oral: in Italy at that time, only in Tuscany did writing resemble speech. From this perspective, the fact that Corsicans spoke differently from the way that an elite minority of them wrote did not undermine Paoli's claim that their (official) language was Italian.

In this diglossic situation, language choices had stylistic and social connotations that were manipulated in both speech and writing. One of the earliest appearances of Corsican in literary works is in the 1817 heroicomic poem *"Dionomachia"* by Salvatore Viale, where there are eleven lines of "dialect" that are used to evoke authentic, local, rustic color. Both Viale and another nineteenth-century author, Nicolo Tommaseo, romanticized the vernacular. Tommaseo published a collection of Corsican songs in what he characterized as a *"langue puissante, et parmi les plus italiens dialectes d'Italie"* [a powerful language, the most Italian of the dialects of Italy] (in Marchetti 1989: 22). Two years later, Viale, in a preface to a second edition of the book, wrote that *"La langue corse est italienne, elle a même été jusqu'ici l'un des moins impurs dialectes d'Italie"* [The Corsican language is Italian, it has even been, up till now, one of the least impure dialects of Italy] (in Marchetti 1989: 22).

Around the turn of the century, when few Corsicans were literate, literary Tuscan was nevertheless available as a register in spoken language in a way that literary French would never be. For example, Vuillier reported in his *Voyage en Corse exécuté en 1890* that shepherds would sit down for their midday meal and, under the shade of a tree, recite the poetry of Tasso and Ariosto. Writing in 1932, Ungaretti recounted hearing an old man recite *"Gerusalemme Liberata"* (published in Italy in 1575) at an evening gathering in a mountain village, with other members of the group joining in at various points to cite out loud from memory (Marchetti 1989: 68–69). This kind of memory was still alive when I did research in 1989: one of my neighbors, born in 1920, told me that one of his vivid childhood memories was of being up in the mountains with his shepherd grandfather, listening to him read and recite from Dante's works. Italian was also a poetic register that was used for stylistic purposes in traditional Corsican oral forms such as the poetic dueling called *Chjami è Rispondi* [call and response]. A former shepherd from Riventosa, born in 1915, also recalled courtship serenades of his youth; in them, men tried to sing and speak *in crusca,* adding as many Italian flourishes as possible to their love songs and poems.

It should be emphasized that we cannot use these accounts of language use as indices of linguistic performance. The boundaries between "Corsican" and "Italian" are blurry in written records from this period, and they were no doubt even fuzzier in oral practice. It was most certainly the case then, as it is now, that what people defined as "speaking Italian" covered a wide range of linguistic performance variables. One of my acquaintances reported to me that what her father does when he claims to "speak Italian" is to liberally sprinkle his discourse with the word *però* 'but', which contrasts with the Corsican synonym *ma.* While I do not have systematic data on this subject, I have observed several casual interactions between Corsican speakers and Italian tourists, and noted the same selective identification of salient linguistic markers of difference. In the cases I have observed, Corsican speakers have deployed a few salient markers in what I heard as a "Corsican" stretch of discourse, but what was clearly, for them, a satisfactory display of "speaking Italian".

In the past, the status of Italian as a "high" register meant that it could be evoked in everyday conversation. In 1926, Maistrale wrote that Corsicans would switch from Corsican to Italian in a story or conversation when they reported on anything that had a formal or authoritative nature. He notes such a codeswitch in the following deposition, where a man uses Italian to make his formal assessment (in Marchetti 1989: 79). The deposition is broken down into three lines below, each one followed by a translation into English. In order to illustrate how much linguistic difference is in play in this text, the original Corsican in lines 1 and 2 is translated into Italian in lines 1a and 2a. In line 3a the original Italian of line 3 is translated into Corsican.

(1)

1	*Dopu avè*	*giratu*	*u*	*chiosu*	*sopradettu,*
	After AUX	go around PAST	the	enclosure	above-mentioned
	'After having gone around the above-mentioned enclosure,'				
1a	Dopo avere	girato	la chiostra	sopradetta,	
2	*in cuscenza*	*è*	*in onore,*		

in conscience and in honor,
'conscientiously and honorably,'

2a   in coscienza e in onore,

3   *ho stimato   il   danno   a   franchi quindici.*
I estimate PAST   the damage at francs   fifteen.
'I estimated the damages at fifteen francs.'

3a   aghju stimatu u dannu a franchi quindeci.

In the section below, I both refer to this short historical example of Corsican–Italian codeswitching and use additional examples to explore some of the linguistic differences between Corsican and Italian. As I will make clear in the following chapter, I do not consider these language boundaries to be natural and self-evident; to a great extent, drawing these lines is an ideological and political decision. Nevertheless, I think that it is useful here to briefly outline some systematic differences between Corsican and "standard" Italian.

1.2. Corsican and Italian verbs

In lines 1 and 1a of the historical text in example (1) we can see a difference in the verb form; the Italian verb *avere,* 'to have' is "truncated" in Corsican, becoming *avè.* Some other examples of this pattern include:

"standard" Italian	Corsican	
parlare	*parlà*	'to speak'
capire	*capì*	'to understand'
nascere	*nasce*	'to be born'
volere	*vulè*	'to want to'

1.3. Articles and endings

Comparison of the Corsican and Italian for the words "after," "gone around," "estimated" and "damage" in lines 1 through 3 in the historical text partially illustrate a set of systematic differences between Italian and Corsican articles. These are illustrated below:

"standard" Italian	Corsican	
il	*u*	[masc. sing. def. art]
la	*a*	[fem. sing def. art]
gli/li	*i*	[masc. pl. def. art]
le	*e*	[fem. pl. def. art]

Corsican and Italian also differ in the masculine singular noun ending. In Corsican, this ending is -*u*; in Italian it is -*o*.

1.4. Vocabulary

This short passage does not illustrate significant vocabulary differences between Corsican and Italian, partly because of the legal domain it refers to. As far as I know, nobody has quantified exactly how much of the Corsican lexicon is shared with Italian. Suffice it to say that this overlap is considerable but probably not more than 70%. Corsicans and Italians who have not studied each other's language need to do a fair amount of work to understand each other.

1.5. Pronunciation

The text does not, of course, tell us much about pronunciation. There are several significant differences between Corsican and Italian. The first is the consonant mutation that occurs in Corsican in intervocalic contexts. Unvoiced stops, fricatives and affricates become voiced: (the intervocalic context in the second column is created by the addition of the articles *u* and *a*). The following examples illustrate this phonological rule:

pane	[pane]	'bread'	*u pane*	[u bane]	'the bread'
terza	[tertsa]	'third'	*a terza*	[a dertsa]	'the third'
farina	[farina]	'flour'	*a farina*	[a varina]	'the flour'
chjesa	[tyeza]	'church'	*a chjesa*	[a dyeza]	'the church'
cane	[k ane]	'dog'	*u cane*	[u gane]	'the dog'

Voiced consonants become approximants or dissapear:

babbu	[babu]	'father'	*u babbu*	[u wabu]	'the father'
golu	[golu]	'throat'	*u golu*	[u wolu]	'the throat'
due	[due]	'two'	*vintidue*	[wintiue]	'twenty two'
granu	[granu]	'grain'	*u granu*	[u ranu]	'the grain'

This mutation does not occur when the consonant occurs (a) at the beginning of a sentence; (b) at the beginning of a clause within a sentence; (c) following a pause or (d) at the beginning of a word that follows an accented syllable (for example, *trè cani* would be pronounced [tre kɑni] and not [tre gɑni]).

The Corsican affricates spelled *chj* [ty] and *ghj* [dy] are sounds that are not found in Italian. There is also a marked intonational/prosological difference between the two languages; Corsican lacks the marked intonational contours that give Italian its "singing" quality.

1.6. Summary

In the sections above, I have highlighted differences between Corsican and Italian. These differences are not insignificant. But they are certainly no more significant than contemporary differences between regional Italian speech varieties (classified as "dialects") and "standard Italian" (see Salvi 1975). It is easy enough to see how Corsicans could experience shifting from Corsican to Italian as movement along a linguistic continuum. "Speaking Italian" in the past was very close to a change of register.

1.7. Diglossia with Italian vs. diglossia with French

The social uses to which Italian was put in some of the examples above are common to all diglossic situations. Today, it is not unusual to find a codeswitch from Corsican to French in exactly the same circumstances as the switches from Corsican to Italian described above. But there are a number of ways in which the social meaning and accessibility of French as a "high" code today is different from the use of Italian in the past. First of all, although Italian was a dominant language, its presence on the island was limited. Italian was not imposed on Corsica except in the sense that Genoa expected to transact its administrative business in Italian, which it did through an elite, literate Corsican minority. This meant that in everyday discourse, Corsicans could tap into the powerful connotations of Italian without necessarily mastering the language or having that mastery critically evaluated. Among themselves, Corsicans could use fragments of Italian–stereotypical linguistic markers of difference–for stylistic effect. For example, in the oral poetic tradition, and even in contemporary Corsican poetry (up through the early seventies) the definite article and possessive adjectives are often "italianized". For example, "my heart," which is pronounced [u mo gɔre] in Corsican and usually written today as *u mo core* would be written or sung *il mio core*.

French, on the other hand, has not been tapped into or evoked in the same ways. In part, this may be a function of linguistic difference. Since French and Corsican are not mutually intelligible to the degree that Corsican and Italian are, Corsicans had to *learn* French, rather than absorb it informally. The continuum between the oral and the written that is suggested by shepherds reciting Italian poetry was thus ruptured when French replaced Italian. And there is probably less fluidity at the phonological level between French and Corsican than between Italian and Corsican. There is only one phonological variable I know to be manipulated for stylistic effect, and that is the replacement of the rhoticized (French) /r/ with a trilled Corsican /r/. This is widely interpreted as an effort to sound "more French," a linguistic move that can be positively evaluated as a "sophisticated" pronunciation style or negatively evaluated as snobbery.

For the most part, however, the abundance of French phonological, morphological, intonational and syntactic influences in contemporary Corsican are neither viewed as intentional nor approved. Like the regional variety of French described below, when pointed out, they are seen as "mistakes" (see also the discussion of the regional variety of French below). In other words, even though both French and Italian have had relationship of dominance with respect to Corsican, that dominance has been expressed in very different social and ideological contexts. The cultural meanings of using French or bits of French in discourse are different from the social meanings of using Italian because of the way that French was transmitted, and because of the economic advantages that it offered in a changing society.

In the next sections, I survey the history of French language politics, and explore the role French schools played in the transmission of an ideology of absolute linguistic differences and values. In school, Corsicans learned that French was a separate, authoritative, superior code. Whereas the authority of Italian had been distant, the authority of French was present and tangible, and insured that the uneducated Corsican's use of fragments of French would indeed be noticed, and most likely, be judged as deficient.

2. French linguistic politics

In part, the differences between Corsican's relationship with these two dominant languages is a hazard of history. That is, if Corsica had remained under Italian control, and if Corsicans had been schooled in the Italian system, they would have had to learn the Italian standard, against which Corsican, like the other *lingue tagliate* 'truncated languages' would have been judged inferior (see Salvi 1975). However, while Italian linguistic unification was a late development of the 20th Century, French monolingualism had been the foundation of the French ideology of cultural and political identity and unity since the ninth century. Since the Revolution, this ideology had been actualized in educational and linguistic policy.

2.1. Language and nation

The *Serment de Strasbourg* of AD 842 is often cited as the beginning of French linguistic politics. In the *Serment*, Louis-le-Germanique and Charles-le-Chauve inaugurated their alliance in a ceremony in which each king pronounced a speech, not in Latin, but in his new diplomatic partner's vernacular. In doing so, they constituted proto-German (*lingua tedesca*) and proto-French (*lingua romana*) as representing a people (the king's subjects) and a territory (Balibar 1987:11–12). As Decrosse writes, the *Serment de Strasbourg* "*associe langue maternelle à la constitution de territories nationaux*" [associates the mother tongue with the constitution of national territories] (1987: 33). The connection between vernacular language and nation in the *Serment* would define future French language policy: by staking their claims to sovereignty, difference and parity with other European leaders on language unity, Louis and Charles prefigured the Jacobin conviction that the unity of the Republic demanded the unity of speech (Achard 1987; Crowley 1996: 127; Jacob and Gordon 1985; Luedi 1992; Weber 1976: 72; Weinstein 1989).

As Balibar puts it, "*Comment la langue nationale forgée pour signifier la personnalité d'un peuple en face de celle d'un autre, va-t-elle pouvoir permettre à ses propres nationaux de signifier les particularités d'une toute autre nature qui les distinguent entre eux?*" [How could a national language that was forged in order to signify the distinction between the personalities of different peoples permit its own people to represent/signify a completely different set of particularities that distinguished them from each other?] (Balibar 1987:16). The answer was, it could not. There had to be one official language. The monolingual standard of French was "*loin d'être une variété parmi d'autres, elle exclut purement et simplement l'idée même de la variété*" [far from being one variety among others, it excluded, purely and simply, the very idea of variety] (Quéré 1987: 62).

The first piece of language legislation aimed at establishing French monolingualism was the edict of Villers-Cotterets (1539), in which François the First declared the language of the *Île de France* the official language of the kingdom. Symbolic value notwithstanding, this declaration had little immediate effect on the variety of languages spoken by François' subjects. By the time of the Revolution (over 200 years later), over six million Frenchmen spoke languages or dialects other than Parisian French. After the Revolution, this diversity was tolerated for a brief period, and official documents were translated into regional patois.

But the Revolutionaries soon seized on language as a symbol of a new kind of national unity, declaring French the authoritative voice of the citizens, who replaced the king and his divine right as "the moral person of the nation" (Balibar 1987: 13). Beginning in 1793, a law was passed mandating that all primary education be given in French. In 1794, the "linguistic terror" began (Graff 1987; Higonnet 1980). In a famous report presented to the General Assembly, the Abbé Grégoire, who had conducted a nationwide survey on language practices, called for the government to "*annéantir les patois et universaliser l'usage de la langue française*" [annihilate the patois and universalize the use of the French language]. In this same report, speakers of dialect were labeled "counter-revolutionaries," and special attention was drawn to Corsica, where Pascal Paoli "*se sert puissamment de la langue italienne pour pervertir l'esprit public...ce dont nous avons besoin, c'est que Paoli n'opère pas la contre-révolution en Corse par les moyens que lui en offre la langue italienne*" [made abundant use of Italian to pervert the public mind...we need to make sure that he does not effect a counterrevolution in Corsica by means of the Italian language] (in Higonnet 1980: 42). By July of 1794, all public acts were required to be in French. Corsica was temporarily exempted from implementation of these decrees, along with other regions where they spoke idioms "*qui n'on aucune espèce d'illustration, et ne sont qu'un reste de barbarie des siècles passés*" [that have no illustrative merits and are only leftovers of the barbarisms of centuries past] (in Higonnet 1980: 42).

The unity of speech, it was argued, was a central element of democracy, since non-French speakers would not be able to fully participate as citizens in the Republic (Achard 1987: 40–43).[21] Secondly, as the reference to "barbaric idioms" in Grégoire's report so clearly shows, language was connected to a moral order. Teaching French to the six million nonspeakers was not just a way of giving them access to participatory democracy but a means of moral and cultural elevation. Almost 100 years after the Revolution, in 1880, an Army report made the connection between literacy and social/moral status explicit: "The young Bretons who do not know how to read, write or speak French...are promptly civilized; they lose the prejudices of their 'pays,' abandon native suspicions, and when they return to the village, they are sufficiently frenchified to frenchify their friends by their influence"(Weber 1976: 299).

The echo of these sentiments could be heard exactly a hundred years later, when the former French Prime Minister Raymond Barre declared: "The foremost of the fundamental values of our civilization is the correct usage of our language. There is a moral and civic virtue in the loyal practice of French by the young people" (Bronckart 1988: 126, cited in Luedi 1992: 153). *Le bon usage* 'correct usage' was, as Luedi writes, "the key term of the centralistic and monoglossic linguistic ideology developed in the 17th Century" (1992: 154).[22] French Enlightenment scholars' efforts to prove the innate, rational superiority of French and to justify its vocation as a universal tongue were carried forward during the Revolution and the Napoleonic period.

2.2. The role of the schools

As Heller writes, "education has an important role to play in the definition of the value of symbolic capital, in its legitimation and in mediating access to it" (1994: 7). The idea that linguistic virtue resided in linguistic form lay beneath French schools' preoccupation with the teaching of *la grammaire générale*, 'general grammar'. The period after the Revolution saw a swell in the production of grammar texts, and the expansion and refinement of grammatical and orthographic rules. Orthographic representation of these rules, writes Achard, were presented to students as if they had always existed, and most importantly, as a model of rational thought (1987: 47). General grammar was, as Higonnet writes, viewed as "the study of logic through the medium of the French language" (1980: 63). In reality, as Cameron points out, "traditional grammar concentrates on rules that are not intuitively obvious" (1995: 104).[23] Therefore, learning grammar was very much about learning to submit oneself to authority, no matter how irrational or arbitrary. In the same vein, Achard (1987: 47–48) points out that the very methods of French grammar instruction transmitted a theory of language as a logical system. This was done by illustrating grammatical principles with a set of phrases far more simple and coherent than those found in linguistic practice. They were models of abstract competence, of *langue* 'language' and not *langage* 'language'. (Poche 1987: 101).

Schoolteachers who went out into the provinces at the turn of the century were thus the front line troops in the government's campaign to create France and French people through language. The guiding light of this mission was the link between language and rationality, civilization, culture, virtue and citizenship. The frenchification of the provinces was rapid. The aims of the schools were embraced by parents and children because of the incontestable pragmatic value of learning French (see Kuter 1989: 77). This is reflected in

Culioli's account of the way his grandfather, a schoolteacher in Corsica around 1911, represented the value of French to his pupils:

> *Dominique apprenait les richesses du français à une vingtaine d'enfants qui s'acharnaient...à ne pas employer leur langue maternelle... "le français, mes enfants," leur expliquait Dominique, "vous servira à se débrouiller dans la vie. Plus de quinze mille des nôtres sont dans l'armée. Comment l'auraient-ils pu s'ils n'avaient pas appris la langue de notre pays, la France? Je vous demande, donc, de ne pas parler le patois...si l'un d'entre vous était surpris à parler le corse, il serait puni. Non par méchanceté, mais parce que vous devez vous astreindre à une certaine discipline. Plus tard, vous remercierez l'école de la République pour ses bienfaits. Bande de bourricots! Faites donc un effort...vous voulez pousser la charrue toute votre vie?"*(Culioli 1986: 172)

[Dominique taught the richness of French to about twenty children who struggled painfully not to use their mother tongue. "French, my children," he explained to them, "will help you to make your way in life. There are more than 15,000 Corsicans in the Army. How could they have done this if they did not speak French, the language of our country, France? I ask you, then, not to speak patois. If you are caught speaking Corsican, you will be punished; not out of spite, but because you must submit yourselves to a certain discipline. Later, you will thank the school of the Republic for its gifts. Herd of donkeys! Make a little effort! Do you want to push a plough all your lives?"]

In Corsica, as in Brittany and elsewhere, parents made sacrifices to send their children to school, and fully agreed with teachers like Culioli that it was the child's primary job to learn French (see Hélias 1978:149 and Wylie 1974: 75). As some of the discourse on the diaspora in Chapter 2 suggests, many Corsicans accepted that the better life they wanted for their children required leaving the island and its language behind. In interviews about early school experiences, middle-aged and older Corsicans made comments that showed how Corsican, like other regional languages, was both devalued as a lowly peasant language in school and perceived as an obstacle to the acquisition of correct French and the social rewards it conferred.[24] Jean-Marie, born in 1950, said, "In school, all the kids whispered and played in Corsican. It was *Oui, Madame* 'Yes Ma'am' to the teacher, then back to our whispers...we were punished for it, made to feel like peasants for speaking Corsican. It was a handicap for learning French."[25] This view was widely shared by teachers. In 1924, the inspector of primary schools distributed a circular in which he devoted a whole section to "*Le dialecte corse, obstacle à l'enseignement du français*" ['The Corsican dialect, obstacle to the teaching of French'] (Anonymous, in Fusina 1994: 249). Octave, born in 1911, said "I remember getting my papers back at school, with *corsisme* 'corsicanism' written all over them in red pencil"[my translations of interviews]. It was Octave's generation that was described by Biron, another school inspector who wrote in 1928:

> *Le dialecte est ici la seule langue vivante. Naturellement, les enfants jouent ou se disputent en corse. Quel entrain leurs débats! Et quelle volubilité dans leurs discussions! En classe, le tableau change. C'est le français qui crée l'atmosphère, mais un français imposé et pour tout dire une langue étrangère...les petits se renferment dans une sorte de timidité sauvage...Quant aux grands, ils jettent mécaniquement leurs réponses dans le moule fourni par les questions. Chez tous, les facultés semblent paralysées* (In Marchetti 1989: 124).

> [The dialect here is the only living language. Naturally, the children play and quarrel in Corsican...what spirit in their debates, what volubility in their discussions! In class, the picture changes. It is French that creates the atmosphere, but an imposed French; really, a foreign language...The little ones take refuge in a sort of primitive timidity...As for the older students, they form their responses mechanically in the mold offered by the question. In all of them, their faculties seem paralyzed.]

The author of the earlier report noted the same "paralysis" and acknowledged that this might entice certain teachers to employ Corsican in order to "*ouvrir l'intelligence des enfants...ou trouver le chemin de leur âme*" [open up the children's intelligence...or find a path to their souls]. He cautioned them to resist this temptation because of "*l'importance primordiale que nous devons attacher à l'apprentissage de la langue nationale [qui] nous oblige presque à renoncer à toute leçon faite en dialecte*" [the capital importance that we ought to attach to the teaching of the national language [which] obliges us to renounce the teaching of lessons in dialect] (Anonymous, in Fusina 1994: 250).

As the Corsican experience of the diaspora shows, the promise of success through French was not an empty one. The fact that Corsicans who learned French and emigrated got stable, well-paid jobs reinforced the explicit message of the educational system, which was that everyone had an equal opportunity to learn French, to become French, and reap the benefits of French culture and citizenship (see Heller 1994: 35 for parallels with French Canadians in Ontario). Together, the economic impetus, and the educational opportunity to learn French brought the Academy home, codified and sanctified the linguistic and social rupture between Corsican and French. As Crowley writes, "those being asked to renounce their linguistic differences in order to speak "nationally" were assured that what they would receive in return would be worth the price" (1996: 69). So, schoolchildren dutifully learned by rote French grammar and spelling that was "completely divorced from speech" (Weber 1976: 337).

2.3. *Language and cultural integration*

The promise of cultural integration through French was a double-edged sword. On the one hand, language was the tool with which France brought its colonies and provinces into the fold of French civilization. Even today, the idea of *la francophonie*, 'the French-speaking world', assumes that sharing the language means sharing culture. In his famous book on the Black French colonial subject, Fanon writes that "The Negro of the Antilles will be proportionately whiter—that is, he will come closer to being a real human being—in direct ratio to his mastery of the French language" (1967: 18). But, as Bourdieu points out, although the school transmits the dominant culture, "by doing away with giving explicitly what it implicitly demands of everyone, the educational system demands of everyone alike that they have what it does not give" (1977b: 493). In effect, education provides the general public with fragments of a cultural/symbolic capital which is possessed in its entirety only by those classes which have access to it outside the educational system. The issue of language, and in particular, linguistic form, has an important role to play in the masking of social hierarchy. As Heller puts it, "By objectifying forms of cultural knowledge...it contributes to disguising the exercise of power through the institutionalization of relations of domination" (1994: 7). As de Certeau, Revel and Julia point out, linguistic value is represented as having an objective, "scientific" rather than a social basis. The discourse of scientific rationality is then used as a screen for the symbolic violence wrought by linguistic domination (de Certeau et. al. 1975: 52). Here, we can see the significance of the focus on grammar and the way it was taught. The removal of language practice from discourse about norms disguises the social origins of those norms and thus makes them look like properties of language itself (Quéré 1987: 69). In other words, school definitions of grammar and *le bon usage* constituted a metalinguistic discourse that naturalized language form as a marker of group identity and value.

What were the results? Emphasizing French as a tool of conceptual precision, as the natural expression of logic and rational cognition, defining French literature and culture as the zenith of Western civilization, and backgrounding the inconsistencies in the grammar and spelling of the language allowed individual failures to master this system to be blamed on the individual. The dominated were thus taught to believe in the rightness of their subordinate status.

Thus the French ideology of language and identity combined the promise of opportunity and integration with the threat of cultural inadequacy. This combination was both a powerful incentive to "buy in" to French and Frenchness, and a source of insecurity which was manifest in both social and linguistic practice. During the colonial period, for example, the large numbers of Corsican functionaries were known as "*plus français que les Français*" [more French than the French]. Corsicans exhibited a similar kind of overcompensation in language practice: Giudicelli remarks that "*les corses 'cultivés' ont toujours employé un français extrême, un français rhétorique à la conquête compensatoire du territoire de la langue française*" [cultivated Corsicans have always spoken an extreme French, characterized by a compensatory rhetoric designed to conquer the territory of the French language] (1984: 194).[26]

2.4. The military: national service and the mother tongue

In addition to the school, the military was an important socializing institution. For many young recruits in the nineteenth century, military service was the first time they had ever left the island as well as the first time they had ever come into contact with other men from all parts of France. Speaking French became a practical requirement in the military context, where it served as a lingua franca that enabled soldiers to give and follow orders and to communicate with their peers. As Ravis-Giordani points out (see last chapter), the idea of the nation was a part of lived experience in the military, where soldiers were being asked to put their lives on the line for France, as Frenchmen. The risk made no sense in the absence of citizenship; therefore, participating in the risk intensified the experience of citizenship. Not only did the military experience cement the association of language, citizenship and patriotism, but it provided a context in which that association was conceptually and experientially legitimate. A French Army manual in the late 1800s made these associations explicit. Recruits were taught that: "1) We call our mother tongue the tongue that is spoken by our parents, and in part, by our mothers; [that which is] spoken also by our fellow citizens and by the persons who inhabit the same *pays* as we do. 2) Our mother tongue is French" (quoted in Weber 1976: 311)

The "myth of the mother tongue," as Vermes and Boutet (1987), Decrosse (1987) and Achard (1987) all emphasize, is critical in the imagination of France. The claim that French is both the national language and the mother tongue naturalizes the boundaries of the nation by equating the visceral link between the vernacular and individual/regional identity and the link of French and citizenship. This assertion of equivalence involves a sleight of hand: that is, the idiom of kinship frames loyalty to the nation in terms of familial and regional loyalties, suggesting that they are complementary and congruent. But the kinship idiom shows that this congruence is clearly fictive: one cannot have two mothers. Being faithful to *la Matrie* 'the Motherland', involves breaking with mother and her tongue. De Certeau has described educational policy in these gendered terms, as *"violence érotique à la terre mère"* [erotic violence to the mother earth], where patois and region together form a sort of dangerous and seductive feminine alterity that was controlled (violated) with the tracing of roads and the intrusion of schoolmasters "spreading the seed" of French and of knowledge in each little village (de Certeau et al. 1975: 33; 155–158).

By the time that the manual cited in Weber was written, we can also see that the way that the connection between language and citizenship was envisioned had shifted in an important way from the beginnings of the French Revolution. French now had to become, and be acknowledged as the individual's "natural," original language (Balibar 1991: 98; Bourdieu 1982: 111). This new requirement for what Bourdieu calls *reconnaissance* 'recognition' of French added a cultural, ideological dimension to participation in a democracy. As Beriss (1990) has pointed out, cultural identity is the foundation of individual rights to citizenship in France. The First World War, with its sheer numbers of recruits and deaths, reinforced the language and citizenship link. As Hélias writes, the soldiers "had all saved France; France was theirs; it had become part of their heritage; so why not the French language as well?" (1978: 150).

To summarize, there are two crucial points about the Corsican experience of schooling and the military. First, in both institutions, language and social ideology were intertwined in practice. The schools and the military not only created a new, shared language of "references and identities of nation, state and authority...the values and morals deemed so crucial" (Graff 1987: 278), but also constituted fields of shared experience which implicitly ratified explicit French language ideology. Secondly, both ideology and practice insured that *"dans ces pays de tradition orale...entre la culture française écrite et la langue non-écrite, instrument de la solidarité du groupe et de l'intimité partagée, il n'y a aucune médiation"* [in these regions with an oral tradition...between the written, French culture and the unwritten language, instrument of the solidarity of the group and of shared intimacy, there was no middle ground] (Furet and Ozouf 1977: 345).

3. Sociolinguistic effects of French language domination

3.1. Prestige and insecurity

The fact that Corsicans absorbed French notions of linguistic hierarchy can be seen in the way that linguistic insecurity in regard to French is coupled with a high social value attached to speaking French. By the time that my neighbor Hervé was dating (the 1930s) the language of courtship had shifted from Italian to French; it was considered *grossier* 'crude' to address a woman in Corsican. The quality of one's French was also a social issue, and Hervé recalled how anxious he had been about his ability to converse in proper French on a double date he went on one summer with two Corsican girls who lived on the continent. In other words, linguistic goods from the dominant market had significant exchange value in the minority market. Other Corsicans I interviewed also identified the status dimension of *le bon usage* of French as the cause of gender-based patterns of language use. Parents, they observed, spoke Corsican less to their daughters than they did to their sons, and girls and women exhibited a preference for French. I will return to gendered patterns of language use below; what is significant here is that prestige is offered as an explanation for patterns of linguistic usage by Corsicans themselves.

Signs of the high value of French and of Corsican linguistic insecurity persist today. Filippi, in his 1992 study of the Corsican regional variety of French, found that many Corsican high school students believed that their French was deficient.[27] There is also a genre of jokes, songs and stories based on Corsican "malapropisms" in French (some of these are idiosyncratic and others are part of a relatively conventional mixed variety Filippi calls *Francorse*, described later in this chapter). I return to this genre of humor in Chapter 8; here let me say only that there is often an undercurrent of embarrassment in the way people talk about these jokes. "I wish I could just laugh, and that's it," said one of my informants, "but I can't. I feel a certain anguish." That anguish is rooted in empathy for the Corsicans who would have been scorned by outsiders and more educated insiders for their "mistakes" or "ignorance". People admire someone who speaks "good French". My neighbor Marcelle told me with pride about how well her daughter spoke French. A local scholar (and amateur collector of Corsican lexical and ethnographic material) made a point to remark in our first telephone conversation, *"Mais vous maniez bien la langue française"* [literally: 'But you wield French well']. Another way in which linguistic hierarchy is inscribed in everyday discourse practices is in the general politeness code (several instances of which are described below) that favors the dominant language (noted by both Dorian 1981: 79 and Woolard 1989a: 70).

In the following sections, I discuss how language shift is manifested in historical and contemporary patterns of linguistic practice, drawing on ethnographic observations, lengthy interview data and sociolinguistic survey results from Thiers' 1984 sociolinguistic survey of almost 800 young teenagers and my own survey data (collected from 164 people) conducted in 1989. Kristol, working on issues of multilingualism in Switzerland, emphasizes that sociolinguistic survey responses cannot be read as accurate reports of practice; rather, they are representations of language use (1996: 127). Thiers makes a similar point, adding that those representations are quintessentially political and ideological in contexts like the Corsican one, where language issues carry heightened social and political significance (1986: 29). These cautions on the interpretation of survey results are important ones, particularly in analyses that depend solely on quantitative data. Nevertheless, quantitative survey results corroborate what the observation of social life makes clear: in the space of a few generations, the practice of Corsican has declined sharply, and that French has replaced Corsican as the primary language of the family.

3.2. Language shift: compartmentalization of language use by age

The economic and prestige value of French played a crucial role in the process of language shift. Like the Gaelic-speaking parents descried by Dorian (1981: 84), and Breton speakers studied by Kuter (1989: 84–85), Corsican parents saw the choice between the dominant and minority language in either/or terms. French was the *langue du pain*, 'language of bread'–that is, of economic value. Those parents whose first introduction to French was in school had experienced their knowledge of Corsican as a handicap; moreover, their teachers had told them that this was so. The school had further instructed them that their home language had no value. French was also the language of power and prestige. The choice was simple.

3.2.1. Childhood practice

Two questions addressed practices of Corsican in childhood. The first was, "Did you speak Corsican as a child?" Respondents answered by checking a category on a scale ranging from 0 (never) to 6 (always). The results are summarized in Table 1. We can see that a total of 55% of the respondents spoke Corsican little, very little or never as a child, versus 45% who spoke sometimes, often or always. Eliminating the high and low end answers "never" and "always," the relative weight of the categories "little" and "very little" becomes apparent: they account for 43% of the total sample, versus 27% for "sometimes" or "often".   We can see the progression of language shift very clearly when we compare the under-30 group and the over-45 group: 72% of people over 45 spoke Corsican sometimes, often or always as children; the same number of those under 30 spoke it never, very little or little.

Table 1. Use of Corsican as a child

	Never	Very Little	Little	Some-times	Often	Always
Under 30	10%	42%	20%	13%	12%	3%
30–45	22%	18%	11%	7%	7%	19%
Over 45	4%	16%	8%	8%	20%	44%

The following table summarizes responses to the second question "If your parents spoke to you in Corsican, how often did you respond in Corsican?" Here, respondents chose from responses on a five-point scale.

Table 2. Response to parents in Corsican

	Never	Little	Sometimes	Often	Always
Under 30	2%	17%	25%	8%	15%
Over 30	0%	11%	8%	16%	38%

Again, we see a clear progression over time with 23% of respondents under 30, versus 54% of respondents over 30 reporting that they responded in Corsican "often" or "always".

Interview data corroborates that the pattern of speaking French to children was well-established after World War II (see Dorian 1981: 105). In Riventosa, Hervé and his wife Germaine (both Corsophones) said they had spoken French to their children. They "didn't know why...it was just what people did at the time". They still tell the story of their oldest, Albert, who was sitting in a high chair when an acquaintance came in. "*U ciucciu, parla corsu?*" ['Does the baby speak Corsican?'] he asked. Before Albert's parents could respond, the baby replied (to everyone's amusement):"*U ciucciu parlu corfu è francese*" ['The baby speaks Corfican (a childish mispronunciation) and French']. The visitor's question reveals how common it had become by the mid-fifties for Corsophone parents to have non-Corsophone children. The fact that Albert did speak Corsican also reflects the fact that Hervé and Germaine, like many parents of their generation, never stopped speaking Corsican to each other and may not have been as consistent as they say they were about avoiding speaking Corsican to their children.[28] Albert, like his sister and brother, is bilingual. Many men of this generation (between the ages of 35 and 45) also report having "learned Corsican in the street"; that is, outside the family in social contexts in which the language still dominated: the cafe, the hunt, sports. This shows that parents like Hervé and Germaine also did not necessarily avoid speaking Corsican to other people's children.

We can see that the postwar generation received mixed messages about Corsican: on one hand, the school and many parents' language choices clearly sent negative messages to children about the utility and status of Corsican. On the other hand, these children could observe first-hand the strength of the affective and social role this language played for their parents and their parents' friends and relatives.

3.2.2. Contemporary practice

This has resulted in a generation of young parents with very mixed competence in Corsican. Corsican is no longer the dominant language of communication between Corsicans in their thirties and forties, although many of them use the language with their elders. As a consequence, even those children who hear quite a lot of Corsican today are likely to perceive it as having a rather restricted social role. Those young parents who have only passive competence in Corsican are obviously not able to transmit the language. And, even those who do speak Corsican have almost all followed the pattern established by their parents of speaking French to their children.[29] This pattern is so ingrained that even the most dedicated language activists have found it difficult to create bilingual or Corsican-speaking households. One such parent told me about the difficulties of putting into practice a deliberate, ideologically motivated decision to speak Corsican to his four boys. He and his wife had actually been prompted to take this decision by the realization that both they and their first child's grandparents had automatically addressed the baby in French. Making Corsican the language of the family did not come easily, and even their boys resisted. They had to resort to force: the children were told that they could not sit and eat at the dinner table unless they spoke Corsican.

Ethnographic observations and self-reports of contemporary practice all paint the same picture of language shift. For example, in my many visits to primary schools, I never once heard a child utter a spontaneous Corsican word; on the playground, the air was filled with high-pitched little French voices. In class, scuffles, arguments, claims for attention from the children ("Teacher, teacher, he's hitting me") and most efforts on the part of the teachers to keep discipline took place in French, even during Corsican language classes. Spontaneous speech in Corsican from children was so extraordinary as to draw comment from other Corsicans. Once, in a supermarket, I heard a three-year old girl who was being pushed in a shopping cart say, "*Collu à u paese*" ['I'm going up to the village'] to the great astonishment and amusement of the women she was with. They had been speaking Corsican to each other, but obviously did not consider it a child's code; right after the little girl uttered the Corsican phrase, they wheeled her up to an acquaintance and repeated what they obviously considered a humorous incident. Similarly, one of the people I interviewed told me what a dramatic effect the first television broadcasts of Corsican language classes in the primary schools had had. Not only was there the strangeness of hearing Corsican in a previously all-French medium (T.V) and domain (school), but there was also the shock of hearing Corsican coming out of the mouths of children.[30]

Over the last ten years, people have gotten much more used to Corsican language being used in the schools, and regularly attend school events in which children use Corsican in school plays and songs. But the child who uses Corsican outside the classroom is still a rarity. This is the case in Riventosa today, despite the fact that the village school has been an experimental bilingual site since 1996. When I visited in 1998, I met little Francescu Maria, a three-year-old who was exclusively Corsophone. His father was completing a doctorate in Corsican studies. He and his wife had made an ideologically motivated decision to speak only Corsican in the household. As a consequence, Francescu Maria did not speak French; he addressed adults in Corsican and they spoke to him in Corsican. Observing these public interactions between adults and a small boy, I was struck with how unusual they still were. I was not the only one to be struck by this, for after Francescu Maria left with his parents for his summer vacation, my neighbors continued to regale me with stories about the little boy. There was no doubt that Francescu Maria was quite precocious, and this was often the subject matter of the anecdotes people told me. But no matter what it was that he said, adults who talked about him always commented on the fact that he said it in Corsican. A good deal of his singularity was obviously linguistic.

Let us turn to the survey data for self-reports of use and competence. Respondents were asked to characterize how often they spoke Corsican by checking one of three categories: 0–50% of the time, about 50% of the time, and 50–100% of the time.[31] Thirty-eight percent of respondents over 30 reported speaking Corsican 50% or more of the time, compared to only 13% of those in the under-30 age range. Similar patterns emerge in Thiers' 1984 study of adolescents: 84% of these students answered "French" in response to the question, "Do you usually speak Corsican or French?" These age-related patterns of use are repeated in the 1991 survey of Corsicans living in the Paris region, in which 41% of respondents under 35 reported speaking Corsican often, compared to 66% of those over 50 (*Forum Paris-Corse* 1991: 63).

I also asked my survey respondents to rate their own level of competence in Corsican (speaking, reading, writing and understanding) on a scale of one to five. Here, 49% of those under 30 rated themselves a 3 (average) or above as Corsican speakers. This figure went up to 57% for respondents between 30 and 45, and rose to 87% for those 45 and older. A similar distribution of self-evaluations of competence can be seen in the survey of Corsicans in Paris, albeit with less dramatic differences. Fourteen percent of those under 30 characterized themselves as "fluent" in Corsican compared to 49% of those over 50 (*Forum Paris-Corse* 1991: 60). In my survey, there was also another question on competence asking respondents to characterize their speaking competence as below average, at the average or above average compared to "the norm".

Table 3. Self-rating relative to the norm

	below average	average	above average
All	32%	43%	25%
Under 30	39%	35%	14%
30–45	27%	46%	11%
Over 45	11%	37%	50%

In Table 3, self-reports as "average" do not show a marked variation from one age group to another.[32] We can see, however, that the oldest respondents are three times more likely than either of the other two age groups to characterize themselves as "above average" speakers of Corsican. And respondents in the youngest group of speakers are three times more likely to characterize themselves as "below average" Corsican speakers.

3.3. Domains of practice: inner and outer sphere

In responses to two open survey questions which asked where, when, with whom and in what circumstances people spoke Corsican/spoke the most Corsican, "the village" was given as an answer 34 times; "family" or "friends" accounted for 81 of 233 total citations. The fact that "family," "friends," "village," "at home," and "with old people" were cited so frequently and in clusters of two or three suggests the extent to which they are associated with the same "inner sphere" environment (Urciuoli 1996: 77). All told, 66% of the total responses referred to this domain, compared to 24% which referred to more public, formal "outer sphere" domains, relationships or activities. This is consistent with the overall reports of Corsican language use in the home (61%) and at work (29%).

These survey results are a metalinguistic discourse which clearly reproduces a diglossic ideology in which French and Corsican are defined a priori as connected to mutually exclusive domains of use and value. It must be recognized that this sort of compartmentalization was embedded in one of the survey questions, in which people had to choose between "home" and work. It was, however, also generated spontaneously by the open-ended question. This diglossic metadisourse was also a ubiquitous feature of structured interviews with people who filled out the questionnaires, unstructured interviews and, as the following chapters will show, public discourse about language.

In the following section, I explore the extent to which this discourse reflects "actual" language practices. In some cases, patterns of practice conform to the "inner sphere–outer sphere" dichotomy for reasons that are consistent with the history of linguistic policy in Corsica: for most of Corsican history, Corsican has not had a public, institutional role. There are many other cases in which the way people use language contrasts sharply with the differentiation of domains of language functions and domains of use that are so neat and clear in metalinguistic discourse. I will argue, however, that in these cases, the oppositions of the diglossic model still constitute part of the shared cultural knowledge used by speakers and listeners to create and interpret meaning.

3.3.1. The "outer sphere": language practices, representations and creativity

The "outer sphere" is the space of relatively impersonal, formal, public, official activities. Corsican is not absent from this sphere, as we will see, but it is generally marked. This markedness is most pronounced in contexts that are prototypically formal and institutional, such as speeches in political chambers. This is illustrated by reactions to the late Andreu Fazi, a nationalist member of the Corsican Regional Assembly, who made a point of speaking in Corsican whenever he addressed the chamber. This set him apart from all of the other Assembly members, even though most were Corsophone, and some of them used Corsican occasionally in the course of the proceedings. Fazi, however, made his Corsican discourse central and formal, and this was noted by journalists writing about Assembly proceedings. They invariably prefaced their reports of what he had said by noting that he had said it eloquently in Corsican. Despite the admiration this eloquence commanded, Fazi's Corsican discourses did not make it into the official record unless Fazi himself provided a text to the Assembly reporter, who was not required (and perhaps, not able) to take dictation in Corsican. This emphasized that the Assembly's "real" business was in French.

Fazi's use of Corsican was meant to challenge the exclusive association of Corsican with the inner sphere in the diglossic model. At the time he held office, we can see that both the official documents and the press reports of the time represented his usage as too exotic to upset normative assumptions. Most other politicians' use of Corsican in the Assembly and elsewhere also did not challenge the diglossic framework: they spoke Corsican for impromptu, personal, often passionate interjections. However, since they used French more than Corsican, these interjections amounted to codeswitches. These codeswitches had a great deal of communicative potential: they could be seen as a display of cultural authenticity designed to establish the speaker's authority to speak "as a Corsican," on behalf of a Corsican constituency. But this rhetorical exploitation of the "inner" in the "outer" sphere does not disturb the status of those categories, or their association with Corsican and French respectively. Like the use of Hawaiian Creole English in the dialogues, but not in the third-person narration of novels in described by Romaine (1995), this "informal" kind of use of Corsican in the Assembly had the overall rhetorical effect of framing Corsican speech as peripheral to the official, public context.

The official language policy in the Assembly that muted Corsican in the written record has been recently changed. In a 1997 resolution on the Corsican language (Number 97/103: 2430), the preamble was written in Corsican. It was not translated into French, but a single line of French that prefaced the page of Corsican underscored the political and symbolic weight of the choice of language: This line read: *"L'Assemblée de Corse adopte au préalable une declaration en langue corse qui constituera un message solennel adressé tant à la société insulaire qu'à l'État"*[Before going any further, the Assembly of Corsica adopts a declaration in the Corsican language which constitutes a

solemn message that is addressed equally to Corsican society and to the state].
This document also contained a commitment to translate all important
Assembly deliberations into Corsican.

Despite the Assembly's recent commitment to bilingual publications, an
equally recent newspaper article illustrates that speaking Corsican in the
political sphere is still newsworthy. Titled *"Le conseiller du Cimbalu
introduit le bilinguisme à l'Assemblée Départementale"* [The representative
from the Cimbalu introduces bilingualism into the Departmental Assembly],
it read:

> *Un élu de la majorité qui s'adresse in 'lingua materna' au préfet du
> département: cela ne s'est jamais vu au Conseil Générale de la Haute Corse.
> Et même si le principal intéressé, Jean-Baptiste Raffaelli en l'occurrence, a
> qualifié son intervention de 'non événement,' l'on doit bien reconnaître qu'en
> agissant de la sorte...l'élu du Cimbalu a bien servi la cause du corse devant
> le représantant de l'État (Corse-Matin 27 June 1998).*

> [a politician from the majority party who addresses the Prefect of the
> Department in the 'mother tongue': that has never been seen in the General
> Council of Upper Corsica. And even if the party concerned, Jean-Baptiste
> Rafaelli as it so happens, characterized his discourse as a 'non-event,' we must
> recognize that in so acting, the representative from Cimbalu admirably repre-
> sented the cause of Corsican before the representative of the state.]

We can also note that the impact of this public discourse in Corsican was
intensified by the fact that Rafaelli is not a nationalist. In a way, because Fazi
was a nationalist, his use of Corsican simply indexed a well-established
nationalist political position on language. In contrast, Rafaelli's departure
from the standard practice of French is not given by his party membership.
The newspaper article also demonstrates that the actual presence of the
Prefect, a non-Corsophone government official, made the use of Corsican all
the more marked. Even in the formal halls of the Regional Assembly, the
debates could be defined as "internal," Corsican ones that would be used as
the basis for later interactions with the state. In the Departmental General
Council, the state is physically present in the person of the Prefect.

While the use of Corsican for the central business of formal gatherings is
marked, there is a kind of institutionalized use of Corsican at the very
beginning of a political or public function. The subsequent switch to French
is often accompanied by metalinguistic commentary. For example, at a small
recognition ceremony, the mayor of the village where it was held opened the
event in Corsican. He then said, *"Je vais vous parler en francais pour que tout
le monde puisse comprendre"* ['I'm going to speak to you in French so that
everyone can understand']. In another event, a Corsican scholar addressed an

international audience in a conference session on Corsican music. His opening words in French were bracketed as an explanation of what he represented as the "real"opening, which was in Corsican. "*Je vais commencer en langue corse,*" ['I'm going to begin in Corsican'] he said, "*pour ceux qui viennent de l'extérieure qu'ils entendent du corse et pour ce qui concerne le chant et la musique, tout cela me vient mieux en corse*" ['in order for those people who have come from elsewhere to be able to hear some Corsican, and because everything to do with singing and music comes to me better in Corsican']. After he spoke some Corsican, he returned to French to continue the presentation. These kinds of commentaries foreground the use of Corsican as a solidarity code and as an "authentic" cultural code at the same time as they acknowledge language shift and mixed audiences (not everyone understands) and confirm French as the language of public communication.

Even in less formal contexts than the Regional Assembly, the language of meetings tends to be French. This is true even in militant, pro-Corsican circles. I was told by a person who had been very active in a nationalist agricultural union that this had been the case in all of their meetings, despite the fact that all of them were Corsican-speaking. When he needled them about the inconsistency between their practice and their ideology, they replied that they would eventually have to present their case to French government representatives like the Prefect, who did not speak Corsican. In this answer, they implicitly evoke a contrast between intimate, small-group interactions (in which Corsican could be defined as appropriate) and the "outer sphere". They then define their meetings outer as part of a wider struggle for political power which is by definition an outer sphere event. This justifies "training" in the language of power.

Bureaucratic/official/formal business is also often conducted in French out of sheer habit: French is the only language in which most Corsicans have ever run, or been part of a meeting or other similarly structured social interaction. My former landlord, a highly successful contractor, was extremely competent in both Corsican and French, and spoke Corsican often during his work day. He told me, however, that he would feel uncomfortable and nervous about speaking Corsican in front of a professional group simply because he had no experience doing so in that language. I attended a wide variety of meetings attended by educated Corsophones who were committed to the promotion of Corsican, and observed that even those who did have experience in public discourse in Corsican sometimes "slipped" back into French.

While the "public" and "formal" character of many settings (meetings, political chambers and some kinds of interviews) is relatively transparent, there are of course many other instances in which the formality or informality of the social context is not unambiguously given. In these instances, language choices can play as large a role in defining the situation as "the situation" plays in shaping those language choices. Take for example the following situation described to me by the sociolinguist Jacques Thiers: when he did taped interviews with his mother on ethnographic topics she not only switched to French but sometimes, used the formal *vous* 'you' with him. In this case, Thiers was both a son and an academic; and while the context was intimate (in the home) the speech event (an interview) was not a casual one. The interview frame, engaged her as an "expert" or authority in the production of knowledge for academic, not social purposes. Given her age at the time (at least 65), it is likely that Thiers' mother was a bilingual for whom Corsican and French use were strictly compartmentalized. He writes that for such bilinguals, "*dès que l'entretien s'oriente vers un niveau plus analytique et critique des thèmes liés à l'ile et à l'ethnicité, le recours au français semble s'imposer*" [as soon as the discussion moves towards a more analytical/critical treatment of themes to do with the island and ethnicity, French seems to impose itself as a language] (1989a: 82). So the mother's use of *vous* might have been a response to the relative formality of the interview frame, in which her son was talking to her in his capacity as researcher and academic. At the same time, we have to recognize the element of choice in Thiers' mother's use of French and formal address and the way in which this choice contributed to way in which this interaction became defined. She could, for example, have used French in her "expert" role but used the informal *tu* to acknowledge or integrate Thiers' role as her son in an interview he did as an academic.

In this case, we cannot predict Thiers' mother's language choice from the context. In fact, her use of vous and French contrasts with the intuition that the intimacy of the mother--son relationship would prevail over all other contextual factors. Her language choice, then, becomes an index of how she defines the context. And here we find that her definition of the context is consistent with, but not predictable from the presence of societal diglossia. Understanding how diglossic ideologies and practices influence individual experiences and practices throughout a lifetime gives us a framework that renders Thiers' mother's linguistic behavior comprehensible. In particular, it allows us to understand how it was possible for his mother not to experience her choice of codes as wildly inappropriate or heavily marked.

Another language choice scenario illustrates the complexity of the variables involved in the definition of situation and hence, in the "marked-ness" of a particular language choice. Philippe, the nationalist shopkeeper in Bastia described in a vignette in Chapter 1, made a point of initiating conversation in Corsican with any customer he judged to be plausibly Corsophone (based on an assessment of age and demeanor). A shop is certainly a public place, but there are lots of different kinds of shops and clienteles that make a particular shop interaction more or less public, more or less formal or intimate. This means that a shopkeeper's initiation of interaction in Corsican in his or her store is not by definition marked, but several specific features of the situation made Philippe's use marked. First of all, the shop was a boutique in Bastia, one of two major cities on the island. It was located on a major street and catered in part to a tourist clientele; it was not really a "neighborhood" grocery store. Philippe did have some regular customers, but he also had a fairly large "anonymous" clientele. While it might not be the case in a village or neighborhood grocery, in a shop like Philippe's in a city, the unmarked choice of public language with a stranger is French. This means that while Corsican is not necessarily marked in this context, it is not, like French, socially defined as unmarked. It is, therefore, not the "safest" interactional route. In this respect, the use of Corsican violates the etiquette of deference to the language choice of one's interlocutor. The requirement for deference is also intensified by the fact that it is a commercial encounter in which the client has a privileged status. Initiating a conversation in French (as neutral) thus allows the client to choose, and does not make that choice an issue in the interaction. Not only did Philippe use Corsican, but he did so in a theatrical style which unequivocally foregrounded language choice. I think that his language choice was motivated almost entirely by his politics; that he considered any other choice ideologically inconsistent. There are a variety of other possible meanings and motivations, which are alternately pragmatic and ideological. He may have foregrounded his choice of Corsican as a way of drawing attention to his own linguistic competence in a display of cultural authenticity and political commitment. My presence as an American anthropologist is a plausible prompt for such a display, though it is impossible for me to tell how much of it was for my benefit. His use of Corsican could also have been a strategy for making and keeping a nationalist clientele. I did not observe Philippe's store in the tourist season, but it may also have been the case that Corsican was part of the product (cultural authenticity) that he sold to tourists.

As Scotton (1986: 406) notes, "listeners typically perceive marked choices as affective statements—and they are, in that they call for changes in the participant relationship." In Philippe's case, his marked use of Corsican amounts to an assertion of his prerogative to define the situation and the relationships in it. The couple who raised their boys as Corsophones, above, reported using Corsican as customers in Bastia in much the same way as Philippe used it as a shopkeeper. They not only spoke Corsican in commercial encounters, but also made it clear to business owners that they would not do business with anyone who did not honor their language choice. In both these scenarios, the initiation of the commercial interaction in Corsican was intended as a political statement, which was the assertion that Corsican had the right to command public space. In interactional terms, the initiation of the interaction in a marked code shifted the frame of reference from a relatively impersonal one in which participants have limited and particular obligations to one another to a far more demanding cultural and political frame in which the interlocutors were effectively forced to respond to the initiator as fellow Corsican citizens with mutual obligations based on a presumed solidarity. The interlocutors were also denied the possibility of neutral response: their choice of a language of response was automatically defined as a symbolic acceptance or rejection of political claims on their cultural identity. Not surprisingly, in both of these situations, some interlocutors signaled their resistance to the initiator's agenda by responding in French.[33]

The markedness of Corsican in public is thus always potential but not always actualized. To come back to the survey responses reported above, it is quite possible that some of the people who did not report speaking Corsican at work did not think about what they did at work as "speaking Corsican" if the job was not defined in terms of language (and almost no jobs are). Observing banks, shops, cafes, post offices and other service industries, it seems to me that patterns of linguistic practice are just as often related to conventional patterns of language choice based on age, familiarity and known or supposed competence as they did to associations of language and domain (see Woolard 1989a: 64, for a parallel account of language choices in Catalonia). So, for example, many bank and postal employees would probably not say they spoke Corsican at work, even though I have seen employees in banks and post offices, explain and conduct an entire financial transaction in Corsican with an old person, expressing the figures in old francs.[34] The pattern of using Corsican with elders can override the generally French frame of a commercial interaction. And, elders can initiate interactions in Corsican without their choice being viewed as marked, as in the following incident: I was standing in a rather loosely defined line in a bank when a man of about seventy came in. He tried to ascertain where he stood in line, and asked a young woman if it were her turn next in Corsican "*Tocca à voi*? ['Is it your turn?'] She waved him forward, saying "*Andate puru*" ['Please go ahead'] in Corsican, the language he also chose to use with the teller. Corsican is also heard frequently in businesses that develop or cultivate intimacy with a clientele (bars, small grocery stores, bakeries), or alternately, operate in a social milieu where intimacy is given, like the village shop.

Corsican is also present in work and other public settings in a ubiquitous, albeit restricted way, as what Laponce (1984: 21) calls the *langue du mot* 'language of the word' in which the focus is on the use of words as symbols or indices of social identities or relations. The *langue du mot* includes such things as Corsican newspaper headlines over a French text, Corsican names for businesses, clubs and associations, as well as the use of brief, formulaic exclamations and interjections. At the airport ticket counter, the agent at her computer says *aspetta* 'wait' in the midst of an interaction in French. Hardly a Corsican pointing out something says *regardez* 'look' in French, it is almost always the Corsican *mi* 'look'. The exclamation *Aiò* 'hey,' the greeting *Cumu va?* 'how are you?' and *Va bè* (which means either 'fine' or with alternate intonation, carries a sarcastic meaning: 'well, that's just great') are also ubiquitous elements of Corsican conversation. These fragments of Corsican add a distinct flavor to the aural landscape, but are not taken as an index of speaker competence, nor as an invitation to carry out a conversation in Corsican.[35] They are what Tsitsipis calls "slim texts". Slim texts are "set discourse material which can be quoted in order to comment on some element of the cultural backdrop or of the immediate situation" (1991: 154–155). For example, in the local travel agency where I accumulated many hours of waiting and listening, I rarely heard an extended exchange of Corsican. But the agents might say while waiting on a customer they knew, *Chì freddu!* 'how cold it is!' Such interjections could also come from customers: for example, one commented, booking a tour at Easter, that "*Tuttu u mondu volenu andà in listessu tempu*" ['Everyone wants to leave at the same time'] in the middle of a transaction in French, provoking agreement, but no further conversation in Corsican.

The fact that slim texts are not interpreted as indices of competence or even of language preference is illustrated in a rather striking way in an interaction I observed with my friend Alphonse, with whom I often went hiking. Alphonse's first language is Corsican, and it is his first language choice with most people he meets on the mountain trails who do not look patently foreign. One day, we were going down a trail and crossed paths with a middle-aged man and his wife who were going up. We paused just long enough for conversation to be struck up. This was done in French. Then the man commented on Alphonse's T-shirt, which said *L'Arcusgi*, the name of Alphonse's marksmanship club. The man said that he belonged to a club of the same name, and told us it was "*in Marseglia*," the Corsican pronunciation of Marseilles, where there is a considerable Corsican population. Alphonse did not respond to these fragments of Corsican with Corsican, but continued to chat in French. The man then used a slightly longer stretch of Corsican in a sentence with a codeswitch: "*Cullemu quassù; credu chì si chjamanu* les espoirs solitaires" ['We are climbing up there; I think they {the mountains} are called *the solitary hopes*']. Somewhat to my surprise, Alphonse never replied in Corsican. When we had parted company with the couple, Alphonse turned to me and remarked, "*Tu sais, il a un club de tir à Marseilles avec le même nom que le mien*" ['You know, he has a shooting club in Marseilles with the same name as mine']. As we continued down the mountain, we passed a shepherd's cabin. Alphonse talked with the shepherd in Corsican, and also exchanged a few words in Corsican with a group of women (relatives of the shepherd) sitting above and off to the side of the trail in the shade of a rocky overhang. As we walked away, he said to me, "*Tu vois, j'ai parlé en corse tout naturellement avec ses dâmes; je savais que je pouvais le faire, étant donné leurs âges*" ['You see, I talked Corsican completely naturally with those ladies; I knew I could because of their ages']. This was my opportunity to ask him about the man and his wife we had met earlier. Did he see them as Corsican speakers? Alphonse replied that the man spoke a little Corsican but had obviously "forgotten" it. I asked how he could tell he had forgotten, and Alphonse replied that he had not been able to understand when the man "said a few names" in Corsican. My perception was that Alphonse was under-representing both the amount of Corsican that the man had used and his level of comprehension: the conversation had flowed without any signs of misunderstanding (such as lack of continuity of subject or repairs). What is more, the *tu sais* 'you know' in his comment to me after we parted with the couple framed the comment that followed as a translation, rather than a reiteration of something we both already knew. This means that at least at some level, he had processed the conversation he was translating as a Corsican one.

In the context of our discussion of slim texts, I think that we can interpret Alphonse's behavior in the following way: the man's initial interaction in French, and the information that he lived in Marseilles caused Alphonse to categorize him as an outsider. The discussion of the diaspora in Chapter 2 shows that this "outsiderness" is not self-evident, since Corsicans living on the continent are not necessarily seen as outsiders, but it is potential. It is possible that this categorization caused Alphonse to deliberately reject the man's bids for access to a shared intimacy code. My acquaintance with Alphonse as a person, however, leads me to believe that it is just as likely that he simply heard the man's interjections in Corsican as instances of the *langue du mot*: significant in terms of affect, but not significant as an index of competence. The man's use of Corsican did nothing to change Alphonse's initial evaluation of him as a nonspeaker. By the same token, Alphonse's initial evaluation of the shepherd's relatives as Corsophones would probably not have been altered if they had responded to him with the same kinds of codeswitches exhibited by the hiker from Marseilles.

To summarize, Corsican is present in the outer sphere in a number of different guises. Having been officially excluded until recent history from public, official, institutional domains, Corsican can be used in those domains as a marked choice that evokes the intimacy, solidarity and cultural authenticity of the inner sphere for a variety of persuasive effects. The markedness of Corsican can be predicted in quintessentially outer sphere domains like the chambers of the Regional Assembly, but it is not unambiguously given in many other contexts, where language choices are part of the way the situation gets defined. While the diglossic model does not predict those choices, it is nevertheless a large part of the shared conceptual and experiential framework that makes those choices comprehensible.

3.3.2. The "inner sphere": practice, affect and the metalinguistic discourse of the village

Just like people's accounts of language practices at work, what they say about their use of Corsican with friends and family in the village context is a metalinguistic discourse that reproduces the diglossic separation of domains of use and value. This does not mean that there is no truth to their assertions that they speak Corsican the most with friends and family in the village. Because of their isolation and limited economic opportunities, many villages in Corsica are depopulated. Those who do live there permanently tend to be retired. Thus the village population, by definition, is dominated by those older people who are most likely to speak Corsican. Not only are old people more likely to know Corsican, but they also provoke the use of Corsican by middle aged, bilingual Corsicans whose language choices are often made on the basis of their interlocutor. Thus a middle-aged Corsican who works in a larger town or city may not use the language in his or her daily life (work or home) but will speak it when visiting parents in the village. The village is also a privileged Corsophone space for Corsican "semispeakers" (Dorian's 1981 term). I knew several people who were not confident about their ability to speak Corsican, and who confined their use of Corsican to the non-threatening context of their villages of origin. The village can also be a place where speaking Corsican can be felt as a social requirement. In Riventosa, the wife of a semispeaker with admittedly limited competence in Corsican confided in me that her husband had to make a *sacré effort* 'huge effort' to speak a little Corsican in the village, something he never did elsewhere. The continued social value of conversing in Corsican is also indexed by some of my survey responses, in which almost all those who rated themselves as below average in speaking competence said they would like to be able to speak better.

It is clear that what people say about speaking Corsican in the village reflects the compartmentalization of their affective and their professional lives that is evident in their testimonies about the meaning and value of village life.

When people told me, "I can't imagine speaking anything but Corsican, it does not occur to me to speak French in the village," they were making explicit a link between language and intimacy: it is in the village that affective relations are concentrated. And this affective, interpersonal domain is the only one in which Corsican still has a significant social role. The connection of Corsican with intimacy in village relations can even override the politeness rule of linguistic accommodation, and the ingrained habit of speaking French with foreigners: after we had lived in Riventosa almost a year, some of our friends stopped making a consistent effort to use French around my husband, who understood almost no Corsican.[36]

Although, as it will become clear below, few people speak Corsican exclusively anywhere, the village is one of the few locations where the use of French (and particularly the exclusive use of French) can be marked. By the same token, the public use of Corsican between strangers in village space can be unmarked. This was illustrated most dramatically to me on a day in Riventosa when a strange man pulled up on the square, where I happened to be alone. He got out of his car and asked me in Corsican where someone lived. Given my age and gender (see discussion below), I was astonished at his assumption of competence (he was no doubt equally surprised by my funny accent). My surprise was based, however, on my knowledge of actual patterns of active competence. I realize now that his speaking Corsican was a way of saying "I am a villager just like you." I do not believe that it would have mattered if I had responded in French. Thus what his language choice signaled was the assumption of at least a passive linguistic competence and an active, shared social competence which included knowledge of the acceptability of Corsican address in the village context. Traveling by car through villages in the central part of the island with my friends Martin and Alphonse (75 and 50 years old, respectively) I saw this principle at work many times over. Martin would hail a stranger to ask directions with an *"Ô"* and tip of the chin (vocal and gestural contextualization cues that Corsican would ensue). On occasion, the advanced years of the people he chose to talk to were a fair guarantee that they were Corsophone. But there were many cases in which Alphonse and Martin began conversation with young people in Corsican. Both the young people who responded in Corsican and those who said they could not speak it seemed to take the initiation of conversation in Corsican as perfectly natural in this setting.

It should be pointed out that the etiquette of Corsican first address in village space described above is a relatively recent consequence of language shift, for it depends on French language competence being able to be taken for granted. A primary school inspector from Riventosa reported that when he used to make the rounds of school villages only a decade ago, and had to stop to ask older people for directions, they often responded in French to his Corsican requests to prove that they could speak the language of prestige. The connection of dominant language competence and social dignity led him to adopt the following politeness strategy: he used French as the language of first address to old villagers, then switched immediately to Corsican once they had responded.[37]

This means that despite the "normalness" of Corsican language encounters in village space, we can see that the force of using Corsican in a public encounter between strangers is derived from the fact that French is the habitual language of public life. It is in fact because French is spoken widely in public, between strangers, even in villages, that speaking Corsican in a village symbolizes "villageness," or social intimacy. As Urciuoli points out, "there is no point where inner-sphere life is truly free of outer-sphere structuring" (1996: 105).

3.4. Gender

The overall picture of language shift I have painted would be incomplete without a discussion of gender differences in practice, and popular accounts of men's versus women's past practices and attitudes. In the survey data, women reported speaking Corsican less frequently than male respondents did. Answers to the question "Did you speak Corsican as a child?" are summarized with reference to gender in Table 4.

If we lump together all responses of "never," "very little" and "little," we find that 64% of the women respondents report low childhood use compared to 50% of the men. There is also a fairly dramatic gender difference in responses of "often" or "always," with 23% of women compared to 42 % of men reporting generally high childhood use of Corsican.

There are also some gender differences in responses to the question on childhood use that asked respondents to report on how often they responded in Corsican if addressed in that language by parents (Table 5). These results show women reporting a lower rate of Corsican response than men. The starkest contrast can be seen in answers of "never" or "little". Women were almost three times as likely to answer "never" or "little" (21% of responses) as men (8% of responses). The gender contrast can also be seen, though to a lesser degree in answers of "often" or "always": 35% of the women respondents answered "often" or "always" compared to 49% of the men.

Another noteworthy gender difference concerns reported percentages of use, summarized in Table 6. Only 4% of women respondents, compared to 22% of the men claimed to speak Corsican over 50% of the time. And considerably fewer men (60%) than women (75%) checked the lowest category of use (0–50%). Men and women, however, report approximately equal use of Corsican in the home (about 60%); it is in the work place that the difference between the sexes widens considerably, with more than twice as many men than women reporting workplace use of Corsican.

Table 4. Gender and childhood use

	All	Men	Women
Never	13%	5%	18%
Very Little	27%	27%	32%
Little	15%	18%	14%
Sometimes	10%	9%	13%
Often	17%	17%	16%
Always	19%	25%	7%

Table 5. Gender and childhood response to parents

	Never	Little	Sometimes	Often	Always
All	2%	21%	25%	16%	36%
Male	0%	8%	21%	14%	35%
Female	1%	20%	17%	13%	22%

Table 6. Gender and reported percentage of use of Corsican

	0–50%	about 50%	50–100%
All	66%	16%	11%
Men	60%	17%	23%
Women	75%	13%	4%

Women also tended to give themselves lower competence ratings as Corsican speakers than men did. In response to the question asking for a rating of speaking competence on a six point scale (0=lowest), 68% of the men, compared to 48% of the women rated their ability between 3 and 5. Table 7, below, also shows that women are less likely to perceive themselves as "above average" speakers than men, and more likely to perceive themselves as "below average" speakers than men.

Table 7. Gender and self-report of competence relative to the norm

	above average	average	below average
Men	26%	42%	23%
Women	13%	40%	35%

How do these representations of practice and competence square with what one can observe in everyday life? It is fair to say that young Corsican women are less likely to be competent speakers of Corsican than young Corsican men, and those who are competent are less likely to make use of their competence outside very restricted contexts. When I was attending classes at the University of Corsica in 1988–1989, I seldom heard female students speak Corsican in classes, cafeterias, libraries, walkways and areas where students typically congregated and chatted. It was not that male students overwhelmingly used Corsican; in fact, the dominance of French in the student body was undeniable. But most of the students who did speak Corsican in public were male. Since 1989, I have not had an opportunity to observe the life of the university over a prolonged period of time, but several student research assistants have confirmed that patterns of language use are still quite gendered. One young man of about twenty who was a research assistant in the summer of 1998 told me that another of my (female) assistants was one of the few young women he knew who spoke Corsican regularly. He also reported that he tended not to initiate conversations with young women in Corsican, despite the fact that he had been brought up by a Corsican-speaking mother, and used Corsican regularly with both his mother and his sister.

Among older women, the relationship between gender and language use is far more difficult to characterize. In intimate and informal settings, among familiars, I have noticed no difference in the amount of Corsican used by women versus men. Women's use of Corsican in "public" settings is less noticeable than men's. But this lack of a public, female voice is not just a question of language; it has to do with gender differences in the occupation of public spaces and roles. Take for example the cafe/bar, a place where even the passing tourist will notice Corsican being spoken. While women are by no means excluded from these public spaces, the inside rooms of cafes are still predominantly male domains. Comparable forms of female sociability, however, are not available to casual public scrutiny. Other contemporary contexts in which Corsican has a significant role include politics, hunting parties, shepherding, and singing of the paghjella, a traditional genre of four part harmony. Women are under-represented in all of these activities, and they always have been. In a sense, participation in traditional forms of male social and political (and hence, somewhat "public") life requires some use of Corsican, whereas a woman's (very restricted) traditional public persona does not require Corsican.

In the course of my research, I was told quite often that women learned and spoke French more quickly and more readily than men. These reports, as I will show below, are hardly neutral, and systematic ethnohistorical work remains to be done on patterns of language use among Corsican women. Nevertheless, my more contemporary survey and ethnographic data suggest that men and women participated in language shift in somewhat different ways. The literature on gendered patterns of language use provides some insights about why women in contexts like the Corsican one might be more enthusiastic learners of French than men. Labov's sociolinguistic research shows that women consistently "lead" men in "shifts from above"; by definition, adopting a dominant language is such a shift (1998: 11–14). Other research that focuses more specifically on gendered patterns of use in minority language contexts shows women shifting away from minority languages when they have easy access to the language of power, and when that language offers them social and economic rewards (see among others Gal 1978; Holmquist 1985 Kuter 1989; Marty-Balzagues 1996; McDonald 1994; Nichols 1983). French was a valuable resource for Corsican women, one which partially compensated for the gender hierarchy of traditional Corsican society (de Zerbi 1987: 222) and gave them a ticket out of an agropastoral economy. In these academic analyses, the key variable is the potential for female social mobility through the use of dominant or standard language forms. Female speakers of minority (or nonstandard) languages do not lead language shift in contexts where they do not have access to economic and social networks where prestige forms advance their interests. This may help to explain the difference between my survey results on gender and those reported by the *Forum Paris- Corse* in1991, where there were no appreciable gender differences in self-reported use of or competence in Corsican. I would suggest that this is once Corsican men and women leave the island, the importance of French in the economic and linguistic marketplace applies equally to men and women, and there are no (or few) economic activities in which speaking Corsican is possible or valued.

So far, I have talked about women's language practices. Let us now turn to metalinguistic discourse about those practices. In Corsican popular and academic representations of women's participation in language shift towards French, women are characterized as being more motivated by prestige than men. In the current climate of appreciation for Corsican culture and general regret that Corsican language use has declined, this kind of motivation is not positively evaluated: women are represented as "buying in" to dominant linguistic and cultural ideologies. Men, by implicit contrast, are more positively depicted as preserving important traditions. The following quotation from a Corsican writer of fiction and nonfiction shows the extent to which this "buying in" is framed as "selling out": "*les mères optaient résolument pour le français, langue dont elles pensaient qu'elle symbolisait la réussite...elles qui, dans l'île, avaient été, durant des siècles, les remparts de la culture...tournaient maintenant le dos...aux valeurs traditionnelles*" [mothers opted resolutely for French, the language they thought symbolized success...those women who for centuries had been the bastions of culture on the island...now turned their backs...on traditional values](Culioli 1986: 274). This theme is also emotionally represented in a *Scola Corsa* poster that has been in circulation for some fifteen years (Figure 2) in which a little child holding its mother's hand looks up and beseeches her, "*O Mà, parlami corsu!*" ['Oh Mom, speak Corsican to me!'].

Figure 2. Oh Mom, speak Corsican to me!

How can we understand this discourse of culpability? First, it is probably the case that women's linguistic practices are defined, a priori, as inferior in contrast to men's (see Hill 1989: 154). This evaluative hierarchy is projected back, historically, in order to legitimize contemporary values. Here, it is interesting to note that it is precisely those people who are excluded from the power codes who are blamed for having had the power to influence societal language patterns. Elsewhere (Jaffe 1991) I have analyzed this scapegoating of the least powerful members of the society as a form of distancing from the collective powerlessness in the face of domination that results in language shift. There is no doubt in my mind that men, no less than women, contributed to family language policies and chose economic paths that required and valorized the use of French.

The contemporary blaming of women for language shift can also be related to strength of the image of the mother tongue (see also McDonald 1994: 100–103).This image operates at two levels. At one level, we find an exaggeration of the commonsense understanding that mothers play a large role in the linguistic socialization of children. This focus, of course, is far too narrow to explain large scale societal phenomena, and ignores all of the other people and institutions that influence children's language practices and attitudes. The other level is more abstract and ideological, and brings us back to Vermes and Boutet's claim (see above) that language shift involves metaphoric violence to the (female) body of the region and the transfer of filial allegiance to the *Matrie* (Motherland). If we follow this metaphor through, we can see how the violated female body of the local culture could be a source of shame and weakness that is at least partially expurgated by blaming the victim.

4. Codeswitching and language mixing

The following brief section on codeswitching and language mixing returns us to a now familiar point: that the boundaries of language use in actual practice are fuzzier than they are in the metalinguistic discourse about that practice.

Codeswitching is, of course, one of the primary ways in which language boundaries associated with diglossia are transgressed. Not all switches, however, breach these boundaries in the same way. There are two kinds of codeswitches which have been abundantly documented in the literature on codeswitching in diglossic situations which draw their meaning from the diglossic division of linguistic use and value. First, there are what Scotton calls "sequential unmarked choices"(1986: 405); codeswitches like the one between Thiers and his mother, above. These are responses to a change in the

Codeswitching {Sequential ⎰unmarked ⎱marked {mark…

frame of the conversation triggered by such things as the topic, or the arrival of a new interlocutor. Thiers' mother switched from Corsican (her habitual language with her son) to French when he presented himself to her as an academic, and asked her to engage in a formal discourse being transcribed and used for academic practices. Conversely, a Corsican male speaking French might switch to Corsican when discussing activities in which the use of Corsican is common, such as herding sheep, hunting or sports.

Another category of switches, ("marked choices" in Scotton's 1986 terms and "metaphorical codeswitching" in Blom and Gumperz' 1972 discussion) make claims on identities and relationships that are defined by the diglossic model. As we have seen in the discussion of politicians, codeswitching to Corsican, or using Corsican in domains in which French is now habitual makes a claim on, or evokes the intimacy and solidarity of village-like relations. One of my acquaintances, Jean, recounted going into the office of an official in Paris. In his story, he said that in the course of a conversation in French, he found out the official was Corsican. The ending to his story was, "and I came out speaking Corsican". It carried the clear implication that the official had extended some kind of favor that went beyond the requirements of his post. "Speaking Corsican" in Jean's account was both the vehicle for a successful claim on intimacy/solidarity and a symbol of its social consequences.[38] Outside the island, shared Corsican identity can be an extraordinarily compelling frame on interaction that overrides other social factors that divide, rather than unify in island life. This affects the way that "speaking Corsican" is interpreted and responded to. Take for example the experience of my acquaintance Jules, a civil service manager working on the island in one of the bigger cities. He knew that many of his employees were Corsophone, and said he often spoke Corsican with them. He noted, however, that some of them seemed quite reticent about using the language with him. In some cases, he said, this might be linguistic insecurity, but he was more inclined to view their lack of response as an unwillingness to give up the distance and formality of French in a situation of unequal social status. In both of the above scenarios, the meaning of using Corsican is clearly linked to intimacy and solidarity; what differs is the extent to which participants embrace that intimacy and solidarity as an interactional frame.

A codeswitch to French in an ongoing Corsican conversation, or the choice of French when Corsican is possible or habitual can also make a claim for authority/status/expertise or sophistication, or establish distance.[39] This distance can be used in various ways as a sociolinguistic resource; it can be "real" or playful. For example, among my older Corsophone friends in the village, French was sometimes jokingly used to create mock distance. So

Martin might say to his cousin Antoine (whom he normally addresses as *tu* and calls by a Corsican diminutive *Antò*): "*Bonjour Monsieur Luigi,*

comment allez-vous aujourd'hui? " ['Hello Mr. Luigi, how are you today?'] and extend a hand in for a formal handshake. The joke, of course, hinges on the strength of their relations in Corsican; people of Martin's generation will occasionally speak French to one another in public contexts where non-Corsophones are present, but outside of these instances they tell me it would "feel funny/unnatural" to speak anything but Corsican among themselves.

4.1. Conscious language choices and an "alternative market"

Several related points can be made here about language choice. First, we can note the importance in everyday life of an alternative linguistic market. In this market, "outside" values are not always positively marked in "inside" interaction. The price of authority/distance is the loss of intimacy and solidarity; in many instances, people work to avoid this loss. The existence of this alternative market guarantees that there will be cracks in the effects of domination: the dominant language is not simply passively accepted as intrinsically superior.[40] As Rampton writes, "prestige languages become the object of intensive play, remodeling and transvaluation, their meaning reshaped in ways that ultimately (though by no means harmoniously) consolidate group solidarity" (1995: 180). We see this in Corsica, in the example above, in the lyrics to "*U mo figliolu*" lyrics (Chapter 2) and in the following anecdote, told to me for humorous effect: a young Corsican woman, recently arrived from the continent, goes into a little store and buys a few items. "*Combien vous dois-je?*" [How much do I owe you?] she asks, using the very proper, literary, inverted interrogative. "*Vingt, cent francs,*" [twenty, and a hundred francs] replies the shopkeeper, his inversion mocking hers (and by extension, mocking her pretensions).

4.2. Heterogenous practices

In addition to (relatively) conscious and motivated language choices and codeswitches in Corsican linguistic practice, there is also a form of uncon-scious, habitual and metaphorically unmotivated codeswitching that takes place in all bilingual communities (Eastman 1992; Gal 1987; Gardner-Chloros 1991; Gysels 1992; Scotton 1986; Urciuoli 1996; Wald 1986). Rather than emphasize the boundaries between two languages and their conventional associations, these practices tend to blur them. It is often impossible to determine what the "matrix" or "unmarked" code is, or to attribute any kind of intentionality or meaning to speakers' linguistic choices. I have often observed Corsicans who are quite capable of carrying on an extended conversation in either language regularly alternating between the two languages, often (but not always) switching at phrase boundaries. These switches often have no discernible intention or triggers. Examples (2) through (5) were collected in casual contexts, where I was among Corsophone friends and neighbors.

(2)   *Ùn era micca ghjunta,* la petite nièce de Jean-Jean?
       'She didn't come, *Jean-Jean's great niece?*'

(3)   *Nous sommes retournés au village,* in quaranta cinque, dopu a guerra.
       'We came back to the village, *in [nineteen] forty four, after the war.*'

(4)   *Il était tout tranquil là,* ma a sapete, hè a moglia chì cumanda. *Elle l'a mis dans une maison de retraite à Ajaccio.*
       'He was completely happy there, *but you know that it's his wife who give the orders.* She put him in a retirement home in Ajaccio."

(5)

1	Pierre:	*Il y a deux ans, je suis*	Two years ago, I came [here]
2		*venu danser la quadrille.*	to dance the quadrille.
3	Jules:	*Quoi?*	What?
4	Pierre:	U cuadrigliu. Era un	*The quadrille. It was a Corsi-*
5		ballu corsu, ind'è	*can ball, in* the church. I came
6		*l'eglise. Je suis passé par*	by here, but you
7	Jules:	*ici, mais tu n'étais pas là.*	weren't home.
8		Induvè era?	*Where was I?*
9		*Je ne sais pas. On m'a*	I don't know. People told me
1		*dit que tu n'étais pas là*	you weren't there, and I did
0		*et je n'ai pas trop*	not really ask any further.
		demandé	

As example (5) shows, conversation following such switching could continue in either Corsican or French and did not necessarily pick up with the language last switched to: Jules follows Pierre's switch into Corsican by responding in Corsican on line 7, but Pierre switches back to French on line 8. As Gal (1989), Gysels (1992) and others have noted, in this kind of codeswitching, intimacy is not so much a function of switching to or from a particular language as it is rooted in the act of alternation itself, and how it indexes a shared ability to manipulate two codes with others. Dorian (1981: 101)

describes some examples of similar mixing as "thoroughly Gaelic performances"; the ones I have described are equally and unequivocally Corsican.

5. Contact-induced varieties

The linguistic landscape of Corsica also includes mixed language varieties in
which there is an interpenetration of both lexical and syntactic features from
Corsican and French. Filippi (1992) identifies two "mixed" codes: *le Français
Régionale de Corse* 'Regional French of Corsica' (abbreviated as FRC), and
Francorse 'Franco-corsican'. The matrix language of both of these varieties
is French. The difference is one of degree: FRC is a reflection of the entire
system of Corsican: phonetics, phonology, morphology vocabulary and
syntax. It cannot be confused with codeswitching; all utterances are in French
(albeit not a standard French). *Francorse*, on the other hand, is closer to
codeswitching in that it involves the transformation (rather than the translation) of Corsican words or morphemes into new non-French words. In some
cases, as Filippi points out, the judgment of whether these lexical adaptations
are hybrids or codeswitches is arbitrary (1992: 200).

5.1. Le Français régionale de Corse

FRC is marked by certain pronunciation features not found in "standard"
French. These include the palatalization of /st/ and /t+cons/, affricatization of
/ks/, and an apical /r/ (Filippi 1992). Corsican consonant mutation is
occasionally applied to French. So, for example, the vocative "*O François,*"
in a "standard" French accent would be pronounced [o frãnswa], but in FRC,
would take the form [o vrãnswa].

FRC also involves idiomatic transfers from Corsican into French. In the
following examples, an English phrase is followed by FRC, Corsican and
"standard" French translations, each followed by an interlinear gloss.

(6)   'Give me another one.'
       a. *Donnez-moi un   de   plus.* (FRC)
          Give   me one in   addition
       b. *Dammi   unu di più.* (Corsican)
          Give me   one in addition
       c. *Donnez-moi encore   un.* (French)
          Give me   again   one

In this example, we can see that the Corsican phrase *di più* is translated directly as *de plus*, which contrasts with the "standard" French idiom *encore un*.

(7)   'It's your turn.'
        a. *Ca touche   à   toi.* (FRC)
           It touch PRES on/at/to   you
        b. *Tocca   à   tè.* (Corsican)
           It touch PRES   on/at/to   you
        c. *C'est   ton   tour.* (French)
           It be PRES your   turn

In this example, the Corsican impersonal construction *tuccà à* is translated as the French *toucher à*. While *tuccà* does mean "to touch" in French, *toucher à* is not used in an impersonal construction: it only means 'to touch'.

In Corsican, you can use the imperfect to talk about hypothetical situations. In French, hypotheticals are expressed with the conditional (or subjunctive).

(8)   'If I did that, I would be in bed for two days.'
        a. *Si je faisais   cela, j'étais   malade.* (FRC)
           If I do IMPERFECT that I be IMPERFECT ill.

        b. *Se facia   quessa, era   malatu.* (Corsican)
           If I do IMPERFECT that   I be IMPERFECT ill

        c. *Si je faisais   cela, je serais   malade.* (French)
           If I do IMPERFECT that   I be CONDITIONAL ill

Unlike French, Corsican makes use of the "hypothetical future" which expresses near certainty about the logical connection between two assertions. Take for example the following utterance:

(9)   'He didn't come–he must be ill.'
        a. *Il   n'est   pas   venu,   --   il sera   malade.* (FRC)
           He   NEG be NEG   come PAST he be FUTURE ill

        b. *Ùn   hè   micca ghjuntu, --   sera   malatu.* (Corsican)
           NEG he be   NEG come PAST   he be FUTURE ill

        c. *Il n'est   pas   venu,   --   il doit être   malade.*
           He NEG be NEG come PAST he must be INF ill (Standard French)

In Corsican, the verbal phrase can be repeated at the end of a sentence. This repetition is not typical of "Standard French," but it does appear in FRC, as in the following example:

(10)   'Your father sings very well.'
       a. *Ton père,   il   chante*   *très bien, il chante.* (FRC)
          Your father he sing PRES   very well he sing PRES

       b. *U   to   babbu, canta*   *bè,   canta.* (Corsican)
          The your father   sing PRES   well   sing

       c. *Ton père   chante*   *très bien.* (Standard French)
          Your father sing PRES   very well

5.2. *Francorse*

In this section, I give some examples of *Francorse*. As in the examples above, I give an idiomatic English translation first. This is followed by the *Francorse* and Standard French versions of that sentence. For the sake of clarity in the explanation of this kind of language phenomenon, I have avoided interlinear translations in favor of explanations of key linguistic points after each example.

(11)   'I fell down.'
       a. *Je me suis charbé.* (*Francorse*)
       b. *Je me suis emplâtré* (colloquial French)

Literally translated, the colloquial expression *s'emplâtrer* means 'to plaster oneself'. The *Francorse* phrase starts with a literal translation of 'to plaster'into Corsican: this is the verb *scialbà*. The /l/ in this verb has been transformed into an /r/ to produce the *Francorse* verb *se charber*.

(12)   'I tore my pants.'
       a. *Je me suis straccié les pantalons.* (*Francorse*)
       a. *Je me suis déchiré les pantalons.* (French)

Here, the French verb *déchirer* 'to tear' is replaced by the *Francorse* verb *straccier*, which is a transformation of the Corsican verb *straccià* 'to tear'.

5.3. Gallicized Corsican

Another mixed code in the Corsican repertoire is what I will call gallicized Corsican. Here the matrix language is Corsican, with influences/intrusions from French. Many of these influences are lexical. In effect, gallicized Corsican is the mirror image of *Francorse*. For example, I have heard people say while speaking Corsican,

(13) *Sò statu pistunatu.*

This means that they got something (a job, for example) through social connections. The verb *pistunà* is a corsicanization of the French word *le piston*, which refers to the system by which you get by or "get over" through patronage. There are also forms that are the converse of FRC, with its wide range of syntactic/idiomatic transfers. Let us return to the phrase used above in example (7), 'It's your turn,' and compare the gallicized Corsican version to "standard" French, Corsican and FRC renditions. Interlinear glosses show the different structures of this phrase.

(14)   a. *Hè   u to tornu.* (gallicized Corsican)
             it is your turn

         b. *C'est ton   tour.* ("standard" French)
             it is   your turn

         c. *Tocca   à   tè.* (Corsican)
             it touches on/at you

         d. *Ça touche   à   toi.* (FRC)
             it   touches on/at you

Here we can see clearly that gallicized Corsican is modeled on "standard" French in the same way that FRC is modeled on Corsican. In example (15), another example of gallicized Corsican is contrasted with "standard" French and Corsican:

(15)   'I left running.'
         a. *Sò partitu   in currendu.* (gallicized Corsican)
             I left PAST in running

         b. *Je suis parti en courant.* ("standard" French)
             I   left   in running

      c. *Sò partitu   currendu.* (Corsican)
        I   left PAST running

Here we can see that the insertion of *in* in the Corsican expression comes from the French construction. Like FRC, gallicized Corsican is also characterized by some pronunciation patterns that differ from traditional Corsican ones. For example, there is the insertion of consonant clusters used in French but not in Corsican (see boldfaced letters):

(16)   a. *ad**m**inistrazione* (gallicized Corsican)
        b. *ad**m**inistration* (French)
        c. *am**m**inistrazione* (Corsican)

Another pronunciation feature involves stress placement. In Corsican, there are a number of multisyllable words in which stress falls on the first or antepenultimate syllable. The word *agricula* 'agricultural', for example, is pronounced with stress on the second syllable(*agricula*). In gallicized Corsican, however, stress is placed on the penultimate syllable (*agricula*) because of the fact that in the French word *agricole*, it is the homologous syllable (*col*) that is stressed. The importance of stress patterns in marking language boundaries is reflected in the way that many Corsicans change the pronunciations of their last names when they are speaking in French, particularly to a non-Corsican French person. For example, a Corsican whose name is "Cesari" may pronounce her name with the stress on the first syllable when speaking Corsican (*Cesari*) to a Corsican, but introduce herself on the phone as *Madame Cesari* (stress on ultimate syllable) when speaking to an travel agent in Paris. Another more recent phenomenon that could be categorized as a sort of gallicized Corsican is French spelling pronunciations of words in Corsican orthography. For example, the letters *ce* in the name "Cesari" are pronounced [če]. In French, this same sequence of letter is pronounced [se]. Madame Cesari might well choose to use this pronunciation in her conversation with the Parisian travel agent, but would be unlikely to do so in Corsican. The pronunciation of personal names is distinct in the degree to which it is sensitive to interlocutor and context. This means that not all gallicized pronunciations of Corsican family names are perceived as code transgressions. This would not be the case for most other words. To take the same pronunciation contrast at issue in the first syllable of the name Cesari, a Corsican who pronounced the Corsican word *certu* 'sure' as [sɛrtu] and not [čɛrtu] would be perceived by other Corsican speakers as speaking in a French way.

    The significance attributed to this mixing by language planners and the general public will be discussed in subsequent chapters; the point to be made here is that the combination of codeswitching and mixing reduces the occurrence of "pure" stretches of either Corsican or French in everyday speech. In the same way that the boundaries between languages can be blurred in practice, the values and experiences associated with Corsican and French can also be ambiguous. For example, the expressed link of Corsican and intimacy, so salient in symbolic language use, is not particularly clear in practice. We know that French has replaced Corsican as the primary language used between parents and children, and that this practice is not new. Indeed, a good deal of French is used in the village context by virtue of the fact that there are significant numbers of younger Corsicans (as well as "mixed" marriages). Although the passive competence of many nonspeakers is high, it is fairly rare for a nonreciprocal bilingual conversation (where one person speaks Corsican and the other, French) to last long. Most significantly, the use of French in the family means that many Corsicans do experience intimacy in that language.

In contrast, Corsican representations of language practices essentialize them; that is, where and when languages are habitually used and what languages are habitually used to do are taken to be inherent qualities or limitations: what they are best or uniquely equipped to do.

6. Conclusion

To summarize, social institutions such as the schools and the military were places where Corsicans both learned French and learned French language ideology. In particular, this ideology naturalized the association of language (with an emphasis on correct linguistic form) with collective (national) identity and with personal identity and worth (being a good person and a good citizen). French language ideology also established a monolingual norm: it was seen as right and necessary that acquiring good French meant losing Corsican. French language policy both reflected French language ideology and ensured the dominance of French in economic and educational domains. This meant that Corsicans learned about the value of French both in the abstract (language ideology) and in the concrete circumstances of their lives. The very same combination of ideology and pragmatics established and perpetuated diglossia; an ideology of separate and opposed domains of practice and value. The pervasive influence of French language ideology and policy did not, however, mean that all Corsicans uncritically submitted to language domination. In fact, the diglossic relationship between Corsican and French heightened the values of intimacy and solidarity associated with Corsican and thus in an indirect way, contributed to Corsican's survival.

Finally, the examination of codeswitching and other language mixtures illustrates the ways in which the idealized image of monolingual, unitary, homogenous language failed to prevent heteroglossic linguistic practices. As we have seen, "mixed" codes are an inevitable outcome of language contact. And it is the context of language shift and diglossia that gives those codes their meanings and values. These include both the value of such codes as interactional resources in communication, and the social stigma that is attached to them in metalinguistic discourse.

In the following chapter, I look at how Corsican language activists working within the context of a nationalist political framework have responded to the sociolinguistic context I have described as they struggle to revitalize the use and social status of Corsican.

Chapter 4
Language Activism Part I

1. Introduction

Corsican language activists have been trying to change the course of language shift for over twenty years. In their effort to combat the pragmatic and the symbolic domination of French, they have deployed strategies in which the pragmatic and the symbolic are intertwined. The pragmatic dimension of Corsican language planning has aimed at creating the institutional and legal structures necessary for the transmission of the Corsican language in the schools. At the same time, activists have worked on changing diglossic language attitudes in the hope of encouraging Corsophone parents to teach Corsican to their children and/or non-Corsophone Corsicans to make the effort to learn the language.

In this chapter and the next, I examine the key events, debates and ideological currents in Corsican language activism. In this chapter, as in the last, the focus is on the ideological and pragmatic forces that shaped the linguistic philosophies and strategies of Corsican language planners. These forces include macrolevel language politics: the influence of dominant European ideas about the link between language, cultural identity and nationhood/political autonomy. They also include how these broad themes have been translated into specific French language policies with which Corsican activists have had to contend.

In the last chapter, I drew attention to the ways in which people both capitulated to dominant language ideology in which Corsican was devalued and exercised a resistance of separation which emphasized the oppositional values of intimacy and solidarity and provided a certain distance from the dominant system. In this and the next chapter, I explore elements of both accommodation and resistance to dominant language ideologies in Corsican language activism. While all Corsican activism resists the domination of French, not all Corsican activism challenges dominant criteria of linguistic value. That is, some Corsican activism is fundamentally conservative in the sense evoked by Heller in her description of Franco-Ontarian mobilization which had as its goal "to integrate Francophones into a national and global network, that is, to gain entry into an existing economic and symbolic marketplace, and not to construct an alternative one"(1994: 61). Another current of Corsican activism does indeed try to construct an alternative symbolic marketplace in which a value is placed on plural, heterogenous language practices. As we will see, the emphasis on practice and a pluralistic model of language and identity challenges in a far more radical way the underlying premises of dominant language ideology. This kind of challenge can be glimpsed in this chapter in the "sociolinguists" position in the public debate with the "purists," and is pursued in more detail in Chapter 5.

One of the things that emerges very clearly in this and subsequent chapters is the extent to which language planning policy and theory are contested terrain on Corsica. As we will see, popular and political support for language planning measures (officialization of Corsican; mandatory Corsican education) have not always been strong. Moreover, even those Corsicans who share a commitment to the promotion and preservation of the minority language differ in both their images of what Corsican is (or should be) and in their ideas about how to promote or conserve it.

These differences of language ideology are not easily correlated with differences in social positions or political agendas. In many respects, these language activists are socially homogenous. The majority of them are highly educated, and many of them have a variety of professional roles and activities in which language is central: they are linguists, writers, teachers. Certainly, scholars can be motivated by a variety of academic interests and agendas, but even here, obvious potential connections do not always pan out: for example, there are scholars of Italian who emphasize the linguistic kinship between Corsican and there are those who do not. The same can be said of language activists' political allegiances. While they tend not to be conservative, the political left in France is a large umbrella, and Corsican language activists can be found in the Communist and Socialist Parties, and, not surprisingly, in Corsican Nationalist or Autonomist Parties. Despite this political heterogeneity, activists' linguistic ideologies do not map neatly onto party platforms: there are nationalists who are linguistic purists and nationalists who are not.

This is not to say that there is no relationship between individuals' social and political positions and their views on language, but rather, that these connections are complex. Not only do different individuals respond in different ways to dominant language ideology and its social effects, but also, as Thompson points out, "dominant language ideology" is not unidimensional. Therefore, reproduction of dominant language ideology does not result in consensus (Thompson 1984: Chapter 2).

In this chapter, I will be exploring the historical origins of what I am labeling an essentialist view of language and identity. I am using "essentialism" as a gloss for key tenet of dominant language ideology: that languages are distinct, bounded, autonomous systems which correspond directly with and define cultural identities. One brand of essentialism is "biological": language is posited as having an identity like a species: it is "naturally" distinct from other languages. In this framework, language is also represented as having a "natural" relationship with identity. In short, both language and identity are framed as biological inheritances. Language purism is an inevitable part of an essentialist perspective, because there can only be one true, authentic code associated with one authentic people. Another form of essentialism can be labeled more "strategic" in nature in that it views unity of language and culture as a key component of national unity, but not as a prerequisite for nationhood.

I will argue that linguistic essentialism has strategic value because it is an integral part of the way that "people" and "nation" have been constructed in European history. It is the only kind of claim on language legitimacy that is recognized by the state, and the state controls resources necessary for the social promotion of Corsican (particularly in education). Furthermore, an essentialist discourse is the only idiom people have experienced to express the legitimacy, value and authority of language. Therefore, it has value in the activist attempt to convince the general public of the value of Corsican (that it is a language) and to encourage them to transmit it or at least support Corsican language education.

At the end of the chapter, I contrast the essentialist perspective with what I am calling the "sociolinguistic" position. Language activists who fall in this camp locate the definition of language in society and its linguistic practices. This position does not conceive of the link between language and social groups as "natural" or "biological" but rather, views those connections as social and political in origin. Language not presented as a completely autonomous system, with clear-cut boundaries and standards. Corsican is what Corsicans speak or what Corsicans collectively agree it is. This perspective proscribes purism, accepts and validates social and linguistic diversity, and makes political or social agendas the basis for language judgments and practices. Here, language as a project of society, a constant process of becoming rather than an essential "being".

What we will see, in this and the following chapter, is that the tensions between strategic and biological essentialism, and between essentialist and sociolinguistic views of language and identity permeate debates over theory and practice within the activist community. These tensions are the basis for differences of emphasis on linguistic (and cultural) boundaries, different definitions of linguistic (and cultural) authenticity, and different prescriptions for actions and change.

2. Language and nation: biological versus strategic essentialism

As we have seen, contemporary Corsican language activism emerged as a significant social force in the early seventies, as part of the Corsican nationalist movement. The Corsican nationalists conceived of their opposition to France as being part of a wider, international struggle of oppressed minorities, and self-consciously modeled many of their strategies on those of the Basques, Catalonians, Bretons, and so on. It was no wonder that language was a central element in these ethnic minorities' claims for self-determination for, as Hobsbawm (1990) and Higonnet (1980) have pointed out, shared linguistic/cultural unity has dominated European definitions of nationhood ever since the "linguistic terror" following the French Revolution. In their analysis of contemporary European popular discourse about language and nationalism, Blommaert and Verscheuren show that the logic of "one language, one nation" continues to have enormous power. They observe, for example, that in European coverage of international events, "the absence of the feature 'distinct language' tends to cast doubt on the legitimacy of claims to nationhood" (1992:11).

To reiterate a point made in Chapter 1: Corsican nationalists deployed a historically entrenched discourse linking language and nationhood in order to support their political claims that Corsica was a repressed, colonized, dominated nation with "natural" rights to self-determination.[41] An early slogan at rallies and on posters was *Morta a lingua, mortu u populu* [The death of the language is the death of the people]. The assertion of the intrinsic, ineffable link between language and people can be traced back to the Romantic philosophers Herder, Fichte and Humboldt, who describe language as the repository of the spiritual, historical and cultural essence of a people. Language played a key symbolic role in a discourse that naturalized and essentialized the cultural identities that were taken as the precondition for political legitimacy. Biological essentialism is a defining feature of much nationalist discourse, and is "often realized as an assumption that national culture is carried by genetic descent" (Herzfeld 1996: 277–278). The importance of language as a criterion of identity was all the more critical in the Corsican nationalist movement because of the fact that it called other traditional aspects of Corsican culture into question, denouncing, for example, the clan and the economic stagnation to which clientelism had contributed. Even though the Corsican language was weakened, it was in greater evidence than other features of their cultural heritage, which centered around a pastoral life that was clearly marginal in the modern context. Within this framework, being and speaking Corsican are conflated. Thus the (deceptively) simple equation of the bumper sticker in Figure 3: *Sò Corsu, Parlu Corsu* [I'm Corsican, I speak Corsican].

Figure 3. Bumper sticker: 'I'm Corsican, I speak Corsican'

Being and speaking Corsican are also represented in nationalist discourse as in stark opposition to French culture and language. The definition of Corsica as a nation makes this necessary within the framework of cultural nationalism: two nations by definition mean two separate languages and cultures. As a brief example, Ghjilormu Ferrandi, writing in the nationalist paper *A Gravona*, compared adopting French language and culture to putting on someone else's clothes. This, he wrote, *"hè sempre qualcosa chì rendi ridiculu è avvilisci l'omu"* [is always something that abases you and makes you look ridiculous]. The author went on to say that *"a cultura di in'altrò chì ùn nega a toia hè cosa chì inricchisci"* [a foreign culture that does not deny your own is enriching]. But French was not included in this category, and readers were exhorted to *"stupà à nantu à una lingua pratenziosa crisciuta nantu à i cadavari d'altri lingui, ma chì, tali ch'edda hè, ùn sprimarà mai cum'è a toia i to gioi o i to peni"* [spit on a pretentious language (French) that has nourished itself on the cadavers of other languages and which, as it is today, will never be able to express your joys and tribulations the way your own language {Corsican}does] (December 1987).

The conflation of language and identity makes possible (perhaps necessary) a number of metaphorical moves. As Balibar writes, "All linguistic practices feed into...the ideal of common origin...which... becomes the metaphor for the love fellow nationals feel for one another" (1991: 98). The following excerpt from another nationalist newspaper shows that speaking Corsican in nationalist circles is often a litmus test of political devotion and that in everyday discourse, being nationalist and not speaking Corsican are viewed by nationalists and their critics alike as inconsistent (see Urla 1988; McDonald 1989; MacClancy 1993). The news feature described five challenges for militants who wanted to speak Corsican, and was written in Corsican. Given the fact that the companion piece (to be described below) was written in French, the language choice for this article suggested that it represented the voices of non-nationalist Corsophones taking nationalists to task about their language choices and capabilities. The first of these voices said: *"Chì hà da esse naziunalista tù, ch'ùn parli mancu corsu!"* ['Who are you to call yourself a nationalist, you who don't speak Corsican!']. The author editorialized: *"Hè u to propiu ziu, CFR [Corse Française et Républicaine; a right wing group] arrabiatu, chì ti parla cusì"* ['This is your own uncle, flaming conservative, talking to you like this']. The fourth challenging voice repeated the same accusation, but here the author described the speaker this way: *"Hè un militanti arrabiatu chì ti parla cusì. Un 'veru' militanti, a sà, cù a vittura stampata di clandestini da capu à fondu"* ['It is a flaming militant who is speaking to you like this. A 'real' militant, to be sure, with his car covered with stickers of underground fighters from hood to fender'] (*Arguments*, 1991: 4). These two voices suggest, in other words, that militants' cultural authenticity was judged by the same linguistic criteria both from within and outside the movement.

These assumptions about consistency of language choice and political identity could be observed in the linguistic orchestration of all nationalist gatherings (rallies, meetings, press conferences): the formal program almost always began with a stretch of discourse in Corsican that was clearly marked as symbolic. The end of the Corsican introduction announced the opening of a less strictly controlled linguistic space, in which the original speaker and others seemed to have dispensation to proceed in French or a mixture of the two languages. But even though the use of French was very common, it was always open to contestation in these contexts. It was not unusual for someone (like the agricultural union member mentioned in the last chapter) to challenge the group to use Corsican. It was also quite common to hear participants in nationalist venues preface their use of French with disclaimers or apologies (of the genre: "I'm sorry, but I'm going to have to speak in French now"). These metalinguistic markers framed the speaker's language of use as *other* than his/her language of political or cultural preference.

Just as language can be the metaphor for the experience of nationality, the nation can be a metaphor for language and self.[42] That is, the equation of language, culture and nation could also be read in reverse. Precedent for this causal relationship could be found as far back as the nineteenth century, as we can see in the following passage from Humboldt:

Every language receives a specific individuality through that of the nation, and has on the latter a uniformly determining reverse effect. The national character is indeed sustained, strengthened and even to some extent engendered by community of habitat and action; but in fact it rests on a likeness of natural disposition, which is normally explained by community of descent (1836, in Crowley 1996: 118).

In the space of a few lines, Humboldt identifies language as an essential inheritance that predates the nation while claiming that part of the essence (individuality) of language is given by the nation.

The simultaneous existence of these two ways of reading the link between language and political identity help us to understand the contradictory values attached to the fact of language shift in the cultural nationalist framework. On the one hand, Corsican nationalists have used the weaknesses of the language as a symbol of the crisis in Corsican culture brought on by French oppression. In *Main basse sur une île*, the 1971 nationalist manifesto, the authors emphasized the profound effects of language shift on the linguistic practices and attitudes of young people. They wrote that the Corsican child under eighteen "*se garde de prononcer un seul mot dans la langue des adultes...s'adresser en corse à une jeune fille serait considéré comme une grossièreté. Demander son chemin à un enfant corse...c'est s'attirer une réponse en français*" [makes sure not to pronounce a single word in the language of the adults...to address a young woman in Corsican would be considered crude. Asking a Corsican child for directions...reaps a response in French] (65). The manifesto authors framed these sociolinguistic observations as symptoms of cultural malaise, noting that "*on ne manquera pas de brocarder...le moindre corsisme [en français] mais...il va de soi que le gallicisme en parlant corse n'est, en revanche, aucunement ridicule*" [the smallest Corsican interference in French invites mockery, but it goes without saying that gallicisms in Corsican are not perceived as ridiculous at all] (65). In sum, these examples were used to illustrate how "*Les Corses deviennent eux-mêmes les agents de leur propre aliénation,*" [Corsicans become the agents of their own alienation] and to mobilize them to reclaim their language and culture (1971: 63).[43]

But there was obviously a danger in this emphasis on linguistic and cultural alienation. For, even though the French state was identified as the villain in the above scenario, the decline of the language threatened the foundation of a nationalist platform that placed heavy emphasis on a primordial Corsican identity. If language = people = nation, then *no* language = *no* people = *no* nation.

The emphasis on language planning was in itself an expression of a strategic essentialism: it amounted to an awareness that, as Balibar puts it, that the People did not just exist, but must be produced (1991: 93).[44] In other words, asserting the link between language and identity partially reflected an existing state of affairs–many Corsicans believed in this connection and considerable numbers still spoke Corsican–and partially, reflected a hope in an unrealized ideal of Corsican unity: considerable numbers of Corsicans were *not* Corsophone.

3. Overview of language activism and language legislation

In this section, I provide an overview of significant events related to the promotion of Corsican in the last twenty five years. This brief review then serves as the backdrop for discussion of salient themes in the history of Corsican language planning in this chapter and Chapter 5.

3.1. The seventies

Corsican militants set about the work of standardization and normalization with enormous vigor in the seventies. A variety of Corsican grammars and pedagogical materials were produced, including the first orthographic manual, *Intricciate è Cambiarini* 'Connectors and Alternators' (the title refers metaphorically to Corsican phonological rules (Geronimi and Marchetti 1971). The association *Lingua Corsa* 'The Corsican Language' was founded by young Corsican intellectuals on the continent, and sponsored Corsican language classes in cities like Paris, Marseilles, Nice and Lyon, which had heavy concentrations of Corsicans. In 1972, the association *Scola Corsa* 'Corsican School' was founded. Modeled explicitly on the language schools of the Basques, *Scola Corsa* organized language courses on the island and launched the public campaign for official recognition of Corsican as a regional language with rights to be taught in the schools. Much of the momentum for this campaign came from the first of what were to become annual *Ghjurnate Corse* 'Corsican Days' at Corté–political, cultural and linguistic rallies that drew thousands of militant students and nationalist sympathizers. Over five thousand signatures were gathered on a petition, and at the end of 1973, a motion proposing official inclusion of Corsican into the provisions of the Deixonne law, which provided for one hour per week of voluntary instruction in "regional languages," was made by a Corsican member of the French National Assembly. This motion was successful, and in 1975, schools began to offer Corsican courses on the limited basis permitted by the law.

Another influential linguistic associations formed in the seventies is the ADECEC. ADECEC members published Corsican lexicons that both collected vocabulary from traditional cultural domains (like pastoralism and cheese production) and actively produced neologisms for modern topics (like "The Car"). Since the mid-seventies, the ADECEC has also sponsored yearly round tables on language, and runs a local radio station called *Viva Voce* [Living Voice] that broadcasts in Corsican. Beginning in 1974, *Scola Corsa* and other cultural/political organizations campaigned for a University on the island. Each year, they organized a "Summer University" at Corté, held on the symbolic grounds of the walled garrison that used to be the headquarters of Pascal Paoli, "Father of the Corsican Nation" and founder of the first University of Corsica. The Summer Universities created part of the social momentum that culminated in the opening of the University of Corsica opened its doors to 500 students in Corté in 1982. In addition to the obvious pragmatic and symbolic value of having a University on the island, it was also seen as an opportunity for Corsican Studies to find full and legitimate expression "at home"; until 1982, students of Corsican language and culture had to pursue their degrees at the University of Aix-en-Provence. Today, over 5000 students attend this University.

In addition to the production of grammars, spelling manuals, lexicons (including two computerized versions) and other pedagogical works, there was a significant Corsican language literary production during the seventies. *Rigiru* 'Return' is a literary magazine edited entirely in Corsican and was founded in 1975 by Dumenicantone Geronimi. Various nationalist newspapers such as *Arritti* 'On Your Feet' and *U Ribombu* 'The Echo' made both practical and symbolic use of Corsican in their pages. The pattern over the years has been fairly consistent: there is at least one "serious" article in Corsican in each edition, usually an editorial. The majority of the articles are in French, but often have Corsican headlines or captions. Also in the mid-seventies, the monthly magazine *Kyrn* instituted a Corsican page, which became two pages around 1984 until the magazine ceased publication in 1992.

Musical groups like *Canta U Populu Corsu* 'The Corsican People Sings' also played a significant role in the promotion of the language. In these groups, political, cultural and linguistic activism were intertwined: they sang in (and about) Corsican as an expression of a cultural birthright; they revitalized the *paghjella*, a traditional Corsican polyphonic song form; they sang about oppression, resistance and political autonomy. Many of the singers were also politically active in the nationalist movement and/or involved in Corsican language education. These groups not only propelled Corsican into public air space in a way that traditional singers of ballads had never done, but they also served as powerful magnets for the recruitment of new, young male speakers who were drawn into a total social practice in which speaking Corsican was required. At its height, *Canta* (as it became known) had several core members and around fifteen to twenty others who performed at various times; many of these members splintered off and formed new groups, recruiting more young males.

3.2. The eighties

The election of the first Regional Assembly in 1982 provided a new political venue for the pursuit of official recognition that had begun with campaign for inclusion in the Deixonne law. Although the Assembly had not supplanted the existing departmental structures, which retained primary control over government resources, it was the first elected body to represent the island as a whole. Corsican language activists looked to the Assembly to play an active role in championing Corsican language rights. In its role as the island's agent to the French government, the Assembly had both a practical/material and a symbolic role to play. Despite the fact that it controlled only a small budget, the one of the Assembly's mandates was to define and prioritize social, cultural and economic goals which affected how resources were allocated from the central government both to the Assembly directly and indirectly, through the *Conseils Généraux* (the governing bodies of the two departments on Corsica).

In the area of cultural politics, legislation passed by the Assembly symbolized Corsican culture, identity and will to the rest of France. A paradigm example of this was the 1988 *Motion du peuple corse* [Motion of the Corsican people], in which the Assembly formally asserted the existence of the Corsican people "within the context of the French Republic," and demanded that this language be inserted in the first article of new legislation on Corsica's status that was being drafted in the National Assembly. This motion was debated at great length in Paris,[45] and was ultimately rejected as unconstitutional by the French Constitutional Council, which ruled that there could be only *one* people in the French Republic. Even though the Corsican Assembly had not made a claim on nationhood, their motion was read as such a claim because of the tenacious hold of the principle of congruent cultural and political boundaries in the definition of the European nation and its citizens. This defeat in no way diminished the symbolic importance to Corsicans of a motion which continues to be referred to as a "historic" and defining moment in Corsican political consciousness.

Corsican language education continued to be a key focus for language activism. The next major policy change after the 1975 inclusion of Corsican in the Deixonne law came in 1982, when a Ministry of Education circular endorsed a more systematic program of Corsican language education, increasing the number of (voluntary) hours of class from one to three in primary schools and allowing secondary students to take Corsican to fill language some language requirements in the curriculum. Beginning in 1982, students taking their *Baccalauréat* (school leaving exam) could also take an optional test in Corsican (the score from optional tests can improve a student's overall test results but cannot detract from them).

Beginning with the first Assembly, language activists pushed for further officialization and institutionalization of Corsican. During the eighties, three separate motions came before the Assembly. The first of these was passed immediately in 1983, and read:

> *L'Assemblée, ayant pris acte du caractère fondamental de la langue comme ciment de la culture, et de l'urgence de mettre en oeuvre une réelle politique de réappropriation culturelle qui traduise la volonté de l'Assemblée de rendre sa langue à son peuple...a décidé de s'engager dans une politique de bilinguisme dans le cadre d'un plan triennal qui sera élaboré en concertation avec l'Etat...d'ores et déjà, parallèlement, l'usage de la langue corse sera généralisé dans le cadre de la toponymie des lieux, des villages, des villes, dans le cadre de l'information et de la formation audio-visuelles, ainsi que pour certains actes de la vie publique.*

> [The Assembly, having officially recognized the fundamental role of the Corsican language as the cement of culture, and of the urgency of putting into practice a concrete policy of cultural reappropriation which translates the desire of the Assembly to give the people its language back...has decided to commit itself to a policy of bilingualism, to be implemented in a triennial plan to be elaborated in collaboration with the state...In parallel, from now on, the use of the Corsican language will be generalized in the names of places, villages, towns, in the context of news and audiovisual training, as well as in certain public documents.]

The practical impact of this resolution was short lived, as it was rejected by then Prime Minister Mauroy. The Assembly was also dissolved a few months later. In 1985 there was the Castellani Motion, which called for Corsican language education to be mandatory for the state, and optional for the student. This motion was tabled, and never voted on. In 1989, a motion that would have established Corsican and French as "coofficial" was debated and voted down. We shall return to these issues in Chapter 5.

Outside of the political context, language activists in the eighties pursued many initiatives begun in the seventies. The production of literary and pedagogical texts continued with vigor, and was kept in the public eye through the press through such vehicles as news articles on new works, radio interviews of authors, a television program, *Detti è Scritti* 'The Spoken and the Written' on current literary events, literary prizes, public debate s/conferences on Corsican literature, and "meet-the-author" book fairs at bookstores. At the beginning of the decade, there were only two radio stations broadcasting in Corsican: the *Viva Voce* of the ADECEC and RCI (*Radio Corse International*). Both of these stations were only able to broadcast to a limited geographical area. In 1984, Corsica got its own branch of the newly decentralized Radio France: *Radio Corse Frequenza Mora* (RCFM), which has pursued an aggressive bilingual policy in its broadcasts. The regional television station, FR3, was moved from Marseilles to Ajaccio, and under Corsican direction, increased the use of Corsican in its broadcasts. Key linguistic and cultural activists from the seventies became University professors at the Corsican Studies Institute, and trained a new generation of young Corsicans who became Corsican language teachers in the schools. Corsican was progressively admitted as a degree subject from the *Baccalauréat* through the Ph.D. (*doctorat du troisième cycle*). The numbers of Corsican musical groups multiplied and enjoyed an immense popularity and there was a small, but steady production in Corsican in theater and film.

3.3. The nineties

Beginning in 1989, the Corsican Region (represented by the Assembly) signed the first of a series of planning contracts with the state. The 1990 contract included a systematic plan for teacher education in Corsican language instruction, provided money for Corsican language laboratories in the Teacher Training Schools, labs and workshops in all secondary schools, the production of pedagogical materials for Corsican language teaching, and a computerized database of the Corsican language. 1990 was also the year that Corsican was admitted as a CAPES subject. This was significant, because the CAPES is a competitive national exam for teachers that confers an advanced teaching degree and civil service rank.

The 1994 contract included several new initiatives. One was the establishment of "Mediterranean classes" in two *Collèges* (beginning level secondary schools for children aged twelve to fourteen). In these classes, students studied Corsican along with another romance language (Italian or Spanish). Another option allowed students to combine the study of Latin, Corsican and another romance language. Beginning in 1994, two recreation centers where primary schoolchildren and their teachers go for week long field trips made Corsican immersion part of their programming. State support was also provided for Corsican language broadcasting on the regional television station, and for continued work on Corsican language databases. As a result of the 1994 contract, four primary schools opened bilingual classes. Labeled "experimental," these classrooms alternate between Corsican and French throughout the day; French and Corsican are both taught as subjects and used as media of instruction *(Cunsigliu Culturale, Suciale è Ecunomicu di a Corsica* 1997: 6).

A 1996 survey of Corsican language education conducted by the Region showed that 195 out of 24,766 primary school students in Corsica were in fully bilingual classes. Roughly 20% (4,870) primary school students received three hours per week of Corsican language instruction. The remainder (approximately 75%) had one hour a week of Corsican. In secondary schools, 35% of the students in *collèges*, 13% of *lycée* students and 30% of students in vocational High Schools were taking Corsican classes. Every secondary school now has a Corsican language teacher, and most of these posts are held by teachers who have the CAPES in Corsican. About a third of all students taking the *Baccalauréat* elected to take a Corsican test. At the University, all students are required to take between sixty and ninety minutes of weekly instruction in Corsican.

4. Major themes and debates in Corsican language activism

In the early days of Corsican cultural nationalism, it was the form of language that became the primary locus of cultural and political meaning and activity. First of all, as we have seen, linguistic form was at the heart of French ideologies of linguistic value. As intellectuals, Corsican nationalists had been nursed on this ideology throughout their long involvement in the French system of education. Secondly, the emphasis on form was directly related to the function of language in the definition of identity. If a language symbolizes cultural and political unity, the "boundedness, distinctiveness and homogeneity of the nation," (Handler 1988: 170), then that language must be unified, bounded, distinctive and homogenous, the mirror of the social body it is held to represent.[46] As Gal writes, when cultural identity is the precondition for political legitimacy, "language is understood as an expression of communal spirit and the uniformity of language is important not for efficient communication and broad participation, but as proof that the speaking subject is an authentic member of the nation, linking speaker and language to the past and its (invented) traditions" (1992: 448–449).

4.1. *Differentiation from Italian: pragmatics and ideology*

As Achard writes, "*les tenants des langues minoritaires, s'ils entendent affirmer leur préférence pour l'orge et leur aversion pour le monopole du blé, entendent, non moins que les autres, bien séparer les espèces*" [Even though the champions of minority languages are vocal in their preference for barley and their aversion for the monopoly of wheat, they are just as concerned as anyone else to clearly separate the kinds of grain] (1987: 56). Drawing clear linguistic boundaries has been of obvious importance for a cultural nationalist agenda, given the essentialist ideology that underlies European claims on political legitimacy and identity.[47]

In Corsica, the struggle for distinction has revolved, understandably, around Corsican's relationship to Italian. Italy's geographical and linguistic proximity made it a "natural" partner for the assertion of difference. As Mewett's analysis of how people define "insiders" and "outsiders" in a Scottish crofting community shows, some of the most socially relevant assertions of difference are with the people "next door" (1986). Being different from distant strangers is obvious—it is being able to make subtle differentiations that bears the weight of proof of the integrity and cohesion of the in-group.[48] Some of the earliest instances of Corsican language advocacy (before it was intensely politicized) were defined by their effort to differentiate Corsican from Italian in writing. In 1896, Santu Casanova founded the weekly *A Tramuntana*, in which he justified writing in Corsican on the grounds that it was a language and not a dialect of Italian. *L'Annu Corsu*, a literary almanac that appeared after the First World War, also militated for a written Corsican as different as possible from Italian.

While a discourse of maximal differentiation from Italian dominates the last twenty years of Corsican language activism, since 1988, there has been an increase in the number of Corsican intellectuals who emphasize Corsican's linguistic kinship with Italian. In the following pages I will sketch the social and political issues that encouraged a discourse of maximum difference up through the 1980s, and discuss the contours of the contemporary debate about the nature of Corsican's linguistic relationship with Italian and the cultural and political significance of linguistic closeness or distance.

My focus is on discourses about linguistic difference and not linguistic difference itself. A word needs to be said, however, about my position on linguistic record. There is one crude but important linguistic truth: that Corsican is linguistically "closer" to Italian than it is to French. This does not require expert verification (and is contested by nobody): it can be measured with very basic tests of mutual intelligibility. As I have suggested earlier, the question of the nature of Corsican's relationship to Italian (how close or distant?) is far less obvious. Neither in this or the previous chapter do I take a position on the validity of one claim over another. This is because I do not think there is any set of criteria for comparing and contrasting Corsican and Italian that is ideologically neutral. The act of choosing and ranking categories of linguistic characteristics and defining the linguistic corpora within which to document them advances a formal definition of language identity, and ignores the pragmatic and political issues that I take to be critical. Even if one is comfortable with a purely formal definition of language, and identifies key aspects of form, the result of a comparison and contrast between Corsican and Italian only has meaning within a wider framework. That is, the meaning of the Corsican–Italian relationship must be measured against the relationship between other linguistic codes. Which ones should serve as the barometer? The relationship between "standard" Italian and Calabrese? Sicilian? Sardinian? Alternatively, the relationship between Corsican and Italian could be compared to the linguistic relationship between "standard" and regional (perhaps even Corsican) French, or between Italian and Portuguese; Portuguese and Castilian; Castilian and Galician. As we will see below, none of these choices is neutral or apolitical, for they automatically posit linguistic labels/identities ("language," "dialect," "regional speech") that are already politically and ideologically loaded.

4.1.1. Historical origins for the discourse of maximal distance

In the latter part of the 1800s and the early part of the 1900s, Italians immigrated to Corsica to work in mines, as agricultural laborers and in the charcoal industry. Many of these immigrants were from the region of Lucca, and these *Lucchese* were, as de Zerbi writes, "*une population pauvre, sobre et travailleuse acceuillie avec défiance et commisération par un peuple...pauvre, sobre et travailleur, tant il est vrai que le bouc émissaire n'est jamais qu'une partie de soi-même*" [a population of sober, poor, hard workers who were received with mistrust by a...sober, poor, hard-working people, so true it is that the scapegoat is always but a part of oneself] (1997: 32). De Zerbi goes on to cite a number of proverbs which illustrate the low regard Corsicans had for the *Lucchese*. In one of them, the comeuppance for a woman whose social pretensions make her overly critical of potential marriage partners is to marry a *Lucchese*: "*A donna chì dicia què vogliu è què ùn vogliu si maritò cù un lucchese*" [a woman who says 'I want this and not that' will marry a Lucchese] (32). We can understand that the status of the Italian language suffered because of the low status of these speakers.

Ottavi writes that it is because of Mussolini's "irredentist" program in the interwar period that "*les Corses ne reconnaissent pas volontiers la ressemblance entre leur langue et l'italien...on tient à marquer des différences et, lorsqu'il n'y en a pas, ou pas assez, on en trouve. Or, que cela plaise ou non, les faits sont là: lorsqu'ils parlent ensemble, Corses et Italiens se comprennent*" [Corsicans do not willingly admit to the resemblance between their language and Italian...we insist on emphasizing differences, and when there aren't any, or aren't enough of them, we find some. Now, whether you like it or not, the facts are there: when they speak to each other, Corsicans and Italians understand one another] (1979: 104–105).[49] Mussolini supported linguistic and cultural movements involving "dialects" of Italian outside his borders, with the ultimate goal of using cultural unity as a basis for political annexation. During and after the Second World War, Corsicans were eager to repudiate this fascist connection. One way of doing so was to de-emphasize those linguistic similarities claimed by Mussolini.

The passage of time has arguably dulled some of these negative associations, though de Zerbi writes in the essay cited above that "*Italophilie de connivence, de proximité et italophobie à dominante raciste se partagent ainsi le coeur des Corses*" [Corsicans' sentiments about Italians are divided between a sense of closeness and complicity and an anti-Italianism of a racist nature] (32).[50] We can see this in the contradictory ways in which Corsicans talk about Italian in everyday conversation. On the one hand, I was told by several older Corsicans that you could always tell the difference between a native Italian and a native Corsican speaking Corsican. Italians would never get certain pronunciations right. Every informant had a different "fool-proof" test case. One of these was the word for "church" [tyezɑ]. Inevitably, they told me, Italians would pronounce the initial sound as a stop, as they do in Italian: [kyezɑ]. Here, phonological habits were represented as "natural," even biological abilities; in short, as insurmountable obstacles to total assimilation that leave the boundaries between "us" and "them" intact[51] (see also Chapter 6). On other occasions alluded to in the last chapter, Corsicans would claim to be able to "speak Italian" with virtually no effort. As I have suggested, what people call "speaking Italian" is often a mixed code. What seems to drive these metalinguistic judgments about the permeability of language boundaries is the degree to which the focus is on communication, rather than political or cultural differentiation. This can be seen in the comments of a reader of *A Viva Voce*, who wrote a letter (in Corsican) in which he said that as a young man, he had been a shepherd who kept his flock on the eastern plain of the island, where he met many Italian workers. "*Passaiu parecchie stonde à fà ragiunamenti cun elli, e pigliaiu assai piacè a sente e capisce a so lingua cusi vicina à a meia, e ghiera forse quessu u puntu chu [sic] u più ci avvicinava"* [I spent many hours chatting with them, and I got a lot of pleasure out of hearing their language, so close to my own, and it was probably this very thing that brought us together] (Grimaldi 1995: 12).[52]

4.1.2. The political context of Corsican language activism

Differentiating Corsican from Italian became crucial in the struggle which began in the late fifties to get the French government to recognize Corsican as a "regional language of France" under the Deixonne law, which had allowed public schools to teach up to three hours a week in Basque, Breton and Occitan since 1951. Corsican had been excluded from this law on the grounds that it was not a regional language of France but an Italian dialect for which the French government was not responsible. It was for the same reasons that the *Conseil National des Langues et Cultures Régionales* [National Council of Regional Languages and Cultures] made up of Basques, Occitans and Bretons was initially reluctant to admit the Corsican linguistic organization *Lingua Corsa*.

Here, we can see that in order to make institutional gains–specifically, in order to enable Corsican to be taught on a minimal and voluntary basis as other regional languages were–Corsican language activists were forced to defend Corsican in French terms. To be admitted to the club of minority languages, even by the members of the club itself, Corsicans had to prove that Corsican was first, a language, and secondly, a regional language of France. They had to prove it was different enough from Italian to extricate it from the category of "Italian dialect" (e.g., neither French nor a language), and they had to prove that it was not so different as to be not at all French, like Flemish or Alsatian.[53]

There was another pragmatic concern once Corsican was being taught: some feared that promoting Italian as a choice for middle and high school students would drain students from Corsican classes in the "zero-sum" competition for student time in very crowded student schedules. What is interesting is that this same concern was not voiced about other language offerings, even though the practical value of English did in fact prevail in students' and parents' scholastic choices. This suggests that Italian and Corsican were viewed as being in the same category; it was their similarity that made them rivals.

4.1.3. The political context of the eighties and nineties

The category "regional language of France" is no longer salient in Corsica's dealings with the French state. Official terminology labels Corsican a *langue minoritaire* 'minority language', and since the late eighties, the French government has pledged its support for these languages. In 1996, the French government asserted that the Corsican language "*fait partie du patrimoine culturel national*"[is part of the nation's cultural heritage] (*Cunsigliu Culturale, Suciale è Ecunomicu di a Corsica* 1997:6).

This does not mean that the status of Corsican as a language has not been publicly called into question by government officials. As recently as 1991, during a Senate debate over the *Projet Joxe* concerning the island, the Minister of the Interior commented that there were no grammars of Corsican but that one "was in preparation" (*Corse-Matin* 16 April 1991). The proposed law under debate was the first significant rewrite of Corsica's political charter since 1982; it provided for greater political autonomy and (among other things) advocated Corsican language education. The Minister's comments, though meant to be supportive of the law, clearly linked "having a grammar" (codification and standardization) with "language" status. He was either unaware of linguistic work on Corsican or was making a distinction between descriptive and prescriptive grammar (only the latter would count). During the same debate, a conservative Corsican senator Charles Ornano discredited Corsican by using (and misrepresenting) the very same formal criteria for linguistic legitimacy, claiming that Corsican had no linguistic unity, no grammar and no spelling (*Arguments*, May 1991: 4).

In other words, in the late eighties and nineties, Corsican activists could be legitimately concerned with trying to "prove" Corsican's status as a language to Corsican and French politicians. From this perspective, differentiation from Italian had considerable importance, since (as we have seen) the criterion of linguistic autonomy goes hand in hand with dominant, formal definitions of language identity.

4.1.4. The emergence of a pro-Italian voice

Despite the national political context described above, a significant pro-Italian voice began to emerge in public discourse beginning in the late eighties. In 1989, Pascal Marchetti, an accomplished Italian linguist, scholar and long-time Corsican language activist (he was one of the co-authors of first Corsican orthography manual), published *La Corsophonie*. The first part of this book is devoted to the historical illustration of the relationship between Corsican and Italian. Marchetti's focus is both linguistic and sociolinguistic: he evokes the socio-political context to explain Corsican's linguistic debt to Tuscan, which he illustrates with abundant linguistic examples.

The same year, almost one hundred well-known cultural and political figures wrote a letter that they circulated in the press in which they advocated the teaching and learning of Italian (text follows below). In the early nineties, there was a brief period in which RCFM had an Italian correspondent who used to call in live from a location in Tuscany and give a report in Italian on the city or region and the cultural events going on there. In 1993, a retired Corsican called Roselli-Cecconi founded *A Viva Voce*, a quarterly magazine that (accurately) billed itself as *"il solo giornale in lingua italiana scritto da còrsi e stampato in Corsica"* [the only Italian language newspaper written by Corsicans and printed in Corsica]. The paper is still in publication today.

It should be emphasized that the number of social actors involved in any of these publications and initiatives is small. But what is significant is that by the late 1980s, a pro-Italian discourse had lost much of its social and political stigma. Among the contributing factors to the emergence of this discourse are the arrival of greater numbers of relatively wealthy Italian tourists, and the European Union, which has facilitated both formal and informal exchanges and partnerships between neighboring regions and countries (see Jaffe 1993b). In the following sections, I describe how italianists view the connection between cultural identity and linguistic form and the position they take on the role Italian has to play in Franco-Corsican cultural and linguistic politics. I then show how these linguistic and political ideologies have been contested.

4.1.5. Linguistic and cultural essentialism: italianists and their critics

One recurrent theme in the pro-Italian discourse is that Corsican and Italian are "natural" linguistic and cultural partners. We can see this in the language of the 1989 newspaper manifesto in favor of the teaching of Italian, which talked about "re-equilibrating" cultural and economic orientations, and that the Europe of 1992 was going to reposition Corsica in its "natural" milieu, among its "traditional partners". *"L'italien n'est pas pour nous une langue étrangère"* [Italian is not a foreign language for us], the manifesto read, *"mais la langue de notre histoire et de notre culture, sans laquelle le corse ne serait jamais devenu une langue à part, et sans laquelle il cessera d'en être une* [but rather the language of our history and of our culture, without which Corsican would never have become a separate language and without which it will cease to remain one] (Poli 1989).

This perspective was implicit in Marchetti's 1989 book, *La Corsophonie* and quite explicit in a 1997 interview for the magazine *A Messagera*. In this interview, Marchetti described Italian as Corsica's *langue historique* 'historical language' and said that Corsicans should remember that this language has been "*utilisée par eux pendant une longue succession de siècles, comme en témoignent leurs anciens chroniques, leurs archives, leurs toponymes et patronymes, leur mémoire populaire, et qu'il ne s'agit point pour eux, d'une langue étrangère, comme le sont l'anglais, l'espagnol, l'allemand, le portugais ou l'arabe...*"[used by them for centuries on end, evidence for which can be seen in their ancient chronicles, their archives, their toponyms and patronyms, their popular memory and that [Italian] is not at all a foreign language for them, like English, Spanish, German, Portuguese or Arabic...] (1997: 34). Not surprisingly, this perspective permeates *A Viva Voce*, whose stated agenda is to act as an agent for the renewal of forgotten but "natural" connections with Italy. A small example: in the editor's comments on a University of Corsica publication about the poetry of a Corsican priest who wrote in the 18th Century, he writes that "*abbiamo letto con interesse queste poesie che dimostrano sopratutto la cultura letteraria di un prete còrso che si serviva con brio della sua lingua, l'italiano*" [we read with interest the poems that testify to the literary culture of a Corsican priest who used *his language*, Italian, with great spirit] [emphasis added] (Roselli-Cecconi 1995b: 11). Less predictable, perhaps, is its appearance in a 1991 editorial of the autonomist weekly *A Fiara*. It read: "*ùn era micca una lingua straniera imposta da l'invasore, ma a lingua litteraria di tuttu u mondu italicu, Corsica cumpresa...è, à listessu tempu, un mezu di cumunicazione à l'internu di ssu mondu, ch'un squassava micca e differenze ma permettia i scambii ecunomichi è i cuntatti umani*" [it {Italian}was not a foreign language imposed by an invader, but the literary language of the entire Italian world, Corsica included...and, at the same time, a means of communication internal to that world that did not squash linguistic differences but made possible economic exchanges and human contacts] (A.-V.P 1991:15). Here we see Italian as a "natural" and equal partner with Corsican being opposed to French as an imposed "non-natural" foreign language.

The notion that Italian was not a foreign culture was also pursued at some length by one of the editors of *Arritti*, a Monsieur Garoby-Colonna in an interview with me in 1988. He pointed out that the cultural status of the evergreen oak had changed as a result of French influence. Unlike *les anciens* 'our ancestors' he said, Corsicans now talked about this tree as *maquis* 'underbrush'–as something that needed to be cleared away. Today, he said, only trees planted in French parks (the chestnut, white oak etc.) were esteemed by Corsicans. The evergreen oak, however, had cultural value in

Italy, where there were entire gardens full of them. For him, the garden metaphor stood for a general rupture with Italian culture, and the resulting loss of a power base from which to resist French cultural dominance. Similarly, the author of the editorial in *A Fiara* that is cited above deployed a very strong version of the Whorfian hypothesis in which cultural essences (and compatibility) are viewed as embedded in linguistic form: "*in secondu locu, a struttura stessa di sta lingua 'alta'...ùn era micca tale, rispettu à quella di u corsu, da fà sorge un'antra manera di percepì a realità...ma lasciava, si pò dì, "incurottu" st'elementu fundamentale d'ogni cultura*" [in the second place, the very structure of this "high" language [Italian]...was not of such a nature, in respect to that of Corsican, to bring forth another way of perceiving reality...but left "uncorrupted," shall we say, those fundamental elements of each culture] (A.-V.P 1991: 15).

4.1.6. The italianist perspective on the politics of linguistic similarity

We can see that one significant thrust of italianist linguistics and the endorsement of Italian language teaching is to escape the pervasive opposition of Corsican and French and to counterbalance the effects of French linguistic and cultural domination. Garoby-Colonna made this point to me in the interview mentioned above: according to him, the study of Italian in the high schools (which was very common up until World War II) had attenuated the cultural alienation brought on by French and French culture.

Part of the value of Italian is its political weight: as a standardized national language with a recognized literary and cultural heritage, Italian has the power to confront French on equal terms. This theme has been frequently voiced in the pages of *A Viva Voce*. In one issue, the editor posed what he obviously considered a rhetorical question, "*E allora è forse il momento di domandarci: il còrso può 'fare il peso' di fronte al francese?*" [Now is perhaps the time to ask ourselves: can Corsican 'carry its weight' in the face-off with French?] (Roselli-Cecconi 1995a: 2). This point was reiterated the following year in a long article by Roccu Multedo whose title, "*Tra il còrso ed il francese: l'italiano*" [Between Corsican and French: Italian] identified Italian as a political intermediary between Corsican and French (Multedo 1996:5). A reader wrote in to voice his appreciation of Multedo's article, adding that "*penso che senza la conoscenza dell'italiano i Corsi non hanno più i punti di riferimento che permettono la protezione della loro lingua. Dimenticando o rinnegando le basi dell'italian, si condanna il corso a morte, perchè le sue*

basi sono le stessi che quelle dell'italiano" [I think that without the knowledge of Italian, Corsicans no longer have the points of reference necessary to
protect their language. To forget or deny the bases of Italian is to condemn
Corsican to death, since its bases are the same as Italian's] (Casanova 1996).

We can note that this argument is anchored in the biological essentalist
view of "natural" language identities. It appears in the assertion of the
"natural" link between Corsican and Italian. It is this link allows Italianists to
assert that *"il terreno guadagnato per l'italiano è anche terreno guadagnato
per il còrso"* [ground gained for Italian is also ground gained for Corsican]
(Peretti 1995: 2). In this respect, they postulate the equivalence of Corsican
and Italian. Thus the editors of *A Viva Voce* are able to print, *"Morta la
lingua, Morto il popolo"* [the death of the language is the death of the people]
in Italian while referring to Corsican.

At the same time, some *Viva Voce* authors use the same essentialist
discourse to affirm the *non-equivalence* of Corsican and Italian in a classic
diglossic framework where Italian is the standard code and Corsican, the oral
variety. Marchetti and Roselli-Cecconi use the examples of Québec, Belgium
(Flemish), the Val d'Aoste and Alsace to assert that *"c'est par rattachement
à la variété normée de leur idiome qu'ils parviennent à conserver leur
originalité linguistique"* [it is with the connection to the standard variety of
their idioms that they succeed in preserving their linguistic originality]
(Marchetti 1997: 34).

It is significant to note that this "linguistic originality" is defined within
the "equivalence" framework, for Marchetti goes on to write that *"le vrai
bilinguisme, en Corse, ne peut être que la maîtrise paritaire du français et de
l'italien, et non pas une mythique équivalence institutionelle de la langue
française et des différentes inflexions rurales propres à chacun de nos
villages"* [true bilingualism in Corsica can only consist of the equal mastery
of French and Italien, and not of a mythical institutional equivalence of
French and of different rural inflections that characterize each one of our
villages] (1997: 34). In other words, Marchetti does not define Corsican as a
unified language; or, put another way, he locates the unity of Corsican in
Italian.[54] While Marchetti does not spell out the implications for those
"different rural inflections," Peretti does. At the conclusion of his two-part
report in *A Viva Voce* on language preservation in Alsace, he writes that as a
result of the increased teaching of Italian that he advocates, *"lo statuto del
dialetto còrso sarebbe modificato nel senso che esso diverebbe un ausiliario
della lingua italiana..."* [the status of the Corsican dialect would be modified
in the sense that it would become an auxiliary to the Italian language] (1995:
1).

4.1.7. Critiques of the italianist position

Relegating Corsican to an "auxiliary" status with respect to Italian is not a necessary ideological component of a general endorsement of renewed attention to Corso-Italian linguistic and cultural relations. Certainly, Italian was a different kind of dominant language partner than French, particularly since the link with Italian was being defined by Corsicans, who fell completely outside Italian governmental influence. Yet if we look at the italianist position in the framework of normative assumptions about the relationship between language and identity we can see how any reference to linguistic similarity with Italian could threaten Corsican's claim to having a unique linguistic identity and a legitimate status as a language. The following extract from a 1991 newspaper article summarizing popular objections to the promotion of Corsican shows that Italian still has the potential to undermine Corsican language legitimacy. Entitled *"Arguments à ras de terre"* [Arguments from Ground Level], the article represented everyday discourse about language in which people argued that Corsican was not a language because *"c'est un patois italien; le corse du sud est du sarde; le corse du nord, c'est de l'italien"* ['it's an Italian patois'; 'Corsican in the South is Sardinian' and 'Corsican in the North is Italian'] (*Arguments*, May 1991: 4).

The presence of this popular, and de-legitimizing discourse was one reason that several Corsican language activists have challenged the italianist trend. These challenges have taken a number of different forms. The first and most obvious target has been the claim that Corsican and Italian are the same. One public response to Marchetti's book *La Corsophonie* was to accuse him of exaggerating similarities. Geronomi takes a slightly different tack by suggesting that Marchetti's comparative framework is biased in its arbitrary selection of "Tuscan" as the sole point of historical reference. Marchetti, he writes, *"écarte systématiquement toute référence à tout ce qui pourrait laisser entrevoir un parentèle plus large"* [systematically leaves out all references to anything that could bring to view a larger {linguistic}kinship] between Corsican and other romance languages. He also questions the framework for comparison by suggesting that the Corsican-Italian comparison is no more and no less justified than a historical comparison of Italian and Provençal, Catalan or Castilian (Geronimi 1997: 34).

Arrighi (a Corsican intellectual who has held several key posts overseeing Corsican language education) calls into question the Italianist framework for comparison in a slightly different way. He writes that: *"Il est certes linguistiquement intéressant de constater que tous les phénomènes jugés propres au corse se retrouvent, mais dispersés, en 'italien'...si l'on appelle 'italien' tous les parlers de l'Italie depuis le Moyen Age*" [It is certainly linguistically interesting to see that all of the phenomena considered to be unique to Corsican can be found in a dispersed fashion in 'Italian,' if one means by 'Italian' all of the dialects of Italy that have been spoken since the Middle Ages] (1992: 43). Here, Arrighi makes reference to the fact that there have always been many "Italian dialects" with no greater distance or closeness to "standard Italian" (a recent, superposed norm) than Corsican. In doing so, he implicitly calls into question the very definition of "Italian" as a "language". By acknowledging similarity only in a very long historical perspective, Arrighi also suggests that italianists have exaggerated the linguistic similarity of *contemporary* Corsican and (standard?) Italian.

Another line of criticism has been to challenge the specific features used by Marchetti to establish the "identity" of the language. Comiti, for example, has criticized Marchetti's emphasis on lexical data, suggesting that the nature of Corsican syntax is both more important as an index of linguistic identity and that it is in syntax that Corsican exhibits the greatest particularities. Furthermore, Comiti questions Marchetti's interpretation of undeniable lexical similarities between Corsican and Tuscan as evidence of diffusion from Tuscan, writing that they could equally well be seen as the results of parallel development (1992: 58). Finally, Comiti recasts the meaning of linguistic difference, writing that "*l'essentiel n'est pas de savoir ce qui rapproche les langues romane–on sait très bien que c'est une langue mère commune–mais plutôt ce qui les distingue suffisament aujourd'hui, pour pouvoir dire qu'il s'agit de langues différentes*" [the key is not how romance languages are similar–we know very well that they have the same mother tongue–but rather, in what ways they are distinct enough today for us to be able to say they are different languages] (1992: 57). In a general way, Comiti, Arrighi and Geronimi can all be classified as taking a strategic, rather than a biological perspective on language and identity. They take Corsica's right to be defined as a language as a political given, and emphasize that it is politics, and not linguistics, that drives the social evaluation of linguistic sameness and difference.

Nevertheless, we can see that none of them completely rejects the notion of linguistic kinship. This can be seen most dramatically in Comiti's extended discussion of the political significance of linguistic difference. He begins with a political assertion: that Corsicans are a people and Corsican is a language. He then goes on to use a metaphor of kinship to insist on the limits of the "blood" relations between Corsican and other romance languages. He claims that all romance languages are "half-sisters," saying that:

[cela] suppose l'existence d'un deuxième géniteur chaque fois différent. Pour ma part il me plaît à penser que le père de chacune des langues en question est représenté par un peuple...Il en resulte que le peuple corse est le père de la langue corse, le peuple toscan (dont on conviendra qu'il n'est pas le peuple corse) est le père de la langue toscane et ainsi de suite (55).

[[this] supposes the existence of a different genitor for each one. My own preference is to think about the father of each of these languages as being represented by a *people*...It follows that the Corsican people is the father of the Corsican language, the Tuscan people (which we will agree, is not the Corsican people) is the father of the Tuscan language and so on.]

What is interesting here is that the "half-sister" relationship allows for "genetic" similarity (the essential, "maternal" link), but preserves a notion of separate, *political* fathers. That is, Comiti uses the metaphor of kinship as an attempt to reconcile potentially de-legitimating linguistic difference and national identity.

Here, we see an unresolved tension between social-constructionist and essentialist views on language and identity. This is because the essentialist argument has played a central role in Corsican language activism, and has been used as the cornerstone of Corsican nationalist claims to cultural and political autonomy. Comiti remains silent on a few key points in the above passage: he does not say if "peopleness" is attributed to a collectivity on the basis of linguistic differentiation, or whether it is the collectivity that asserts its peopleness, and this assertion legitimizes the definition of language boundaries.[55] His metaphor remains ambiguous: is the father "pater" or "genitor"; must biological paternity be proven?

Geronimi breaks more clearly than Comiti with dominant biological models by defining linguistic kinship as an aspect of lived experience. Furthermore, he situates the very nature of that experience within a political framework. He emphasizes that Italian was a dominant language that stood in the same kind of relationship to Corsican as French does today, and cites the work of the historian Graziani to illustrate the presence of Corso-Italian diglossia in sixteenth-century Corsican documents. For Geronimi, the collective memory of this dominance overshadows linguistic similarity, and denies Italian any privileged affective or cultural status on Corsica. He uses his experience of the authenticity of place name pronunciations as an illustration, writing: *"Pour moi qui habite Aiacciu, je ne fais aucune différence entre l'officiel tosco-français 'Porticcio' et l'acculturé 'Paurtich' si je les place l'un et l'autre en regard du local, et donc légitime 'Purticchju'"* [For me, living as I do in Aiacciu, I do not make any distinction between the official, tuscan-french '*Porticcio*' and the acculturated '*Paurtich*' if I judge them both against the local, and thus legitimate '*Purticchju*'] (1997: 35). That is, he is just as alienated by the tuscanization of the name of the town as by the way that it is pronounced in French.

4.2. *Language unity: the drive for elaboration*

The complement to Corsican's definition as a language on the basis of its differentiation from other, external codes is an argument for internal linguistic unity and purity. Let me first take up the notion of language unity, and why language activists found it important to stress.

Once again, there was the political reality of Corsicans' dependence on the French government for dispensation to teach Corsican in the schools. In the ultimately successful struggle for the inclusion of Corsican in the Deixonne law, linguistic militants had to contend not only with the accusation that Corsican was an Italian dialect, but also, with the government's objection that Corsican was not sufficiently unified or codified to count as a language. Countering these ideas about Corsican held by French politicians has been and continues to be important in activists' efforts to secure government support for Corsican language education.

Corsican language planners were also acutely aware that many Corsicans viewed their language as lacking unity and structure, and that these judgments were a part of a whole complex of language attitudes that were obstacles to Corsican's revitalization. The authors of *Main basse sur une île* wrote that they faced, in the Corsican population at large,

> *l'arsenal des arguments fallacieux utilisées par le civilisateur: la langue locale est pauvre, incapable de rendre les nuances de la pensée, sa pratique est nuisible et constitue une entrave à l'apprentissage et au bon usage du français; c'est un "patois" qui laisse un accent–ridicule quand il n'est pas parisien ou marseillais à la rigueur...on en conclut que le corse ne s'écrit pas...*(1971: 63)

> [the arsenal of fallacious arguments used by the colonizer: the local language is poor, incapable of expressing nuances of thought, its use has a negative impact on the process of learning good French; it is a patois that leaves an accent which is [seen as] ridiculous, since it is not Parisian, or at very least, from Marseilles...from this, it is concluded that Corsican cannot be written....]

It would not be long before linguists in the autonomist movement (trained in sociolinguistics) began to use the term diglossia to name the problem described in the manifesto. The study of diglossic situations around the world, as well as on the island, highlighted the intimate link between attitudes toward a language and its social practice. Like Basque language activists described by Urla who had also experienced rapid language decline, Corsicans activists also held that "diglossia was both a sign and cause of language shift" (1988: 387). The remedy for diglossia was to engage in what the sociolinguist Heinz Kloss termed *ausbau* 'elaboration' (see Thiers 1988a: 91). Strategies of elaboration included normalization (inserting Corsican into high status domains of use previously occupied by French alone) and standardization (achievement of linguistic unity also attributed only to the dominant language).

This meant grammars, dictionaries and teaching materials in Corsican had multiple purposes. Practical tools for Corsican language education and people writing in Corsican, they were also a symbol of Corsican's ability to perform "high" linguistic functions and of its unity as a language. If we look closely at some of these texts, we find that the issue of regional dialectal diversity in Corsican looms large. Marchetti, who was the author of *Le Corse Sans Peine* [Corsican Without Difficulty], a language-learning manual accompanied by an audio tape written in the early eighties, took great pains to include vocabulary and speakers from different parts of the island throughout the book. Moreover, he did not explicitly identify them as different linguistic subsystems. The "unity in diversity" of Corsican was asserted through both through this silence and by the dramatization of interdialectal comprehension in the fictional dialogues at the beginning of each chapter.[56]

More often, however, the issue of diversity merits explicit acknowledgment. This is true, for example, in Comiti's 1992 book, *Les Corses face à leur langue*, discussed in more detail below. Comiti succinctly explains why, writing that *"Les Corses éprouvent, donc, des difficultés à dépasser les problèmes de la diversité. Je dis 'problèmes' car ils sous-tendent un paradox qui n'est pas un des moindres: d'une part la langue n'est conçue qu'à travers la notion d'unité et d'autre part c'est le respect de la diversité qui préoccupe le plus"* [Corsicans experience difficulty getting past problems of diversity. I say "problems" because there is an underlying, and not inconsequential paradox: on the one hand, the language is only understood through the notion of unity and on the other hand, it is respect for diversity that is the chief preoccupation] (70).

We see this very struggle in another recent text: a small section titled "grammatical notes" in a 1997 bilingual Corsican-French dictionary. On one page, the authors write, *"La diversité de notre langue reste assurément un obstacle à son unification"* [the diversity of our language remains without a doubt an obstacle to its unification] (Culioli et. al.: 310). On the next page, however, they downplay the extent and the significance of this diversity, making reference to *"légères différences qui existent entre la language corse pratiquée dans le nord de l'Île et celle du sud"* [small differences between the

Corsican spoken in the north versus the south of the island], and cautioning readers not to "*donner à ces différences plus d'importance qu'elles n'en ont*"[make these differences out to be more significant than they really are] (311).

We can see that dominant ideologies of language establish "unity" as an important criterion of linguistic legitimacy. "Unity" is entailed by the essentialist bias of such ideologies, in which "one" language embodies "one" culture. From this perspective, the diversity which figures largely in the way that Corsicans experience and conceive of "speaking Corsican" is defined as a problem.

4.3. The boundary with French: the "purists" vs. the "sociolinguists"

This problem–of the relationship between practice and ideology–underscores the debate of the mid to late eighties between the "purists" and the "sociolinguists". These labels oversimplify, as we will see, but they do signal important differences of opinion about the nature of linguistic identity, the process of norm-setting and the social and political responsibilities of linguists and educators. One of the key points of contention was the importance of preserving the boundary between Corsican and French. It is this boundary that is called into question by many contemporary spoken language practices; in particular by the frenchified Corsican in evidence in everyday speech. Should it be tolerated, embraced, defined as "Corsican" on the grounds that it is a language variety used by Corsicans, or should it be sanctioned in favor of a Corsican less "contaminated" with French?

4.3.1. The purist position

Language purism in the Corsican case is highly predictable. Thomas' cross-cultural and historic analysis of linguistic purism shows that purism is widespread in situations in the context of nationalistic movements (1991: 137), where there is language contact with a socio-politically dominant language (133), during the "pre-standardization" period of linguistic elaboration, in which it is often "xenophobic in nature and moderate to extreme in its intensity" (117). As we have seen in Chapter 3, French influences can be found in Corsican pronunciation, in the lexicon and in grammatical structures. As we will see, the amount of importance attributed by linguists to "impurity" in these different formal domains varies.

4.3.1.1. Linguistic targets for purist censure: pronunciation

One kind of pronunciation influence (or "problem") mentioned in Chapter 3 is a result of people reading written Corsican using French sound-spelling conventions. Pascal Marchetti deplored this phenomenon in his regular newspaper column on language. (In the following citation, *Querciolu* and *Macinaghju* are the names of two villages; phonetic transcriptions are mine). He wrote, *"on prononce le premier syllabe de Querciolu 'ker' au lieu de 'couer', et 'massi' au lieu de 'madji' pour les premiers deux syllabes de Macinaghju"* [people pronounce the first syllable of Querciolu 'ker' [kɛr] instead of 'couer'[kuɛr], and say 'massi' [mɑsi] not 'madji'[mɑʄi] for the first two syllables of Macinaghju] (Marchetti 1991). There is less mention (either by linguists or in everyday commentary) of other pronunciation influences such as the transfer of French syllable stress patterns to Corsican described in Chapter 3. One possible explanation for this is that "correct" pronunciation is so closely associated with competence that Corsicans who are unsure of their control over pronunciation simply refrain from speaking Corsican; thus these "errors" show up much less in everyday speech than the gallicisms that have become part of almost all Corsicans' repertoires.

4.3.1.2. The lexicon

Lexical "impurities" are frequent targets for what Cameron calls "verbal hygiene," perhaps because "foreign" elements are so frequently absorbed into the vocabulary, where they are readily visible even to the non-specialist (Thompson 1984: 201; Hill and Hill 1980; Dorian 1994). In Corsican, the vocabulary of "modernity" is almost exclusively made up of French or French-based terms. This is because the introduction of French and French education took place before the technological revolution. There was no particular pressure to develop a "modern" Corsican lexicon; French was there as a ready resource. For decades, Corsican speakers have used French words (sometimes with nativized pronunciation, sometimes not) for modern technology, institutions and practices. The word for 'car' in Corsican is thus *vittura,* based on the French *voiture* (and not on the Italian *macchina*). In many cases, words that enter Corsican via French are not any more French than they are Spanish or Portuguese (for example, *aviò* for 'airplane'). But they tend to be perceived as being French unless they are clearly derived from words that exist in Italian but not French (like the Italian *tifosi* 'football fans', which contrasts with French *supporters*, taken from English). This means that Corsican linguistic space is inherently "impure". Shapiro makes the point that in puristic discourses, linguistic and moral purity are often closely associated (1989: 23). We can see how, in the political context of Corsican language activism, a similar metaphorical move can equate "impurity" with collective cultural inauthenticity.

One remedy for this is, of course, the invention of neologisms. The only organized effort to do this has been conducted by the ADECEC, which published pamphlets of neologisms in the early eighties on such topics as mathematics or the parts of a car. The radio (see Chapter 9) is the most active domain for neologism invention today. We can see the importance of this brand of purism for the larger goal of recapturing public, official, prestige domains from French. While the early ADECEC pamphlets had little practical impact, they did fill a symbolic function. Gaps in the Corsican vocabulary were often cited in a form of folk biological essentialism as "proof" that Corsican could not express abstract thought, and was inherently not adapted to the modern world. The invention of neologisms was part of an effort to change attitudes towards Corsican from within the diglossic model: the creation of a "pure" Corsican vocabulary (even if it was not widely adopted) was meant to convince Corsican speakers that they could use their code beyond the confines of the affective relations and rural life with which the language was conventionally associated.

Reviving an authentic vocabulary is one of the themes of features on correct usage that are a regular enough fixture of the island press to be recently parodied.[57] Pascal Marchetti, cited above, is one of the linguists who has had a regular newspaper column on language. In one of these, he described current usage as a "loss of linguistic memory," citing as an example the "blunder"of believing that *mammata* means 'mother', where it actually means 'your mother'. Young people do not know this, which leads them, he writes, to respond incorrectly to such a question by saying "*Iè, mammata sta bè*" [Yes, your mother is doing well] in response to the question "*Mammata sta bè?*" [Is your mother doing well?] (*Corse Matin* 27 May 1991).

But by far the most common target for Corsican prescriptivists has been the use of French calques where a Corsican word already exists. Table 8 depicts prescriptive guidelines printed in the March 1988 number of *A Spannata*, a paper dedicated to the promotion of southern varieties of Corsican. It is an extract from a feature called *U Corsu Schiettu* 'Pure Corsican'; its subtitle was *Éviter le gallicisme* 'Avoid the gallicism'(Rotily-Forcioli 1988).

Table 8. *U Corsu schiettu 'Pure Corsican'*

Pour dire: 'To say'	*la salive* 'saliva'	*un juif* 'a Jew'	*une pe- tite tasse* 'a small cup'	*un vieux soulier* 'an old shoe
A	*ùn diti micca* 'don't say'		*unu juiffu*	*una piccula tazza*	
B	*Pudeti dì* 'you can say'	*a saliva*	*un ghjudeiu*	*una tazzina*	*vechju scarpu*
C	*ma ditti piutostu* 'but say rather'	*u stupu*	*un abreiu*	*una chicara*	*scamaronu*

The phrases in row A are most clearly identifiable as calques on French. This is the kind of usage frequently targeted in other similar newspaper features, where Corsican terms like *usciu* 'door', *fulminente* 'match' and *pidone* 'mailman' would be prescribed as replacements for their common equivalents *porta*, *allumetta* and *fattore* (derived from the French *porte*, *allumette* and *facteur*).

Some other criterion of authenticity is operating, however, in the preference for row C over row B. For the phrases 'saliva' and 'old shoe', the operative criterion appears to be greater distance from French; the choices for 'jew' and 'little cup' emphasize distance from both French and Italian. The importance of the "authentic" Corsican words in row C is twofold. Not only do they police the linguistic boundary with French, but they also invoke the authority and authenticity of a historic Corsican. This "archaising purism" has a long history in what Thompson calls "traditionalist nationalism" (1984:137).

4.3.1.3. Semantic and syntactic distinctions and the autonomy of linguistic codes

Jean-Joseph Franchi (long-time promoter of Corsican, writer, onetime pedagogical counselor and editor of the Corsican-language literary review *Rigiru*) pleaded in a 1984 text for the retention of "authentic" vocabulary on more explicit and complex grounds. He pointed to a process of semantic shift/loss in which Corsican terms had become reduced to the meanings of their "false friends" in French, and the Corsican equivalents of those false friends had dropped out of use. Two examples:

(17)
Corsican term: *fruttà*
Original meaning: 'to bring in revenues'
"New" meaning: *frotter* French verb 'to rub'
Corsican term(s) lost: *strufinà* 'to rub'

(18)
Corsican term: *impregnà*
Original meaning: 'to impregnate'
"New" meaning: *impregner* French verb 'to infuse/fill'
Corsican term(s) lost: *insurpà; timparà; penetrà* etc.

Here it is not just the loss of a traditional vocabulary, nor its substitution with words of French origin that is at issue, but the loss of *distinctions* internal to the code. Franchi identified these distinctions as one of the keys to the unique identity of Corsican (Franchi 1984: 3). This position is made even more explicit in 1988, in Franchi's side of a long written debate with Jacques Thiers about the value of sociolinguistics in the Corsican context. Franchi evokes the structuralist insight that "all languages have their own logic" as the foundation of minority languages' claims to linguistic parity with dominant languages. He locates the key to this logic in syntax. For this reason, he censured popular usage in which there had been an "abandonment of characteristic forms" in the "alignment" of Corsican syntax with French. For example, he wrote that the conditional phrases *s'è fussi stancu, ùn ci andaria* and *s'è era stancu ùn ci andava* were being used interchangeably. Both of these sentences translate as "If he/she were tired, he/she wouldn't go there," but the former sentence has a subjunctive-conditional verb sequence and the latter, an imperfect-imperfect verb sequence. This was not a case of direct modeling on French, in which conditional sentences are formed with an imperfect-conditional verb sequence. Rather, it was an example of Corsican speakers unconsciously viewing having a *single* conditional format (the case in French) as the norm. In doing so, Franchi argued, they failed to exploit the subtle difference in meaning of the two kinds of conditional sentences in Corsica: the one with the subjunctive characterizes the situation as "unreal" as opposed to simply "improbable" (imperfect-imperfect) (1984:1–2). Franchi comments that "*u lessicu, puru stroppiu, ferma corsu, è a funetica dinò, ma a sintassi, ma tuttu l'assestu di a dicitura hè francese schjettu...u 'corsu novu' hè francese*" [the lexicon, even if distorted, remains Corsican, and so does the phonetic system, but syntax–the whole framework of speech–is pure French...the "new Corsican" is French] (1988: 25).[58] In other words, from the structuralist/formalist vantage point, the loss of distinctions internal to the code and loss of distinctions with external codes displayed in these kinds of examples signal "loss of linguistic identity".

4.3.1.4. The politics of linguistic representations

The above perspective is one of the sources of Franchi's criticism of sociolinguistics. In his 1988 exchange with Thiers, he accuses sociolinguists of "promoting" everyday usage of frenchified Corsican rather than fulfilling what he considers their social responsibility to research and illustrate the logic of Corsican as an autonomous linguistic system. We will take up Thiers' defense below; what I would like to point out here is that Franchi's position is actually a sociolinguistically informed view of the politics of linguistic representation. That is, it is based on the recognition that in the highly politicized context of minority language promotion, where there are a limited number of language specialists and linguistic texts, any description of Corsican will be read as "the norm" and thus take on a prescriptive character.

It is this representational consciousness that drives another theme in purist commentary: the critique of inconsistency in the writing of Corsican. For example, Perfettini, president (and twenty-year member) of *Scola Corsa* criticized the laissez-faire approach to spelling that would allow both *dillali* and *di la li* 'tell it to him'. He advocated the former spelling because the doubling of the consonant *l* signaled a rule of pronunciation: when the verb ends with a stressed vowel, the articulation of the following consonant is forceful or emphasized. Perfettini ended his column with the following statement (emphasis in original text): "*Toute langue a ses règles, le corse est une langue. Ceux qui se font le devoir d'écrire correctement en français doivent avoir la même rigeur lorsqu'il s'agit du corse*" [Every language has its rules, Corsican is a language. Those who oblige themselves to write correctly in French should apply the same rigor to Corsican] (1994). Perfettini's comments show that orthography–written form–has significance as one of the public symbolic spaces in which language identity, unity and legitimacy is displayed. Perfettini writes his column about a particular rule, but what is really at issue is rules themselves. These theme is also taken up by Franchi, who wrote that people do not "passively accept everything that anyone says" in French as correct. He contended that the result of policing French, but not Corsican linguistic form is that "*la langue forte se défend, et la langue faible accepte d'être pidginisée*" [the strong language defends itself, and the weak language allows itself to be pidginized] (1984:2).[59] Here we see the larger, political issue raised by the acceptance of French influence in Corsican: the maintenance of language boundaries is not just about linguistic integrity/authenticity. In other words, an "essentialist" perspective on language and identity does involve a political consciousness. "The rules" not only have value for linguistic identity, but they also constitute an exercise of a social and political prerogative to define good and bad speech; to be active agents rather than passive recipients of processes of linguistic change.

4.3.2. The sociolinguists' perspective on the meaning of French influences

No less than the "purists," sociolinguists like Jacques Thiers have documented French : Corsican "interference". In his 1989 book, Thiers does not remain neutral about some of the examples he provides. He introduces the following example as one that is *"peuplé de monstres"* [filled with monsters], and as *"un énoncé qui heurte notre sensibilité linguistique commune et l'idée qu'intuitivement nous nous faisons du corse"* [an utterance that clashes with our shared linguistic sensibility and our intuitive understanding of what Corsican is]. The phrase is: *"U so dumiciliu si trova certenamente in fondu di u boulevard"*[literally: his domicile is definitely found at the end of the boulevard] (1989a: 67). There is one word, *certenamente*, which is patently different from an "authentic" Corsican word (*certamente*), but the "monstros-ity" of this sentence lies in the fact that is a word-for-word transfer of the French sentence: *"Son domicile se trouve certainement au fond du boule-vard."* Thiers does not provide an "authentic" Corsican version of this sentence, but it would likely involve a different word order (beginning with *sicuru* or *certu* 'it is certain') the use of the word *casa* 'house' instead of *dumiciliu* 'domicile' and possibly, the use of *strada* 'street' or *stradone* 'big street' instead of *boulevard*. Not unlike Franchi, Thiers implicitly emphasizes the role of syntax in defining uniquely Corsican patterns of expression.

But, having given several examples of "monsters," Thiers went on to write that *"ce sont des énoncés réellement prononcés par des gens qui, au moment même de s'exprimer n'ont trouvé que ces ressources-là pour dire ce qu'ils avaient à dire. Ces énoncés...peuvent aussi provoquer de belles colères et de propos définitifs sur l'abâtardissement du corse. N'importe: ce qui est dit est dit!"* [these are utterances actually spoken by people who, at the moment of self-expression, only found these resources to say what they had to day. These utterances...can also provoke considerable anger and authoritative pronounce-ments about the bastardization of Corsican. No matter: what is said is said!] (1989a: 67). In this passage, Thiers focuses attention on the speaking person and his/her communicative purposes. By giving such clear priority to communication, Thiers implicitly qualifies his (and others) "intuitive" linguistic judgments about the authenticity of linguistic form as emotionally understandable but intellectually and philosophically unjustified.

Thiers thus does not accept the purist premise that French influences deform the essence of the Corsican language because he defines language as practice, not as form. This is also evident in another section of his book in which he analyzes in great detail two bilinguals' practice of Corsican in a formal, interview situation. He notes inconsistencies in pronunciation (shifting sometimes towards Italian, sometimes towards French), loss of semantic distinctions of the sort mentioned by Franchi, patent translations of idiomatic expressions from French, and nervous self-corrections (1989a: 76-80). But the conclusions he draws from the speech corpus are far from negative. He writes that Matthew (one of the subjects)

> *démontre à l'analyste la souplesse et la flexibilité de la langue minorée. En effet, malgré la persistance d'un certain compartimentage thématique et linguistique qui relève du cadre ancien de la diglossie...on peut affirmer que les membres de la communauté Corsophone bilingue sont aptes à aborder...en langue corse, quel qu'en soit le thème...sans rencontrer d'obstacle majeur qui serait inhérent à l'état d'une langue considérée...par la majorité de ses locuteurs et par les linguistes, comme strictement réservée à l'expression vernaculaire et incapable d'accéder aux thèmes de la modernité sans perdre son identité linguistique* (1989a: 81).

> [demonstrates to the analyst the suppleness and flexibility of the minoritized language. In effect, despite the persistence of a certain linguistic and thematic compartmentalization that comes out of the early diglossic context...one can affirm that members of the Corsican bilingual community are capable of grappling with any theme...in Corsican...without encountering any major obstacles that should be inherent in a language considered..by the majority of its speakers and by linguists as strictly restricted to vernacular expression and incapable of attaining themes of the modern world without losing its linguistic identity.]

In this passage, evidence of the speaker's recourse to both Corsican and French linguistic structures is not cast as a serious deficiency, but as "a certain linguistic and thematic compartmentalization" which ultimately does not detract from the "suppleness" and "flexibility" of Corsican. In a significant contrast with the purist position, Thiers' definition of Corsican *includes* French-influenced forms; the performance of the bilinguals he describes is characterized as no loss of linguistic identity.

Thiers also sees the public struggle for legitimacy for the Corsican language revolving around communicative functions (the expression of modernity) rather than on form (the representation of Corsican as an autonomous code). Moreover, he questions the very process of identifying "a single norm," asking, "*comment, en l'absence de descriptions antérieures, retrouver les structures 'anciennes' dans 'l'esperanto' moderne, dans le 'sabir francorse' d'aujourd'hui?*" [in the absence of previous descriptions, how does one discover the "old" structures in the modern "esperanto," in the "sabir francorse" of today?]. He suggests that there is no neutral ground for linguistic analysis, and that a linguist who presumes to describe a "pure" Corsican should "*craindre de forcer, par abstractions répétées un système idéal donné comme la langue et authentifié par sa propre description?*" [be wary of imposing [inventing], through repeated abstractions, an ideal system called the language which is authenticated by his own description?] (1986: 83).

Thiers suggests here that when there is no social and sociolinguistic stability and consensus, no individual has the right to decide what the norm will be. Unlike the purists, he does not take the position that there are any autonomous linguistic principles that justify one choice over another; there is no linguistic "essence," there are no "natural" linguistic boundaries: Corsican is what Corsicans say it is. Thiers also points out that the legitimacy of the academic enterprise itself is grounded in social formations. To engage in the process of evaluation of whether a particular study has satisfied abstract linguistic principles depends precisely on the preexisting agreement about what language is that does not exist in Corsica.

There is another implicit assumption of the sociolinguistic perspective which is revealed in a 1988 letter to a newspaper written by one of Thiers' students. This letter was in response to a comment by the Rector of Corsica that sociolinguistics was "obsolescent," and that what students needed was a more "classical" (read "formal") linguistic training. She wrote: "*A vulè mantene una lingua pura, si corre u riscu, sinno di cundannàlla à a morta, omancu di staccàlla di a rialità linghaghjaghja*" [Trying to maintain a pure language runs the risk if not of condemning that language to death, then at the very least of isolating it from everyday linguistic practice] (Carbuccia:1988). Another (anonymous) newspaper commentary in the same year titled "Corsican: avoid ultra-purism" elaborated on the potential for purism to damage the language:

> *Il leur faudrait simplement un peu plus de tact....[pour ne pas] créer des blocages chez les débutants ou de dénigrer la parole de locuteurs pourtant honorables...Là où cette purisme risque d'être assez dangereuse, c'est lorsque les gens prétendent interdire toute innovation parce qu'ils estiment que l'innovation est fautive, parce que toute innovation porte atteinte à la pureté de la langue. Ils ne voient pas que ce sont les "fautes" d'hier qui ont permis aux langues d'évoluer* (*Le Corse: eviter l'ultra-purisme*, 1988).

[They [prescriptivists] just need to have a little more tact...[so as not to] create stumbling blocks for beginners or to deride the speech of honorable speakers...This purism is the most dangerous when it forbids all innovation because they believe that all innovation is wrong, because all innovation threatens the purity of the language. They don't see that yesterday's "errors" made it possible for languages to evolve.]

There are several points we can elaborate on here. One is that the terms of the public debate ("anything goes" vs. "all speech is corrupt") tended to oversimplify the range of opinions in both the purist and the sociolinguistic camps. In contrast to the purists, the sociolinguists clearly recognized much everyday, "impure" speech as part of "speaking Corsican"; on the contrary, the everyday is seen as the motor of a natural and legitimate process of linguistic change. But their objections to purism are not completely philosophically motivated. One of the key "dangers" of purism cited by the sociolinguists is its potential to discourage those who are currently speaking or learning Corsican. This is a pragmatic concern that does not necessarily reject the desirability of making discriminations between oral forms in an *ideal* world, but does reject it in the unstable circumstances of Corsican language revitalization. In other words, all speakers of Corsican are considered such a vital and scarce resource that language activists cannot afford to scare them off by creating linguistic insecurity in Corsican. This perspective has its social parallel in attitudes towards Corsicans of the diaspora; although resident Corsicans may harbor resentments and ambivalence towards them, they are too vital a cultural and social resource to be written off. Here, social, cultural and linguistic vitality of Corsican are being measured in concrete, local, tangible forms: by the numbers of people in the village, and by the numbers of people still speaking the language.

The debate between the purists and the sociolinguists demonstrates Cameron's point that both prescriptive and descriptive linguistics have their own orthodoxies: they are linked with different visions of the foundations of social order (1995: 5–6). For the purists, sources of linguistic authority are rooted in formal systems of linguistic structures which, because of language domination and shift, are only imperfectly reflected in everyday usage. Thus, it must be sought in the past–which is reflected in the speech of only certain Corsicans. From this vantage point, the social implementation of language planning is by definition a top-down process of the kind employed by France. For the sociolinguists, the collectivity is the only legitimate or practical source of linguistic authority; for language planning to be successful, it must work from the bottom-up. As I have pointed out earlier, the "bottom-up" approach is difficult to reconcile with language planners' desire to rejuvenate an interest in minority languages that is not necessarily shared by the majority of the minority population. It also poses practical problems for practical requirements for minority language promotion and education, as we will see in subsequent chapters.

4.4. Critical grammar as synthesis

The tension between "top-down" and "bottom-up" approaches is acknowledged most explicitly by the linguist Jean Chiorboli, whose work I will cite here as a kind of bridge between the two opposing positions I have described. In 1994, Chiorboli published *La Langue des Corses*, a book on Corsican grammar intended for a popular audience. In a press conference, he underscored his anti-prescriptivist stance: "*Une des ambitions du travail est en effet de susciter chez les corsophones une prise de conscience concernant leurs habitudes linguistiques. Il ne s'agit pas a priori d'expliquer aux Corses comment ils doivent parler, mais d'abord de leur montrer comment ils parlent...le souci principal du livre n'a rien à voir avec une attitude puriste*" [One of the ambitions of this work is in effect to stimulate an awareness among Corsophones about their own linguistic habits. Its primary goal is not to explain to Corsicans how they ought to speak; it is to show them how they do speak...the underlying desire of this book is far removed from a purist attitude] (1994: 5).

Yet the kind of "critical grammar" practiced by Chiorboli does not take the position that no position can or should be taken on the relative desirability of specific linguistic features and usage, or that every linguistic description is by definition biased and therefore an illegitimate exercise of power in the business of norm setting. In fact, he wants to persuade the general reader that language management is just as vital and legitimate a social function as economic planning. His grammar is written as a tool for social and political decision making. Chiorboli responds to Thiers' challenge (from what usage shall the norm be drawn?), which he rephrases thus: "*Comment le linguiste peut-il éclairer les choix langagiers de la communauté tout en conservant une démarche scientifique?*" [How can the linguist elucidate the linguistic choices of the community and still maintain a scientific method?]. His answer is to cast a wide net (for speakers/writers and domains of use) and then to scrupulously describe the origins of the data:

> *Eh bien en fournissant toutes les charactéristiques possibles concernant les structures linguistiques en concurrence: fréquence, origine, ancienneté, rapports avec les modèles des langues officielles du champ linguistique roman, notamment le français et l'italien...Qui utilise telle expression?*

Existait-elle déjà en latin?...est-elle utilisée en corse seulement ou également dans d'autres langues-soeurs?...la rencontre-t-on seulement à l'oral ou est-elle fréquent aussi à l'écrit? Esc-ce que les grammaires corses existantes l'admettent? Est-elle utilisée par tous les auteurs reconnus? Y a-t-il contradiction entre les prescriptions des grammaires et l'usage des 'bons auteurs'? (1993).

[Well, it's by laying out all of the competing characteristics concerning linguistic structures: frequency, origin, relationship with models drawn from official romance languages, notably Italian and French. Who uses such and such an expression? Did it already exist in Latin? Is it used only in Corsican or does it also exist in other sister languages? Does one encounter it only in speech or is it also common in writing? Is it accepted in existing Corsican grammars? Is it used by all recognized authors? Is there any contradiction between the prescriptions of the grammars and the usage of the "good authors"?]

Like Thiers, Chiorboli ultimately underscores the social and political origins of language change. The way that he articulates the impossibility of neutrality, however, is slightly different from Thiers. Chiorboli locates "grammar" equally in linguistic and metalinguistic action, and he believes that he can come close to an impartial description and analysis of a wide range of often contradictory linguistic practices and ideologies. But he implicitly and explicitly acknowledges that there is no way for the interpretation and social use of his data to be neutral. He writes that: *"La réponse que je donne à ces questions est susceptible de fournir des critères de sélection pour ceux qui veulent réduire la variété, ou de simples informations pour ceux qui...pensent avant tout que* 'varietà fa richezza'" [The response that I give to these questions [above] can then be used to come up with criteria of selection for those who wish to reduce variety or as simple information for those who...believe that above all, '*in variety there is richness*']. In effect, Chiorboli points out that all stances towards norms and standards–even a sociolinguistic one (with which he is sympathetic)–are in fact acts of language politics that are based on hierarchies of social and linguistic value.

5. Conclusions

In this chapter, we have seen evidence for a strong essentialist bias in the history of European discourse about language and nation/identity. At the same time, this "dominant language ideology" provides support for different definitions of the relationship between formal linguistic boundaries and cultural/political identity. In the essentialist perspective, language identity inheres in formal linguistic properties; as a consequence, it is extremely important to establish and maintain linguistic boundaries between Corsican and Italian and between Corsican and French. Proponents of an this kind of view identify authentic language identity as located somewhere other than everyday practice: it is an abstract system based on an ideal speaker/writer whose authority may be derived from the linguist's analysis or from history/tradition/literary use. In this respect, all "purists" are essentialists.

In contrast, the perspective taken by people like Thiers and Chiorboli locates linguistic identity in popular usage and in political action. Since boundary setting is seen as a political prerogative, it is not dependent on any specific linguistic correlates. The strategic view of language identity emphasizes the social, rather than the abstract linguistic origin of standards and norms. There are no absolute, independent sources of authority for the definition of what counts as Corsican, or what counts as good Corsican; Corsican is what Corsicans speak and what they define as their language. It is the political that makes room for the blurring of boundaries between Corsican and Italian, and for the acceptance of *Francorse* as legitimate. By laying open criteria of judgment, these linguists relinquish, to some extent, a privileged prescriptive position for themselves.

This chapter also shows that the practical and ideological context of language planning tips the balance of power towards the biological position. Given the reliance of Corsican language planners on institutional structures controlled in large part by the French government, the framework for persuasion and interpretation of Corsican's linguistic status was by definition a dominant, French, biological essentialism. Not only is this perspective the one that frames all dealings with the French state, but it is also embedded in the very act of writing about or writing in Corsican. Writing has so many practical and symbolic values, that it is an indispensable to all language activists, no matter what their philosophy of linguistic identity. But the interpretation of writing, as we shall see in subsequent chapters, draws the focus onto form, standards and authority and thus always implicitly invokes a biological essentialist perspective.

This chapter also illustrates the point made by the authors of *Main basse sur une île*: that dominant language ideology is not just a form of external pressure. It is also embedded in the "internal" political economy of language, since the absorption of dominant linguistic hierarchies is reflected in the diglossic popular attitudes and practices described in this chapter and the previous one. This chapter's discussion of the influence of popular attitudes and practices on language planning strategies is taken up in greater detail in the following chapter, which analyzes the sources of resistance to the language legislation described briefly above. The following chapter also looks at how popular responses to language planning strategies have led to the further elaboration of "plural" perspectives that attempt to challenge both the essentialist content of dominant language ideologies and the oppositional structure of identity formation within a diglossic model.

Chapter 5
Language Activism Part 2

1. Introduction

Like Chapter 4, this chapter revolves around the politics of linguistic difference, taking up as a main theme an issue that has been raised in the previous chapter: what competing images of language organize language action on Corsica? In the first part of this chapter, I examine this question through the analysis of popular and political discourse surrounding proposed Corsican language legislation. Successful language legislation has been briefly sketched in Chapter 4; here we will look at both the motions that passed and the motions and amendments that failed to be approved, delving into Assembly transcripts and sociolinguistic survey responses to tease out the linguistic philosophies and ideologies shaping public opinion.

The main story in the first part of the chapter revolves around the repeated failure of motions making Corsican language instruction mandatory. This failure has not, as the overview of language activism in the last chapter shows, prevented significant gains in the institutional status of Corsican, nor has it prevented a language bill with far-reaching implications and significant budgetary support from passing the Assembly in the summer of 1997. Yet even in this most recent resolution, which makes enrolment in Corsican language classes the default choice, and requires parents to take active steps to exempt their children from those classes, the word "obligation" is conspicuously absent, and was struck from the wording of the final document by a majority vote during Assembly deliberations.

I read the rejection of "official" and "obligatory" status for Corsican in proposed language legislation between 1985 and 1997 as an index of popular opposition to language planning measures these that has its roots in a passive resistance of separation in which the meaning and value of Corsican is carefully cordoned off from the official, authoritative and authoritarian domains of the dominant language. Described in this way, this sort of resistance illustrates the pervasive hold of essentialist models of language and identity and does not challenge a diglossic system in which the minority language is excluded from the powerful linguistic marketplace occupied by the dominant language. Yet, I will also argue that this resistance of separation shows evidence of a political consciousness; it reflects an understanding of the relationship between linguistic prescriptions and social power that we have seen in the "strategic essentialism" of some language activists. That is, in arguments against mandatory bilingual education, we will see Corsicans resisting Corsican language planning from the same position that some Corsican language planners resisted French domination.

I argue that this popular resistance is one catalyst for changes in the discourse and strategies of language activists that I document in the second part of the chapter, which takes up where Chapter 4 leaves off, and brings the description of academic language planning ideologies up to date. These changes include the replacement of *mandatory bilingualism* with *coofficiality*, of *diglossia* with *polynomy* and of *mother tongue* with *Lingua Matria*. These discursive shifts signal a movement away from a Corsican monolingual norm; that is, toward a model of Corsican language identity that is not created in the image of French. In the context of a resistance of separation, lodging Corsican in an alternate field of values from French clearly has its advantages. At the same time, a "plurilingual" norm violates deeply rooted understandings of what a legitimate language is, and complicates the use of Corsican as a marker of bounded identity.

1.1. Background for the debates: the early eighties

While I will be drawing in some contemporary quotes from Corsican Assembly members' 1997 debates, I will be doing so primarily to mark the continuity of certain themes. The bulk of my data, however, comes from an earlier time frame, and here I will briefly sketch the context in which these early debates on language took place.

In 1983, the first Corsican Assembly operated in a climate of optimism. The very creation of the Assembly was the work of a new, Socialist government, whose President (François Mittérand) had publicly affirmed his commitment to the preservation of Corsican cultural and linguistic diversity in a visit to the island. In the deliberations preceding the vote of the final motion, politicians from all political persuasions took the opportunity to voice their attachment to Corsican language and culture. No one in the chamber, not even an Assemblyman who got up to say that he wanted to make a full claim on Corsican identity despite the fact that he did not speak Corsican, disputed the "essential" link between Corsican language and culture. No one opposed the teaching of the language. But the Assembly was deeply divided over the issue of mandatory Corsican language education, with those opposing it in the majority: the final resolution on language adopted by the Assembly in 1983 (see Chapter 4) is a strong statement of support for Corsican, but it does not prescribe how it will be taught.

The 1983 legislation was immediately rejected by then Prime Minister Mauroy, who stated that given the pressing needs to educate French schoolchildren in ever-expanding domains of knowledge (presumably technical and scientific), it was not possible for the government to impose instruction of Corsican language and culture on those who did not want it. At the time of this rejection, the Corsican Assembly was plagued by other political problems which led to its dissolution.

The next move came in 1985, when Castellani, an autonomist representative to the Assembly, brought a new motion on bilingualism to the floor. The Castellani motion was based on the results of a 1984 round table on bilingualism organized by the CCECV to which political leaders from all parties had been invited. The motion called for Corsican language teaching to be made obligatory for the state while remaining optional for the student, which had been the consensus opinion to emerge from the round table. As an aside, it is important to recognize that obliging the state to provide Corsican language education for the primary grades makes taking Corsican classes the default choice, since parents have to go out of their way to pull their child out of a part of the curriculum.[10] Despite the wide political representation at the round table, its consensus dissolved in the Assembly. The lengthy debate on this motion resulted in an impasse: unable to agree on either the principle or its execution, the Assembly effectively tabled the matter by voting to convene another ad hoc committee to study the question.

1.2. *Sources of data and survey results*

In the following section, I draw on two main sources of data: published deliberations from Assembly sessions in 1983, 1985, and 1997 and interview and questionnaire data gathered as part of my 1988–1989 data collection on language attitudes. In this research, I questioned people about their support for mandatory Corsican language education. My written survey included the question: "Should the teaching of Corsican be mandatory?" Respondents were asked to write short rationales for their answers and these answers were explored in interviews. I also asked respondents to characterize the quality and quantity of current Corsican language education and to say whether or not they thought it was sufficient. The sample size for the written survey was 160, and I followed up with interviews with 60 of those people. My sample was not as demographically representative as I had hoped;[11] most importantly for this discussion, it was probably ideologically biased since those who made themselves accessible to me were more likely than not to be in favor of mandatory Corsican language education.

The statistical results can be summarized as follows: 50% of the sample was in favor of mandatory Corsican language education; 33% was against, and 3% was undecided. We can note that 16% of the respondents did not respond at all to the question, which is an indicator that the question was a sensitive one. Given the built-in bias of my sample, I am inclined to see these results as exaggerating the extent of public support for mandatory bilingualism in 1989, an interpretation that is supported by the political outcomes, above. It is also interesting to see how responses to this question correlate with responses to another survey question which asked people to comment on the quality and quantity of language teaching in the schools at the time. Twenty-two percent of those who thought that Corsican was not taught enough in the schools were either against making that teaching mandatory or had a null response to the question. To put it another way, 44% of those who were against mandatory Corsican education were, in principle, in favor of increasing the amount of Corsican taught in the schools. This shows the extent to which it is the mandatory nature of the instruction, and not the instruction itself, that is at issue.

2. Support for mandatory Corsican

2.1. The primordial link

One current of support of mandatory teaching of Corsican was based on the notion of Corsican as a cultural birthright. In the 1983 debate, the autonomist Assemblyman C. Santoni referred to the "millions of dead Corsican ancestors" in a speech he read from a written text in Corsican (that was included in the official record) saying, *"...si a nostra lingua veni à spariscià, ùn campanu eddi, chè à traversu à la nostra lingua, postu chì in la nostra lingua ci hanu datu tuttu cio c'eddi avianu aquistatu, è si a lingua veni à spariscià, eddi tornanu à mora è i intarraremu una siconda volta"* [...if our language dies out, they only live through our language, because it is in our language that they gave us everything they accomplished, and if the language dies out, they will die once over and we will have to bury them for a second time].[12] Here, the link between language and culture is both primordial and exclusive: the only possible vehicle for Corsican culture is the Corsican language.

There were several survey respondents who, somewhat less dramatically, came out in favor of having Corsican as a mandatory subject on the basis of its natural link with a Corsican culture that they thought it was important to preserve. One respondent did this by writing simply, *"Parce qu'il est parlé"* [Because it is spoken]. Others went into more detail:

"Sur le territoire corse, il serait normal [de l'enseigner]...en tout cas, cette instruction ne pourrait pas être nocive. Les allergiques peuvent toujours s'installer ailleurs..."
[On Corsican territory, it should be normal [to teach it]... in any case, teaching it could not do any harm. Those who are allergic can always go and live somewhere else...]

"Il est important pour toutes les régions de retenir leurs identités, leurs traditions, tout ce qui leur rend différentes, afin de ne pas tout fondre dans l'anonymat."
[It is important for all regions to retain their identities, their traditions, everything that makes them different, in order to avoid melting into anonymity.]

"Raisons! Parce que c'est notre vie, notre culture, nos racines...bien que je me reconnaisse autant dans la culture française. Mais ce que nous avons, nous devons garder."
[Reasons! Because it is our life, our culture, our roots...even though I identify myself equally with French culture. But what we have, we need to hold on to.]

In written survey results, other respondents voiced a nationalist/autonomist position on language that made the link between cultural identity and political sovereignty explicit:

"Étant la langue de la Nation Corse, elle devrait avoir la même importance que le français dans la vie courante en France."
[Being the language of the Corsican nation, Corsican should have the same importance as French in contemporary French life.]

"S'il reste optionnel, il souffrira un coup mortel en peu de temps. Il est absolument nécessaire qu'il soit une langue à part entière, c'est-à-dire, coofficielle avec le français. Comment peut-il avoir un Peuple Corse sans l'affirmation et l'expression de sa langue? Comment parler de la culture corse sans parler de la langue corse?"
[If it remains optional, it will soon suffer a mortal blow. It is absolutely necessary for it to be an independent language, that is, coofficial with French. How can you have a Corsican people without the affirmation and expression of its language? How can you speak of Corsican culture without speaking about the Corsican language?]

"Du moment qu'une langue est le véhicule–et de la vie intellectuelle et du quotidien–d'un peuple ou d'une ethnie, elle devrait être obligatoire."
[From the moment that a language is the vehicle–of both everyday and intellectual life–of a people or an ethnic group, it ought to be mandatory.]

In reference to the question of political parity, two respondents evoked Resolution 192 of the European Council, which affirms the rights of linguistic minorities. This resolution was aimed at establishing aggressive programs for the promotion of regional/minority languages and culture by member states. France did sign on to the resolution but had made few changes in its linguistic policies at the time of the poll.

2. 2. *Acknowledging language shift: a sense of urgency*

Those who were in favor of making Corsican language a mandatory subject were unanimous in painting a dire sociolinguistic picture: they saw the threat of language death as a real and immediate one. Ferrandi, an Assembly member in 1983, remarked that while a policy of "encouragement" rather than "obligation" struck him as philosophically "more desirable," he was afraid that *"à travers cette politique d'incitation on ne noie le poisson, excusez-moi de le dire"* [with this policy of encouragement, one will end up, if you'll excuse me for saying so, drowning the fish]. *"Imaginons,"* [Let us imagine] he went on to say, *"aujourd'hui la France soit annexée par les États-Unis, et que sur les televisions françaises, et que dans la presse française, on parle anglais. Je me demande ce que deviendrait le français dans deux cent ans; il aurait regressé, il serait certainement une language de plus en plus minorisée"* [that today, France was annexed by the United States, and on French televisions and in the French press, one spoke English. What would French become in two hundred years, I ask myself: it would say that it would regress, it would certainly be increasingly diminished]. The analogy was clear: after two hundred years of French language domination, Corsican was on a downhill path.

It was not just the fact of language shift that gave a sense of urgency to politicians like Ferrandi, and language activists like Castellani (who authored the 1985 resolution and was an autonomist Assemblyman in 1983). They were also motivated by the limited practical results of a decade of language revitalization efforts. Insofar as education was concerned, Corsican's feeble institutional status under the Deixonne law was one obvious problem. This law had not provided for the pedagogical/institutional structures (teacher training, textbooks, scheduling, examinations) which make language teaching effective. Moreover, the optional nature of the instruction meant that it depended on the motivation and support of parents, teachers and administrators. In any given school district, lack of support from any one of these constituencies could undermine the Corsican language teaching effort. It was clear in 1983 (as it is today) that the absence of mandates led to uneven quantity and quality of education. A child might have two years of excellent Corsican language teaching followed by none at all. Corsican might be offered during prime hours in one school and at 8 a.m. on a Saturday in another. One teacher's version of Corsican teaching might involve having children recite a few poems or songs in the language, while another might employ a full range of language teaching strategies and incorporate the use of the language throughout the school day.

As one Assembly member said in the course of the debate preceding the 1983 motion, "*l'expérience facultative est bâtarde et source de dépense inutiles. Le choix est donc entre tout ou rien. C'est pourquoi nous sommes favorables à l'enseignment du corse de la maternselle à l'université, malgré le côté contraignant de cette solution*" [the experience of being an optional subject has been a wretched waste of money. It's an all or nothing choice. That is why we are in favor of Corsican classes from preschool to University, despite the constraining nature of this solution].[13]

But the reason that weak educational structures were cause for such concern was because language planners had also *not* seen a significant effort to reverse language shift in the general population. There had been no mass movement towards "reacquisition" of Corsican such as the early militants had seen in the adult Corsican language classes organized in Paris and elsewhere on the continent in the seventies. Those politicians who supported mandatory Corsican classes made explicit reference to past and current failures of Corsican speakers to transmit the language to their children. So, for example there was Luciani, who said in 1983 that the linguistic problem they faced was one for which they all had "coresponsibility". He included as "coresponsible" the French state, and "Corsicans as a whole," since "*il est vrai que la langue s'apprend d'abord à la maison, et que nos propres parents, trop souvent ont oublié de nous l'enseigner*"[it is true that the language is learned above all in the home, and that our own parents forgot all too often to teach it to us].

The case for mandatory education thus cast blame historically as well as contemporaneously; the school was a means of correcting the failures of transmission of the past and sidestepping the problem of unsupportive/apathetic parents in the present. In other words, with their support of mandatory bilingualism, they abandoned hope in the Corsican language as a popular cause. This abandonment was clearly difficult to reconcile with the image of the language as a "natural" foundation of Corsican cultural identity. Some responded to this difficulty by talking about Corsican language education as a way of "sensitizing" people to the value of the language. In doing so, they implicitly separated identity (which remained constant and authentic) from sensibility or consciousness (which fluctuated in response to historical/social conditions). Others adhered to a more

Whorfian view that speaking a heritage language could recreate a lost cultural unity. For these people, mandatory Corsican classes were a last resort in the face of a lack of collective will–they offered the possibility of convincing a handful of individuals, who might be the vectors of a greater collective linguistic conscience in the future.

Fourteen years later, in the course of 1997 Assembly deliberations, the comments of an Assemblyman (Stefani) showed that shifting the locus of cultural preservation from the public/familial to the educational domain had been a pivotal, and contentious issue. He voiced his approval of the proposed motions saying,

> *"Il y a des principes fondamentaux qui sont repris dans ce document, notamment que l'enseignement doit être le pilier de la réappropriation de la langue, ce qui n'était pas le cas jusqu'à aujourd'hui puisqu'on renvoyait sans cesse aux familles."*
>
> [There are some fundamental principles that are taken up in this document, particularly that teaching should be the foundation of the reappropriation of the language, something that has not been the case up until now because [responsibilty] was always placed on the family.]

Some survey respondents and language planners viewed Corsican language education as a viable way of actually creating new Corsican speakers. Others were skeptical about the level of fluency and practice likely to be achieved by school instruction, but were committed to providing some sort of stopgap in the face of failures of parental transmission.

2.3. The pragmatic effects of symbolic action: legitimacy and language attitudes

Many people looked at the value of Corsican language education as having a more indirect effect on practice. They evoked the link between status and attitude, saying that official, mandatory status for Corsican would convince parents and students that the language was being taken seriously, and prompt them to take it seriously as well. As one of the respondents wrote,

> *"Le choix des sujets optionnels est fait le plus souvent pour des raisons utilitaires. Si le corse reste optionnel, il continuera à être peu choisi et disparaîtra."*
>
> [The choice of optional subjects is most often made for utilitarian reasons. If Corsican remains optional, it will continue to be chosen infrequently and will disappear.]

The continued salience of this utilitarian focus can be seen in the comments one teacher made at a roundtable on Corsican language teaching in 1993. *"Quand'è vo dumandate à un parente chì hà cinque figlioli 'Cuuficialità, chì ne pensate? Bislinguismu, chì ne pensate?' dice "Chì i mo cinque figlioli dumane appiinu u stentapane!"* [When you ask a parent with five children, 'What do you think of coofficiality? What do you think of bilingualism?' he/she says, 'I think that I want my five children learn how to earn a living in the future!'] (*Arritti* 1993, 1386: 9).

The school curriculum emerges in this discourse as providing both symbolic and pragmatic incentives for people to speak Corsican. First, the school is an institution which both prepares students for the job market and constitutes, in itself, a significant marketplace for the conferral of rewards (grades) that have economic repercussions. A subject that is treated seriously by the school acquires utilitarian value. Quastana (who has held several positions overseeing Corsican language education since the late eighties) put it this way in the 1997 Assembly deliberations:

> *"On dépense des millions de francs* 'è ùn c'è mancu un zitellu chì sorta di a scola parlendu u corsu'...*pour sauver la langue corse, il n'y a qu'une solution, c'est de rattacher la langue à la réussite sociale. C'est-à-dire: si on veut réussir, il faut parler le corse; le corse doit être dans les examens, le corse doit être dans les concours d'entrée des administrations, le corse doit être au baccalauréat avec un coéfficient important, au moins égal à celui du français."*

> [We spend millions of francs and '*there isn't one kid who comes out of school speaking Corsican'*...to save the Corsican language, there is only one solution, which is to connect it to social success. That is to say, if you want to succeed, you have to speak Corsican; Corsican should be in exams, Corsican should be in the administrative entry tests, Corsican should be part of the *baccalauréat* [High School exams] weighted significantly [with respect to the overall grade], at least as significantly as French.]

In addition to the fact that the school is a significant part of the linguistic marketplace, parents and students also read the content and implementation of the curriculum as a symbolic indicator of the social status of a particular subject. This emerges in comments made to me by both students and their parents. Students told me that the fact that Corsican classes were scheduled late in the evening or early Saturday morning, or the lack of seriousness or rigor (on the part of students and teachers) in some Corsican classes were clear signs that the subject was undervalued by the school. Some parents reported to me that their children had dropped Corsican as a result of these kinds of experiences and observations. It was also clear that exams played a significant role in shaping both parental and student attitudes. Some parents reminded me that at the *Collège* (ages 11–14) level, optional subjects had no exams, which was a sufficient reason in and of itself for students to dismiss them as unimportant. The impact of exams on parents' attitudes and behaviors was confirmed for me by a discussion with a woman who taught Corsican classes in an after school program at a youth center. She had seen her enrollments rise dramatically when parents realized that their children were going to be tested in Corsican at school.

Some other brief examples from my fieldwork suggest how the insertion of Corsican into the taken-for-granted authoritative practices and routines of the school served to socially legitimate the language among people who were not actively involved in ideological debates over Corsican language education. Having gotten to know two mothers of primary school children through a Parents' Association, I went with them to sit in on some Corsican lessons. The two women participated with great enthusiasm in a very basic Corsican spelling test their seven-year old children were taking, and sang along with the class when the teacher led them in Corsican songs. The mothers did not do very well on the spelling test, even though they said they had learned a little from their children's homework. Both said they would like to go to the classes at the school more often, but did not want to disrupt the class. Neither woman spoke Corsican often; neither one would have been likely to make the effort to drive twenty miles to the closest major city to take adult evening courses in Corsican which were offered there, but insofar as this instruction concerned their children, they had become involved. In the village of Riventosa where I lived during my fieldwork, I also saw the way that children's Corsican homework engaged children in talking in (or at least about) the language with their elders.

2.4. Summary

If we look at the rationales given by politicians and my survey respondents, we see that legislation aimed at officializing Corsican and making it a mandatory school subject had both practical and symbolic goals. It was intended to: (a) be a practical tool of language transmission: preventing language death by stepping in where the family was not; (b) raise the status of Corsican among Corsicans and indirectly contribute to its maintenance through extra scholastic (family) transmission; (c) claim the same unchallenged linguistic and cultural authority and legitimacy accorded to French (to the state and to Corsicans and (d) symbolize cultural identity and unity (with various goals, including political autonomist ones).

These goals have both persuasive and coercive elements, which are linked to the tension between the image of Corsican as a primordial heritage (reflected in the possessive in the phrase "giving the people *their* language back") and the problem of decline in Corsican language practice and competence. The phrase "giving the people their language back" also places agency squarely in the hands of language planners; they are not talking about officially sanctioning existing, minority language practices and language values, but rather, about creating new social fields of value by allowing and requiring the practice of the minority language. In other words, the text of the 1983 motion reveals the militants of the eighties trying to work the attitudes–practice relation in reverse by tapping into the power of (imposed) practice to influence attitudes. In doing so, they attempted to harness not only the symbolic power of dominant models of language, but also the material power of the process of domination itself. The enforced practice of French, just as much as ideological hierarchies, had led to the devaluation of Corsican. The institutions of French public life had forced French on them; now they would use those same institutions to force Corsican on themselves.

3. The argument against mandatory Corsican: "choice" and oppositional value

Those who opposed mandatory Corsican disagreed on the legitimacy of the use of any form of coercion as well as about the meaning and value for Corsican culture of teaching Corsican in the schools. The most frequently cited reason for opposing mandatory bilingualism was an objection to any limits on freedom of choice. Survey respondents came to this position from a variety of philosophical perspectives. As the numerical survey results suggest, there were those who were for Corsican language instruction, but against the idea of it being imposed. This was the case for Bungelmi, an Assembly member who said in 1983,

> "*Nous proclamons notre opposition a l'obligation...par contre nous reclamons des moyens toujours plus importants pour l'enseignement du corse a tous les niveaux.*"
> [We proclaim our opposition to obligation...on the other hand, we advocate increasing support for the teaching of Corsican at all levels.]

A survey respondent replied in a similar vein, writing,

*"Liberté de choix, mais les structures pédagogiques ont besoin d'être
beaucoup plus développés qu'elles ne sont."*
[Freedom of choice, but pedagogical structures need to be much better
developed than they are now.]

Some respondents articulated the argument for freedom of choice with
reference to universal principles of democracy and human rights:

*"Nous ne sommes pas un état totalitaire... lisez l'Article 10 de la Déclaration
des Droits de l'Homme."*
[We aren't a totalitarian state...read Article 10 of the Declaration of the Rights of
Man.]

*"Imposer le corse serait une atteinte grave à la démocratie et aux droits de
l'homme...les jeunes sont usités de leurs travaux à l'école, où ils apprennent
l'indispensable pour survivre; est-il raisonnable, pour soi-disant raisons
culturelles, leur imposer encore un sujet?"*
[To impose Corsican would be a serious threat to democracy and to human
rights...young people are worn out by their schoolwork, where they are taught what
they need to know to survive; is it reasonable, for so-called cultural reasons, to
impose yet another subject on them?]

In the 1997 Assembly debate on language, these sentiments were expressed
in the strongest form by the Assemblyman Chiarelli, who (after saying in
Corsican that he "loved Corsican as well as anyone and spoke it pretty well)
asserted:

*"Il y a une chose qui me heurte c'est cette obligation detournée, à mon avis,
du corse, du fait même qu'on oblige les gens à l'inscription.....Je crois que
puisqu'on parle de corse, nous sommes très attaches à "a Santa Liberta".
Alors, toutes obligations me heurtent en bon démocrate."*
[There is one thing that affronts me, that is what is in my opinion a misguided
{insistence on} obligation, that resides in the very fact that we oblige people
to register {for school}...I think that since we are speaking about Corsican, we
are all very attached to our '*Sacred Liberty*'. So, all obligations offend me as
a good democrat.]

I would argue that the use of this human rights discourse with regard to a
school subject is rhetorical hyperbole,[14] but this does not mean that it
exaggerates Corsican cultural resistance to that which is imposed. If we
explore this resistance, we find that it has several facets and origins.

3.1. "Choice" and language hierarchy

In the penultimate quotation, for example, the rhetoric of "freedom of choice" is clearly related to the undervaluation of Corsican. Comments like the last one echo Prime Minister Mauroy's rationale for rejecting the 1983 language bill. In the 1985 debate, several members of the Corsican Assembly voiced objections on the same order ("how can we fit this into students' busy schedules?"). Just below the surface of this discourse is language hierarchy. While there is no reason to make the effort to "fit in" or "impose" a subject that is not "important" or "necessary for survival," there are no objections raised to the imposition of "important" subjects. French language and culture are important and necessary, Corsican language and culture are not.

Some respondents in the survey who opposed mandatory Corsican made this practical and symbolic language hierarchy even more explicit, saying that Corsican should not be taught because it was a "dialect". In the 1985 Assembly debate, several Assembly members evoked the "dialect" status indirectly by citing Corsican dialectal diversity as an insurmountable pedagogical obstacle ("But which Corsican shall we teach?" they asked). Others labeled it a language but said it was disqualified as a school subject because it was "neither official nor a vehicle of everyday communication," or "without power or utility". One person wrote, *"À quoi bon ça sert ailleurs? Le français est la langue des relations internationales"* [What is it good for elsewhere? French is the language of international relations]. A student at the University commented, *"Les gens du village me disaient,* Amparate prima u francese, dopu pudete amparà u corsu" [People in the village said to me, *learn French first, then you can learn Corsican*].[15] He also told me that even though his parents and other villagers liked the fact that he studied Corsican at college, and that he spoke to them, they continued to reject the idea of mandatory Corsican education.

3.2. "Choice" as the cornerstone of language value

The attitude of these villagers was not uncommon, and is reflected in other arguments given by survey respondents in which they insisted on the intrinsic value of Corsican language and culture, but located that value in the individual's voluntary choice to speak the language. This sentiment is a logical outcome of the experience of diglossia: as we have seen, few Corsophones have learned Corsican outside the voluntary, affective domain, and Corsican is important to them *because* it is not imposed like French (see McDonald 1989:154). Here, we see a familiar pattern, in which Corsican identity is asserted on the basis of maximal distance from things French. This makes sense of the Corsican politician's assertion in the 1985 debate on the Castellani bill, that he had the impression that he was contributing to the death of his mother tongue. We have also seen this essentialization of oppositional identity in early reactions to the officialization of Corsican spellings of place names on road signs: recall the mayor of Venaco's advocacy of using a French grapheme as a sort of prophylactic between strangers and the local code of intimacy.[16] The fact that mispronunciation of a place name by strangers is seen as polluting indicates the extent to which Corsicans view Corsican linguistic space as private.

As a consequence of these attitudes, learning Corsican in school was viewed by some people as a contaminating, deauthenticating act (see the following chapter). One person wrote that anyone who wanted to learn Corsican was not really Corsican, because "*un Corse serait trop fier, mettre son enfant dans un cours de corse*" [a Corsican would be too proud to put his child in a Corsican language class]. This last remark returns us to the theme of familial transmission of the language, and paints a picture of social change brought about by years of linguistic and cultural activism. That is, it is only in a context in which speaking Corsican is positively valued, and in which maintenance of cultural identity is cast in terms of individual (civic) responsibility that the failure to speak or transmit the language would be a face-threatening act. The comment also implicitly acknowledges that these "failures" of transmission have taken place.

Other respondents, however, explicitly denied widespread change in the sociolinguistic landscape. Like some of their opponents on the issue of mandatory Corsican teaching, they painted a portrait of the language in good health in comments such as:

"*Dans chaque maison, il y en a qui parlent corse. Il ne faut pas qu'il soit obligatoire. Peut-être qu'il continuera à être parlé spontanément.*"
[In every home, there are people who speak Corsican. It is not necessary for it to be mandatory. Maybe it will continue to be spoken spontaneously.]

"*Le corse s'apprend en famille. Il faut le parler.*"
[Corsican is learned in the family. It has to be spoken.]

"*Habitant en Corse, tout le monde finit par le parler et le comprendre.*"
[Living in Corsica, everyone ends up speaking and understanding it.]

This genre of comments is fairly common, both among politicians and by ordinary people. How do we explain such assessments in the context of widespread and seemingly obvious significant language shift? One kind of explanation has to do with the range of personal experiences afforded by a situation of language shift plus diglossia. The diglossic exclusion or reduction of Corsican from many public and institutional domains has never prevented interactions in Corsican in the private sphere of intimate and family relations. Arguably, this exclusion has intensified the meaningfulness of such inner-sphere use of Corsican. The habitual Corsican speaker does indeed "choose" to speak Corsican in many situations, and does not feel particularly constrained by the presence of French in official life. These frequent speakers were more likely to be over 45, but there were also some young people who grew up in contexts where Corsican was widely spoken. One young man enrolled in the Law School at the University of Corsica told me that his desire to learn to read and write Corsican stemmed from his early astonishment, as a child entering school, that French, which he heard spoken around him, was taught, but the Corsican which he had also always heard, was not. Most importantly, the diglossic compartmentalization of language practices means that people cannot infer with total confidence private language choice or language preference from public sphere practice. In effect, diglossia in contexts of language domination helps to mask the effects of language domination and the extent of language shift, since people who hear French being used can always imagine its users in another, Corsican-speaking context.

An alternate, and I think equally compelling way of reading these statements in the context of negative attitudes about mandatory Corsican teaching is to view them as a metalinguistic discourse that reflects the image that these Corsicans are prepared to accept of the state of the language. In the same way that having to learn Corsican (or having one's child have to learn Corsican) could be individually deauthenticating, the requirement to teach it could be seen as collectively deauthenticating.

3.3. The discourse of "choice": Corsican identity and the rejection of that which is imposed

In addition to the issue of the need for language intervention, there was also the question of the consequences of doing so. A number of respondents felt that imposing Corsican would have a negative cultural effect, by provoking student rejection:

> "*Toute imposition est la source de résistance.*"
> [Every imposition is the source of resistance.]

"La langue ne devrait pas faire partie d'un système contraignant comme l'enseignement obligatoire. Le corse doit rester une langue que l'on aime parler, et parle volontiers...les aspects pénibles de l'apprentissage d'une langue, comme la grammaire, pourrait le faire perdre son charme; il y aurait aussi le risque que cet enseignement ferait parler mal le corse, parce que les cours de langue mettent l'accent toujours sur l'écrit, et pas l'orale. Le corse doit être parlé spontanément, comme il l'a toujours été jusqu'au présent."
[The language should not be part of a restrictive system like mandatory education. Corsican should remain a language that one likes to speak, and speaks willingly...troublesome aspects of language learning, like grammar, could make it lose its charm; there would also be the risk that this instruction would lead to poor oral Corsican, since language courses always emphasize the written over the oral. Corsican should be spoken spontaneously, as it has always been up until now.]

"Non. Ce qui est imposé est souvent rejeté et la mauvaise santé du corse ne permet pas ce risque d'echec...l'idéal serait que le corse soit choisi spontané-ment."
[No. That which is imposed is often rejected, and the ill-health of Corsican does not permit this risk of failure...the ideal would be that Corsican would be chosen spontaneously.]

Comments like these last ones index Corsican assumptions about human motivation and attitudes towards the exercise of power that I have sketched in Chapter 2. One pole of Corsican identity defines the individual in terms of his or her attachments and obligations to others. Corsicans expect other Corsicans to be motivated by self-interest broadly defined in terms of some sort of collective (family, regional, political) concerns. Collectively, the struggle for material and symbolic resources is viewed as a zero-sum game. This means that meeting one's social obligations automatically pits one against others doing the same thing. This is consistent with another pole of Corsican identity, which revolves around the public display of autonomy and independence. Other Corsicans' agendas are, therefore, likely to be viewed with suspicion. And resisting them is a valuable form of identity work in and of itself. Language planning measures are not exempt from this kind of logic, and are not automatically assumed to be benign, disinterested acts which benefit everyone equally. Bungelmi, mentioned above, explained his rejection of mandatory education within this framework. He prefaced the comments below with: *"Nous refusons l'illusion du monolinguisme français, comme du monolinguisme corse"* [We refuse the fallacy of French monolingualism, and by the same token, Corsican monolingualism]. This monolingualism, for Bungelmi, is intimately linked with the idea of a norm, and he balks at the imposition of a norm for Corsican

"*Toute langue a vocation d'être ecrite. Mais selon quelle norme?...Nous repoussons, quant à nous, l'obligation, la contrainte. Nous sommes pour une politique d'incitation à un bilinguisme assumé, mais pour une mise en place progressive, ce qui suppose que les problèmes de norme soient progressivement reglés par les masses et non par les autorités. On ne peut, ni on ne doit essayer d'agir par decret en ce domaine. Et qui est fondé à prendre de tels decrets?*"

[Every language is destined to be written. But according to what norm?...For our part, we reject obligation, constraint. We are for a policy encouraging people to take up the cause of bilingualism, but with a progressive implementation in which, presumably, problems of the norm will be progressively solved by the masses and not by the authorities. One cannot and should not act by decree in this domain. And who has the right to do so?]

3.4. Choice and the mother tongue

If we review what people say about resisting imposition, we see that they differ in their assessment of how well the process of spontaneous choice is working for the language. What they share is a perspective on the relationship between Corsican language and culture which is romantic, but is not necessarily essentialist. That is, they do not identify Corsican itself (either in the abstract or as spoken practice) as being critical to Corsican identity. Rather, they base the importance of Corsican for Corsican identity on the quality of the attachment speakers have to the language. The love of the language is what counts, and this cannot be taught. The imposition of language courses is not so much deauthenticating as it is unmeaningful. As one respondent put it: "*L'apprendre à l'école est mécanique, pas maternel. Il est enseigné comme s'il était l'anglais. Le corse doit être ressenti comme une partie de l'esprit, de la vie*" [Learning it in school is mechanical, not maternal. It is taught as if it were English. Corsican should be felt to be a part of the spirit, a part of life].

This sentiment was shared by Petru Mari, a bilingual journalist, who remarked in a 1993 rountable on language teaching that not many Corsicans seemed convinced that their children should learn Corsican in school, and went on to say that: "*Eppò puru s'elli a fessinu, in casa ùn ci n'hè unu annant'à deci chì parla u corsu naturalemente. Face chì puru s'elli puntessinu à fà chì i figlioli scelganu u corsu, seria una materia cum'è l'altra, inutile cum'elli a piglianu diciaremu l'istruzzione civica*" [Even if they were, there are only about one in ten who speak Corsican naturally. This means that even if they were to make a point of encouraging their children to choose

Corsican as a subject, it would just be a subject like any other one, as useless as those who take civics say that course is](*Arritti* 1991, 1386: 9).

As Wald (1986:115) writes, when a minority language is standardized, *"il perd par le même mouvement ce qui pourrait le rendre 'maternel': son indifférenciation et son antériorité à toute catégorisation"* [it loses in this very movement that which could make it "maternal": its lack of differentiation and its historical resistance to all forms of categorization]. Heller describes a similar reaction of Franco-Ontarian parents, who feared that anglophone access to their schools "would change the nature of the linguistic resource distributed, taking what had been a symbolic emblem of ethnic identity and turning it into a mere technical means of communication" (1994:110). The potential for a minority language to suffer from its institutionalization is also reported by McDonald, who writes that enrolments in Breton language classes at the *Collège* level dropped after these classes were made part of the regular curriculum. "Breton was now a subject to be treated like any other subject," she writes, and students were dismayed that it was "no longer fun," and carried the risk of academic failure (1989: 65–66). Both the definition of the school as the polar opposite of the domain in which the value of Corsican is located, and personal experiences of the French school system undoubtedly contributed to these respondents' skepticism that anything to do with local culture, or deep emotional value could be transmitted in the schools.

As Wald suggests, the allusion to the mother tongue is also part of a discourse in which the social and economic determinants of language choices are minimized. This comes out very clearly in a recent report on the bilingual nursery school that was opened in Corté. In it, the author wrote that fundamental problem had to be faced: *"Si toutes les mères corses parlaient corse à leurs enfants dès la naissance, pouvait-il y avoir une seule force extérieure capable de porter atteinte à notre langue, qu'il s'agisse d'un État, de l'argent, ou de je ne sais quoi?"* [If all Corsican mothers spoke Corsican to their children from the moment of their birth, could there possibly be any single outside force capable of damaging our language, be it a state, money, or I don't know what?] (Piroddi 1994:14). This perspective is reflected in the *Scola Corsa* poster reproduced in Chapter 3 (*"O Ma, parlami Corsu"*)

4. Lingua Matria

In 1988 and 1989, the CCECV's language committee undertook to change some of the terms of public discourse about language. Their first publication in 1989 took on the notion of the mother tongue, and was titled *Lingua Matria*. Both this term, which the committee coined, and the format of the document were intended to mediate diglossic concepts of language. First of all, it was trilingual, with a Corsican, French and English version.[17] Although the English version had no practical value, it had a great deal of symbolic significance. First of all, bringing in a language other than French had the value of undermining the status of French as the sole point of reference and authority (something we have seen in the italianist position in Chapter 4). Secondly, making the document trilingual indexed a shadow audience or readership that went beyond the boundaries of the island. This was a rhetorical device which did not depend on an actual anglophone readership to put the reader on notice that the perspective and themes of the document were intended to be a shift from customary discourse about language and identity on Corsica. Thirdly, including a language of international power was a declaration of independence from the idea of domination. It proclaimed that the value of Corsican could only be complemented, not threatened, from contact with the Other, powerful or not.

The title, *Lingua Matria*, stands in implicit opposition to the notion of the *Lingua Materna* [mother tongue] so often used to describe Corsican. *Lingua Materna*, as we have seen, evokes the domain of the family and the intimate bond between mother and child; it is connected with a discourse of "essential" identity. In contrast, *matria* [Motherland], the feminine version of *patria* [Fatherland], is connected with a discourse of political identities, invoking the national, political domain and relationships between citizens.

The reasons for this shift in label are explained in the following passage: "Corsican is no longer the first language acquired, even though the status of maternal language is still attributed to it. Thus this source of confusion and even conflict needs to be replaced with a new idea which is consistent with reality: the language is neither maternal nor foreign, but a creative source of identity: LINGUA MATRIA" (CCECV 1989a:15). The authors also emphasized the hybrid nature of Corsican linguistic practice and cultural identity, suggesting that neither Corsican dual identity nor Corsican bilingualism were balanced and that Corsicans had internalized criteria of value from the dominant culture with which they disparaged their own identities. One of the lines of the document read, "to pursue the metaphor of a citadel under siege, we are aware that we are not only within its walls, but also outside, with the attackers."

It is interesting to compare the notion of the *Lingua Matria* with the model of linguistic kinship proposed by Comiti in the last chapter. Both Comiti and the CCECV committee members started from the assumption that Corsicans had the right to claim Corsican as the language of the Corsican people. Because of the close association of "maternal" with "essential" identity, Comiti uses a *paternal* metaphor in his assertion of the political basis for linguistic autonomy. With *Lingua Matria*, the CCECV evoked the sureness of maternity in a new term which fuses the affective with the political. The text makes it clear that *Lingua Matria* is not a cultural essence (or an innate ability) but rather, a cultural right that every Corsican could claim. The act of claiming it (for example, by learning it in the schools) is an expression of cultural authenticity; it does not make Corsican a "foreign language," or divest it of its symbolic value (as we see in the discourse opposing mandatory Corsican teaching). The document emphasized the contemporary value and power of a language claimed by the community; Corsican was not a vestige of the past but rather, a resource for a changing world. This view of identity formation and legitimation is a radical break with dominant, "boundary-oriented" models; the logic of identity proposed revolves around collective will and practice.

5. Coofficiality

Later in 1989, the CCECV launched the concept of *coofficiality* as a replacement for mandatory bilingualism. The CCECV, it should be noted, is a consultative council to the Assembly, and their proposal was not a formal motion, but rather, a position paper intended to persuade both Corsican politicians in the Assembly and to sensitize the general public. The following long excerpts from their booklet include both the explanation and the official motion brought before the Assembly:

Coofficialité/*Cuuficialità*
La présence des deux langues, français et corse, est une réalité sure le territoire insulaire.
Le problème est celui de leur statut, c'est-à-dire la place officielle de l'une et de l'autre. La coofficialité est donc une mesure juridique visant à rendre officielle l'existence des deux langues.
Cela veut dire que désormais des actes rédigés en corse ou en français auraient la même valeur légale.
le principe introduit donc une notion de liberté, chacun pouvant désormais utiliser oralement ou par écrit la langue de son choix au cours des relations et des actes publics et non officiels.

Oghji, si sô calmati i passioni, cresci a cuscenza di l'identità è veni a lingua-u bisognu di a lingua-ad appuntillà issa cuscenza.
Si cheri una lingua à paru, micca par minui l'altra, micca pè strappà li pezzu. Nô! piuttostu pà arrichiscia. Arrichi un populu chî si appughjarà à dui lingui. Chî oghji, populi d'Auropa parlendu una lingua sola, ùn asistarà più.
Allora, eccu a parolla: cuufficialità.

Parolla nova, parolla paura, parolla portatimori.
Pà oghji basta à lascià andà, avanzà issa idea.
U so essa si farà pedipedi, un passu dopu
à l'altru, ch'ellu ùn avissi nimu à pianta si par
istrada chî i più belli avanzati sô quilli ch'ellu
faci un populu incù tutti i soi.

RESOLUTION

Le Conseil de la Culture, de l'Education et du Cadre de Vie a adopté le 13 novembre 1989 à Ajaccio, à l'unanimité des membres présents et représentés, en plénière, le texte sur la cooficialité préparé par le groupe LINGUA:

1) la langue française est la langue officielle commune à l'ensemble des régions,

2) la langue corse est, elle aussi, officielle sur son territoire, l'île de Corse,

3) chaque citoyen utilise à sa convenance, dans tous les domaines, l'une ou l'autre langue,

4) l'autorité publique doit garantir l'emploi courant et officiel des deux langues en créant les conditions nécessaires pour aboutir progressivement à une réelle cooficialité.

The presence of the two languages, French and Corsican, is a reality on the territory of the island.

[*Cooficiality*/Cooficiality

The presence of the two languages, French and Corsican, is a reality on the island territory.

The problem is their status, that is, the official position of each one. Cooficiality is thus a legal measure aimed at making official the existence of these two languages.

This means that henceforth [public] acts written in Corsican or French will have equal legal value.

The principle [of cooficiality] thus introduces a notion of freedom, henceforth everyone will be able to use the language of his/her choice in speech or writing in both public and unofficial interactions and documents.

Today, passions have calmed down, a sense of identity is growing, and the language–the need for the language–is coming to the aid of that growth of understanding.

The call is for an equal language, not one in order to diminish the other, not to eke out a living. No! Rather, a language to enrich–a people which can rely on two languages is enriched, in that today, European peoples speaking only one language will no longer exist.

So, here is the word: cooficiality
New word, word of fear, word of noise
For today, it is enough to just let the idea go forward
Its essence will emerge little by little, one step
at a time, so that no one will have to stop along

the way since the most beautiful steps forward are the ones
made by every member of a People.

RESOLUTION:

*The Council of Culture, Education and Quality of Life adopted in its
session of 13 November 1989 at Ajaccio, with the unanimous vote of members
present and represented, the text on coofficiality prepared by the group
LINGUA:*

1) the French language is the official language shared by all of the regions,

*2) the Corsican language is also official on its own territory, the island of
Corsica,*

*3) each citizen uses, according to his/her wishes, in all domains, either one of
these languages,*

*4) public authorities must guarantee the common and official use of the two
languages by creating the necessary conditions for the achievement of a
genuine coofficiality.*]

The document and the motion on coofficiality represented some significant
changes in philosophy compared to the two previous motions on bilingualism.
First, and most obviously, they gave French an equal, legitimate place in the
life of the island. This strategy contrasted with the previous two motions
which had, at least symbolically, proposed a Corsican monolingual norm as
a counter force to the French monolingual norm. Like the *Lingua Matria* text
that was its philosophical inspiration, the bilingual format of the coofficiality
text, as well as its content, stress that Corsican identity is expressed both
through Corsican and French. In doing so, the motion on coofficiality
departed from the implicit position of the 1983 and 1985 resolutions, which
was that Corsican is the only true expression of Corsicanness. This was not,
I should add, the only position taken in by Assembly members, and several of
them explicitly acknowledged Corsicans' bicultural and bilingual heritage.
Yet these messages were offset, in the 1983 Assembly deliberations, by the
fact that so many politicians made a point of declaring or demonstrating their
Corsican language competence as a claim on legitimate Corsican identity. We
have already read one such example above (Chiarelli); in another, Jean
Baggioni (in the course of opposing mandatory Corsican) declared that
bilingualism was "in him," since *"J'ai appris à dire* 'Oimè' *avant de dire
'J'ai mal.' J'ai appris à dire* 'O mà' *avant de dire 'Maman'"*[I learned to say
'*Oimè*' before I learned to say 'I hurt'. I learned to say '*O mà*' before I learned
to say 'Mom']. We also see the force of this implicit assumption about
language and identity in an intervention made by Pierre Pasquini, who stood
up and testified,

"Regardez-moi, je suis incontestablement et je ne m'en suis jamais caché, un Corse qui ne parle pas corse. Voyez quel paradoxe...je vous comprends tous, suffisamment lorsque vous parlez corse pour que vous m'ayez ému...il peut y avoir des garçons ou des hommes de bonne volonté, comme moi...qui ne parlent pas corse...Et en ne la possédant pas, je me sens profondément de culture corse et tout autant que chacun d'entre vous."
[Look at me, I am undeniably and I have never hidden from the fact, a Corsican who does not speak Corsican. What a paradox...I understand you all well enough when you speak Corsica to be moved by what you say...it is possible to have boys and men with good intentions, like me...who do not speak Corsican...And while I do not possess the language, I feel profoundly Corsican in a cultural way, just as much as every one of you.]

He went on to say that the happiest moment of his life had been when he felt the need to bring back his parents' remains "from thousands of miles away" to be buried in his natal village, and to know that he would be buried there too. It is notable that in order to counterbalance the symbolic power of language, he turns to what is a highly compelling collective image of a primordial attachment to place sustained through the trials of migration (and loss of language). *"Ça, c'est corse!"* [Now that, that's Corsican] he said. Nevertheless, his claim on Corsicanness did not remain uncontested. Only a few moment later, another Assembly member (D. Santoni) stood up and said,

"Personne bien entendu ne conteste qu'il soit Corse, et c'est vrai, on peut être Corse aujourd'hui sans parler la langue corse. Mais on ne pourra pas toujours l'être. S'il est Corse aujourd'hui, c'est parce qu'il y a encore des gens qui parlent la langue corse...et si un jour personne ne parlait plus corse, je doute que les gens puissent invoquer cette qualité de Corse."
[No one, of course, challenges that [Pasquini] is Corsican, and it is true, one can be Corsican today without speaking the Corsican language. But this will not be possible forever. If he is Corsican today, it is because there are still people who speak Corsican...and if one day no one spoke Corsican any more, I doubt that people would be able to claim this quality of being Corsican.]

This is not to say that the Corsican and French parts of the coofficiality document are strictly equivalent. In fact, the Corsican parts of the text are distinguished by their verse-like visual format, by their poetic meter, and by an affective dimension that is missing in the French text. These devices metaphorically accentuate Corsican as the language of deep feeling and meaning. This resonates with some of the essentialist images of Corsican strategically deployed on both sides of the bilingual education debate. The coofficiality text does identify the quality of Corsicans' attachment to Corsican as a key component of Corsican identity. Yet this document strategically disconnects the cultural status and authenticity of the Corsican language from actual practice. Corsican is not the language of Corsica because of the number of people who speak it. Rather, its value and connection with Corsican identity is linked to Corsicans' participation in the wider European community, where the authors state that monolingualism will be an exception and a handicap. There is a overt effort to depoliticize the language question: "passions have calmed," states the document (in Corsican). It insists that cooficiality means equal, noncompetitive relations between the two languages.

In a preface to the cooficiality text, the chair of the committee which drafted the motion stated explicitly that the idea of cooficiality was an attempt to keep the public eye on the issue of legal parity, and to move them away from thinking about individual bilingualism (Bassani 1991:12). We can see the reason for this: individual experiences may lead Corsicans to underestimate the need for linguistic intervention.

No explicit mention was made of schooling, and the document foregrounded individual freedom to choose a language in all domains of life. In fact, the section in Corsican almost implied a complete lack of concrete policy, proposing instead to let the idea of cooficiality percolate until it gained public acceptance. The end of this passage ("the most beautiful steps...") also spoke to a voluntarist view of culture and the value of language.

However, if we look at all of the texts in the published booklet, we find some of the philosophical positions of the resolution itself are not represented with perfect consistency by all the authors. In all three of the booklet's prefatory texts, the justification of coofficial status for Corsican was made using language that undercut the legitimacy of any French expression of Corsican identity. In one of these texts, a member of the language group wrote, "*La langue est un des sanctuaires de l'identité, elle est moyen de se reconnaître, de se savoir d'un lieu...elle est, surtout, une manière de penser*" [Language is one of the sanctuaries of identity, it is how we know who we are, where we come from...it is, above all, a way of thinking] (Bassani 1991:13). Elsewhere in this article, the author returns to pre-*Lingua Matria* terminology, defining Corsican as the mother tongue of Corsican children because it was the language linked to their culture. Similarly, the political scientist Olivesi characterized the language in his preface to the document as the "*le vecteur fondamental*" [fundamental vector] of a strong Corsican cultural identity being threatened by France (Olivesi 1991:24). These supplementary texts also spelled out some of the ways in which the process of implementation of cooficiality would take shape (such as the right to have Corsican represented in the schools, media, place names and public acts), and they did not propose waiting for popular consensus to begin the process.

In the end, the Assembly voted down the motion. The text of the decision read:

> *"La langue corse est un des principaux éléments constitutifs de notre culture. Vouloir l'imposer, la rendre officielle irait à l'encontre du but recherché qui est de faire naturellement retrouver un idiome qui s'est un peu perdu et appauvri. Pour le Corse, son usage doit représenter un plaisir et un privilège de pouvoir communiquer dans la langue de ses ancêtres."* (cited in *Kyrn*, 18 May 1990: 13).

> [The Corsican language is one of the principal elements constituting our culture. To set about imposing it, making it official, would run counter to the desired goal which is for an idiom which has become slightly lost and impoverished to find itself again naturally. For Corsicans, speaking it should be a pleasure and a privilege to be able to communicate in the language of their ancestors.]

The text of the decision remains anchored to the essentialist view of language and cultural identity; so much so, that the authors refuse to acknowledge any crisis for the Corsican language (it is "slightly lost"). We read echoes of public reactions to the idea of mandatory bilingualism: the opposition of "natural" and "imposed" (since Corsican is learned "naturally" and is the "natural" language of the culture, to impose it is to deform its essence). The focus is kept on individual bilingualism, rather than on the issue of legal parity.

We can see that all the efforts made by the CCECV to defuse some of the objections that had stood as obstacles to previous motions fell on deaf ears. Coofficiality was simply read as "imposition and officialization," and rejected out of hand on the same bases as opponents had rejected mandatory bilingualism. On the one hand, this may have represented a refusal in the political class to "hear" the message of coofficiality. On the other hand, it may also reflect the fact that the politicians had also "heard" the continuing echoes of the essentialist position in the CCECV documentation. As a consequence, they may have reacted on the basis of their own traditional notions of "primordial" identity rather than being prompted to revise their categories of value and identity. As we have seen in the survey responses on mandatory bilingualism, an essentialist perspective can be just as easily translated into opposition as support for minority language legislation. In the attempt to reconcile "old" and "new" models of language and identity, both the CCECV document and the prefaces in the publicly distributed booklet send hesitated between those models. In effect, the dual nature of the document may have muffled its potentially radical message.

Another equally likely possibility is that Assembly members heard very clearly the policy implications of the motion on coofficiality that were absent in the motion but quite obvious in the rest of the text. They also are likely to have heard the policy implications of the motion on coofficiality that were absent in the motion but quite clear in the rest of the text. In fact, the concrete implications of the motion were almost as far-reaching as any of the previous ones, given Corsican's striking lack of politico-legal status.

6. From diglossia to polynomy

The movement from *bilingualism* to *coofficiality* was paralleled by a shift in academic circles away from *diglossia* as the organizing sociolinguistic concept towards the notion of *polynomy*. In 1990, the Institute for Corsican Studies organized an international conference on *Langues Polynomiques* [Polynomic Languages]. The originator of the term, Jean-Baptiste Marcellesi, defines a polynomic language as:

> *une langue à l'unité abstraite, à laquelle les utilisateurs reconnaissent plusieurs modalités d'existence, toutes également tolérées sans qu'il y ait entre elles hiérarchisation ou spécialisation de fonction. Elle s'accompagne de l'intertolérence entre utilisateurs de variétés différentes sur les plans phonologiques et morphologiques, de même que la multiplicité lexicale est conçue ailleurs comme un élément de richesse* (1989: 170).

> [a language with an abstract unity, recognized by its users in several modalities of existence; all of them are equally tolerated and they are not ranked or functionally specialized. It is accompanied by phonological and morphological intertolerance between users of different varieties; moreover, lexical multiplicity is seen as a source of richness.]

Since the 1990 conference mentioned above, Corsican academics have actively promoted the idea of Corsican as a polynomic language in a conscious attempt to substitute the notion of "unity in diversity" for ideologies of linguistic identity that link it solely with a single standard. In fact, in the opening session of the conference, polynomy was represented explicitly as contesting dominant ideas about norms and normalization (Filippi 1992:14). This contestatory intent can be seen very clearly in Marcellesi's published responses to questions raised during the 1990 conference. In his remarks, Marcellesi made explicit some of the key tenets of the "sociolinguistic" approach that, as Thiers' thesis advisor, he had had a role in disseminating on Corsica. Polynomy, he asserted, was a way of denouncing what he called "*l'idéologie sécuritaire*" [the comforting ideology] that makes people require a single norm (1991: 21). He said: "*Il n'y a pas lieu d'exiger des enseignants ni des élèves dans une quelconque cohérence dialectale et de prétendre enfermer les locuteurs dans une variété*" [There is no reason to require any sort of dialectal coherence of either teachers or students, or to expect to lock speakers in to a single variety] (1991: 34). He characterized Corsican as a "very polynomic language" because, in contrast to French, Corsicans did not stigmatize linguistic variability. For Marcellesi, linguistic unity resided in the collective image of language boundaries; it did not therefore depend on linguistic uniformity. Put simply, Corsicans decide what Corsican is. According to Marcellesi, the current social definition of the language allowed for significant variation between speakers.

This was an interesting and significant shift from the public dissemination by intellectuals of the term diglossia in the early eighties. Talking about diglossia had focused attention on the power of the dominant language; it explained language practices (including those which disfavored Corsican) in terms that situated individual choices within a matrix of social forces. It exhorted Corsicans to undo diglossia both by speaking Corsican and by practicing and promoting literacy in Corsican. In contrast, the concept of polynomy did not advocate a power reversal, but rather, a redefinition of what power was. The discourse of diglossia, while critical of the techniques of language domination, nevertheless represented diglossic language attitudes and practices as undesirable: they were something Corsicans were urged to shed. In contrast, the discourse of polynomy represented Corsicans as a superior speech community measured against new norms of inclusivity and tolerance.

Alain di Meglio, a conference participant, sociolinguist and teacher, commented that the idea of polynomy had "dedramatized" the issue of Corsican language education for teachers and for the general public, short-circuiting the oft-repeated query "But which Corsican shall we teach?" in which dialect differences were presented as insurmountable obstacles to a teaching program (1992b:22). Elsewhere, (1992a:127) he wrote that many parents and teachers had rejected Corsican language education because they believed that teaching a language required imposing a single norm that they did not recognize as "their" language (Bungelmi's position, above); a polynomic perspective allayed these concerns. Another teacher and researcher, Paul Filippi, commented that a "polynomic consciousness" could be seen in people's use of mixed forms, which sometimes served as a "*espace de liberté où les sujets inscrivent une construction d'identité*" [a free space in which subjects engrave their own constructions of identity] (1992: 30). I heard an echo of his comment in the public remarks of a musicologist describing his research at a cultural forum in 1993: *"Je vais parler en corse et en français,"* [I'm going to speak in Corsican and French] he announced after having switched from one to the other in his first sentence, *"et parce que je parle tous les deux mal, je n'ai aucune honte de passer de l'une à l'autre"* [and because I speak both of them badly, I am not at all ashamed to pass from one to the other]. Moracchini, commenting several years later, wrote that the idea of polynomy had allowed people to take linguistic action while prohibiting Corsican's status as a language from being contested (1998:153).

The conference, however, revealed the difficulty of applying the idea of polynomic language against a backdrop of deeply rooted ideas about linguistic legitimacy and in the face of the practical requirements of teaching. Several people who would never have qualified themselves as "purists" expressed their doubts about the radical inclusiveness of a polynomic language. So, for example, Filippi followed his comment above with the dramatic qualification that this "free" space was found *"entre le crainte de mal parler le français et la crainte de mal parler le corse"* [between the fear of speaking French badly and the fear of speaking Corsican badly] (1991: 31). That is to say, the notion of polynomy had not evacuated the potential for linguistic alienation. Nor did it seem that tolerance of diversity was extended to *mixed* forms, whether they were mixtures of Corsican and French or mixtures of Corsican dialects. This point was emphasized by another conference participant (Jean-Marie Arrighi), who commented that *"Un corse mêlé est mal accepté par un public qui d'ordinaire reconnaît à la fois un parler comme corse et comme provenant d'une partie de la Corse"* [a mixed Corsican is not readily accepted by a public which ordinarily simultaneously identifies a way of speaking as Corsican and as coming from a [particular] part of Corsica] (1991: 45). In other words, boundary maintenance was very important at the local level. The issue of regional identification will be explored in detail in the next two chapters; here I will only mention my use of Southern Corsican vocabulary when talking to people in the center of the island. I had been studying the language manual *Le Corse Sans Peine*, which featured dialogs in a variety of regional dialects that were not explicitly identified to learners (who were assumed to be Corsicans who could readily identify regional varieties). Despite my obvious status as a foreign learner, and the tolerance for oddity and error that went along with it, my saying *tola* 'table' in a region where they used the term *tavola* 'table' struck listeners so odd that it distracted them from listening to what I was saying. Even as a foreigner, I had to learn and stay within regional linguistic boundaries.

Although Arrighi acknowledged that almost everyone spoke *Francorse* as the language of everyday interaction, he dismissed Marcellesi's implicit assertion that the users of this mixed code saw it as a unified system, commenting that "*Chaque microrégion, voire chaque individu, élabore son propre composé et juge ridicule, scandaleux ou non-corse celui du voisin*" [Each microregion, even each individual, develops their own [French–Corsican] composite and judges that of their neighbors to be ridiculous, scandalous or non-Corsican] (1992: 44). This assessment of language attitudes was one of the reasons that Arrighi took the opposite position from Marcellesi on dialectal coherence in the classroom.[18] During the conference, he also alluded to the need to set boundaries; to define what is acceptable and unacceptable in the classroom and in the use of language to do the work of identity. In remarks that summarize neatly some of the dilemmas of minority language education that are illustrated at some length in the following chapter, Arrighi wrote that recent efforts to teach Corsican "*placent les Corses dans une contradiction entre l'attachement générale á une diversité à laquelle nul n'est prêt à renoncer si peu que ce soit et le minimum de normes, même provisoires, qu'exige cette situation nouvelle. A partir du moment où existent des examens et des concours, il existent des critères, dits ou non, de choix*"[place Corsicans in a contradictory position between the general desire not to relinquish the smallest bit of linguistic diversity and a minimum set of norms–albeit provisional–that is required by this new situation. From the moment that exams and competitions exist, criteria of selection–spoken or unspoken–exist as well] (1992: 41). Moracchini leveled a slightly different criticism, which was that it was disingenuous to pretend that one could function without a standard in the educational domain. Professionals who did so, he wrote, were "*conforté... par un discours érigeant l'absence de norme en...norme, mais non sans recourir aux outils de la norme...et à les transformer en 'vérités' validés par la situation institutionelle*" [comforted...by a discourse that institutionalizes the absence of a norm as a...norm, but not without recourse to the tools of the norm...which are transformed into 'truths' validated by the institutional context](1998: 152).

In an echo of Franchi, Marchetti and Perfettini (see last chapter), Arrighi also addressed the role of standards as a way of preserving linguistic identity. As an example, he cited the "*cambiarini*" (those consonant mutations that characterize Corsican phonological space); writing that the failure of new learners of Corsican to pronounce them correctly (under the influence of spelling, which represents only the "hard" phonological variant) should not simply be accepted as an acceptable variant of Corsican. "*Polynomie, oui; anomie: non*" [Polynomie, yes; anomie, no], he concluded. "*Même s'il y a cinq variétés d'une certaine forme ne nous autorise pas à en créer une sixième*" [Just because there are five varieties of a particular form does not authorize us to create a sixth] (1992: 45). In other words, employing a shared code was a way of showing–and perhaps experiencing–respect for a language (see Perfettini in the last chapter). The liberty of individual writers to write as they pleased stood in the way of collective acts of linguistic identification, which required some rules and boundaries.

7. Conclusions

In this chapter, we have seen the way that public opinion about language planning measures on Corsica has been shaped by dominant language ideologies and their effects on experience documented in Chapter 3. Supporting language legislation on the status and teaching of Corsican required abandoning the resistance of separation born out of the diglossic experience. It also called into question the "primordial" link of language and cultural identity. This essentialism was embedded in everyday life in multiple ways: not only was it part of dominant ideology in a broad, European sense, but it was also very much a part of the discourse of Corsican linguistic and cultural activists. In the late eighties and early nineties, the discourse of language activism began to change in response to lack of widespread public acceptance and support of language planning measures. Language planners at the university and in the CCECV attempted to replace the monolingual, monocultural norm with more plural perspectives on language and identity: *Lingua Matria*, *coofficiality* and *polynomy*. The underlying philosophy was that Corsican language practices were heterogenous, and that heterogeneity included linguistic symptoms of French language domination. Given this sociolinguistic reality, monocultural and monolingual norms were bound to exclude most Corsican speakers, and to alienate them from the language planning process. This was one lesson they could draw from the failures of language legislation in the Assembly. These failures also demonstrated how "primordial" views about the link between language and identity stood as obstacles to all language planning efforts, which were by definition *not* "natural".

This discursive shift, however, was not complete, and it did not have immediate, unambiguous results. The "coofficiality" motion was not distinguished in political and public opinion from the mandatory bilingualism one that it replaced. This is in part because all efforts to push Corsican into the official sphere risk being rejected as "inauthentic" uses of the language. But it is also because there was a coercive intent behind the motion granting coofficial status to Corsican and French. In the case of both the *Lingua Matria* document and the academic discussion of *polynomy*, we see evidence of the continued importance of essentialist cultural and linguistic imagery and the boundary maintenance to which it is connected. We can see that Corsican language planners are caught in what Dorian has characterized as a "difficult balancing act" between drawing on the power of *separate* identity in the quest to revitalize a minority language and acknowledging the plural linguistic and cultural nature of minority identity and lived experience (1994: 490–491).

Chapter 6
Language learning: its social evaluation and meaning

When I first heard someone say "*Parla corsu cumè noi*" [She speaks Corsican just like us"] I was flattered. I was in Riventosa, sitting out on the low wall on the village square that caught a nice afternoon sunlight, perched with the crowd that always assembled there before dinner on long summer evenings. This line up was known as the skewer (brochette); we were as idle as chunks of meat on a grill. Cars would drive by, to be scrutinized, evaluated, and situated in the order of things by ten to fifteen pairs of eyes. The stray German, Italian or continental (French) license plate (not from a department heavily populated by Corsicans) would be immediately remarked and the car and its contents impaled on the steady gaze of the village. There were strangers, there were those who belonged, and then there was another category of people who had ties of kinship or friendship in the village who stopped their cars to "do" the brochette, shaking hands, exchanging pleasantries. It was to one of these people that I was introduced: the American "*chì parla corsu cum'è noi!*" I demurred, I hoped modestly. But I was made to perform: "Tell her what you ate for dinner!" This scene was to be replayed many times, and despite my embarrassment at being forced to do my trick for people who often quite understandably did not care, I knew that none of it was meant maliciously, that it meant that I was "their" American, that I had become a part of the community, partly by dint of my efforts to learn Corsican.

The village context was my first experience of what it meant to Corsicans to have a stranger come in and try to learn a minority language whose precarious status in Corsican society symbolizes and gives voice to an equally precarious, ambivalent and problematic sense of identity. In this chapter, I describe in some detail the way in which Corsicans reacted to and explained my language learning process. I then compare and contrast my experiences with those of Corsican learners of Corsican. Both my own story, and how it contrasts with Corsican students' show the social stresses associated with learning a minority language when that language is both threatened, and treated as a major element of identity and belonging. Both the outside learner, and the institutionalized setting of the language class frame and give meaning to speaking Corsican in ways that conflict with the powerful imagery of the mother tongue, as well as with many Corsican speakers' linguistic experiences. The final section of the chapter shows some of the challenges of putting a "sociolinguistic" or pluralistic language planning ideology into action in the classroom by exploring the ways in which issues of linguistic authority and cultural authenticity shape pedagogical strategies for teachers of Corsican.

1. Reactions to a foreign learner: boundaries and community

Even though the comment "She speaks Corsican just like us" was a premature judgment of fluency, it was preceded by a fairly long period in which my learning was ignored and/or denied. The first reaction to my efforts to learn Corsican was surprise; like the Welsh speakers described by Trosset (1986), people in Riventosa did not see why a foreigner would be interested in learning the language, and were skeptical about an outsider's ability to do so. These reactions stemmed to a great extent from the fact that the link between language and community on Corsica has always been experienced as powerful, closed and exclusive. The language of the island has always in itself been an island of intimacy. Historically, Corsicans have had little or no experience with learners of Corsican, since few outsiders had considered it worth the effort. And the current language education system had not yet produced enough learners to make them a socially familiar category of person. Many Corsicans in Riventosa and elsewhere had married non-Corsicans, but few if any of them learned Corsican. It was not uncommon to find "continental" spouses who had been married to Corsicans for over twenty years who had never tried to learn the language. In Riventosa there was a case like this, of a woman who had been married fifty years and had returned with her Corsican husband every summer. Only recently was her lack of desire to assimilate been called into question. I remember the semijoking comments directed at her on the square: "Fifty years and you could have picked up a word or two!" But this was a recent phenomenon (perhaps incited by my presence). Her response, however, speaks for an atmosphere that prevailed for many years: "When I got here, I thought it was my duty to teach them how to speak French properly," she said.

There were other non-Corsicans married to Corsican speakers who claimed to understand Corsican very well, just from having heard it for so many years, but who did not speak it or express any desire to do so. In a subtle way, they too depreciated the language in their implicit claim that it could just be "picked up" with little effort, and was not worth the effort to speak. Their disinclination to learn Corsican was matched, in some cases, by their spouses and families' disinclination for them to learn. Some continental spouses (usually women) told me that they had initially made the effort to learn and speak Corsican, but had been discouraged by their in-laws, who teased them (albeit lightly) whenever they tried to speak. I never had the impression that this mockery was taken as hurtful by the non-Corsican women. But it was clearly a form of boundary maintenance, in that it denied the in-marrying spouses full participation in the code of intimacy.

The outsider groups that were the most successful Corsican language learners were those with the least social and economic power. Many Corsicans told me about Italian or North African manual laborers who had come to the island and been forced to learn Corsican to get along with Corsican work crews whose language of everyday use was Corsican. But these uprooted people were already part of the landscape by virtue of their powerlessness, and in a sense, had never counted. My learning of Corsican stood out in comparison, since I was a young academic from a country that evokes power, with a language of power as a mother tongue.

1.1. The underestimation of competence

My foreignness and my pragmatic, determined, academic approach to language learning set me at first so irretrievably outside the normal conceptual boundaries of the community of Corsican language use that some people simply refused to admit that anything I said was Corsican. "That's Italian," they would say, and proceed to speak French to me. I was dismayed. I would go back home to my language cassettes, to reemerge the next day on the pretext of buying bread from the delivery van in order to meet people and try again. I had taken Italian six years before, and it is highly probable that I did mix Italian and Corsican vocabulary and pronunciations. But it was the symbolic, oppositional role played by Italian (close but distant) that was the catalyst for these evaluative comments. Anything spoken by an outsider that was not perfect Corsican was by definition Italian. Sometime between April, when I "spoke Italian," and August, when I was first advertised as fluent, I crossed boundaries that were partly linguistic–to be sure, I spoke better–but mainly, I think, social. For my familiars, I went from being completely foreign to being thought of as within the linguistic and social community–an oddity, but an assimilated oddity: *their* American. One was either in or out. I was in. Therefore, what I spoke was Corsican. This linguistic inclusion was eventually extended to my husband by our neighbors and the people he worked for despite the abundant evidence that he understood almost no Corsican; in situations of social intimacy they often "forgot," talking around him and sometimes addressing him as though he did.

The fact that the assertion *Parla corsu cumè noi* had more to do with social than linguistic boundaries was also illustrated by differences in front versus back region behavior among some of my closer friends. The same people who made grand claims about my competence on the square did not maintain the fiction of my fluency in private and felt free to correct me, to tell me they had not understood, that I really had italianized a word, or to switch to French with me in order to carry on a conversation in a more efficient way. This discrepancy between the public and the private was in itself a sort of intimacy; the same intimacy afforded by codeswitching. The following excerpt from my journal illustrates this point: Hervé was one of my close friends:

> Sunday, 13 November 1988.
> Yesterday I said *"senza problema"* in front of Hervé and Charles. Hervé repeated *"senza prublema"* with his mocking voice.
> *"Ne te moques pas de mon accent"* [Don't make fun of my accent], I said. Hervé said, *"Ce n'est pas du corse. Problema."* [It isn't Corsican] [repeating the word with a non-Corsican *"o"*]). I replied, *"Aghju dettu prublema."* [I said prublema] [insisting on the *"u"*]. *"Mais on ne dirait pas cela en corse, c'est du français: sans problème."* [But you wouldn't say that in Corsican. It is French: no problem.] said Hervé.
> *"Allora cum'è si diceria questa allora in corsu?"* [Then how would you say in Corsican?] I asked him. *"Dumanda à Madamma Cristofari."* [Ask Madame Cristofari.] was Hervé's only reply.

I did not, of course, share the same intimacy with everyone, and in some people's minds, I never shifted out of the category of the "outsider" who by definition does not speak Corsican. Their categorization of me as a non-speaker was impervious to concrete evidence that I understood, or actually spoke. One neighbor persisted in translating into French even the most basic of Corsican words and phrases up until the time that I left. Sometimes, other people who had heard me respond to questions in Corsican would begin to talk about me in Corsican as I walked away, long before I was out of earshot: Corsican retained for them the status of a secret code that could be used with impunity around foreigners.[19] The fact that some people who did not know me well did not infer much competence from my public discourse can also be explained by their knowledge of the linguistic behavior of Corsican semi-speakers, whose ability to exchange formulae of greeting and parting that are absolutely no indication of a deeper knowledge of the language. Thus, one day I was in someone's house when another visitor (an elderly man from the village) came in. We greeted each other. He hesitated a few moments and then asked me if I liked hearing Corsican. I said yes, and with evident relief, he launched into a discussion in Corsican with the host. Many a time, we had exchanged greetings in Corsican on the square, but he was not sure what this meant, and did not want to alienate me in a more private, social context.

As some of the events I have mentioned show, the public report of competence and the private assessment of competence can be two distinct activities which evoke the community in different ways. The report of competence is above all, a social performance that reflects, proposes, establishes, contests, or comments on social relationships. In some cases, the social relationships evoked were essentially superficial and only involved me, the reporter and an audience in a casual sort of way. After having heard *Parla corsu cum'è noi* for the fiftieth time, I certainly recognized it as a social formula that reflected the extent to which language was the primary idiom of social inclusion. This was certainly the case the time that I overheard my hostess telling her sister in Marseilles about the group that was assembled in her dining room for a holiday meal. In French, she said: "and we have a young American here who speaks Corsican just like us."

1.2. The exaggeration of competence

As far as my actual competence was concerned, after a year of fieldwork and a great deal of hard work, I could carry out a reasonable, basic conversation in Corsican, and follow 90% of a meeting or class on a subject that did not involve a specialized vocabulary. What little I was able to say, I pronounced fairly well. But I emphasize that the range of my conversational ability was far from remarkable. As Trosset (1986:175) notes in her article about Welsh learners, "because native speakers usually expect little from learners, they tend to exaggerate the latter's achievements, and thus the learners may be perceived as more linguistically competent than they really are."

However, subtle exaggerations of my competence were also made by advocates of Corsican language and culture. In some cases, I thought that this was done for my benefit—to be polite and encouraging to me as a language learner. On another occasion, I was speaking in French with a man who told me how impressed he was with my Corsican—that he had heard me come into a bookstore the week before and ask for a certain French–Corsican dictionary which was out of print. He said he had thought that I was Corsican, I spoke so well. Later, I reflected on the exchange in the bookstore and realized that I was sure it had taken place in French, the store owner being someone to whom I had never spoken Corsican. While it was quite possible that this man had heard me speaking a little to someone else during the course of the same evening, in which we had attended the same literary meeting, it is significant that he specifically remembered a conversation that took place in French as having been in Corsican. Somewhere along the line he had made the yes/no evaluation of my ability to speak the language, and retrospectively attributed his moment of revelation to an event, a request for a dictionary which was consistent with his positive image of me in respect to the language.[20] But in other cases, I saw myself as a catalyst for a discourse in which I was a rather trivial addressee. In one such instance, I heard one of my acquaintances agreeing wholeheartedly with another that I spoke exceptionally well; the woman who initiated this exchange had a pretty slim listening knowledge of my ability and the other one, whom I had just met, had only my own report that I had been learning Corsican to go on. These assertions about my competence were a metalinguistic discourse that served to fortify an image of the language shared by both Corsican conversational partners. Asserting the success of a minority language learner, as Trosset points out, asserts the language's right and ability to continue to exist (1986: 174).

Both the under- and overvaluation of my ability to speak Corsican were related to my status as a "linguistic categorical anomaly": I confounded the diglossic organization of all language into "Corsican" and "not Corsican" (see Trosset 1986: 171–2). Fitting me into existing categories was easier than inventing a new one.

2. Social drama: learners as performers

My experience of being forced "on stage" to display my Corsican competence was an experience common to other anthropologists learning minority languages. As Trosset writes, "the role of Welsh learners was an almost continually performative one." She reports becoming aware that people had asked her questions not because they cared about the answer, but to hear her use the language (1986: 179). Being thrust into a performative role in the village was somewhat embarrassing, but was also flattering, since what my stage managers were showing off was my inclusion in their group.

The meaning of these forced performances in the militant context was quite different, both for me and for those who prompted them. For members of the island intelligentsia, for whom the defense and promotion of Corsican was a consuming part of their lives, I served as a handy weapon in this campaign. One of the more extreme and embarrassing instances of sensationalization of my competence took place during a literary gathering at a bookstore. I sat next to an acquaintance who was also a Corsican language author. He turned around to a T.V. announcer sitting behind us and said: "This is an American who speaks Corsican...have you met her? isn't that interesting?" The announcer barely managed to hide his lack of interest (or, his unwillingness to make too much out of my presence). Once the guest of the evening had finished talking about his writing, there was a discussion period. My acquaintance kept poking me and whispering "Go on, ask a question in Corsican, go on..." Annoyed, I took out my notebook and wrote to him in Corsican: "I will ask a question when and if I please." He was momentarily discouraged, but undaunted. A few minutes later, he raised his hand and asked the presenter a question, then, while he still had the floor, announced: "Well, are you all aware that we have in our midst an American who speaks Corsican? Now, (to me) what do you want to say?"[21]

This sort of behavior made me extremely uncomfortable, but I understood my value as a public symbol. For activists who had been battling the attitude that Corsican cannot be learned except in the home, I was a highly visible, exploitable example to the contrary: "Corsican *can* be learned–see, a foreigner has learned it." The interest of an outsider, since it had been so rare up to that point, was also an occasion to express cultural pride–to claim broad and universal value for Corsican and Corsica. It was this sort of symbolic value that led the president of the CCECV to propose me as the "student" to appear on a national television show *Du Coté de Chez Fred* [Fred's Place] on the subject of Corsican culture and language. I originally hesitated to accept, imagining that Corsican students would resent the idea of an outsider representing them. It turned out, however, that the student union had approved of my choice on the grounds that I would make a bigger impression on a French viewing audience than any one of them.

But I was also used to, or unintentionally aroused another social sentiment: shame. The assertion "she speaks Corsican just like us" implies that "we" all speak Corsican. Because this was not the case, some Corsican semispeakers remarked to me or to other Corsicans that I probably spoke Corsican better than they did, and that this was a source of shame. In some cases, they may have been reacting to my relatively stable command of an academic/literary register to which they had probably never been exposed growing up. That is, their comments reflected a diglossic compartmentalization of competence. In other cases, this kind of comment was a judgment of brute competence in ordinary social usage. I was often in no position to evaluate my interlocutor's competence; self-conscious semispeakers usually did not speak Corsican in public. The expression of shame was particularly acute among those who were supporters of the linguistic and cultural revitalization effort. It was clear that sometimes, my language acquisition was made into a moral issue by language promoters: they wanted to make others feel guilty by using me as an example. Although it was quite true, of course, that Corsicans could learn Corsican as I had, it was not the case, as the section below will show, that the process and its implications for individual identity were the same for native versus foreign learners.

Thus as a language consciousness-raiser (Clayton 1978 in Trosset 1986: 174) even a moderately successful foreign learner could be a source of linguistic insecurity. Among the more competent speakers in the intellectual and cultural milieu, my speaking was far from being on a par with their own, but that was not the case with my ability to write in Corsican. I noticed that when I attended literary/academic/cultural gatherings, my note taking drew quite a lot of (somewhat surreptitious) attention. Apart from being curious at what I might write down, people wanted to see what language I wrote in. Because I had learned a lot of Corsican from books, my oral and written competence were about par. This is almost never the case for Corsicans; as the survey results demonstrate, only a handful are competent writers. In classes or meetings that were conducted in Corsican, people looked at my notes in Corsican and often made some sort of admiring comment (often, indirectly—for example, to the person next to them). I began to look at what journalists or other students wrote: most of the time, it was in French. I think that my note taking in Corsican was interpreted as a sign of great competence and total immersion in the language which they did not possess. Their own French notes reminded them of the written competence they lacked. They were unused, and perhaps unable to imagine a foreigner's learning process, to realize that my notes were simply a function of how I learned the language.

3. Myths of acquisition: more boundary maintenance

Despite the fact that my language learning was used, sometimes successfully, to induce guilt and shame among Corsicans in regard to their own cultural and linguistic fidelity, other Corsicans' explanations of how I had learned Corsican just as successfully de-emphasized the personal or cultural significance of my ability to speak Corsican.

I have labeled one particularly widespread assumption of how I had learned Corsican the immaculate conception model. The presumed scenario is that I arrived in the village, and simply by virtue of the sporadic and limited conversations that I had on the square while buying bread or throwing out my trash, I became fully fluent in Corsican. In this scenario, language learning is spontaneous and "natural" in an authentic cultural space. The image of me sweating over a grammar book or listening to cassettes was so incompatible with many people's experiences and concept of Corsican as maternal and innate that it was often simply rejected. For example, when I answered the question posed by many people from outside the village about how I had learned Corsican, they usually ignored my references to using books and tapes and seized upon the fact that I had lived in a village as a full and sufficient explanation of my competence. It was true that compared to city life, living in a village facilitated the process, and multiplied opportunities for contact with people who habitually spoke Corsican. But it was hardly a situation of total immersion–the first, and enduring instinct was to speak French to a foreigner. I am sure that all those who accepted the village explanation in and of itself were aware, at heart, of how unusual it is for village people to speak Corsican to a stranger. The immaculate conception/ village immersion myth served to maintain the order of things, to leave undisturbed a cultural image of a natural, innate link between language, community and localized place. This myth demanded an exaggerated version of my social integration and immersion, but this was easier to swallow than the unfamiliar image and the social implications of Corsican as an academic discipline.

In another explanation of how I learned Corsican my competence was attributed to personal qualities that I was born with: personal talent, high intelligence, a flair for language. Characterizing my learning as exceptional and innate downplayed the effort involved. It also set the act of learning Corsican firmly outside the norm for which the average person could be held accountable: an entire population could not be expected to be exceptionally endowed. The course of one conversation I had illustrates the mechanism by which the individual feat is garnished, in order to be stripped of unwanted implications for society as a whole. I was speaking in Corsican to a Corsican recently transferred from Paris, where he had actually taught some language classes. He and his companion agreed that I spoke well, and initially, expressed regret and shame that most of their compatriots did not make a similar effort. One of them said, "You should be given a medal!" A bit later, a Corsican acquaintance of mine approached us and he returned to the topic of my linguistic accomplishment. This time he exclaimed, and everyone agreed, that it was a "gift," an *individual* gift.

In the same vein, people often expressed amazement at how quickly I learned, even after I had been living on Corsica for almost a year. "She learned it in what–three months?" If I protested that I had been there twelve months, the response was still: "So well, in only a year." I could not escape the label of the gifted linguist, it was too important for people to maintain it. As a normal learner, I would invite the troublesome consideration of where to place the social responsibility for the process of language shift and its reversal.

Another common kind of remark, also designed to disengage the responsibility of the Corsican, was the flip side of the exaggeration of my competence: "You know Italian, don't you?" This comment devalued both my labor of language learning and the uniqueness and dignity of Corsican as a distinct language. In effect, I encountered in popular Corsican discourse the arguments that had once been used against Corsican by the French (that Corsican is so close to Italian that it must be labeled a dialect, or that it has too much internal variation to be considered a language) to justify the fact that its use has declined and to discourage or devalue my interest.

We can thus understand why Corsican language activists, in using me as an example, insisted on Corsican's learnability and downplayed the social context of learning Corsican. Even as a foreign learner, the social context made the process of learning difficult: there were few "natural" social contexts in which Corsican was required and I was forced to use it. In fact, I had to force Corsican conversation on people whose first instinct was to speak French with me. Corsican learners of Corsican also stimulated Corsican identity politics. However, as we will see, the efforts of insiders trying to learn to speak Corsican was fraught with different cultural and political implications.

4. The Corsican learner: problems of identity

Maria è Filippu so corsi. Un parlanu micca corsu.
[Marie and Philip are Corsican. They don't speak Corsican.]
Paulu è Savieriu parlanu corsu è francese.
[Paul and Xavier speak Corsican and French.]
Dice Filippu, "Sò corsu, ma ùn parlu micca corsu."
[Philip says, "I am Corsican, but I don't speak Corsican."]
Dice Saveriu, "Ampara, è prestu saperei!"
[Xavier says, "Learn, and soon you will know how!"]
"Un basta micca à esse corsu per sapè parlà corsu."
["It does not suffice to be Corsican to know how to speak Corsican."]

This dialog comes from the *Corsi di Corsu* [Corsican Course], a beginning audiovisual method developed by a member of *Scola Corsa* (Perfettini and Agostini 1987). It highlights the tension that results from the imperfect fit between a dominant model of perfect congruence between language and collective identity and the reality of minority language loss that courses like this one attempt to combat. In this dialog, and in the course in general, the author evokes the model of linguistic and cultural fit in order to prod Corsicans who do not speak the language to learn it. The gentleness of that prodding illustrates the author's recognition of the fact that an essentialist view of language capacity makes the hard work of language learning culturally problematic. The declaration "It does not suffice to be Corsican to speak Corsican" is an index of the strength of commonly held ideas about "natural" language acquisition that tend, as we have seen, to devalue or define as unnecessary any formal methods. From this perspective, being Corsican is supposed to be enough. Every true Corsican is represented as a potential, natural, authentic speaker. Those who do not speak simply have not actualized instinctual cultural abilities.

The social framing of the process of learning Corsican that we see in the audiovisual program is an integral part of the pedagogical process from kindergarten through college. What we see in minority language pedagogy is that issues of value and legitimacy that go unmentioned in the teaching of dominant languages are foregrounded and made explicit (see Heller 1996). The very visibility of the struggle for legitimacy is an index of its vulnerability to social contestation, something that children in the Franco-Ontarian schools described by Heller immediately grasped and used (1996: 146). The audiovisual method *Corsi di Corsu* suggests that teachers cannot just teach language, they must anticipate and confront the way in which the foregrounding of language as a marker of authentic cultural identity is fraught with conflict at all levels and can translate into personal uncertainty for the individual language learner.

4.1. The problem of the "prise de parole": inauthenticating error

The problems of being a Corsican language learner are dramatically illustrated in the conduct of Corsican language classes I attended at the University. I remember the first day of the first-year Corsican language class at the Corsican Studies Institute in 1989, when the teacher asked the students why they had chosen to enrol in Corsican Studies. I waited, with interest, expecting to hear a youthful, militant discourse. Teaching Corsican was a political and ideological statement; taking the program must be too. To my surprise, I heard a painful, strangled silence. Few students volunteered anything, and the responses that were ultimately extracted from them were hesitant, both linguistically and conceptually.

When I talked later with Thiers, the professor, he said that he was far from surprised at their difficulty with the *prise de parole*. His choice of this phrase, rather than just saying "speaking" is revealing. Literally translated, the phrase *prise de parole* means 'the taking of the word'; the expression is used to mean 'taking the floor,' and it implies an act of speech in a public place in which the speaker claims a right to assert a point of view. It is easy to understand how difficult it was for many of these students to claim the word, the floor and an opinion given their often uneasy relationship with Corsican as a practice and as a cultural symbol. Many of them had little experience using Corsican in a formal, public context. In this, they were not alone. One of my acquaintances, a respected artist who was a regular attender of literary and cultural gatherings, told me that she never spoke Corsican in these contexts. She was intimidated by both the public forum and the presumed critical ear of "language experts" in attendance. One of the things that my friend and the students had picked up on was that approved language use in the militant setting of Corsican studies classrooms was, as Heller writes about Franco-Ontarian schools, based on "a concept of bilingualism as a pair of fully developed monolingualisms, as distinct from a unified form of competence drawing from a range of language varieties" (1996: 145; see also 1994: 142).

So, in the context of the Corsican–French opposition which fueled the explicitly political context of the Corsican Studies classes, the silence of the first day can be interpreted as the fear of *inauthenticating* error. There was, first of all the problem of competence. By declaring a Corsican Studies major, students had expressed a desire to connect with their Corsicanness, and had made a claim on cultural authenticity. Their struggles with the language in the first year class, however, reminded them that they had to learn what they "ought" to know. Students with limited knowledge of Corsican also knew that some lexical and grammatical features were considered "purer" than others. Like the different varieties of Haitian Creole described by Schieffelin and Doucet (1992: 2), this authenticity was defined in terms of distance from French. It is also possible that the students' silence was a form of passive resistance to the implicit hierarchy in the classroom's interactional order; that is, the identity of the legitimate language may have been reversed, but the structures of power had not (see Martin-Jones and Heller 1996).

4.1.1. Competence and "authenticity"

The students' presentations (one a week, on a topic of their choice) were revealing in regard to both competence and their views of cultural authenticity. Many of them gave reports on traditional aspects of Corsican agro-pastoral life (such as the presentation on "The Chestnut"). Few students were at ease with the requirements of extended discourse about a serious topic. They groped for words, they corrected verb endings in midstream, shuffled their feet, coughed and laughed nervously, and hesitated over syllable stress in midword. When they expressed this nervousness linguistically, it was most often in French; *enfin* 'finally' and *bon* 'good' punctuated linguistic space as transitions or fillers.[22] Speaking Corsican in a classroom was clearly a marked activity. Once, I was in a class and we were forced to move classrooms.

Almost all of the light chatter ("Where are we going?" "Is it this room?") that accompanied the activity was in French; this was true of other instances when students were out of the "front region" of the classroom. This dominance of French, particularly for young people in a classroom context, was understandable. Few of them had spoken Corsican regularly at home, and even if they had, being responsible for an academic discourse in a University context was a new role and register for the minority language.[23]

4.1.2. Competence and political engagement

In the context of the Corsican Studies Institute, these issues of competence and language choice were never neutral. There was an acute consciousness of the discrepancy between linguistic/cultural/political ideals and linguistic usage of the sort indexed by the editorial comment cited in the previous chapter, where the nationalist newspaper *U Ribombu* characterized militant action on behalf of a language that they were incapable of using as an "enormous contradiction".[24] That is, the issue of language choice was always foregrounded, and often, assumed to be an index of political commitment. Being pro-Corsican demanded the practice of Corsican.[25] I recall talking to a graduate student in Corsican and asking about an American she had met. "*Di chì età hè?*" ['About how old is he?'] I asked, and she replied, "California". After a moment of mystification, I realized she had read my question as "*De quel état est-il?*" [French for 'what state does he come from?']. That is, she had filtered both Corsican vocabulary and syntax through French, prompted no doubt by the fact that America has states. When I rephrased my question in Corsican, "*Quant'anni hà?*" ['How old is he?'–literally, how many years does he have?], she seemed a bit taken aback and embarrassed, since she was a good speaker of Corsican, an advanced student, and was an active political and linguistic militant. In front of a foreign anthropologist, in the university setting, her utterance was no longer just conversation, it was an index of her competence and identity. Although I said nothing, another student might well have made a remark since, as McDonald remarks about a similar Breton context, calques of French "are seized upon as inauthentic in moments of conflict over identity which otherwise pass unnoticed" (1989: 206). For students in Corsican Studies, those moments of conflict were incipient in most of their University interactions, given that the very existence of the Corsican Studies program represented a cultural and political commitment. It was on these grounds that some students spoke to me disparagingly about teachers at the Institute who conducted courses in French. In meetings and public statements which had to do with cultural politics, there was an obligatory "*prise de parole*" in Corsican which was meant to symbolically displace the authority of French. At student union meetings, this usually took the form of a spokesperson reading a prepared statement written in Corsican before switching to French. These readings were usually marked by the same paralinguistic signs of lack of familiarity, confidence and/or competence that I saw in the classroom presentations.

We can see that there is an interesting compartmentalization of symbolic significance: it is in "front region" discourse that standards of linguistic authenticity are most stringently applied. French was implicitly accepted in "back region," informal communication of the sort I overheard going from one classroom to the next. Among linguistic/cultural activists, however, there was always the potential for the "back" to be pushed up front–for an individual to define Corsican as "required" in a particular situation by using Corsican in a way that marked it as a choice. This sort of use of Corsican is almost impossible to distinguish from "unmarked" switches without reference to prosodic and performance variables. The "key" of these performances is exaggeration. Speakers might exaggerate intonational contours or raise their volume. Or, they might place more dramatic emphasis than the situation required on uniquely Corsican linguistic formulae of hailing and greeting in the opening of an interaction: for example, saying "*Ô*" plus a Corsican diminutive of an addressee's name (for me, this was *Ô Lisà*, the diminutive of *Lisandra*, my first name in Corsican). What counts as "exaggeration" is, of course, a matter of interpretation based on very subtle points of discrimination that are inferred from a total context, and the histories of interaction leading up to that context. While difficult to quantify, it seemed clear to me that in some contexts, people spoke in ways that put their choice of language on display, thereby making language choice and competence a salient interactional issue for all concerned.

So fear about competence was not a chimera, it was based on a very real knowledge that French linguistic reflexes were both extremely difficult to eliminate and ran the risk of social censure in the militant context. Figure 4 depicts a sign that was put up at the Corsican Studies Institute to announce a very important meeting for Corsican Studies students. The author of this hastily scribbled note was anonymously rebuked by another student who circled *assai*, wrote *gallicisme* next to it, and penned in *très*; the word the author had translated "incorrectly" as *assai*. *Assai* means 'much,' or 'enough' but not 'very' or 'significantly' as does its French cognate *assez*. An "authentic" Corsican choice, not offered by the anonymous critic, might be *impurtantissimu*, with the magnifying suffix *-issimu* replacing *assai*.[26]

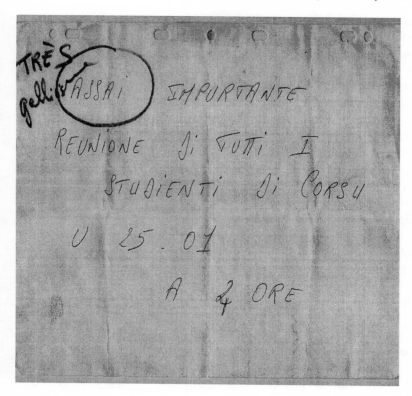

Figure 4. Purist note of rebuke

This is a very clear example of the kind of minority language purism we have encountered in Chapter 4.[27]

4.2. Learner's Corsican

Another sort of popular purism also made speaking a learner's Corsican risky for young Corsicans, even in informal contexts. To return to the comparison with my own learning process, there were very wide differences in the rigor with which what I said versus the linguistic production of a Corsican were socially evaluated. I could make mistakes and neither I, nor anyone else held these mistakes against me. This was not the case for Corsicans, for the deeply embedded image of Corsican as a mother tongue did not admit to any intermediate stages in language competence; it was something you either had or did not have. Thus even though it was quite clear that people accepted and were accustomed to Corsicans who had only passive competence in Corsican, it seemed to me that Corsicans did not want to hear another Corsican speak an "intermediate," regionally mixed or academic Corsican. This is corroborated by a 1991 article in the paper *A Fiara*, in which the author described a non-Corsophone (Corsican) friend's efforts to learn Corsican, "*ùn fussi chè per scambià quattru parolle cu i so paisani senza aduprà u francese*" [if only to be able to exchange four words with his fellow villagers without using French]. This friend went to a bookstore and bought an audiovisual method that was based on a northern variety of Corsican. The friend lived in the South. The writer commented that "*quellu chì pruverebbe à parlà stu corsu in Auddè o in Pitretu, essendu ellu stessu di u locu, ferebbe ride u paese sanu è forse ci resterebbe in pruverbiu*" [the person who tries to use this [Northern] Corsican in *Auddè* or *Pitretu* [Southern villages], where he is a native, will make the whole village laugh and maybe even become immortalized in a proverb] (*Ma u corsu*, 1991: 12). We see here a person who has been, as the article author acknowledges, born too late to "learn Corsican in the street"– that is, cut off from social transmission, being held to local standards of authenticity as a book learner of Corsican. This explains, in part, the frequent criticisms of announcers on the regional radio and television. Similar criticisms are made about the Corsican taught at the University. People have told me that they have spoken to students with degrees in Corsican Studies, and "they can't speak Corsican." We return, in these comments, to the opposition of the "natural" and the "learned/imposed"; "speaking Corsican" involves by definition those kinds of competencies that are acquired outside these formal, academic contexts.

This everyday purism had the effect of banishing learner's Corsican from the informal, public sphere. This is reflected in the habits of Corsican semispeakers, who tend to avoid speaking it altogether, or limit themselves to the occasional greeting. As I have mentioned, there is a sociolinguistic etiquette which prevents salutations from being interpreted as indices of competence, and in general, competent speakers do not try to press semi-speakers beyond these superficial exchanges.

5. Pedagogical strategies

In the face of this dramatization of competence as an index of cultural authenticity and ideological/political commitment, how was the teacher to define and deal with error? Encourage practice? Improve competence? Influence linguistic choice? As McDonald (1989:197–199) writes in her account of children's Breton language classes, there was a constant conflict between structure (an integral part of French pedagogy) and antistructure; imposition (of test criteria, for example) and naturalness (the image of the mother tongue).

5.1. A sociolinguistic approach to variation and authenticity

The professor in the first year Corsican Studies class was Jacques Thiers, the sociolinguist introduced in the last two chapters. In keeping with the philosophy described in Chapter 4, Thiers sought to dispel the specter of a single authoritative, authentic or "pure" Corsican language or identity to which none of his students could measure up. Following one student's presentation on traditional marriage, engagement and mourning practices in Corsica, he questioned the presenter and the class about both continuity and change in the structure, value and practices of the Corsican family. By moving the discussion squarely into the present, he counter-balanced the ahistorical voice of the report, in which the fact that no distinction was made between dying/extinct customs and current practices lent the past unquestionable authority. Thiers made essentially the same point in his responses to French interferences in his students' Corsican speech: that linguistic change, and linguistic hybridization was the rule and not the exception.

This was one of the themes developed in a homework assignment following a presentation on agriculture. Students were told to come up with Corsican equivalents for phrases like *l'Office pour la Repression des Fraudes* [the Office for the Repression of Fraud], *randonnées équestres* 'horse trail rides' and *tables d'hôtes* 'private inns'. These were all phrases which student presenters had either translated literally into Corsican or said in French. The following week's discussion centered around the cultural content of the terms, emphasizing linguistic and cultural nonequivalence. Could one, Thiers asked, even express the idea of a *table d'hôte*–people in private homes selling meals–in a language whose idioms reflected a society in which this category of behavior did not exist? The answer was "no," to the extent that one could view the two languages as reflecting independent, bounded cultural identities. To the extent to which language reflected cultural contact and mix, the answer was also "yes". Thiers pointed out that choices in translation reflected cultural philosophies. One could either emphasize cultural boundaries by using French terms while speaking Corsican, giving up on translation where "traditional," "authentic" vocabulary fails, or take the opposing strategy of accepting less than perfect and strictly speaking, "inauthentic" transliterations or approximations that achieved a communicative purpose. The implicit message of the class was that in *either* case, there was linguistic and cultural hybridization.

Although this discussion of the limits of the Corsican lexicon raised questions of authenticity, it was relatively neutral at the level of personal choice and ideology, since the lexical gaps were the result of historical events outside of individual control. Corsican vocabulary reflected the fact that the language had been excluded from the domains in which technological and bureaucratic terminology was developed. Syntactic and idiomatic French interferences, however, were a thornier problem, since they seemed to be more closely associated with individual competence, and thus "authentic" identity.

5.2. Sociolinguistic choices

In response to French interference in his students' speech, Thiers attempted to present an array of linguistic *choices,* whose relationship to various philosophies of authenticity and to languages (French, Italian and "traditional" Corsican) was described but not judged. Thus when a student referred to forms as *foglie* 'papers' (based on French usage), he offered as alternatives *documenti* (which he identified as more Italian) and *scartafacci,* the Corsican word for *dossier.* There was, however, an unavoidable tension between a radical relativism (all choices are equally legitimate) and an equally rigid purism (there is only one authentic choice). In another instance, a student said *mette in piazza,* a calque of the French *mettre en place,* meaning to establish or set in motion. Thiers pointed out that *piazza* referred in (authentic?) Corsican solely to the town square, and offered *mette in postu* as an alternative. It was hard not to read *mette in postu* as the better choice, since it retained a lexical distinction in Corsican.

Thiers' avoidance of the label of "error" was, first of all, a response to both his students' varied and inconsistent competence and the cultural and political values attached to competence. The problem for Thiers and for teachers of Corsican at all levels, was that Corsican was not just another language for either their students or themselves. To be sure, the Corsican Studies Institute was the place in which students' and teachers' ideological and political frames on the meaning of language were far more congruent than they were, for example, in other university programs or in primary or secondary education. Yet even children in grade schools with very limited knowledge of Corsican had captured a sense of its value as a language of community and intimacy. Of particular interest to me in my observations of primary classrooms and discussions with teachers was that children reading aloud from elementary texts in Corsican "translated" what they were reading into their own regional pronunciation. This was striking because most of these children came to the class without ever having really spoken in Corsican. In their limited repertoire of linguistic knowledge was a grasp of the most socially significant linguistic markers: the ones that linked them to place.

Like the children in Francophone schools in Ontario (Heller 1994; 1996: 146), Breton language schools (McDonald 1989: 199), and multicultural British school settings (Rampton 1995: 84), Corsican pupils quickly grasped the political and symbolic import of language selection and use. This was particularly true of children in one of the "model" classrooms I visited. They had been observed and even filmed so many times that their Corsican lessons had all the ring of practiced performances. The teacher in this classroom and her husband were both extremely dedicated teachers and language activists. They reported that their son, whom they had raised exclusively in Corsican, had rejected the language from about age six to ten. They saw this very clearly as a rejection of the political agenda which, even as a child, he had learned came attached to the language.

Because Thiers and other teachers were convinced that they had to encourage their students' sense of cultural property rights in the Corsican language, they were hesitant to correct too much. The resource they were in charge of–young people who were speaking Corsican (albeit in a restricted context)–was too scare a resource to squander. In other words, teachers of Corsican had seen that a heavy-handed imposition of strict standards in these social circumstances could, as some of the opponents of mandatory Corsican claimed, risk a reflex of rejection by the student.

Thiers was committed both to promoting the use of Corsican and to a model of language in which boundaries were defined by social practice rather than by formal linguistic features. By acknowledging, confronting, even accommodating French linguistic interferences in Corsican, he attempted to undermine black and white judgments of purity and authenticity which stifled the *prise de parole* of his students.

5.3. Limits to "choice": linguistic judgments in the classroom

Nevertheless, replacing "error" with "choice" did not eliminate the requirement to make linguistic judgments and hierarchical distinctions if one maintained, as he did, that there were still two separate languages. The boundaries had to be drawn somewhere. And Thiers did have his own thresholds for interference. Some of the things that he corrected, (thereby defining them as "not Corsican") in the classroom included: (a) Saying *Face cinq 'anni* 'five years ago', (a calque of the French *ça fait cinq ans*) instead of *cinq 'anni fa*, the usual way of saying 'five years ago' in Corsican; (b)

Confounding *ci hè* 'there is' with *ci sò* 'there are' because the French *il y a*
covers both singular and plural; (c) Misplacing the syllable stress, saying, for
example, *industria"* rather than *industria"* following the French stress pattern
of *industrie*; (d) inserting consonant clusters where there are none in Corsican
(*administrazione* for *amministrazione*) based on the French (see Chapter 3).

Quéré notes that with the process of standardization, *"une langue se met
à exister comme entité abstraite et autonome constituée en dehors, en surplus
et au-dessus des pratiques. Elle leur sert à la fois de norme (à laquelle elles
doivent se conformer), d'étalon...de moyen de représentation"* [a language
begins to exist as an autonomous and abstract entity that is constituted
outside, in addition to and at a level above [linguistic] practice. The standard
serves both as an ideal to which those practices are supposed to conform, and
as a badge...a means of self-representation](1987: 62). Given what we know
about the teaching of French orthography and grammar, we can see how
slippery the pedagogical slope is: no matter how they are framed, the drawing
of linguistic boundaries with rules of usage were likely to be read as indices
of the authority of Corsican as an abstract, autonomous system. And of
course, at one level, they were meant to: as we have seen, part of the value of
teaching Corsican as a proper (or mandatory) subject was that institutionaliz-
ing the language sent the message that it was dignified and important enough
to be taken seriously. The dilemma that Thiers' class illustrates is that in
actual practice in the school context, the very elements that made Corsican
"serious" were those that also risked alienating students: the enforcement of
standards through exams which carried the risk of failure.

6. A return to the problems of linguistic and cultural boundaries

Thiers' sociolinguistic approach emphasized the socially constructed and
indeterminate nature of linguistic judgments and social boundaries. At one
level, he was trying to encourage his students to invent their own tradition, to
assert a modern, hybrid Corsicanness and Corsican. The problem was that in
order to avoid a "purist," "elitist" and ultimately derivative discourse about
language, he had to assert the autonomy of Corsican by acting *as if* it were a
language of equal power and legitimacy to French, *as if* his students could
decree what the Corsican of the future would be. These positions were
academically defensible, but they were extremely difficult to sustain in the
university classroom because of the following social conditions: (a) the
continued hold of dominant ideologies of value and identity, (b) the cultural
and political salience of Corsican and (c) the weak practical base of linguistic
competence of most young Corsicans.

One of Thiers' attempts to restore complexity and continuity to the history of Corsican–French relations was to draw his students' attention to FRC (Corsican Regional French described in Chapter 3). This was meant to illustrate that linguistic influences travel in both directions, that the nature of contemporary Corsican expression includes a wide range of varieties of both Corsican and French, and that the life of language in society consistently eludes complete control by any political or social group. In other words, he was trying to focus his students on continuities in the social process of linguistic change.

The implicit message of this emphasis on process was that all languages are equal before the forces of history. It was true that the Corsican variety of French tweaked and teased the normative, *Académie Française* 'French Academy' ideology of the language. But this did not, in the end, really compensate for the wide range of changes French had worked on Corsican. The influence of French caused students to make the errors of syntax and pronunciation that even Thiers identified as "not Corsican". From this perspective, the example of a Corsican variety of French had a sour aftertaste, since it was anecdotal evidence of a Corsican conceptual dominance that was no more. It was also difficult to dispel the stigma of this kind of French, which figures in Corsican oral culture (jokes and songs) as funny/shameful bilingual malapropisms made by Corsicans for whom French was a second language (examples follow in Chapter 8).

Thus it was obvious that Corsican interference in French, no matter how gratifying an inroad into gallic purity, had not been and was not a threat to the status or power of French as a linguistic and political system. The influence of French on Corsican, however, had not only eroded the practice of Corsican, but also seemed to be making inroads into its formal autonomy as a language. Nor had Frenchness ever been undermined by the recalcitrant provincial speaker; he or she was simply classified as backward and inferior. Corsican-ness, however, did not enjoy this autonomy from all things French; few Corsicans could afford to reject a Corsican speaker whose Corsican was influenced by French. In fact, few Corsican speakers were free from this influence.

Thiers would have agreed with Hill's claim that the definition and perception of language contraction is only relevant if the central focus is on autonomous languages as systems, rather than on individual and collective access to linguistic and social codes. She notes that *speakers* of Mexicano have not lost stylistic and sociolinguistic options. These options are simply distributed across two languages, Spanish and Mexicano, which also have distinct and complementary roles in the articulation of power versus solidarity (1989: 163). As we have seen, the same can be said of Corsican and French.

Outside the university context, older Corsicans make ample and unselfcons-cious use of both Corsican and French, switching codes with little regard to issues of dominance and purity even when their codeswitches clearly reveal a gap in Corsican vocabulary or the existence of registers or domains that have been usurped by French.

But this speaker and function-centered approach to language mixing depends on a certain level of competence in both languages. It also requires a nonpoliticized social context in which linguistic choices are made. To a great extent, what Thiers presented to his students as the *opportunity* to choose was really a requirement. It was this requirement that stifled the *prise de parole*. One student articulated this quite clearly in his presentation, asserting that the linguistic productions of young people (for whom the "unmarked" linguistic choice remained French outside the militant context) were constantly sensationalized, overdramatized, their meanings for the individual eclipsed by their social and political connotations. To emphasize the social context of language in the classroom was to stress its communica-tive function, but it was precisely this function that was backgrounded by the political context of the Corsican utterance (see Trosset 1986: 179). As the student pointed out, the social evaluation of a young person's speech focused almost exclusively on form, not on content. As Brown (1993: 83) writes in reference to Louisiana French, "the choice of a word is a commitment, a risk, a conflict. What word to choose: *'je vais,' 'j'vas,' 'mo va'*?" In the same way, it was difficult for young Corsicans to "just talk" if their every locution was a series of symbolic crossroads, if saying *orditura* or *pidone* (for 'context' or 'mailman') classified you as a traditionalist/purist pitted against the opposing camp of the sociolinguists who would accept the more gallicized *cuntestu* or *fattore*.

7. Conclusions

My own language learning experiences emphasize the tenacious hold of the monolingual norm and its "essential" constructs of language identity, the role of language in the marking of social boundaries, and the way that competence becomes dramatized and politically loaded in the context of language revitalization. All of these themes are echoed in the analysis of the meanings and perils of learning the minority language for Corsicans themselves. In the classroom context, we can see that academic contextualizations of notions of authority, leading to dispensations like "*Un basta micca à esse corsu per sapé parlà corsu*" [It does not suffice to be Corsican to know how to speak it] could not efface the fact that the burden of proof of authenticity fell to members of the minority, and that the rules of evidence were defined by the majority. Students who were still not comfortable carrying on an extended conversation in Corsican were confronted with the part that they would play in the collective fashioning of Corsican linguistic destiny. The academic lesson was that Corsican was only one possible way of representing Corsicanness. The practical lesson was that it was usually the primary symbol of cultural identity. Calling norms and standards into question undermined an unreflexive faith in Corsicanness itself. The students could not just speak, they had to take positions; they could not just *be* Corsican but had to constantly engage in representing Corsicanness. This self-conscious representational activity led, as we have seen, to an emphasis on the symbolic rather than the communicative function of language; this in turn widened the rift between ideology and practice, threatening notions of cultural legitimacy.

Chapter 7
Cracks in the public performance of Corsican literacy: the Second Annual Corsican Spelling Contest

Having a Corsican spelling contest was first conceived of in 1987. The idea was generated by members of RCFM and FR3, the regional radio and TV stations, and by members of the linguistic association *A Falce,* a conglomerate of most of the cultural associations on the island. The model for such a public event was the yearly International Francophone Spelling Championship that culminated in a very popular national broadcast in which French speakers from all over the world vied for large prizes with their mastery of the capricious orthography of French. The French championship celebrated French linguistic form as the vehicle through which all members of *la francophonie* could experience cultural unity and display the value of their cultural capital.

A spelling contest thus offered a number of potent symbolic possibilities for language activists. It dramatized a key area of language standardization. It tapped into the power of the written code to symbolize linguistic and cultural unity. It contributed to the normalization of Corsican both in its celebration of Corsican literacy and in its use of a medium (TV) dominated by French. A spelling contest was also a popular event, which had the potential to present spelling as a normal, everyday activity of ordinary people. Finally, it was a game. It was an opportunity to involve the Corsican public in a lighthearted way with a topic which, up to that point, had been restricted to serious, academic, contentious and highly politicized contexts.

This chapter focuses on the final round of the Second Annual Corsican Spelling Contest, which was broadcast in 1988 during a ninety-minute television program. In addition to showing the contestants taking the final dictation, the show featured interviews with all of the contestants, most of the sponsors and organizers, as well as performances by well-known Corsican actors and musicians, and climaxed with the announcement of the winners. This broadcast provides a focused, performative event that allows us to look at people engaged in the active interpretation and production of linguistic ideology. On the one hand, there is the effort by the Contest planners to appropriate dominant symbols of power and legitimacy. On the other hand, there are the participants' comments and exchanges, many of which challenge the value of a unified, authoritative, written Corsican that is the major premise of both the Spelling Contest and much Corsican language planning practice and ideology.

1. The meaning of orthography

1.1. The role of writing in minority language promotion

Here I want to briefly draw attention to an obvious feature of Corsican language promotion: the central role of writing. Texts like grammars and dictionaries, as we have seen in Chapters 4 and 5, both describe and symbolize Corsican's claims on legitimate status as a language. Writing is essential from the vantage point of an ideology in which *form* is at the core of linguistic identity. As Annamalai writes, "when an oral language becomes written, it becomes a tool for the reorganization of the political and social structure of the linguistic community...the written form is perceived as permanent, visible...[and] sacred" and the focus on form rather than content is related to the central role of symbolism in language revitalization (1989: 227–230).

Texts and written tests are also central elements of the educational system. Again, written pedagogical materials and written examinations have both practical and symbolic value. Writing is also a necessary vehicle for achieving standardization, since it is through reading Corsican that Corsicans are able to apprehend, and potentially recognize and accept standardized forms. Writing also has other symbolic and political values. The use of writing in prestige literary genres creates a corpus whose presence or absence confers authority and legitimacy within dominant linguistic models: in the 1991 debate over the *Projet Joxe*, a non-Corsican member of parliament (who was against Corsican language education) used the question "*Où sont vos Rimbaud*? [Where are your Rimbauds {famous poets}?"] as a rhetorical challenge to the legitimacy of Corsican as a language. Finally, all writing in education, the media and politics has the value of displacing French domination of the public sphere.

These multiple values of writing make it a critical component of all Corsican language planning, despite the fact that language activists vary considerably in their notions about what kinds of written texts should be granted authority, and the status of the written vs. the oral in the identification of linguistic unity and the project of standardization. To write, one must spell. And so, orthography becomes a potent and often contested symbolic focus for issues of social and symbolic control (see Brown 1993; Graves 1991;

McClure 1985; Schieffelin and Doucet 1992; Sebba 1996 and forthcoming; Winer 1990).

1.1.1. The role of orthography in establishing and legitimizing boundaries

Orthographies are never simply transparent vehicles for getting a language down on paper; they are selective representations of linguistic form in a language that always (implicitly or explicitly) invoke a comparative framework. That is, orthographies by definition symbolize, naturalize and legitimize differences and/or similarities of a cultural or political origin. Decrosse writes that orthographies played an important supporting role for the idea of the mother tongue, for alphabet systems *"ont été conçus la plupart du temps comme un attribut national, qui permet à chaque population de s'identifier comme unie et autonome"* [were conceived of, for the most part, as a national attribute that made it possible for each population to identify itself as unified and autonomous] (1987: 32). That autonomy implied difference from other populations, and establishing distance through orthography has been used in support of political boundary-making where linguistic differences were scant. Two obvious examples involve the use of the Cyrillic alphabet: to distinguish Moldavian and Romanian in the former USSR and to differentiate between Serbian and Croatian. This symbolic differentiation went hand in hand with symbolic alliance: the Cyrillic alphabet represented the East and the Eastern block and the roman alphabet, a Western cultural, political and/or religious orientation. The adoption of a roman (over an arabic) alphabet by General Siyad in Somalia and the use of the roman alphabet in Ataturk's language reform in Turkey used the East–West symbolism afforded by choices in writing systems. In other instances, establishing distance from other languages through orthography is particularly important because that linguistic difference is contested. Orthographic differentiation from "standard" forms has been very important in the case of creoles (and for Scots English) in order to combat the common perceptions of these languages as variants or "dialects" of standard languages (French or English).

Additionally, as a body of prescriptive rules that identifies one right way of using language, orthography is itself a symbolic medium for political and social control. This link is made quite clear in the following two commentaries. The first is an excerpt from a letter to a Corsican nationalist weekly, in which the writer protests the newspaper's inclusion of poets who used French orthographic conventions. In an echo of arguments made by Perfettini and Franchi (Chapter 4), he wrote: *"A grafia di a nostra lingua ùn hè à bastanza stabile è i danni di issa scrittura ùn sò ancu spariti...Chì ognunu parli secondu l'usu di u su rughjone, quessu hè un bè...Ma u scrive dumanda una certa disciplina"* [The orthography of our language is not very stable, and it is not sufficiently protected against the damages done by this bastardized writing...writing demands a certain discipline] (Polidori 1988: 15). Polidori's emphasis on "discipline" indexes the fact that control of writing standards both reflects and confers cultural and political power. Spelling is where outside influences can be symbolically banished, where the internal consistency and systematicity of the code can be displayed and policed, and where social actors can, through their conformity, invoke the presence of a social and linguistic authority. The second example is a small, humorous piece by a journalist in *Corse-Matin*, one of the two major daily papers on the island. This piece reported on the clue that had been given to a contestant in a television game show in which players searched for hidden "treasure" in different parts of the country. A recent episode had been set in Corsica, and one written clue given to the contestant read, *tianoualouzoucorsu*, which used French spelling conventions to approximate a phonetic rendition of the Corsican phrase *tianu à l'usu corsu* 'Corsican style stew'. The journalist used this example to remark, *"Et dire qu'il n'y a pas si longtemps, la langue corse a échappé de justesse à une graphie très phonétique, mais peu ragoûtante, assez voisine du 'tianoualouzoucorsu'"*[And to say that not so long ago, the Corsican language only barely escaped a very phonetic–but not very tasty–writing system that was quite close to *'tianoualouzoucorsu'*] (Mondoloni 1998). Although the journalist makes explicit mention only of the way that Corsican is "phonetically" expressed through French orthography, he implicitly recognizes another feature of this "spelling," which is that the words are all run together, since he marks word boundaries in his "translation" of the phrase. In short, the game show spelling represents Corsican as an unintelligible oral stream of sound, heard through French ears. In contrast, a Corsican orthography represents the language as intelligible, ordered and legitimate.

1.1.2. Difference from French and Italian

The decade leading up to the Contest had seen some fairly heated debates about spelling which polarized island intellectuals around different ideologies of identity. "In many instances," Brown writes of similar debates about Louisiana French, "the final choices for orthographic representations have amounted to making a social statement of allegiance either to the European motherland or to Louisiana" (1993: 81). In Corsica, predictably, orthography has been a symbolic site for the assertion of linguistic difference from Italian and cultural autonomy from French/France.

Orthographic differentiation from French, however, has had a slightly different significance than differentiation from Italian. The source of this difference can be seen in the following critique (taken from the same letter writer, above) of the use of French orthographic conventions in Corsican spelling (these would include, for example, *ou* to represent the sound [u], or *ty* to represent the voiced affricates like [dj]). Polidori wrote: "*ci sò sempre uni pochi di scrittori o pueta, ancu di grazia pocu letti, dicciarbellatti da a nurmalisazione di a lingua francese è chì s'inchjoccanu à scrive u corsu incu una funetica francese*" [there are still a few writers and poets, fortunately not widely read, who, brainwashed by French normalization, blindly continue to write Corsican with French phonetics]. He labeled this "*une graphie patoisante*"; that is, an orthography that confers the low status of a "patois" (Polidori 1988). In other words, the use of dominant orthography to depict difference carries with it a dominant ideology in which that difference is viewed as a defect (see Preston 1985). For this reason, as Polidori's letter suggests, orthographic distance from French had more or less become the norm at the time of the Spelling Contest.

Although Italian was a standard language, Corsicans had little to no experience of language dominance from within the Italian system. As a consequence, while differentiation from Italian was important for Corsican as a marker of linguistic boundaries, using Italian spelling conventions did not carry a heavy symbolic burden of social stigma. Given the linguistic closeness of Corsican and Italian, and the regularity of and relatively phonemic character of Italian orthography, it would also have been difficult for Corsicans to break radically with Italian conventions. Corsican and Italian share the same orthographic representations of all vowel sounds and stops, and use several of the same principles of consonant combination (such as consonant doubling and, the use of "h" to "harden" a consonant before a vowel).

The goal of differentiation from Italian has thus made it all the more important to use orthography to foreground features of Corsican that are not shared with Italian. One of these distinct features of the Corsican phonetic repertoire is the presence of the voiced palatal affricates [tj] and [dj]. The choice of the graphemes *chj* and *ghj* to represent these sounds is one of the most visually striking aspects of *Intricciate è Cambiarine*, the first Corsican spelling manual, which proposed these trigraphs as a replacement for the use of the Italian conventions *ci* [ʧi] and *gi* [ʤi], which, not being palatals, were inaccurate representations of the Corsican sounds.

1.2. Internal coherence: Corsican as an autonomous code

In discussion at a 1986 roundtable on orthography sponsored by the linguistic association ADECEC, the assembled linguists and writers made it clear that they considered it very important for orthography to visually represent the way Corsican sounded. They saw this unique sound as a key aspect of its linguistic identity, and something that distinguished it from Italian. But they were also very interested in using orthography to depict significant features of Corsican grammar and phonology. As Achard writes, "*l'usage orthographique, base de l'unité de la langue, est supposé...relever d'une logique explicitable*" [orthographic usage, the base of the unity of a language, is presumed to be based on demonstrable logic] (1987: 50). We can see that spelling not only encodes difference/boundaries, but is also the most visible, tangible evidence of all of the criteria of "languageness": internal linguistic unity, regularity, codification and autonomy.[78]

So, for example, a number of homophones with Italian were given accents in order visually cue Corsican consonant mutation rules. Thus 'three' is written *tre* in Italian but *trè* in Corsican, because *trè* is one of the exceptions to the rule of Corsican pronunciation in which unvoiced consonants are voiced following a vowel. Without the accent, **tre pere* [three pears] would be pronounced [tre bere]; with the accent, it is (correctly) pronounced [tre pere].

In another example, *Intricciate è Cambiarine* distinguished between three grammatical functions filled by the same monosyllable [e]: (a) third person singular of the verb *esse* 'to be': written *hè*; (b) the conjunction 'and': written *è*; (c) the feminine plural definite article: written *e*. This convention was not accepted by everyone. During the 1986 ADECEC roundtable mentioned above, one participant (the linguist Antoine Veuvet) argued that what he called the "bastard" (unpronounced) *h* was unnecessary, and advocated using *è* for the verb, like Italian, and *e* for the other two uses. Pascal Marchetti, one of the authors of the spelling manual, countered that there were written contexts in which failing to make these distinctions would create ambiguity. He used the title of the spelling manual itself as an illustration, saying that if *Intricciate è Cambiarini* were written without the accent on the *e*, the first word could be read as an imperative (second person plural) and the second two words as a noun phrase (DET+N) that was the direct object of the verb. The intended meaning of the title, "Interconnections and Changers" could be misinterpreted as "Interconnect the Changers". Veuvet responded that people in most languages dealt quite adequately with homonyms, using context to disambiguate.

1.2.1. Esthetics/pronunciation vs. structure

In Veuvet and Marchetti's exchange, we glimpse the competition that recurs in the Roundtable discussion between using orthography to display grammatical and phonological rules and relationships and using spelling to represent the language in an esthetically pleasing way. Veuvet did not like the way that the *h* in *hè* 'is' looked, and was willing to sacrifice clarity for beauty. Other participants linked visual to verbal esthetics. Jacques Fusina, a University professor and poet, talked about the way that the *ritrattu mentale* 'mental image' evoked by particular spellings influenced a mental phonology, saying that when he saw complements of the verb written as separate words after it (*di la mi* 'tell it to me') instead of attached to it (*dilammi)* he was "*ubligatu à ripigliami duie volte*" [obliged to read it two times] to get the sense and sound right. For others, the esthetics were purely visual. So Marchetti, who had argued for the *h* in *hè*, admitted that he had violated the principles of logic and consistency that he thought should drive orthography by providing two allowed forms for 'that': *istu* and *stu* (the "*i*" is not always pronounced) but only one for the word 'this'(*issu*), even though this word was always pronounced [su]. This was because the alternative (*ssu*) was, in his words, "*goffu cum'è un peccatu murtale*" [ugly as mortal sin]. François Perfettini (Academic Inspector and co-author of the audiovisual method mentioned in Chapter 6) countered by placing priority on the connection between the visual and the verbal, saying that putting the unpronounced *i* at the beginning of *issu* "*mi disturba è mi dispiace assai*" [greatly disturbs and displeases me]. Where Fusina had talked about how orthography could make a fluent speaker stumble, Perfettini brought in his perspective as a school inspector, saying that the unpronounced *i* also had the potential to deform authentic pronunciation patterns among Corsican language learners. He commented that, "*Frà i zitelli chì avianu amparatu u corsu in scola è chì l'avianu vistu scrittu...ne sentu certi chì dicenu 'issu,' allora chì, per vita mea, ùn l'avia mai intesu dì*" [Among those children who have learned Corsican in school and who have seen it written...I have heard some who say "*issu*," something I have never heard said in my whole life.]

While these comments show a variety of opinions about esthetic criteria and their functions, they have in common the notion that orthography can be esthetically "true" or "false" to essential dimensions of linguistic identity. As we will see, below, many Corsicans expected Corsican orthography to be true to their regional pronunciations.

2. The symbolic meanings of the Spelling Contest

The Contest was an unqualified success in the way that it succeeded in occupying media space and time. The Contest was kept in the public eye from August 1988, when the first, written test which was distributed in the banks and disseminated by the press, through the November semifinals in which contestants were given a dictation that was broadcast on television, up until the final televised contest in December. In the 1988 contest, there were also periodic spots about the contest on the radio and television, as well as quarter-page sections in the newspaper in which *A Falce* urged people to enter and presented spelling and grammar hints for potential participants (see Figure 5).

Figure 5. A Falce orthography advertisement

During the final broadcast, several of the guests marveled out loud at the mere existence of an hour and a half broadcast that was entirely in Corsican. It was calculated by the television station that over 15,000 viewers had tuned in to the final. This in itself proved the viability of Corsican as a media language, and answered the question which had been posed and debated in the recent past (March 1987) on a television show on the language. In this show, the guests (many of whom were involved in the planning for both the 1987 and 1988 spelling contests) had argued about whether they should make sure to discuss "serious" topics in French "in order to make sure that everyone understands".

The contest also dramatized progress in the domain of Corsican language literacy that the organizers probably (and correctly) felt was not common knowledge. People learned, for example, that the contestant pool had begun with 800 people who sent in the first of the three successive tests. Even though this number represents a small percentage of the Corsican population (280,000), as a raw number, 800 contestants nevertheless struck me at the time I was doing research as a fairly decent critical mass. Outside of the University context, my encounters with people who read and wrote in Corsican were very sporadic, as was the case for anyone in Corsica. Thus for most of the viewing public, I suspect that the Contest provided a snapshot of the wider picture of Corsican literacy that was not a part of routine awareness.

2.1. The cracks in the mirror

The form and intended functions of the Spelling Contest allow us to classify it as a "secular ritual". One of the features of these rituals is their instability: they are vulnerable to critique precisely because they dramatize values that are at once potent and uncertain (Moore and Myerhoff 1977). They can be challenged by alternative models of value from within the minority community or they can be found wanting in dominant terms. Both of these vulnerabilities emerge in the broadcast, and reflect the conflict between the two different models of resistance to which I have referred, above.

The first area of vulnerability concerns the way in which literacy is represented. The media drama of the final suggested, because of its relatively explicit analogy with the French contest, that the contestant pool was representative of a wider, literate population–that the 800 initial entries were a small fraction of all competent spellers. My own surveys and observations of everyday life suggested to me that the 800 initial entrants represented a fairly large percentage of all Corsicans who read and wrote regularly. In this sense, the Contest made an implicit claim that writing was a social norm that contrasted with the reality of social practice.[79] Secondly, there was far less social consensus about language standardization than the existence of a contest implied. The orthography that served as the Contest standard was widely used, but not consistently; Corsican print media and literature exhibited a noticeable range of orthographic variation. This variation can be observed even within the Corsican citations in this book. For example, in the *Falce* promotional piece below, there is the repeated use of a circumflex accent where an accent is the norm: *ciô chî* 'those who' is usually spelled *ciò chì.* The *Falce* text also separates words in expressions like *Pô dà si* 'it could be' which are run together by many writers as *podarsi* or *podassi*.

In the broadcast of the Spelling final we find that in the comments of contestants, MCs and performers, all of the following underlying premises of the idea of a Spelling Contest were challenged: (a) that writing is normal and important; (b) that there is a standard orthography; (c) that the contestants are representative and the contest a popular one; (d) that the spoken language is stable; (e) that it is important or appropriate to emphasize literacy; and (f) that there is consensus over the cultural value of linguistic standardization.

2.2. The role of writing

The first challenge to the official message of the Contest emerges in the very text contestants had to spell. Although the Contest was billed as a popular and populist event, which presumes a community of use and of value, the content and the representation of the dictation qualified this message. The dictation was read by Geronimi, one of the authors of *Intricciate è Cambiarini*, whose orthography (with a few modifications) was serving as the contest standard. The first few lines of the dictation were, "It is good that I have applied myself to learning to speak Corsican, to listening to it and also, to learning how to write it." If we apply the conversational maxim of Quantity ("Say no more and no less than is necessary") to this assertion, the fact that it is made at all, and made in such explicit terms implies that the value of speaking and writing Corsican *cannot* be taken for granted (Grice 1975). This emerges clearly in one of the promotional news columns printed by *A Falce* before the final:

> *Quand'ella sarà compia a statinata, chî vo sareti sazii di festivali, alegrii...chî vo sareti stanchi di tutta issa ghjenti nuda guasi câ incristu, imbuvaliti da i frombi di tuttu ciô chî pô fà rimori, ramintetevi, vi ferma à participà à u Campiunatu d'ortograffìa corsa. Vi sentu dighjà dî: "Ah! eiu ùn so scriva" Pô da si, ma imparà vuleti imparà? Allora, feti a vostra prima prova. Andeti à un creditu agriculu, R.c.f.m, FR3, La CORSE o Falce è pigleti un fogliu di participazioni è po vultetivi in casa, incrucchetivi à tavulinu è focu à ceppa. Prima quistioni! è dighjà l'affare in ciampa.*
> *Mà ùn lighiti ghjurnali? ùn asculteti radiu? Ci hè ogni ghjornu spiigazioni pà participà à issu campiunatu. E' po dumandeti intornu à voi. Di sicuru truvareti sempri à qualichissia prontu ad ciutavi. E' cusî avareti fattu ancu voi qualcosa par fà campà a vostra lingua.*
> *Sapiiti chî u prima attu militanti hè di parlà a lingua, di leghja è scriva in corsu. A leia billicali incù a vostra tarra hè di sicuru a lingua è micca com'ellu a ci vulia fà creda ghjorni scorsa l'ambrascu chî dicia ch'ella hè issa leia billicalii: a carta d'allitori.*

A lingua: ùn ni parleti, parletila e ancu: Lighitila è scrivitila (A Falce 1988: 5).

[When the long summer is over, and you are sated with festivals and other amusements, when you are tired of all of these people [on the beach] almost as naked as the day they were born, if your head is spinning with the reverberations of all kinds of noise makers, keep in mind that you can still take part in the Corsican Spelling Contest. I can already hear you say, "Oh, I don't know how to write!" Perhaps, but don't you want to learn? Alright, give it a try.

Go to a *Crédit Agricole* [bank], *RCFM* [radio station], *La CORSE* [newspaper] or *a Falce* and get the contest form and then go back to your house, pull yourself up to your familial table and hearth. First question! and already you've gotten the process underway.

But don't you read the paper? Don't you listen to the radio? Every day, there are directions about how to participate in this contest. And you can always ask your neighbors and familiars. You will surely find someone who is ready to help you make the plunge. And in doing so, you will have done something to help your language thrive.

Understand that speaking the language, reading and writing in Corsican is an essential militant act. It is certain that the *language* is the umbilical link you have with your *tarra* [place of origin]; this link is not, as they would have had you believe in the past, your voter registration card.

The language: if you don't speak it, speak it, and also, read it and write it.

The typical contestant who is the presumed audience for this promotion is uncertain about his/her ability to compete, and probably really does need help from a neighbor 'to take the plunge'. Turning to a neighbor is clearly a way of using human contact to get over the shock of the unfamiliar. In another piece of significant imagery, the act of filling out the form is depicted as taking place at home, at the table/hearth. The word *ceppa* in the Corsican phrase used here (*tavulinu è focu à ceppa*) literally means "roots" and is used to talk about descent groups. As a rhetorical strategy, this linkage of spelling and "primordial" images of Corsican identity draws attention to its own novelty. Unlike all the other promotions for the contest that I read, this one also underscored the identity politics associated with literacy in general, and participation in the contest in particular. In sum, the rhetorical strategies by which the promotion sent the message that writing in Corsican *should be* taken for granted underscored the extent to which it could *not* be taken for granted, and encouraged participation as a way of changing the status of writing in Corsican society.

To return to the broadcast, the action of the camera sent the same implicit message as the promotion, above, and the words of the dictation by focusing in so closely and clearly on the contestants' writing hands that their styles of script could be made out. I interpret this as an attempt at representational realism–that is, as a conscious effort to frame the act of writing as natural. But while the fascination of the camera with the writing hand may make writing "real," it is also an index of the exoticism of the act; it commands the camera's eye precisely because of its novelty.

This prelude sets up a tension which runs through the entire show: the tension between the *representation* of the language and the role of writing demanded by the nature of the contest and the event's *representativeness* of the social life of both oral and written Corsican. The exotic quality of writing and knowledge of Corsican through the written word is highlighted in the MC Petru Mari's introduction of the contestant Albert Fontana:

(19)

	1	Mari:	Ci hè quì Albert	*Here are Albert Fontana,*
	2		Fontana, Ange Mantini è	*Ange Mantini and*
	3		François Ollandini. Al-	*Francois Ollandini. Albert*
	4		bert Fontana, voi site	*Fontana, you are*
→	5		unu di i scarsi candidati	*one of the few candidates*
	6		chì ùn sò micca	*who are not spec...I mean*
	7		spec...vogliu dì,	*to say,*
	8		prufessiunali.	*professionals*
→	9	Fontana:	Inno, sò amatore, *bon*;	*No, I am an amateur,well;*
	10		mi ci mettu dapoi	*I have been at it for sev-*
	11		qualchi anni cusì, ma in	*eral years, but at home,*
	12		casa, interessendumi à a	*on my own, taking an in-*
	13		lingua, a manera di	*terest in the language, and*
	14		scrive la dinò.	*also in how it is written.*
	15	Mari:	Chì fate cumè mistieru?	*What is your profession?*
	16	Fontana:	Sò cummercente in	*I have a small business in*
	17		Bastia.	*Bastia.*
	18	Mari:	Interessenduvi à a lin-	*Taking an interest in the*
	19		gua, di chì manera	*language–in what did you*
	20		l'avete fattu prima?	*first [take that interest]?*
	21	Fontana:	A a so manera di scrive-	*In the way in which it is*
	22		la. Sapendu la parlà, più	*written. Knowing how to*
	23		o menu–ùn dicu micca	*speak it, more or less–I*
	24		cunnosce tuttu u	*won't say I know all the*
→	25		vucabulariu, ma sapendu	*vocabulary, but knowing*
	26		la parlà, cercu à sapè	*how to speak it, I seek to*
	27		cumu elli si scrivenu	*learn how certain sounds*
	28		certi soni.	*are written.*

	29	Mari:	Di rutinu, cumu si pò	*In the course of everyday*
	30		amparà una grammatica,	*life, how do you learn*
	31		a sintassi?	*grammar, syntax?*
	32	Fontana:	Aghju lettu e gram-	*I read the grammar*
	33		matiche, sicuramente,	*books, to be sure,*
	34		aghju lettu anche e	*I also read*
	35		puesie–i scritti...	*poetry–writings...*
→	36	Mari:	Per voi, essendu qui cusì	*For you, being here like*
	37		stasera, à mezu à a	*this tonight among these*
	38		ghjente, chì sò pru-	*people, who are profes-*
	39		fessionali, certi scrivenu	*sionals, some write*
	40		libri, voi, cumu vi sen-	*books, you, how do you*
	41		tite?	*feel?*
	42	Fontana:	Appena, appena accantu,	*A little, a little marginal*
	43		diceremu, ma enfin, ùn	*shall we say but after all,*
	44		hè micca...ùn pensu	*it isn't, I don't think one*
	45		micca chì ci vole à fà a	*should make dis-*
→	46		differenza...a lingua	*tinctions...the Corsican*
	47		corsa, da presu à me,	*language, in my view, is*
	48		ghjè di tutti, è tuttu u	*everyone's, and everyone*
	49		mondu, ci pò ghjunghje	*can arrive at this*
	50		à questu livellu–è po, sò	*level–and at any rate, I*
			a prova.	*am the proof*

Applying another of Grice's (1975) conversational maxims (Relevance) to Mari's questions, we can assume that they are designed to elicit answers that Mari believes will contribute significant and relevant information to the audience. His questions reveal what has already been illustrated in the last chapter: that the process of learning grammar and spelling are remarkable and interesting because they are so out-of-the-ordinary. The MCs' questioning strategies also show how peripheral and/or inauthenticating the MCs assume an academic approach to Corsican to be. This is foregrounded in an interview by the MC Castellani with a contestant who was a graduate student in the Corsican Studies Institute. He asked the contestant what he studied. When the contestant began to describe his own sociolinguistic research, Castellani cut him off by asking "Aren't you taking Karate lessons?" Although it would be risky to read too much into this question, since it is common for MCs to move quickly from one topic to another on this sort of show, this particular switching of gears seemed to have struck the contestant as abrupt; he hesitated a moment, as if somewhat taken aback with the relative superficiality of the question, before offering a suitable, sociable, lighthearted response.

Thus, paradoxically, the content of the dictation, the action of the camera and the MCs' questioning strategies reveal the marginality of what the contest is trying to represent as normal by highlighting and dramatizing the act of learning and practicing literacy in Corsican.

2.3. Language and social hierarchy: the question of elitism

Not only does the broadcast undercut the implicit claim that writing is a normal, widespread activity, but it also connects writing to status hierarchy and the exercise of authority. This surfaces in the MCs' dogged return to the theme of elitism. We see this in Mari's interview with Fontana, above. Mari is careful to single Fontana out as one of the "few nonprofessionals" among the finalists (lines 5–7). Recognizing that he is being set up by the MC as an extraordinary case, Fontana attempts to de-dramatize his literary competence and to present his acquisition of literacy as a natural outgrowth of his oral knowledge of the language (lines 25–28). This naturalization of the extraordinary is undercut by the MC's next question, in which he refers to the "celebrity" nature of the other contestants (lines 36–41) and implies that Fontana might feel a bit overwhelmed or intimidated. Fontana persists in his own version of the event, acknowledging his respect for those around him, but insisting on the popular nature of the contest and offering himself as a symbol of the average person's access to the code of literacy (lines 46–50). This requires a delicate presentational balance: Fontana has to portray himself as both enough like the other contestants to give the impression that the contest was conducted on a level playing field, but different enough from them to convince the audience that literacy is accessible.

Both Mari's questions and Fontana's response show that Fontana's "averageness" was marked; the question was, whether it was proof of the contest's elitism or its populism. The MCs collectively emphasized elitism, relentlessly pursuing a line of questioning and introduction that painted most of the contestants as "professionals" or "specialists," a label that the contestants tried equally hard to resist. The passage below, is from an interview with a middle-aged local intellectual who had no formal training in Corsican.

(20)

1	Mari:	Etienne Pasquini...Avemu	*Etienne Pasquini...Once*
2		dinò un insegnante.	*more, we have a*
3		Allora, per voi dinò, a lin-	*teacher. So, for you*
4		gua corsa hè dinò un	*also, the Corsican lan-*

5		mistieru, di una certa	*guage is a profession,*
6		manera?	*so to speak?*
7	Pasquini:	Sò direttore di una scola di	*I'm a school principal*
8		à Castagniccia. Ùn hè	*in the Castagniccia. It is*
9		micca un mistieru, hè	*not a profession, it is*
10		piutostu un piacè. L'aghju	*more a pleasure. I did it*
11		fattu soprattuttu per piacè.	*above all for pleasure.*
12		Ùn aghju micca fattu	*I have not studied*
13		studii di lingua à	*language at the Univer-*
14		l'Università.	*sity.*
15	Mari:	U vostru piacè di a lingua,	*What gives you the most*
16		cumu u pigliate?	*linguistic plea-sure?*
17		Scrivendu puesie?	*Writing poetry? singing*
18		cantendu per è machje?	*in the maquis?*
19	Pasquini:	Diceraghju...facciu, per u	*I'd say...I do, always*
20		mo piacè sempre, incù	*out of pleasure, with the*
21		l'ADECEC facciu richer-	*ADECEC I do lexical*
22		chi lessicali, recerchi nan-	*research, research on*
23		tu à i parolli, i nomi di...	*words, the names of...*
24	Mari:	Cunnuscite i nomi di e	*Do you know the no-*
25		capre?	*menclature of goats?*
26	Pasquini:	I nomi di e capre, aghju	*The names of goats, I*
27		fattu una inchiesta incù un	*did a piece of research*
28		pastore indè un locu	*with a shepherd in a*
29		muntagnolu, è m'ha	*mountainous zone, and*
30		spiegatu a manera di	*he explained to me how*
31		chjamà e capre, aghju fattu	*goats are named, I*
32		un travagliu di	*turned this into a classi-*
33		classificazione, finitu	*fication, which once*
34		dopu, l'aghju datu à	*finished, I gave to the*
35		l'ADECEC, chì l'ha	*ADECEC, which print-*
36		stampatu.	*ed it.*
37	Mari:	Dinò, site specialisti di a	*You are also an expert*
38		caccia.	*on hunting.*
39	Pasquini:	Eh, micca a caccia...aghju	*Not on hunting...I did a*
40		fattu una ricerca lessicale	*piece of lexical research*
41		nantu à a caccia.	*on hunting.*

Here, Pasquini makes a great effort to resist the application of the word "professional" to his relationship with the Corsican language. In his discussion of his work within the ADECEC, he emphasizes his amateur role and de-emphasizes his own expertise, describing his work as transcription, as a vehicle for the cultural knowledge of traditional experts like shepherds and hunters. In sum, he stresses his "natural" relationship with Corsican language and culture, which reveals that he views the academic relation imputed to him as inauthenticating.

The MCs' pursuit of the theme of elitism may be explained by the fact that the same issue had been raised the year before in the first Spelling Contest, after which the MC Mari and one of the judges had both recommended that the contestants be divided into two categories the following year: "professionals" and "amateurs. This, said the 1987 Contest judge, would help to popularize the language, rather than promote a Corsican *à part* 'separate,' that is, detached from everyday speech. It is perhaps because this change had not been made that Leca, Mari and all the other MCs took the position they did during the 1988 program.

The MCs also had, I believe, an ambivalent relationship with writers and other intellectuals. On the one hand, they were linked with them by their shared commitment to the promotion of the language, and by their extraordinary command of Corsican in a nonhabitual domain of use. On the other hand, those involved in the media saw their enterprise as much more firmly anchored in the "real world" and its demands. They characterized themselves as "professionals", but insisted that they were *media* professionals, not professionals of language. In an interview, Petru Mari told me, "*Nous sommes Radio Corse, pas Radio Sorbonne*" [We are Radio Corsica, not Radio Sorbonne]. He, and other radio and television professionals presented their use of Corsican as instrumental rather than ideological; popular rather than purist. Their goal was to communicate, rather than to enforce linguistic standards.

2.4. "They" have an academy: the question of linguistic authority

The issue of elitism is connected to the question of linguistic authority that is at the core of the contest and its subtext. This theme is taken up in the commentary of *Teatru Mascone*, a comedian who was one of the celebrity guests on the broadcast. Because of his stage presence and his ability to be both funny and incisive, Mascone's commentary plays a particularly effective subversive role in the broadcast. In it, he emphasizes the distinctness and incompatibility of French versus Corsican linguistic values, and challenges the notion that the promotion of writing is important or appropriate at this stage of Corsican sociolinguistic history.

(21)

1	Leca:	Allora per voi, a lingua	*So for you, the Corsican*
2		corsa ghjè un strumentu	*language is an instrument*

3		di travagliu?	*of your trade?*
4	Masc:	Innò, hè a mo lingua, hè	*No, it's my language, it's*
5		a mo lingua. Sta sera,	*my language. Tonight, we*
6		vedemu tutti questi	*see all these linguists,*
7		linguisti, specialisti, si	*specialists, which almost*
8		dà quasì l'impressione	*gives the impression that*
9		chì a nostra lingua hè in	*our language is com-*
10		piena salute, ch'ella hè	*pletely healthy, that it has*
11		quasì successa à una	*almost got itself an Acad-*
12		Accademia. Ma eiu	*emy. But I have an expe-*
13		aghju una sperienza di a	*rience of the language*
14		lingua ind'è u paese (un-	*from the village (unintel-*
15		intelligibile) è vogliu dì	*ligible) and I want to say*
16		chì a nostra lingua hè	*that it is sick, it needs to*
→ 17		malata: hà bisognu di	*be cured. So, sure, it*
18		esse guarita. Dunque, hà	*does need to be written.*
19		bisognu di esse scritta,	*We Corsicans who know*
→ 20		certu. Simu pochi corsi à	*how to write it are*
21		sapè lu scrive;	*few;*
22		ci n'hè di più chì u sanu	*more of us can*
23		parlà chè chì u sanu	*speak it than can*
24		scrive, ma si a nostra	*write it, but if our lan-*
25		lingua smarisce di u	*guage disappears from*
26		carrughju, mi pare chì ùn	*the streets, it seems to me*
→ 27		serve micca à nulla	*that it doesn't do much*
28		scrive la...scrive la, vole	*good to write it...writing*
28		dì "va bè." Ci vole scrive	*is saying "it's fine." We*
29		u corsu, ci hè una	*must write Corsican,*
30		nuvella, un struitu corsu,	*there is a novel, an intel-*
→ 31		ma u struitu,	*ligentsia, but this elite, it*
32		c'est nous, hè un	*is us, it's an illusion, our*
33		illusione, a nostra lin-	*language...*
34		gua...	
35	Leca:	(ridendu) Aspetta,	*(laughing) Wait, I will*
36		diceraghju, hè...	*say, it is...*
37	Masc:	Innò, in realità,	*No, really,*
38		riconnoscu chì quandu	*I recognize that when I*
39		parlu di un struitu,	*talk about an intelligent-*
40		ùn mi mettu à l'infora, mi	*sia, I'm in it, I don't ex-*
41		mettu dentru, è mi face	*clude myself, and it*
42		piacè. Sò per a rinascita	*gives me pleasure. I am*
43		di a mo lingua,	*for the rebirth of my lan-*
44		è ch'ella sbucchi ind'è	*guage; may it flourish in*
45		tutti i lochi. Ma vogliu dì	*every domain. But I want*

→	46		chì i mezi sò i mezi, è	*to say that means are*
	47		chì i mezi finu à oghje sò	*means, and that to date,*
	48		stati troppu impostu	*the means used have in-*
	49		nantu à a tecnica è micca	*sisted too much on the*
	50		abbastanza nantu à a	*technical, and not enough*
	51		pratica. E mi dispiace à	*on practice. And it pains*
	52		vede chì à nantu à certe	*me to see that in certain*
	53		generazioni, a lingua hè	*generations, the language*
	54		morta. Quessa hè una	*is dead. This is a*
	55		realità chè ci vole à dil-	*reality we must express.*
	56		la. I mezi sò i mezi. Ci	*Means are means. We*
	57		vole chì noi u parlimu,	*need to speak it, those of*
	58		noi chì u parlemu, ci	*us who speak it, and each*
	59		vole chì u corsu piglii a	*Corsican has got to take*
	60		decisione di ùn micca	*the decision not to ask the*
	61		dumandà à u Statu di	*state to defend his*
	63		difende a so lingua.	*language. It isn't*
	64		Ùn hè micca cusì	*all that difficult–to hear*
	65		difficiule– à sente parlà	*some Corsicans talk, sav-*
	66		certi corsi, salvà a lingua	*ing Corsican, speaking*
	67		corsa, parlà corsu hè	*Corsican, is like wanting*
	68		cumu vulè castrà i	*to castrate grasshop-*
	69		grilli...	*pers...*
→	70	Leca:	Innò, un si...	*No, it isn't...*
	71	Masc:	Salvà a lingua hè cumu,	*Saving the language is*
	72		hè difficiule quantè à	*like, is as difficult as cas-*
	73		castrà i grilli.	*trating grasshoppers.*
	74	Leca:	Eccu.	*There.*
	75	Masc:	Allora, un affare chè ùn	*In other words,*
→	76		ci ghjunghjeremu mai.	*something that we can't*
	77		Ma salvà a lingua,	*ever accomplish. But we*
	78		pudemu riesce se	*can save the language if*
	79		vulemu, sè i corsi chì u	*we want to, if Corsicans*
	80		parlanu, parlanu.	*who speak it, do so.*
	81	Leca:	Quandu vo fate u vostru	*When you perform, is it in*
	82		spettaculu, ghjè in corsu,	*Corsican, in French?*
	83		in francese? Ci sò e duie	*Don't you use both lan-*
	84		lingue?	*guages?*
	85	Masc:	Iè, ma quessa hè una	*Yes, but this is also a re-*
→	86		realità dinu, chì simu un	*ality, that we are a bilin-*
	87		populu bislingu. Ma issu	*gual people. But this spel-*
	88		campiunatu d'ortograf-	*ling contest, it looks like*
→	89		fia, appare chè hè un	*it is somewhat derived*
	90		pocu dirivatu di le *u*	*from the the French con-*

91		campiunatu francese.	*test.*
92	Leca:	Mmm...	*Mmm...*
→ 93	Masc:	Alors, bon, ma elli anu	*So, well. but they have an*
94		una Accademia, una lin-	*Academy, one sole lan-*
95		gua unica. Noi simu un	*guage. We are a bilingual*
96		populu bislingu, dunque	*people, so we speak in*
→ 97		parlemu à a nostra	*our own special fashion,*
98		manera à noi, è hè un	*and it is a*
99		pocu più difficiule per	*little more difficult for*
→ 100		noi, manighjemu duie	*us, handling*
101		lingue, è finu à sti	*two languages, and up to*
102		ghjorni, avemu scrittu	*now, having only written*
103		una sola–chì, aghju	*one–which, I've heard, is*
→ 104		intesu, hè strappazzu!	*very difficult! It isn't*
105		Ùn hè micca faciule!	*easy!*
106	Leca:	Cunnuscite, voi, ciò chè	*Do you, do you know*
107		vule dì questa parolla	*what this word*
108		"strappazzu"?	*"strappazu" means?*
109	Masc:	Iè. Hè una parolla chì	*Yes. It is a word with a*
110		porta u so sensu è mi	*specific meaning which*
111		pare chè hè statu precisa,	*seems to me to have been*
112		a parolla. Diceraghju	*quite precise.*
→ 113		"strappazzosu"!	*I'd say extremely difficult!*

Mascone's approach to the issue of elitism is an interesting contrast to both the MCs' and the contestants'. Although he immediately dismisses Leca's attempt to cast his relationship with the language as a "professional" one, he is not trying to affirm the populist nature of the contest. On the contrary, he asserts that he, and everyone else in the broadcast is an elite, by virtue of being able to read and write Corsican. He goes on to undercut the Contest's reason for being by stating clearly (in lines 27 and 28) that the activity of elites is irrelevant to the salvation of a "sick" language. The language can only be saved, he says, if all Corsicans commit to speaking it (lines 76–80). Moreover, by saying that the Contest "almost gives the impression" that Corsican has an Academy, he underscores the fact that it does not. This is a reminder to the "elites" running and participating in the contest that they do not have the power to prescribe. His comments also undermine the Contest's claim to reflect and promote a socially accepted orthographic standard.

Not only does Mascone question the existence of a linguistic standard, but he also questions the efficiency and appropriateness of sociolinguistic authority that a standard implies. He does this in two ways. First, he highlights the widening gap between the spoken life of the language and its formal expression in spelling and writing (lines 20–24). This points to the failure of a literacy-oriented language planning policy to create more Corsican speakers (lines 46–51). His remarks that spelling in French is *strappazu* 'very difficult' (line 104 and 113) cast the act of writing as a "requirement" to submit to a capricious, authoritarian outside force, and suggests that Corsicans may rightfully feel reluctant to enter into a similar relationship with "their" language.

Second, Mascone draws out the kind of difference between "us" and "them" that make the modeling of the Contest on the French International Spelling Competition questionable. In doing so, he forcefully asserts the counter values of intimacy, solidarity and egalitarianism in opposition to the dominant language. In his codeswitch to French in the phrase "the elite is us," (lines 31–32) Mascone metaphorically links French with, and excludes Corsican from the domain of authority and hierarchy. He highlights the social and experiential boundaries between French and Corsican, then suggests how the contest has transgressed them by attempting to model itself on a French one (lines 89–90). "They" have an Academy, *one*, unified language (lines 93–94). "We" are not only bilingual, but also, people who "talk in their own special fashion" (lines 97–98). That special fashion includes, as we have seen, FRC (the Corsican regional variety of French) and codeswitching. This is indeed a "polynomic" approach to language identity, for Mascone identifies hybrid linguistic practices with being Corsican. He also embodies such practices in his comedy routines. In the broadcast, both his good-natured exchange with Leca over the wording of a proverb (beginning on line 69), and the clip from a stage performance that is broadcast at the end of his interview emphasize language unity based on shared oral practice in both French and Corsican, rather than on written linguistic codes. In his commentary and in his performances, Mascone suggests that an emphasis on the written, rather than the oral, is an academic approach to language value that articulates poorly with the plural nature of Corsican language use. Moreover, he suggests that spelling conventions themselves are manifestations of an elitist view of language standards.

2.5. Language standards and linguistic alienation

Mascone's and the MCs' discussion of elitism further suggest that officialization establishes standards that can have the undesirable effect of alienating "average" Corsicans from a language which is culturally "theirs" even if they have become estranged from its practice. It is the nature of a Spelling Contest that some spellings are defined as right and others as wrong. When, as

Mascone suggests, there is an accepted canon, the concept of error is relatively free of personal and social repercussions and tensions (see also Trosset 1992, in reference to Wales).[80] When there is no Academy, and no absolute consensus, this is not the case. As we have seen in the last chapter, because Corsican has no accepted canon, "errors" are loaded with personal and social repercussions and tensions.

This potential for alienation can be seen in both the 1987 and the 1988 contest. In 1987, a long time member of a linguistic association entered the first round (which was relatively easy) and made it to the second. When he received his losing entry back in the mail, covered in red pen marks, he wrote back to one of the jury members to say that he was going to abandon his current project to publish a collection of local folktales in Corsican, as well as the bimonthly regional paper he edited, since his Corsican was obviously woefully inadequate. This shook up the person who had corrected his entry so much that he paid the man a personal visit in order to persuade him that he was not a failure.

In the 1988 Spelling Contest broadcast, a conversation with one of the sponsors illustrated the way in which the officializing process can create linguistic insecurity in speech. Romei's conversation with Petru Leca goes like this:

(22)

1	Leca:	Allora, dite ci perchè voi	*So, tell us why you're*
2		site qui sta sera.	*here tonight.*
3	Romei:	Ahem. *Oui.* Hè vera chì	*Ahem.* Yes. *It's true that*
4		ghjè un'onore, una man-	*it is an honor, a way*
5		era pè una banca re-	*for a regional bank,*
→ 6		giunale, 'Creditu	*'Creditu Agriculu' and*
7		Agriculu' è a diceraghju	*I'm going to say it*
8		in francese perchè ùn	*in French because I don't*
9		cunnoscu micca a parolla,	*know the word,]* the os-
→ 10		*l'osmose* fra	mosis *between the admin-*
11		l'amministrazione è	*istration and employees. I*
12		l' impiegati. Sò cuntentu	*am happy to be here,*
→ 13		d'esse quì, *même un peu*	even a bit
14		*ému...*Ci sò affari chì si	moved...*these are things*
15		facenu spessu pè i	*that are usually done by*
16		specialisti. Ma	*specialists. But*
→ 17		questu...Creditu Agriculu	*this...Creditu Agriculu*
18		hà bisognu di ghjente	*needs people like us,*
19		cum'è noi, è, cum'elli si	*and is, as they say,*
→ 20		dicenu, *est le lien entre* a	the link between *the peo-*

21		ghjente chì venenu	*ple who come to*
22		sollicità...fà un	*solicit...to make a*
23		prestu...questa ghjenti chì	*loan...these people who*
24		sò i impiegati...ci	*are the employees... to-*
25		vole...esse inseme...	*getherness is necessary.*
26	Leca:	Parlendu di	*Speaking of the organ-*
27		l'organizazzione è i soldi,	*ization and the money, so*
28		per chè tutti sapissi, a	*everyone knows, the bank*
29		banca a datu [listu di	*has given [list of*
30		premii] Allora, ghjè una	*prizes].[81] Now, is this a*
31		manera di fàssi a pub-	*way of getting publicity?*
32		licità? Certi dicenu chè a	*Some people say that the*
33		banca ùn face chè a	*bank is just getting pub-*
34		publicità. Allora, ghjè un	*licity. So, is this a real*
→ 35		veru matrimoniu frà a	*marriage between the*
36		banca è a lingua corsa?	*bank and the Corsican*
37			*language?*
38	Romei:	Iè, ghjè un veru matrimo-	*Yes, it is a real marriage.*
39		niu. Spiegeraghju un pò.	*I'll explain, briefly.*
40		Una banca, una banca	*A bank, a regional bank*
41		regiunale cum'è a nostra,	*like ours is not just about*
42		ùn hè micca chè soldi.	*money.*
43		Avemu 90% impiegati	*We have 90% Corsican*
44		corsi, chì campanu in	*employees, who live in*
45		Corsica, è ci sentimu tutti	*Corsica, and we all feel*
46		questa ecunumia, chì	*concerned about this*
47		avanza incù tanti	*economy that advances*
48		difficultà. Si sente...Mi	*with so much difficulty. It*
49		pare chè un mezzu, un	*is felt...It seems to me that*
50		bon mezzu...hè di	*one good way...is to sup-*
51		sustene una lingua è una	*port a language and a*
52		cultura chì c'aiutanu à	*culture that helps us to*
53		capisce. Vi dò un	*understand. I'll give you*
54		esempiu. Mi hà fattu	*an example. I have been*
55		piacè sta sera di stà à	*pleased to hear people*
56		sente i parlati di tutti i	*tonight speaking from all*
57		regioni, cuntentu di pudè	*regions, pleased that I*
58		capisce à tutti...	*could understand every-*
59			*one...*
60	Leca:	Dopu questu campiunatu,	*After this contest, will*
61		serete qui per a terza?	*you be there for the*
62	Romei:	Ùn dice mai chè ùn ci	*third?*
63		seremu. Ma, incù l'altri	*Don't even suggest we*
64		organizatori, feraghju	*wouldn't be. But, with the*

	65		u.....di più...ci vole	*other organizers, I'll go a*
→	66		esse perchè, *bon,*	*step further... we must be*
	67		ùn hè micca	*because,* well, *it is not*
	68		ognunu chì...parlu corsu,	*everyone that...I speak*
	69		chè aghju amparatu in	*Corsican, that I learned*
	70		carrughju, à u caffè, in	*in the street, in the café,*
	71		famiglia, per fammi	*in the family, and to make*
	72		capitu...	*myself understood...*
	73	Leca:	Allora, hè capitu chè per	*Well, it is understood that*
	74		u prossimu, ci vole fà	*for the next one we need*
	75		parechje categorie per i	*several contestant cate-*
	76		candidati–liceani contru à	*gories–High School kids*
	77		insegnanti etc. etc. per	*versus teachers, etc. etc.*
	78		permette à tutti di	*so that everyone can par-*
	79		partecipà. Avà, vogliu	*ticipate. Now I'd like to*
	80		presentavvi Teatru	*introduce Teatru*
	81		Mascone.	*Mascone.*

Romei's relative lack of confidence and competence speaking Corsican contrasted sharply with all the other participants in the program. He was, however, fairly representative of his age group (he is about 40) in his obviously compartmentalized knowledge of spoken Corsican. This compartmentalization was immediately noticeable in his nervous, involuntary lapses into French (beginning on lines 10, 13, and 20). The performance features that marked these as "lapses" rather than smooth or unconscious codeswitching included hesitations preceding the French words, (indicated by dots) hesitant speech in Corsican and a nervous facial expression. He also makes explicit mention of his use of French, leading up to the word "osmosis" in lines 6 through 9 with an elaborate and apologetic disclaimer, which has the function, as Thiers (1988a: 301) points out, of signaling that the use of French is a last resort.[82] No sooner did he resume speaking in Corsican than he was confronted with another term of phrase, *même un peu ému* [even a bit moved] that he could not translate quickly into Corsican (lines 13 and 14). The fact that this happened again (with the words "the link between") suggests that *at these moments*, he was indeed translating French into Corsican, rather than thinking in Corsican.

The meaning of Romei's codeswitching and his disclaimer in the broadcast has to be interpreted in the context of everyday Corsican patterns of speech. In fact, the contest imposed a frame which was at odds with the meaning of codeswitching in ordinary discourse in the informal social contexts the bank director evokes. In a casual conversation, it is unlikely that either the Bank director or his audience would have been conscious of a switch to French. Romei becomes self-conscious about his switch because of the Spelling Contest's monolingual Corsican standard, a framework within which any use of French is cast as a deficiency. Here, we see evidence of the "linguistic terrorism" (Hill 1985: 735) from within the minority language community that Mascone argues against: as we have seen in Chapter 6, "correct" or "pure" use of the minority language is used as a test of cultural authenticity.[83]

For a nonperformer, the experience of the broadcast was, first of all, unfamiliar and a source of nervousness. More important, it was an official, formal event for Romei: he was there in his capacity of representative of the bank. He was a senior man; representing the bank was part of his job. But it was a role that he had no doubt experienced almost exclusively in French. Two of the phrases which resisted Corsican so stubbornly ("osmosis" and "link between") were probably the stock phrases which he drew out, on such occasions, as part of his repertoire of official discourse. His use of the word *bon* 'good/well' (line 66) and his comment about being overwhelmed with emotion were evidence of strong French verbal instincts that emerged, in his nervousness, in the context of a speech in a register normally reserved for that language. Romei spoke Corsican, but probably, like most men his age, spoke it in the café, with his friends, on everyday topics, in informal contexts. He was not even used to referring to the name of his bank in Corsican. The first time he pronounced *Creditu Agriculu* (line 6), his tonic accent was uncertain: it wavered between the Corsican (penultimate syllable) and the French (ultimate). The second time he approached the name (line 17), he could be heard to slow down and prepare his pronunciation, in which he gave the words the Corsican pattern of accentuation.

It is interesting to compare his uneasy confrontation with French terms to Leca (one of the most experienced and respected Corsophone announcers, one of the few that almost everyone describes as a "good speaker" of Corsican), who has had extensive practical experience expressing himself in Corsican on almost any subject. Elsewhere in the broadcast, Leca uses a French word with a Corsican article (*u presse*) when he could have selected the "more Corsican" *a stampa*. Leca may say *u presse*, but as an accomplished speaker, this usage is a *choice* rather than a sign of linguistic limitations. Returning to Romei, and his difficulties, Leca picks up Romei's stumbling reference to the "link" between the bank and the people in a follow-up question to Romei[84] (line 35) where he uses the Corsican word *matrimoniu* 'marriage' to replace Romei's lapse into French (with *lien* 'link'). *Matrimoniu* was hardly out of the range of Romei's vocabulary or competence in Corsican. What was out of reach for him was the practice which would have enabled him to tap into Corsican linguistic patterns in a full range of social contexts.

In Leca's final comments, he uses Romei's comments about his limited competence as an opening for the theme pursued by all of the MCs in the show: that this year, it is elitist, but next year it will take on its true populist color by instituting different levels of competition. In this sense, Romei, in his discomfort and limited command of the language, is used as a symbol of the common man and his alienation from an academic standard for Corsican.

2.6. *Regional diversity vs. a standard orthography*

In popular discourse on Corsica, the question of the legitimacy of any linguistic standard inevitably leads to the topic of regional diversity. The topic came up in the 1987 Spelling Contest, and also surfaced with some unanticipated consequences in the 1988 final. In 1987, regional linguistic identification was cited by the judges as one of the principal causes of error: contestants were described as having "translated into their own *parlatu* (regional dialect)". In a reversal of the process observed among schoolchildren reading Corsican, the spelling contestants only "heard" the *meaning* of the words spoken in the dictation. When they went to write them down, they spelled them as they were pronounced in their own region. For example, a contestant from Porto Vecchio might have heard [nɔstra] 'ours' but written *noscia*, [nɔʃa], his regional variant of the word.

In 1988, the regional identity of the contestants was consistently foregrounded by the MCs' attention to where the contestants were from. While this is a standard question for an MC to ask in such a context, it evoked the essential role that language differences play in Corsican discourse about social and geographical space. In this discourse, linguistic difference is made congruent with judgments of social distance; the socially distant are labeled "unintelligible". Given the continued social salience of microregional identity, linguistic differences are given considerable social play. This popular discourse of difference is often intended and read as a challenge to language activists' claims that Corsican is one, unified language.

We can see the perceived relationship between regional variation and language unity and legitimacy in several interchanges in the Contest broadcast. In one example, one of the MCs asked a contestant (Castelli) whether his "mixed" (Northern and Southern) regional and linguistic heritage made it easier for him to do the dictations, which included a variety of Corsican regional dialects. Rather than answering "yes" or "no," Castelli immediately replied that the Corsican language was *one*. That is, he recognized that the Corsican discourse of language difference was antithetical to the Spelling Contest's symbolic function, which was to affirm for Corsican a linguistic identity equivalent to French.

Castelli responded firmly and categorically to a question articulated at the most general level (North: South) at which diversity is recognized. In the following interview, the MC Castellani interviews another contestant, Santu Rinaldi. This interview shows that the more localized the level of linguistic identity evoked the more difficult a discourse of unity becomes.

(23)

1	Castellani:	Accantu à me hè Santu	*Here next to me I have*
2		Rinaldi, di Scorca.	*Santu Rinaldi of Scorca.*
3		Avete publicatu	*You've published*
4		opere...	*works...*
5	Rinaldi:	Nantu à l'ortografia	*On Corsican spelling. It*
6		corsa. Era una fantasia.	*was a whim.*
7		Aghju scrittu un	*I wrote a little tiny book*
8		libracciolu d'ortografia,	*on spelling*
9		chì m'hà inspiratu	*inspired by* Intricciate
10		*Intricciate è*	Cambiarine.
11		*Cambiarine.*	
12	Castellani:	Site piutostu per l'uni-	*Are you generally for the*
13		ficazione di a lingua?	*unification of the lan-*
14			*guage?*
15	Rinaldi:	Ah...hè una questione,	*Ah...that's a question,*
16		quessa, chì fà	*that one, that embroils*
17		imbrogliu à tuttu...	*everyone...*
18	Castellani:	È u vostru vulè, in	*And your position? In a*
19		corte parolle?	*few words?*
20	Rinaldi:	Eiu diceraghju chè si	*I'd say that it will*
21		ferà, sicuramente, ma si	*surely happen, but we*
22		po digià pensà à certi	*can already think about*
23		affari, per esem-piu, in	*some issues, for ex-am-*
24		u mo paesi ci ne sò	*ple, in my village, there*
25		parolle, per es-	*are words, for example,*
26		empiu,"a fiarrula," la	a fiarrula, *the flame,*
27		flamme, allora, ùn	*well, as for myself, I*
28		l'aghju trovu, eiu, in un	*have not found it in a*
29		diziunariu corsu.	*Corsican dictionary.*
30		Ci hè "a fiaccula," è "a	*There's a* fiaccula, *and a*
31		fiara," chì dicu quandu	fiara, *which I use when I*
32		parlu incù a ghjente di	*talk to people from other*
33		altri paesi. Pensu chè ci	*villages. I think that we*

34		hà dà pudessi	*ought to be able to ac-*
35		ghjunghje à a	*complish*
36		unificazione, ma u	*unification, but*
37		scrittu–v'aghju à parlà	*writing–I'll give you*
38		di un altra affare. Ci hè	*another example. There*
39		"cavallu," è "cavaddu".	*is* cavallu *and* cavaddu
40		Simu d'accordu?	*'horse' Agreed?*
41	Castellani:	Iè.	*Yes.*
42	Rinaldi:	È "zitella" è "zitedda".	*And* zitella *and* zitedda
43			*'little girl'.*
44	Castelli:	Iè.	*Yes.*
45	Rinaldi:	È ci hè "sullu" è	*And there's* sullu *and*
46		"suddu," è tra è duie,	suddu *[on] and be-*
47		"suldu," ghjustu un	*tween the two,* suldu,
48		esempiu, una manera di	*just as an example, a*
49		parlà. O ci hè	*way of speaking. Or,*
50		"caldu" e...	*there is* caldu *and...*
51		Facemu l'accortu,	*Let's make it brief, as*
52	Castelli:	perchè ci tocca à...	*we have to...*
53		Se vulemu à fà una	*If we wanted to make a*
54	Rinaldi:	pruposta, vogliu dì chè,	*proposal, I want to say*
55		per esempiu, "u	*that, for example,* u
56		cavallu" po esse	cavallu *'horse' could be*
57		"cavallu," ma pudemu	cavallu, *but we could*
58		scrive la, "cavaldu,"	*write it* cavaldu, *in order*
59		per fà piacè à i	*to please the*
60		suttanacci. Devemu	*southerners.[85] We should*
61		metteci d'accordu...	*agree...*
62		Parlendu di a fiara, a	*Speaking of the flame,*
63	Castelli:	passu à Petru	*I'm passing it to Petru*
		Leca...	*Leca...*

In this interview, the MC asked Rinaldi about the "unification" of Corsican. In contrast to "unity," an abstract concept, "unification" implied action: policies that will transform the existing state of affairs. At first, Rinaldi was very reluctant to make any kind of pronouncement on this topic, for the same reason that Castelli did not want to emphasize internal language boundaries. But when he was finally prodded into a response, he embarked on a long discussion of linguistic variety at the level of the village, the smallest unit of social/linguistic identification. In his village, they had a unique word for "flame" which he had not found in any dictionary of Corsican. That is, his regional variety had been read out of the norm in the processes of unification/normalization that had occurred so far. This shows that for Rinaldi, the process of unification ultimately implied a sacrifice of a valued sort of linguistic and social differentiation to the standard.[86] These sentiments are echoed in Hélias' discussion of Breton. He writes that "If Breton were standardized, it would no longer be their own private posses-sion...the professionals persist in wanting one single orthography and no other, which would take away what is left of its freedom..." (1978: 340–342). A similar outlook figures in the preface to a French–Auvergnat dictionary, and expresses Rinaldi's implicit position in explicit terms: *"l'unification d'une nation occitane impliquerait la mort de l'auvergnat comme des autres dialectes. Elle nous dépouillerait de notre héritage plus radicalement que ne le fait la francisation"* [the unification of an Occitan nation would lead to the death of Auvergnat and other dialects. [Unification] would divest us of our heritage in an even more dramatic fashion than Frenchification] (Bonnaud, in Poche 1987: 96–97).

The specific example from his village launched Rinaldi on what is an extremely conventional everyday discourse about regional difference. Other than his initial example, ("flame") all of the words he selected came from a standard stock of examples of linguistic diversity which I have heard from people from all parts of the island on countless occasions. This discourse usually leads to the conclusion that Corsican is too diverse to be taught or written (see McClure 1985: 209). While Rinaldi did make it clear that these differences in pronunciation were not obstacles to oral communication, their written status was another thing altogether. In conversation, speakers have a variety of ways of conveying social and political stances: by accommodating to their partners' language variety, they can establish a relationship of equality and mutual respect. A written standard, however, is stripped of these interactional possibilities: it becomes almost purely political. If we combine this with the esthetic expectations mentioned above, we can see why Corsican speakers expected to be able to "see" the way that they pronounced things reflected in orthography, and saw themselves as victims of political domination when their varieties of Corsican were silenced by "standard" spellings.

This issue surfaced in many guises in the 1986 ADECEC Roundtable on orthography. For example, there was one long exchange that concerned how to represent initial consonants. Regional variation posed a problem for the identification of the underlying form (phoneme) because of rules for consonant mutation that varied from one dialect area to another. One participant claimed that the *v* in such words as *vulà* 'to fly' and *ciarvellu* 'brain' should be written with a *b* and not a *v* since they were pronounced as [b] throughout the island. Others provided counterevidence that these words were pronounced with a *v* in certain regions, and justified the use of *v* on this basis. In the North *vulà* is pronounced [bula] after a period, accented vowel or consonant, and [wulà] following an unaccented vowel. In the South, it is pronounced [vulà] and [wulà], respectively. One participant said it would be unfair to write the word with a *b* because *"Quandu vulà hè scrittu cù una "v", eiu, essendu d'insù, prununzia naturalemente "bulà", ma u Fiumurbacciu dicerà "vulà". Invece chì scrivendu "bulà" cù una "b", u Fiumurbacciu, leghjendu, ùn riccunoscera micca a parolla secondu a parolla"* [When '*vulà*' is written with a '*v*', I, being from the North, naturally say '*bulà*', but someone from the *Fiumorbu* [a region] will say '*vulà*'. In contrast, if '*bulà*' is written with a '*b*', the person from the *Fiumorbu* won't recognize the word from its pronunciation]. This comment underscores the idea that people have the right to see their speech in writing, albeit with an interesting inconsistency: the northern speaker imputes linguistic alien-ation/miscomprehension to a speaker from another region while representing his own ability to pronounce the *v* as [b] as "natural". In the article (cited in the previous chapter) about the Corsican language learner from the South, the author also represents spelling that does not transcribe local speech as an obstacle to comprehension: *"un omu di quaranta anni, puru avendula intesa, pò difficilemente mettesi in capu una pronuncia cum'è questa quì: 'Bi ribedu (w)elli zidé, ciò ch'elli 'igenu 'abertuttu' quand'elli vede scrittu 'vi', 'belli' ecc."* [a forty year-old man, even having heard [the language] will have a hard time getting the following pronunciation into his head: 'I'll tell you again my dear boy, what they said above all' when they see in writing '*vi*', '*belli*' etc.]. The italicized phrase in the original text, above, would normally be rendered *"Vi ripetu, belli zittelli, ciò ch'elli dicenu dapertuttu"*; the text highlights the difference between pronunciation and speech (A. V-P 1991: 15). Another speaker of a southern variety gave me yet another interdialectal rationale for separating the direct and indirect objects in the imperative. In Corsican, you can write "say it to him" in two ways: *dillalu* [say + direct object + indirect object] or *di la lu*. In the latter "connected" version, the *l* is doubled. Proponents of this spelling say that it serves to represent the length of the consonant following a stressed syllable. My acquaintance from the South, however, objected on the grounds that the doubling of *l* could be "confusing" to him. When he saw two *l*'s, he automatically translated them into two *d*'s. He did this because the medial [l] versus [d] was one of the most salient phonological distinction between the North and South, and since the northern dialect is more heavily represented in the written materials of all kinds. But this phonological rule does not cross morpheme boundaries; northern and southern pronunciations of the imperative form above would not differ. In such a case, the reading "translation" produced a nonexistent word: **diddadu.* In this conversation, I suggested that since this was a nonsense form, he would be unlikely to be confused. He persisted in his position, which I think that we can take two ways. I think he was using "confusion" to describe the experience of having the eye arrested in its movement across the page. He was an advanced reader, and a student in Corsican studies, and he had come to expect to read Corsican smoothly. These double consonants caused him perhaps a split second of extra processing, but in that moment, he became aware of spelling; he stopped the pure flow of information. Secondly, there is the question of dialectal politics. As a Southern speaker, he had already accommodated to Northern dominance in the written domain, and he resisted having to do so in yet another way.

Another reason why Corsicans expect spelling to "look like" the way they say it has to do with the link between language and intimacy, and the way that this is tied up with very local, village identities.

To return to the contest, Rinaldi did not in fact propose that his dialect be represented as the norm. He actually advocated graphic mixtures that incorporated elements from the pronunciation of both northern and southern dialects. He suggested that it was more equitable for all speakers to be equally alienated from the "look" of the word on the page, and that having a single (and "mixed" if necessary) spelling for each word was needed in the graphic representation of linguistic unity. In effect, his proposal insisted on a much greater level of consistency in reference to regional variation that currently existed in the guidelines provided by *Intricciate è Cambiarini*. As an example, we can note that while the authors and supporters of this manual were unwilling to let both *bulà* and *vulà* be valid spellings, they accepted both *cavallu* 'horse' (Northern) and *cavaddu* 'horse' (Southern). In both his discussion of regional linguistic diversity, and in his proposal for a new spelling standard, Rinaldi implied that the treatment of diversity in the Spelling Contest contributed to internal social divisions rather than to a concept of pan-Corsican unity.

Leca and Castellani, embarrassed by the duration and content of Rinald's message, cut him off. It was clear that his comments touched a nerve, for Leca felt obliged to respond to them in defense of the contest. While he avoided any reference to rules, error or authority, he remarked that organizing such a contest "was not easy" and that they could not discuss regional differences of pronunciation because "the contest had to go on." He went on to congratulate everyone for being there, "all together," which implicitly recognized the sense in which unity, consensus and unification did not preexist the contest but were in the process of being forged by the partici- pation in it. Leca's comments assume that the acceptance of the authority of the Spelling Contest required significant compromises and sacrifices at the level of regional diversity.

Other MCs, however continued to ask about diversity, and the contestants' responses continued to question the Contest's spelling standard. For example, when Petru Mari asked the contestant Angelu Migliacci about the difficulty of the final, this contestant said that he had had problems understanding the speech from the Marignana region since he was more used to two other regional dialects. Mari then pursued the same line of questioning with Albert Fontana, another one of the five first place winners. Consistent with his policy of linguistic representation demonstrated earlier, Fontana denied that there were any particular difficulties in the text and asserts that written Corsican is as normal as any other language. Mari then concluded that regional diversity was not a factor for the finalists. His next interviewee, however, contradicted this statement; being from the South, Ange Mantini said, did cause him some difficulties. "So there *is* a difficulty in the choice of dialect," said Mari. This comment must have reminded Mantini of the political and ideological ramifications of his comments, for he scrambled to recast his representation of the language in a way that is consistent with the goals and ideals of the contest. His reference to mutual intelligibility invoked a "natural," oral unity of the language; his comments on the normalness of difficulty in a test situation (individual inadequacy in face of a norm or standard) asserted what was, at heart, contested. In the context of his previous remarks, it was clear that in taking this position, he relinquished some of his hold on autonomous, regional linguistic identity.

As we have seen, the intense experience of local linguistic identity has been the only framework, in which the concept of linguistic identity, and therefore, of concepts of competence and error have been understood by the majority of Corsican speakers. As Poche writes, "*Si une langue oral se compose d'un très grand nombre de variétés proches...chacune sera perçue comme une forme stable sans qu'aucune ne puisse prétendre à la qualité de standard linguistique*" [if an oral language is made up of a very large number of neighboring varieties...each one will be perceived as a stable form without any one of them being able to claim itself as the linguistic standard] (1987: 95). This seems to be the case in Corsica. Most Corsican speakers do not view "homogenized" Corsican as "authentic". "Authentic" speech is local speech.

The standards for competition in the Spelling Contest also conflicted with the way that "authentic" local speakers accommodated to one another in conversation, in which it was assumed that both could speak their own variety and simply have passive (receptive) competence in their partner's dialect. To do well in the Spelling Contest, however, required contestants to use the orthographic code to transcribe the speech of another region. This required a reflexive consciousness of linguistic interpretation processes that was quite unusual.[87] In a sense, the standards for competition were in conflict with the orthographic philosophy implied by the choice of passages in the contest's dictation: all were marked as belonging to a specific linguistic region. The contest thus promoted one orthography, but did not promote one variety of Corsican as standard. This orthographic philosophy implies that people should use the code to write the way they speak.

3. Conclusions

In the broadcast, we can see some of the unintended consequences of forms of linguistic resistance that do not challenge the dominant models of identity and criteria of value. First of all, the Contest provided a forum for, perhaps even provoked a contestatory discourse emphasizing the countervalues of solidarity, egalitarianism and intimacy–the resistance of separation. The Spelling Contest was unable to have a single, authoritative voice because it left a diglossic model of linguistic identity and value intact. Since the value of Corsican and the value of French are defined (for Corsicans) in opposition to each other, to evoke one is to invoke, at least implicitly, the other. Because of this perpetual "dual voice," the Spelling Contest could not tap into the capacity of dominant discourses "to prescribe while seeming to describe" (Bourdieu 1991: 128). The prescriptive dimension of the contest did not cause the rules to be taken for granted; rather, it ended up laying their ideological premises open for evaluation and dissent.

If we look at the form that this dissent took in Mascone's comments and in the discourses about regional linguistic variation, we can see once again that the very act of emphasizing Corsican as a language of authority and power violated Corsican categories of linguistic value and identity. In the Spelling Contest, the authoritative voice that the organizers attempt to appropriate for Corsican is defined as "French" and classified as "other". I would argue, as Reed-Danahay (1987: 87) does in a parallel case involving French farm children in school,[88] that this distancing maintains the value of Corsican as a private refuge, essentially untouchable by French or France.

The Spelling Contest also allows us to reflect on how the glorification of writing at a time when there was a declining number of Corsican speakers with highly compartmentalized sociolinguistic competence affected the way that norms and standards were interpreted. The French competition that the contest was modeled on was grounded in a practice (learning to spell French) that was a rite of scholastic passage experienced by all members of the Francophone world. But the standards of the Corsican contest were completely detached from any collective cultural experience or practice. The focus on form rather than practice drew exclusionary rather than inclusionary boundaries.

Adopting the dominant notion that the value of language is primarily linked to its properties as a formal, autonomous code also de-legitimized Corsican cultural and linguistic heterogeneity. In the broadcast, we can see how the framework of the contest led some of the participants to view the regional linguistic diversity and codeswitching/language mixing that characterize everyday communicative practice as transgressions of linguistic and cultural boundaries which constituted a threat to the integrity of Corsican.

The Spelling Contest returns us to a theme that we have seen in the last three chapters: that Corsican language planners are in a double bind. To the extent that a dominant ideology of linguistic value is part of popular consciousness, they are led to employ its terms in order to convince Corsicans of the legitimacy of their language. In doing so, however, they set in motion a series of culturally conditioned responses to domination/authority which act as obstacles to the program of linguistic revitalization that planners wish to promote, and create new forms of linguistic insecurity and alienation.

These points were not lost on the organizers of the Second Annual Spelling Contest. In 1989, the contest had age and competence categories, was held in a High School, and was not broadcast. The following year, it was quietly abandoned.

Chapter 8
Moving language off center stage: media and performance

In the last four chapters, we have seen the dilemmas, ambiguities and limitations of forms of resistance that do not challenge the premises of dominant models of power and value. Some of the unintended consequences of language activists' attempts to build the authority, status and practice of Corsican through literacy and officialization are: (a) minority language hierarchy (purism) which leads to the alienation of learners and Corsophones who are not literate in Corsican or who speak an "impure" or otherwise "deficient" variety; (b) the rejection of language planning measures such as officialization or mandatory education on grounds that are rooted in either a diglossic logic ("How can you teach/impose a mother tongue?") or a dominant language ideology in terms of which regional dialectal variation is cast as an insurmountable obstacle to any form of language unification or standardization; (c) overdramatization and overpoliticization of communicative and expressive activity that burdens and thus discourages practice;[89] (d) an inability, in both activist models and popular reactions to them, to recognize the plural, mixed nature of Corsican linguistic practice and cultural identity

But the story of Corsican language revival is not simply the story of the trials of standardization, normalization and officialization. There is also another voice in the defense of Corsican that I began to hear in 1989 and which I have tried to track in subsequent research. This is the voice of Corsican creative practice in which the Corsican language is used, but in which it is not the central focus, nor the sole marker of Corsican identity. The first, and largest part of this chapter examines the use of Corsican in the media and other performing arts and compares and contrasts its sociolinguistic implications with the literacy-oriented strategies emphasized so far. The thesis is that media practice reflects and implicitly validates the abundant language mixing (and the plural cultural identity that it indexes) that characterizes Corsican communicative practice as well as foregrounds communication rather than linguistic form and standards. Taken together, this de-dramatizes the issues of language choices and competencies as barometers of "authentic" cultural identity. Media practice thus allows for linguistic play and creativity that blurs, rather than emphasizes linguistic boundaries (see Thiers 1989: 104). The second part of the chapter describes some initiatives in the public and academic domains in which, as in the media examples, the burden of representation of Corsican identity is shifted away from the Corsican language in its relation with French and resituated in a broader linguistic and cultural context.

1. Radio: *Radio Corse Frequenza Mora*

Radio Corse Frequenza Mora (RCFM) is the Corsican branch of France's decentralized regional radio network. It is an extremely popular station which, according to a recent survey, commands approximately a 70% share of the listening market. Programming is bilingual. In a typical broadcast day there are regularly scheduled features such as news, weather, community announcements and, comedy spots that are done in both Corsican and French. In the case of the news, the Corsican versions alternate in a planned pattern with the French ones. Considerable broadcast time is also given over to loosely structured programming in which bilingual disc jockeys introduce songs, conduct radio quiz games, take listener call-ins, or broadcast live from cafes and villages around the island. This radio space is characterized by linguistic plurality: the humor is bilingual and bicultural, and both the DJs and their listeners regularly switch languages in every conceivable way, as will be seen below. The radio space is also plural in a number of other important ways: (a) RCFM's Corsophone announcers come from all parts of the island, and represent a range of regional varieties of Corsican;[90] (b) the programming includes different registers of Corsican; (c) particularly in the comedy and listener call-ins, you can hear both a distinctly regional (corsicanized) variety of French and a distinctly modern (frenchified) variety of Corsican; and (d) listeners and radio staff exhibit a range of levels of competence that is an accurate representation of the current sociolinguistic picture.

In these ways, RCFM fulfills the mission described to me by the director in 1992, which was to be a *radio de proximité* 'radio of proximity': a mirror of life on the island, including its heterogenous communicative practices. His goal, he reported, was to broadcast the language one hears in the bistro, "where there is that bilingualism, that jumping from one language to another". As an afterthought, he said that perhaps this was a bad sign from a linguistic point of view, that perhaps it meant that the Corsican language was in decline, but that it was the reality.

1.1.   Contests and standards: A Ghjustra Paesana and l'Accademia di i Stralampati

In the Spelling Contest, the issue of standards emerges as a alienating and divisive one. This was not, however, the case in two other contests that were a regular part of RCFM's programming for several years. The first was called *A Ghjustra Paesana* [The Village Joust]. This was a year-long series of contests that pitted two teams (representing clubs, villages and other associations) against each other in three event categories: history/current events, poetry, and vocabulary/spelling. By definition, all of the players were Corsican speakers and spellers, since one of the contests was to see which team could make the longest word out of a series of letters. Because it was a team effort, however, not every player had to be an expert speller; often individuals were recruited on the basis of their particular ability in one of the other three events. Not only did the variety of events counterbalance the emphasis on literacy skills, but it also valorized every single player's contribution and dissipated literacy-based anxiety. I happened to be at a *Scola Corsa* meeting in which they discussed who was going to go to the upcoming semifinal. One man[91] was very hesitant, mostly about the spelling. "Come on," someone said, "we need you for the part where you make up poetry." His face brightened. "Oh, *that's* easy," he said, and agreed to go.

The settings of the recording sessions (cafes, festivals, town halls) also contributed to the convivial and lighthearted atmosphere; there was always an enthusiastic audience of fellow villagers and café regulars. The listening audience was also actively included in the program: the winner of the impromptu poetry contest (each team had to make up a poem on a given topic in ten minutes) was decided by an audience telephone vote. The DJ who ran this program, Petru Mari, was a well-liked radio personality who drew a crowd.

The popular and populist appeal of the *Ghjustra* contrasted sharply with the reception of the Spelling Contest. One of my neighbors, a woman of about sixty who often participated in RCFM contests to do with language and was a competent reader and speller, had dismissed my suggestion that she enter the Spelling Contest by saying that it was rigged and that there was favoritism. This was really a roundabout way of alluding to the dominance of intellectuals in the finals. But two years after Riventosa formed a *Ghjustra* team and hosted the contest in the village, she was still talking about the event. For her, it represented a high point in village history.

As a faithful listener to the *Ghjustra*, I was struck by the fact that there was never any evidence of dissent or rancor over spelling standards, despite the role the word-composition event played in the joust. This is not to say that there was no disagreement; teams often challenged the validity of the other team's word or the way that they had spelled it. Like players in a Scrabble game, contestants often stretched the limits of credulity, and Mari would say, "Hmmm...has anyone actually heard of this word? What exactly did you say it meant?" But if contestants made a convincing case that a word was an obscure regional term, they usually won a challenge. Spellings were also contested. Once, there was a question as to whether or not a double consonant was required. It could not be resolved on the air, and Mari said, "We'll have to defer that ruling until tomorrow, so we can look it up in the dictionary." There was not a peep of dissension from either team, despite the fact that they could have well asked, "*Which* dictionary?," given the fact that there is no one authoritative standard. On another occasion, Mari told a contestant who complained about a trigraph, "*Si vous voulez gagnez le gâteau à la chataigne, vous devez accepter que les trois lettres "chj" representent le son [tj]. C'est compliqué, mais c'est comme ça*" [If you want to win the chestnut cake, you will have to accept that the three letters "chj" stand for the sound [tj]. It's complicated, but that's the way it is] (Thiers 1988a: 142).

What is interesting here is that Mari endorsed a spelling convention, but did so in a way that both implicitly acknowledged the arbitrariness of orthographic rules at the same time as it discouraged ideological readings of those rules. In the *Ghjustra*, spelling a sound a particular way was framed as purely instrumental (to win the chestnut cake); the wider sociological implication was that a community of speakers could/should also accept spelling conventions for their instrumental value. In discussions I had with Mari and the RCFM station director about how they went about creating new words in Corsican for their Corsican news broadcasts (to fill lexical gaps like "tanker" or "environmentalism"), they also emphasized the instrumental. They reported using various documents to make up words: ADECEC lexicons, a variety of Corsican dictionaries and Italian dictionaries. They took the position that expediency was the key and intellectual models of authority were not the issue. As we will see, it was impossible for them to remain neutral in the endeavor of creating neologisms, and individual journalists did have preferred and dispreferred sources of linguistic authority. So their representation of their practice was not entirely consistent with what they did, but it was also not completely inconsistent. In the case of the *Ghjustra*, Mari was indeed willing to suspend some of his personal preferences for the sake of the game.

The point was that spelling was not the only contest in the joust, nor was it the sole focus of the word composition game, which also involved vocabulary. Moreover, the ludic quality of the whole event was foregrounded. The importance of the playful dimension was alluded to by Lisandru Bassani in a newspaper interview about his new edition of a traditional Corsican flashcard game. He said,

> *Je voudrais dire que nous avons voulu faire éclater un peu l'angoisse que nous transportons souvent en nous au sujet de la langue et de son devenir. Je crois que jusqu'à présent cette angoisse s'est portée elle-même sur les documents et la pédagogie, les documents étaient souvent trop austères et trop sévères. Il nous faut sortir de ce cycle et je crois que l'aspect ludique de ce [jeu de] loto est un bon moyen* (Bassani 1989: 11).

> [I want to say that we wanted to blast away a bit at the anguish that we often carry within us about the subject of the language and its future. I think that this anguish is borne in documents and in language pedagogy; the documents have often been too austere and severe. We need to get out of this cycle and I think that the ludic aspect of this lotto [game] is a good way to do so.]

In the other parts of the *Ghjustra* the teams had to answer trivia questions on current or historical events. They also made up questions to ask each other, usually about their region of the island. In contrast to the discourse on regionalism in the Spelling Contest, the role of regional identity in both the spelling and the quiz portions of the *Ghjustra* was integrative rather than divisive. Participants were rewarded for their knowledge of regionally specific lexical items—just the kind of knowledge that they were likely to associate with Corsican linguistic identity and legitimacy. In the *Ghjustra*, regional linguistic diversity was evoked as a unifying cultural constant rather than an impediment to a pan-Corsican identity. Like the greetings exchanged by strangers in villages, the regional aspects of the *Ghjustra* proclaimed "I am a villager just like you."

The *Ghjustra* also served another function in the promotion of a consciousness of "unity in diversity" by broadcasting speakers from all over the island. Despite the fact that Corsicans travel the island much more than they used to, many people still find the speech of other regions quite exotic. I recall, for example, being at a dinner party in 1989 where RCFM was playing in the background. They happened to air an interview in Corsican of a schoolteacher and her students in the South. This caught the attention of the host and the other Corsican guests, who were all northerners, and they proceeded to listen and repeat words and pronunciations that were different from the way that they spoke. Despite the fact that the radio program focused their attention on difference, it also demonstrated dialectal intercomprehension. In this respect, by bringing varieties of Corsican the language into general circulation, we can see that media has the potential to persuade the public of a linguistic unity based on use, rather than on abstract linguistic or academic grounds (see Thiers 1988a: 334).

Mari's attitude towards spelling was part of his general philosophy of language: he made an issue of neither practice nor competence. So, although he carried out the majority of the show in Corsican, he did not avoid French or discourage its use. On one occasion, he gave the letters to be used in the spelling competition to the two teams in both Corsican and French; on another, he repeated a date in French, acknowledging but not criticizing the fact that many Corsicans are French-dominant in some everyday language acts like counting. There were also contestants who asked or answered questions in French; this was not remarked on. Nor did Mari avoid or discourage gallicisms in Corsican, acknowledging, again, their widespread existence in everyday speech. His use and attitude towards purity and authenticity seemed to me to be consistent with those of many habitual speakers of Corsican that I knew; that is, it was not intellectualized and was not particularly consistent. So, for example, he was capable of using a gallicism in one breath, and an obscure item of Corsican vocabulary in the next. My friend Martin the retired shepherd did the same thing. I recall asking him the word for 'heavy'. He said, immediately, "*lordu*," (from the French *lourd*) and then after a short pause, "*pisivu*" (literally, 'weighty,' the older Corsican term). The second translation was implicitly marked, in this interaction, as the more "authentic" but it was also quite clearly the least frequently used. Martin also made it clear that authenticity was not a huge issue for him, remarking that *pisivu* was "more Corsican," but doing so with without any particular emphasis. Both terms adequately communicated the same thing and he was equally likely to use either one.

In general, on the radio, tradition was not overemphasized, but nor was it ignored. There was another show, *L'Accademia di i Strampalati* [The Academy of the Maladroit], in which a poem, or song, or proverb was read on the air with a certain number of errors. Listeners could call in and win by correctly identifying mistakes such as wrong words, faulty pronunciation or grammar. This game resembles French language pedagogy of the nineteenth century described by Achard, where children were taught to correct texts with deliberately placed errors long before they were able to write well themselves. Underlying this practice was a premise that "the language was, in a certain way, presumed to be known" by the students (Achard 1987: 50).[92] The radio game also drew on and presumed social and linguistic competence, a stock of "traditional" as well as other kinds of knowledge which a good number of listeners shared. One woman of about fifty told the story of how she had won this game without even knowing that it was a contest. An infrequent listener, she heard song lyrics recited on the radio and called in to voice a complaint that they were incorrect. She was tickled pink to win a prize for her vigilance.

1.2. Language alternation and language mixing on the radio

L'Accademia di i Stralampati is only one of numerous games that RCFM has used to solicit the listener call-ins which are a regular part of morning radio shows. The following transcripts of some of this programming illustrate both the way in which the DJs alternate between Corsican and French in their own patter, as well as the mixture of the two languages in their conversations with listeners.

(24)
Listener call-in: deferring to language choice

1	DJ:	Salute Jean	*Hello Jean.*
2	Jean:	Salute.	*Hello.*
3	DJ:	Jean, ci chjamate di, d'in-	*Jean, you're calling from*
4		duve chjamate?	*where?*
5	Jean:	Di Folelli.	*From Folelli.*
6	DJ:	Allora.	*Well.*
7	Jean:	*Bon, je vais vous parler*	Good. I'm going to speak
8		*en français.*	to you in French.
9	DJ:	*Je vous en prie.*	Please go ahead.

(23) Listener call-in: unmotivated switching (the caller is trying to guess a song title from a very brief recording that was aired)

	1	DJ:	Santa, d'Aiacciu	*Santa, from Ajaccio.*
	2	Santa:	Bonghjornu.	*Hello.*
	3	DJ:	Cumu Andemu?	*How are we [you] doing?*
	4	Santa:	E bè, cumu sti vechji.	*Oh, like old folks.*
	5	DJ:	Fa bellu tempu in	*Is the weather nice in*
	6		Aiacciu?	*Ajaccio?*
→	7	Santa:	*Oui, très beau, très beau,*	Yes, very nice, very nice,
	8		*oui.*	yes.
	9	DJ:	*Alors vous allez à la*	So you'll go to the beach
	10		*plage cet après-midi?*	this afternoon?
	11	Santa:	*Bah...*	Bah...
	12	DJ:	*Ou vous restez à*	Or you'll stay in the
	13		*l'ombre...*	shade...
	14	Santa:	*C'est à dire que j'ai un*	The thing is, I have a

15		*problème de conjoncti-*	problem of conjunctivitis
16		*vite, alors la plage...*	so the beach...
17	DJ:	*Ah, oui, c'est mauvais: le*	Ah, yes, it's bad, sun and
18		*soleil, et puis l'eau de*	sea water have a bad ef-
19		*mer ça fait mauvais effet.*	fect. Yes, you stay where
20		*Ah oui, vous restez au*	it's cool, one is comfort-
21		*frais, on est bien au frais,*	able in the coolness, don't
22		*ne vous inquiétez pas.*	you worry. Toussainte,[93]
23		*Toussainte, je vous*	I'm listening [go ahead].
24		*écoute..*	
→ 25	Santa:	Sta megliu fora chè in	*It's better outside than in*
26		casa.	*the house.*
27	DJ:	Iè, hè vera.	*Yes, that's true.*
28	Santa:	Ùn hè micca "U Caten-	*It wouldn't be "The*
29		acciu"?	*Catenacciu"?*
30	DJ:	"U Catenacciu"?	*"The Catenacciu"?*
31	Santa:	Iè.	*Yes.*
32	DJ:	Mancu appena.	*Not at all.*
33	Santa:	Bah,.ùn face nunda.	*Bah, it doesn't matter.*
34	DJ:	Ma cumu emu da fà? A	*Well, what can we do?*
35		vedeci ô Santa!	*See you later, O Santa!*
36	Santa:	*Allez*, bona ghjornata.	Ok, *have a nice day.*

(24) Listener call-in: passive competence assumed

1	DJ:	Avemu subitu Marilou.	*Right now we have*
2		*Marilou bonjour. Vous*	*Marilou* Marilou, hello.
3		*allez bien?*	You're doing well?
4	Marilou:	*Très bien, et vous*	Very well, and yourself?
5		*même?*	
6	DJ:	*Oui oui, avec le soleil ça*	Yes, yes, it's always great
7		*va toujours bien. Mari-*	when it's sunny out.
8		*lou, d'où vous appelez?*	Marilou, where are you
9			calling from?
10	Marilou:	*De Migliacciaru.*	From Migliacciaru.
11		Migliacciaru. A	Migliacciaru. Is it
12	DJ:	Migliacciaru il y a du	sunny in
13		*soleil?*	Migliacciaru?
→ 14	Marilou:	Iè, iè	*Yes, yes.*
15	DJ:	Sicuru. Hè in u Fium-	*Sure. It's in the*
16		orbu, Migliacciaru?	*Fiumorbu, Migliacciaru?*
17	Marilou:	*Voilà*, in Fiumorbu,	Yes, in [the] Fiumorbu,
18		*oui.*	yes.
19	DJ:	Bè, ci hè u sole in u	*Well, it's sunny in the*

20		Fiumorbu.	*Fiumorbu.*
21	Marilou:	*Oui.*	*Yes.*
22	DJ:	Allora, tuttu va bè.	*So, everything is fine.*
23		*Migliacciaru, c'est en*	Migliacciaru, it's on the
24		*plaine. Voilà, voilà,*	plain. So, so, good, great.
→ 25		*c'est très bien.* Chì	*What do you want to*
26		vulete sente voi?	*hear?*
27	Marilou:	*Queen, le groupe*	Queen, the group Queen.
28		*Queen.*	
29	DJ:	*Po po po po, Queen.*	Po po po po, Queen.
30		*Vous êtes dans le vent,*	You're in the wind,
31		*eh?*	eh?
32	Marilou:	*Ah, oui.*	Ah, yes.
33	DJ:	Vi piace à Queen.	*You like Queen.*
→ 34	Marilou:	*Dommage qu'il soit*	It's a shame he died
35		*mort jeune, oui?*	young, isn't it?
36	DJ:	Ah, ma quessa, *c'est la*	*Ah, but that,* that's life,
37		*vie,* chì vulete?	*what can you say?*
→ 38	Marilou:	*C'est la vie.*	That's life.

In example (22) with Jean from Folelli, the DJ politely defers to Jean's expressed desire to speak French, and ceases to address him in Corsican. More often than not, the caller does not voice a language preference in the opening sequence as Jean does, but either falters in Corsican or simply switches to French with no explanation after an exchange of greetings in Corsican. On the radio, as in everyday communication, greeting exchange is not taken as an index of competence in Corsican. Both faltering and switching usually prompt the DJ to switch to the caller's selected language with no comment,[94] as is the case in example (23) above, where the DJ follows Santa's switch to French in line 7, and her switch back to Corsican in line 25. This conversation is a very good model of the kind of unmotivated codeswitching that one often hears between Corsican bilinguals, and which as a practice, itself indexes and creates a certain intimacy (see Chapter 3).

While deference to one's interlocutor's language choice is the stated politeness norm in Corsica (as it is in many bilingual contexts), it is not necessarily the only socially accepted form of language choice. In example (24) the conversation begins in French. The DJ switches to Corsican in response to Marilou's first utterance in Corsican ("yes" on line 14). The DJ continues to address Marilou in Corsican repeatedly in the remainder of the exchange, even though she never utters another Corsican word. Yet I would argue that the DJ does not place a very heavy burden of comprehension on Marilou; he does not publicly "test" her Corsican competence. The only direct question he asks her in Corsican ("What do you want to hear?" on lines 25 and 26) is highly predictable, since the purpose of her call is to request a song. His other Corsican utterances are statements, rather than questions, to which Marilou is not required to respond directly. She is able, as in lines 34 and 38, to expand on or echo the propositional content of his comments.

Significantly, Corsican speakers to whom I played this excerpt did not all evaluate Marilou's competence in Corsican the same way. Originally, I had read Marilou's continued use of French as a sign that she could not speak Corsican. But when I asked my interviewees whether they thought the DJ's codeswitching was appropriate or polite, some said "yes," justifying their answer with comments like, "He could tell the lady spoke Corsican."

The gap between Marilou's performance and these listeners' judgments can be explained in two ways. First, there is the general sociolinguistic context in which this particular conversation takes place.
As we have seen, this context makes it difficult to infer language competence (and even language preference) from short stretches of public speech. But there is another, conversation-internal explanation: my listeners were also able to "hear" Marilou as a Corsophone because of the DJ's use of codeswitching. This switching metalinguistically represented the conversation as a bilingual one (and thus, Marilou as a Corsican speaker) while, as we have seen, making it possible for her to participate in a bilingual exchange with a minimal amount of linguistic competence.

I have heard other on-air exchanges in which a Corsican–French conversation (with each person speaking a different language) has lasted throughout an entire exchange. What is significant in these examples is that the language alternations show and implicitly validate heterogenous bilingual practice. Like vernacularization in urban, transethnic contexts described by Wald, this kind of radio practice "renders hybridization banal and everyday" (1986: 119). The above exchanges also air, and implicitly accept the very uneven linguistic competence that is the mark of language shift.

This is also the case in the following two transcripts of comedy spots. The first is a passage from a daily parody of horoscope reports that ran in 1992; the second is an excerpt from a daily routine aired beginning in 1994 that was so popular that the comedian did a live performance in the summer of 1994. The character, "Madame Mozziconnacci," is a parody of a gossipy woman who lives in Ajaccio and relates in breathless and relentlessly mixed Corsican and French, her daily life.

(25)   Comedy: horoscope satire

1   *Se vo ùn sapete ciò che vo avete à manghjà oghje, v'aghju à dà*

If you don't know what you're going to eat today, I'm going to give you an

2   *un'idea. Allora, fatevi piuttostu duie canneloni* à la brousse
    idea. Ok, make yourself a couple of *cheese* canneloni

3   *Allora, v'aghju à spiega.* Vous faites une daube. *Cumè vo fate*
    Now, I'll explain it to you: *You make a stew.* Like you

→ 4 *d'abitudine un tianu in* daube, *cu essu alivu**démailloté,[95]
    usually make a stew in *stew,* with those olives *without bathing suits,*

5   *cu i so* champignons, *fate rivene,* vous faites une daube et vous
    with those *mushrooms, you sauté, you make a stew and you*

6   laisser consommer. Vous prenez un café. Alors, ensuite, vous prenez
    let it reduce. You have a cup of coffee. So, next , you take

7   votre brousse et vous l'écrasez, et vous le mélangez avec les épinards
    your cheese and you mash it and you mix it with the spinach

→ 8 *Pigliate a carne macinata,* vous machinez bien votre viande avec ses
    You take the ground meat, *you grind your meat well with those*

→ 9 olives*démaillotées, *ùn ci hè più nocciu...*
    **olives without bathing suits,* there are no more nuts....

(26) Madame Mozziconnacci

1   *Coco, ça va? Aspetta Coco, t'hai à fà dì. Piglia u to caffè.*
    Coco– *how are you?* Wait, Coco, I've got things to tell you. Have a coffee.

2   *Prima, je vais raconter...qu'est-ce que tu veux, tu veux les personnages?*
    First, *I'm going to tell...what do you want, you want characters?*

3   Je vais te raconter *un personnagiu, mì, Coco, micca cunnisciutu.*
    I'll tell you about a character, look, not a well-known one.

4   C'est dommage. *Era longu longu, magru magru. Iè, si chjamava*
    It's a shame. He was very tall and very thin. Yes he was called

5   *Zeze Untu.* Il avait un peu de goutte, *ellu facia i fascini,*
    Zeze Untu. He had a little *gout* he made up bundles of firewood,

6   *eru u specialistu di fascini. T'avia u so carettu, è u so sumere,*
    He was the faggot specialist. He had his wagon and his donkey

7   *è partia ti rendi contu, tamanta strappata prima*
    and he used to leave, picture it–it was was so tough in those times,

8   il n'y avait pas les automobiles *chì ci n'hè avà.*
    there weren't the cars that there are now.

In the both the horoscope parody and the last comedy sketch, we see numerous examples of intrasentential codeswitching. The horoscope parody (along with the conversation in Example 23) was used in interviews to prompt people to talk about the frequency, purpose, effect and desirability of codeswitching in everyday conversation. Everyone identified the intrasentential switching as "common" or "normal". The French spoken in the horoscope parody was also strongly marked as "regional" by the speaker's heavy Corsican accent and by the Corsican interferences in French. These interferences/malapropisms are found on lines 4 and 9, where olives are describe as *démailloté/démailloteés* 'without bathing suits' instead of *dénoyauté/dénoyautées* 'pitted' and on line 8, which features the verb *machiner* which is not French, but a frenchification of the Corsican *macinà* 'to grind'. There is also a repetition, *tianu in* daube 'stew in stew'. All of these features were pointed out to me in interviews; almost all my respondents found them (as well as the accent and timing) very funny. The joke about the olives without bathing suits was circulated on the public square as a result of some of my interviews in Riventosa.

This kind of comical codeswitching has been documented by Woolard in Catalonia. Part of its appeal, as she points out, is that "the actual use of both languages...is an important denial of the boundary identifying force of the two languages" (1988: 70). Put another way, the production and interpretation of bilingual puns and codeswitching depends on the ability to "operate in both frames simultaneously"; its force is "derived precisely from [participants] ability to move across different linguistic and cultural frames" (Heller 1994: 167). In this creative framework, the dramatization of difference (the opposition of the two codes) does not necessarily highlight their inequality. Rather, difference seems to be exploited in the articulation of a hybrid identity. Rampton takes this line of analysis in his explanation of felicitous language "crossing" (the use of group linguistic patterns by someone outside the group) among British adolescents, who can "recognize, exaggerate difference in communication in a set of stylized and often playful interactions that up to a point at least, constitute a form of antiracism" (1995: 21).

2. Corsican reimagined: reference to Italian and other languages

In the next two excerpts (also drawn from the horoscope spoof) the comedian parodies in turn, an affected Englishman speaking Corsican, the speech of a Corsican youth who lives in Paris (speaking in a style which has approximately the same connotations as "Valley Girl" talk) and finally, a traditional Corsican song.

(27)
Horoscope: a Briton speaking Corsican

1   *Capricorni: Salute à tutti Capricorni. Ah, cumu ferete per esse cusì*
Capricorns: Hello all you Capricorns. What have you been doing to get so

→ 2   *ennervati? Ùn a sò, eiu–appena di* "self-control"? "Keep cool,"
         stressed out? Me, I don't know–a little bit of *self-control*? *"Keep cool,"*

3   *cumu si dice ind'è noi. Rimarcate, eiu aghju pussutu vede ch'ellu*
         as they say where I come from. Note that I have been able to see that

→ 4   *si dice anche ind'è voi. Ho ho ho...*so long, *Capricorni!*
         you say this too. Ho ho ho...*so long* Capricorns!

(28)

Horoscope: Parisian Corsican and song parody

1   *Leoni: vous vous dispersez complètement. Vous avez tout fait votre petit*
         Leos: you are spreading yourself altogether too thin. You've all come

2   *bout de chemin. C'est dingue, mais il ne faut pas se décompenser à ce*
         your way, It's crazy, but you shouldn't deprive yourself to that

3   *point-là faut aller à la campagne, sais pas, il parait qu'il y a de bonnes*
         point, You've got to go to the country, I dunno, It seems there are good

4   *vibrations:*
         vibes there:

5   Pare chì à a campagna
                It seems that in the country

6   ci hè u sole è vibrazzione è aria pura
                there is sun and vibrations, and clean air

7   aria pura è vibrazzione
                clean air and vibrations

→ 8   ùn ci vole micca a "flippà"
                you don't have to flip out

9   o allora scambia di rughjone
                otherwise you can change regions.

In example (27) there are three examples of Corsican–English codeswitching: the use of "self control," "keep cool" and "so long"(in lines 2 and 4). The word *flippà* 'flip out' on line 8 of example (28) also evokes English, albeit via French. Reference to English in Corsican is extremely rare, as is the English accent in Corsican that is part of the performance of (27). I only ever heard two everyday examples of Corsican–English language play, and I was arguably an audience that would have prompted such usage. The first was a joke about a Corsican in America that involved a scatological pun on the city name "Chicago," since it sounds like *ci cagu* 'I shit there' in Corsican. The second was a question and answer joke: Question: "Do you speak English? Answer: *"Innò, spicà figatelli"* ['No, to unhook sausage'] with the play on the Corsican verb *spicà*, pronounced [spika], which means "to unhook" (the sausages referred to were often hung from the rafters). Before this radio broadcast, I had seen such language play only once in performance, during a television special aired in 1989 during a three-month long general strike on the island. Called *I Scrianzati* 'The Badly-Brought-Up Ones,' it spoofed all participants in the strike. In one sketch, entitled "The crisis seen from elsewhere," the comedians imitated foreigners speaking Corsican, doing a Chinese, a Russian, a Kanak, and even George Bush, who proclaimed in a heavy accent that he loved Corsica, and chewed *ficatellu* (a traditional sausage) flavored gum. There was also a Portuguese woman who said, with sibilant Portuguese -*s* sounds, "I'm Corsican, like you. I eat *ficatelli*. I do evenings around the fire. I'm Corsican."

Of course, the humor of foreigner talk in *I Scrianzati* and on the radio was precisely that it was inhabitual, unexpected. It was derived in part from the incongruity of speakers of major languages trying their hand in Corsican. But the improbable image of a Corsophone world was also a reworking of idealized images of Corsican. It proposed an image of linguistic and cultural contact in which Corsican was not a closed or exclusive code, but one that could be learned (and mangled) by outsiders. Outside learners, as we have seen in Chapter 5, legitimate language status or power by representing Corsican as "the" language you must learn to operate on Corsica. Although this is clearly no longer the case from a strictly economic or pragmatic perspective, it was the case for low status workers in many living Corsicans' memories. The Portuguese woman in the sketch reminded Corsicans in a lighthearted way of a not-so-distant past in which outsiders had to adapt to Corsican, for it was the language of the domestic or agricultural work in which they engaged. Even though these days are gone, these sketches had the potential to suggest Corsican as "the" language of Corsican *culture* (rather than economy) that outsiders might wish to learn as a form of cultural integration.

2.1. Italy on the radio

The radio has also been a site for a renewed interest in Italy and Italian. In 1991, Sciacci, then director of RCFM drew on the notion of idea of cultural and linguistic complementarity and initiated a morning broadcast featuring an Italian correspondent. The correspondent called in live from an Italian city, where he reported on current cultural events in Italian, thus dramatizing the operating assumption of mutual intelligibility between Corsican and Italian. Corsican announcers talked back to him in italianized Corsican, a language variety that I had heard on occasion in Corsican's interactions with Italian tourists. In return, RCFM sent tapes to an Italian station in which journalists described cultural events going on in Corsica, in Corsican. The idea was to encourage Corsicans and Tuscans to use the ferry (it is only a four hour trip from Bastia to Livorno) to attend concerts and so on. To reinforce this point, one clue per day was broadcast about the identity of a famous Italian historical figure. The person who correctly guessed who it was won a weekend in Florence. All of these measures were a way, the station director told me, to remind Corsicans of the "other continent" as a point of cultural reference.

3. Theater and storytelling

In a different medium, Francis Aïqui's play *Boswell, Paoli, Bonaparte,* makes use of French, English and Corsican in its dramatization of three famous historical characters and their impact on Corsica. The three languages are allowed to trespass on each other's territory. For example, Jean-Marie Arrighi, who collaborated on the script, pointed out that Boswell occasionally speaks in Corsican, but as an Englishman, with English syntax (for example, he had him say, "*So andendu à Cervione*"–'I am going to Cervione'–instead of the correct "*Vo à Cervione*"). Jacques Thiers noted in his review of the play:

> *L'ancrage lexico-grammatical des langues est lui aussi subordonné à la finalité du théâtre...Qu'il soit anglais, français ou corse le texte ne garde aucune prééminence sur les costumes, le jeu des comédiens, le chant et la musique: tout fait sens à un seul et même niveau: c'est bien du théâtre, non de la langue mise en scène* (Thiers 1990: 42).

> The lexico-grammatical anchoring of languages is itself also subordinated to the finality of the theater...Be it English, French or Corsican, the text never prevails over the costumes, the comedian's play, the songs or the music: everything has meaning at a single level: it is theater proper, *not language put on the stage* (my emphasis).]

Another of Aïqui's plays (*Gran' Testa* 'Big Head') makes use of the diglossic relationship between Corsican and French as a vehicle for the depiction of characters' stances, personalities and relationships. In this play, Aïqui uses the two languages to express the two sides of the deeply conflicted protagonist. Ghuvan Luca Rancelli, the actor who played the leading role of 'Big Head' in the play, remarked in a 1991 interview that "*Quand'ellu parla in francese, ùn hè micca ellu cum'ellu deve esse*" [When he speaks French, he is not as he is supposed to be]. His "real" self is expressed in Corsican, which is the "language of emotion" in the play. It is also the language through which the character of the servant addresses the audience, the language in which the servant *"fa capisce ch'ellu ùn hè micca sempre accunsentu cù Gran'Testa"* [makes it known that he doesn't always agree with *Gran' Testa*] and in which he resists the orders *Gran' Testa* gives him in French (Ferrandi 1991: 7). Even though Aïqui and Rancelli explicitly acknowledge that they view the use of Corsican on stage as a "militant act," the artistic possibilities of both languages drive the way they are deployed. Moreover, there is no effort to exclude French: Aïqui comments that artists should say to themselves, *"ce sont deux langues avec lesquelles nous allons vivre, essayons alors de les faire chanter toutes les deux..."*[these are two languages with which we are going to live, let us thus make them both sing]. It is important to note that the interview was conducted in both French and Corsican; Aïqui speaking always in French and the interviewer and Rancelli using Corsican. Aïqui himself is half Canadian, and does not often speak Corsican, as he did not learn it as a child. Rancelli's final comments in the interview made reference to the plural linguistic character of the play and its potential effect on linguistic tolerance: *"mi pare ch'è s'elli accetanu a situazione quì, l'hanu da accetà megliu a rombu in u carrughju"* [it seems to me that if they [the audience] accept the situation here [on the stage], they will be more likely to accept the noise in the street" (Ferrandi 1991).

In another performance genre, a Corsican storyteller also put Corsican on stage along with French in a way that acknowledged the nature of their sociolinguistic relationship without making language hierarchy a source of tension. Franchi, one of the leading "purists" of the debate of the previous decade and winner of the Spelling Contest, had become director of Corsican Language and Culture at the Corsican Rectorate, which oversaw all primary and secondary education. One of the educational strategies that he promoted by his own example was a particular kind of bilingual storytelling. He performed one of these stories at a storytelling festival in the summer of 1994. The performance was bilingual, but not evenly so: the dominant language was French. Despite the fact that French carried the story line, Corsican was present in some interesting ways throughout the story. Franchi used Corsican in repeated formulae such as, "and the giant said...." where the giant always said the same thing. It was also used on all occasions in which the context made it possible for even a non-Corsophone listener to guess the meaning. Words or phrases that were introduced this way were then reintroduced at later points in the narrative without the contextual clues: each story was thus a linguistic apprenticeship. There was enough Corsican in this performance to make it more than window dressing, yet it was geared entirely towards the French-dominant child. This in itself evacuated the issue of identity and authenticity. In addition, the act of learning Corsican was inserted so skillfully into the storytelling process that it shed the symbolic charge that it could have in other kinds of educational contexts.

4. The newspaper

In 1989, a member of the RCFM journalism staff attempted to bring this same sort of philosophy/practice to print media. In June of 1989, the daily newspaper *Le Corse-Le Provençal* changed its name to *Le Corse*, and set up a Corsican editorial staff that was independent of the mainland office. As part of this corsicanization of the paper, a weekly Corsican language page was inaugurated. In addition to editorials, cartoons and reporting on cultural/social events, it included a roundup of the weeks news. This variety of genres was significant in the context of existing patterns of Corsican use in the weekly magazine *Kyrn* and the nationalist newspapers *U Ribombu* and *Arritti*. Articles in Corsican were most often restricted to "cultural" pieces or to (short) nationalist political editorials; they were "marked" as carriers of "Corsican only" material.

René Sciacci, former RCFM director, was appointed the editor of this page. He wrote an opening editorial in which he vowed to base his approach to written Corsican on the philosophy of the radio, whose "first truth" was to broadcast the news, "as if we were explaining it to friends". This meant that he intended to write in accessible, everyday language, without excessive concern for purity of form: *"Cusì dunque, à i risichi dinu di truvà sbagli numerosi, si prupone quì di davvi à scobre un corsu chì ùn si leghje micca per u piacè di a lingua, ma per u piacè di ramintassi l'attualità di l'ultimi ghjorni..."*[consequently, with the risk of making numerous errors again [as they had on the radio], this is a proposal to give you a chance to discover a Corsican that is not to be read for the pleasure of the language, but for the pleasure of being able to recall the news of the last few days...] (Sciacci 1989).

Sciacci's radio experience had convinced him of the power of the symbolism of practice. He believed that attitudes to newspaper reporting in Corsican would change as they had to radio news, where *"...pianu pianu, a ghjente s'hè messa à riagisce nantu à u cuntenutu è più nantu à a manera di dì e cose...*[people had come to react, bit by bit, to the content, and not just to how things are said]. He wanted his readers to recognize Corsican news writing as *"un postu di travagliu cumè un altru"* [a type of work like any other], and to encourage them to *"francà...u passu psicologicu di u scrittu"* [to cross the psychological barrier of writing in Corsican]. The Corsican page was, unfortunately short-lived, and it is impossible to tell whether or not this de-centering and de-dramatizing of written Corsican inspired people who were not comfortably literate in Corsican to read the news in that language.

5. Some persistent "old" politics of representation at play in the media

Despite a rhetoric in which they downplayed the political and pedagogical aspects of radio practice, radio professionals could not avoid the fact that no language choice in any forum could ever be completely neutral on Corsica. There are times in which the symbolic dominates the expressive, even on the radio. There is a hint of this in the on-air exchange with Jean from Folelli, above. Although Jean does not exactly apologize for speaking French, the fact that he announces his switch rather than just switching shows that he has perceived Corsican as the preferred, or standard language of this particular radio interaction. While I would argue that overall, the DJs' common practice of greeting their callers in Corsican is usually more neutral than Jean assumed, the fact is that DJs do sometimes needle their callers or interviewees about language choice, by failing to follow their lead to French. The following transcript is of a conversation the DJ Jean-Paul had with a caller:

(29)
Listener call-in: caller's competence ignored

1	DJ:	*C'est bien d'avoir pro-*	It's good that you pro-
2		*posé Duteil parce que*	posed Duteil, because
3		*Duteil, comme Yves*	Duteil, like Yves
4		*Duteil, est domicilié en*	Duteil, has his residence
5		*Corse.*	in Corsica.
6	Jo:	*Oui.*	Yes.
7	DJ:	*Parce que "Sonny's*	Since "Sonny's Boy,"
→ 8		*Boy," aghju u so in-*	*I have his address, so to*
9		dirizzu, diceremu sarebbe	*speak, and it is mainly in*
10		piutostu in Corsica.	*Corsica.*
11	Jo:	*Oui. Boh,* ùn face	Yes. Well, *it doesn't mat-*
12		nunda.	*ter.*
13	DJ:	Mi dispiace ô JoJo.	*Sorry, Oh JoJo. Where*
14		Induve site?	*are you?*
15	Jo:	In Bonifaziu.	*In Bonifacio.*
16	DJ:	*Ah, ô la la,* di Bonifaziu,	Ah, o la la, *from*
17		una chjama di Bonifaziu.	*Bonifacio, a call from*
18		Induve state in	*Bonifacio. Where you live*
19		Bonifaziu?	*in Bonifaziu?*
→ 20	Jo:	O, ùn facciu nunda.	*I'm doing nothing.*
21	DJ:	U vostru indirizzu.	*Your address.*

→	22	Jo:	Face bellu tempu.	*It's nice out.*
	23	DJ:	Iè, face bellu tempu ma	*Yes, it's nice out, but*
	24		induve state voi? u vostru	*where are you, your ad-*
	25		indirizzu, induvè hè a	*dress, where your house*
	26		vostra casa?	*is?*
	27	Jo:	In Golfu di Santa Manza.	*In the Gulf of St. Manza.*
	28	DJ:	Ci hè un pocu di mondu?	*Are there quite a few peo-*
	29			*ple there?*
	30	Jo:	Un pocu.	*A few.*
	31	DJ:	A vedaci, ô Jo.	*Goodbye, Jo.*
	32	Jo:	A vedaci.	*Goodbye.*

In this exchange, the DJ began in French. It was he, rather than his caller, who decided to switch to Corsican (on line 8). The caller Jo's responses do not provide any decisive clues about his level of competence, or even about his preferred language. Jo's responses on lines 20 and 22 show that he has twice misunderstood the question "where do you live?," mistaking it first for "what are you doing?" (indexed by his response on line 20) and then, "how is the weather?" (his response on line 22). These problems of communication did not cause the DJ to switch back to French, in which he could at least have tested the hypothesis that Jo had limited competence in Corsican (rather than other possible causes for his responses such as a hearing problem, or a disinclination to talk about where he lives). It is of course possible that the DJ was pursuing a line of questioning without particular consciousness of his language choice; in this case, he was failing to keep accommodation to the caller on the top of his priorities.

Another, even clearer example took place during a program called *Decalage Horaire* 'Time Difference' in which the radio paid for and broadcast conversations between Corsicans and friends and relatives living in distant places. A DJ was talking to a Corsican woman who had emigrated to Canada some twenty years before. After a few exchanges in which he asked questions in Corsican and she answered in French, she finally protested, saying that she was terribly rusty in Corsican and that she had told him all of this before the show to prevent just such an on-air embarrassment. In both of these examples we see DJs (either consciously or unconsciously) failing to make use of bilingual space to create the maximal possible communicative comfort for their caller.

5.1. Sociolinguistic responsibility vs. professional ideals

Nor could RCFM avoid a sense of social responsibility in regard to the language, and the difficult choices that it implied. When the radio station had opened in 1982, the first directors had responded to what they perceived as a state of linguistic crisis; they felt it was crucial to speak as much Corsican as possible on the air in order to compensate for the almost complete void in the broadcast media at that point.[96] As a result, they pressed all possible members of their staff into service, including some whose command of Corsican was limited. This emphasis on quantity over quality drew intense criticism, particularly about the news. People called in to the station with complaints I was to hear in my own interviews, such as: "You have to know French to understand that Corsican," or "It sounds like they are reading French and translating in their heads." Here we can see radio language confronting the same discourses of cultural authenticity as other more explicit and literacy-based forms of language activism. In response, the station organized Corsican language courses for their employees that were taught by a University professor. Eventually, the 1989 director told me, they just "closed their ears to the criticisms and went about the business of doing their jobs, which was to report the news". Of course, deciding to report the news in Corsican was still an ideological rather than a purely pragmatic communicative choice: all of his listeners understood French. And this meant that those newscasts by definition focussed listeners' attention on language choice and language form. Later in the interview he talked about his continuing difficulty in finding people who were both qualified radio professionals and fluent Corsican speakers. He was not willing to sacrifice radio expertise for linguistic competence. Still, he did recognize the enormous power, and thus the social and pedagogical role of the media. From this perspective, he felt a responsibility to engage competent speakers and to worry about language in a way that conflicted with his professional ideology that communication should come first. The conflict ran deep. He felt, as he put it bluntly, as if he had "*le cul entre deux chaises*" ['his ass perched between two chairs'].

If we look at the newscasts, we can also see elements of the purist linguistic ideology from which many radio professionals distanced themselves in metalinguistic discourse. For example, up until 1997, in the Corsican versions of the news, taped interviews in which the interviewee had spoken in French were suppressed in order to maintain a pure Corsican linguistic space. At the level of vocabulary, the journalists who wrote regional news in Corsican or who translated the national and international news from AFP reports also did make an effort to create a radio language that was not markedly dependent on French. Thus they attempted to create neologisms that were either semantic expansions of existing Corsican words or to base those neologisms on Italian rather than French. This was in fact Petru Mari's strategy when he became a journalist in 1993, despite his earlier comments about sources for Corsican words. In some cases, this meant rejecting popular usage: for example, RCFM coined the term *spegnifocu* 'fireman' (literally, "put out the fire") in order to avoid the commonly used term *pompieru* which is a corsicanization of the French *pompier*.

Nor was the reference to Italian without ambiguity. The 1991 initiative with the Italian correspondent did not survive a change of directors, and the (new) director in 1993 told me that he felt that he had to "be careful" about the amount of Italian–even the proportion of Italian songs–that he broadcast. If they played too many Italian songs, people inevitably called in to complain. He returned to his theme of the radio as a "mirror" of everyday life: the fact was that the primary culture of reference was French, and his listeners wanted to hear the French standards.

5.2. Popular purism: reactions to codeswitching and neologisms

In the inevitable scrutiny to which the Corsican spoken on the radio was put, there were also mixed reactions to both the mixing of languages in the informal conversations and comedy spots illustrated above and to neologisms in Corsican newscasts. When I played newscasts in Corsican to people and drew their attention to various neologisms, they could be quite critical. One young woman who was a self-described non-Corsophone said the fact that she could understand them at all was damning proof of their inauthenticity. While everyone agreed that all of the kinds of language mixing heard on the radio were an accurate mirror of society, and while many people agreed that it contributed to the "convivial" atmosphere of the shows, mixed language practices were also read as signs of linguistic degradation, although people differed considerably in how they evaluated the seriousness and the import of this degradation (see Cadiot 1989: 570).

Some older (over 65) Corsicans did not notice codeswitches at all until they were prompted (see Cadiot 1989: 571). When they thought about it, they almost invariably concluded that the kind of codeswitching and language mixing seen in examples (23) and (25) were the results of someone's lack of linguistic competence. Some said the speaker who switched was "unable to stay in one language;" a problem with which they empathized from personal experience.[97] Other older Corsophones interpreted the codeswitching in both of these examples as the polite accommodation of the DJs to the language their caller understood best. These judgments are all the more interesting reflections of these informants' sociolinguistic consciousness because they are not at all grounded in the passages they listened to: other than in examples (22) and (29) there was no evidence of lack of competence on either the DJ's or the caller's part. These older people were not inclined to criticize language mixing: they acknowledged that it would be "better" to be able to use just one language at a time, but they thought it was a difficult standard to require of someone.

Among those I interviewed were also younger Corsicans with a greater political and cultural awareness. Some of them were almost embarrassed to laugh at the horoscope satire, since, they said, it represented a "bastardized" form of language that they saw as an emblem of French domination and an obstacle to Corsican's future status and survival. This theme appears in the lyrics of a "militant" song written in the seventies titled *A lingua* 'The Language'. One of its verses reads:

> *Questu misciu di corsu è francese*
> This mixture of Corsican and French
> *Divene una insalata*
> Is becoming a salad
> *In ogni città è in ogni paese*
> In every city and every village
> *A nostra lingua hè malata*
> Our language is sick
> *Questu misciu...*
> This mixture...
> (Casale and Luciani 1980: 371).

Here we can productively go back to the parallel with "crossing". Rampton emphasizes that "crossing" is not equally felicitous in all contexts; the most successful exaggerations of difference take place in "recreational contexts" and "among equals" (1995: 21). On the one hand, radio broadcasts were consumed in and were thus "like" the private, convivial contexts in which Corsicans were "among equals" and could and did tell jokes about Corsican malapropisms in French. On the other hand, radio was also a public medium, and the public frame invited a) dominant modes of interpretation and b) consciousness of linguistic hierarchy.

This is revealed in the comments of one woman I interviewed, with whom I was chatting about the character Madame Mozziconnacci. I had not yet recorded example (26) above, and so the discussion was based purely on her memory of the program. My interviewee told me how much she liked this comedian. When I alluded to the character's mixed language, my respondent denied that it was mixed, asserting that Madame Mozziconnacci "always spoke Corsican". In other words, so closely was a pure, monolingual norm linked with value in her mind, that she retroactively read out abundant heterogeneity in her recollection of something she had liked. The radio examples led others to express their distaste for *Francorse* or FRC and provided me with stock examples of everyday usage that they disparage. One interviewee called such usage *du petit nègre* 'little Negro,' recalling a term from a racist and colonial context used to stigmatize the French spoken by the colonized. This shows that there can be multiple and ambiguous results when stigmatized language forms are dramatized. Rampton's report on the use of Stylized Asian English (a stigmatized form) in school drama presentations underscores this point. He writes, "In school based groups that were organized to encourage discussion and reflection, adolescents could attempt to reclaim Asian Englishes from the representations they were given in dominant discourses...But this was only ephemeral [and did not] generate any authority or commitment outside well-demarcated events" (Rampton 1995: 242).

In 1993, RCFM staff was also divided over the desirability of the amount and nature of the codeswitching practiced by the DJ in the transcripts above. Mari, who had moved up from DJ to journalist by that year, expressed the opinion that codeswitching within a speaker's turn on the floor was regrettable evidence of decline in Corsican competence, and that codeswitching within the sentence was even worse. Despite his comment that it was "Radio Corse and not Radio Sorbonne," Mari felt that RCFM should mirror the best, not the worst in contemporary language practice, a view he shared with the director. The best was monolingualism.

The interviews about radio language illustrate that concepts of purity, homogeneity and boundedness are part of most Corsicans' metalinguistic inventory. These interviews, however, also make it very clear that these concepts are a rather small part of people's everyday consciousness about language. For example, although many people asserted before they heard my taped newscasts that there was too great an influence of French in the Corsican news, there were far fewer people who were able to spontaneously pick out an example of poor usage from the flow of the broadcast. There was also very little consensus among respondents about what counted as "good" or "bad" Corsican; even individuals were not always consistent in their criteria of judgment. Few were able to offer a "more Corsican" way of saying something they had identified as "too French".

It was clear to me that outside of the interview context in which attention was drawn to issues of form and authenticity, the "language question" was backgrounded in listening practice. For the most part, people just "heard" the news as news rather than as a linguistic laboratory. This was even more the case with the nonnews programming. What RCFM had succeeded in doing was to make actual, rather than ideal Corsican language patterns part of a public institution and a background noise in the kitchens and living rooms of a wide segment of private life.

6. Conclusions

In many of the examples I have described in this chapter, it is clear that bilingual speech patterns recognize and sometimes celebrate multiple and hybrid identities, in marked opposition to models of identity and value in which all that matters is being "not French" or "as good as French". These ideas are familiar ones; they are the ones promoted by the "sociolinguists" in the move for coofficiality and through the concept of polynomy. What the data in this chapter suggest, however, is that the use and promotion of Corsican in the media and performing arts does not automatically invoke dominant models of linguistic evaluation the way that top-down, literacy oriented language planning strategies (even "plural" ones) inevitably seem to do. At a very basic level, this is because the main focus of the performances I have described is to entertain and communicate; it is not on language. When that focus shifts–as in the examples of the newscasts–to language as a symbol, familiar notions of purity and boundedness make their way to the top of people's consciousness.

The example of the radio also demonstrates something else: that certain kinds of media events and practices bridge and mediate the public and the private. Unlike academic treatments of language, radio discourse demonstrates the potential to become a seldom-noticed part of the texture of the Corsican sociolinguistic context, to become part of the routinized linguistic habits that define, for Corsicans, what constitutes "their" language. This *practical* basis for the link between language *use* and identity contrasts with the logic of *formal* and *oppositional* identity that is invoked by standard strategies of minority language promotion.

Chapter 9
Conclusion

By way of conclusion, I would like to reflect on the implications of the Corsican case for larger issues concerning the nature and outcomes of minority language activism. The Corsican case is interesting–and suggestive–because it is not a clear-cut case of minority language planning "success" or "failure". As Chapters 4 and 5 make clear, "Corsican language activism" is not a unified, coherent and consensual strategy, but rather, a range of strategies, launched from a variety of different ideological and political positions, and having a variety of results. The particular constellation of social, cultural, economic and political factors I describe may be unique, but my sense is that the complex interrelationships between ideology and action we see in Corsica is more typical than atypical of similar minority language contexts. In this chapter, then, I will try to synthesize my observations of the Corsican situation at the same time as I suggest broader comparative themes and issues.

I begin with a discussion of the nature and possibility of resistance to material and symbolic domination. In her 1994 book *Crosswords*, Heller writes, "The debate internal to the Francophone community is whether it is necessary (or possible) to set the rules of the game within a separate market. If so, the question remains whether that market should revolve around similar or different material or symbolic resources" (1994: 96). Below, I consider what the Corsican data suggests about the extent to which minority language activists can enact a "radical" resistance; defining the "rules of the game" (or the currency of the language marketplace in which they act). I also review some of the consequences of deploying similar versus different symbolic or material resources. On the basis of this discussion, I propose that one of the key comparative issues in the study of minority language movements has to do with the availability and cultural fit of sources of linguistic legitimation and authority. Finally, I discuss the importance of ethnography for the theorization of language movements. Whether we are concerned with the nitty gritty of "what works," or conceptualizing social processes, ethnography is critical if we are to understand the social and cultural repercussions of language policy.

1. Responding to dominance: stances and consequences

Let me return to Cameron's important point that all models of language have their own orthodoxies (1995: 5–6). These orthodoxies include ideas about what language is, but they also include much more than that–they propose and embody images of a social world and of identities and relationships. When Corsicans take a stand against mandatory Corsican classes, they invoke an image of a Corsican speech community organized around the affective and the voluntary. When members of the CCECV launch the concept of the *Lingua Matria*, they invoke a community of identity founded on sentiments of attachment rather than on linguistic competence. When the MCs in the Spelling Contest needle contestants about their "professional" relationships with the written language, they propose an egalitarian model of language legitimacy for Corsican that contrasts with the French language hierarchy they know so well. When Thiers encourages his students to critically evaluate neologisms, he offers them an image of a society under construction, in which they have just as legitimate a claim to set "the rules" as anyone else. When a Spelling Contest participant performs a riff about a word from his village, he taps into a powerful, shared discourse of intense attachment to local language and culture; a world in which Corsicans are united by an idiom of difference. When Franchi argues that French syntactic influences on Corsican should be rigorously policed, he invokes a particular kind of bilingualism and a particular kind of Corsican self, where the two languages/identities cohabitate but do not blend.

All of these stances are coherent responses to the experience of linguistic and cultural domination, and they draw our attention to the complex and sometimes contradictory nature of this experience. On the one hand, assimilation and accommodation to dominant society is rewarded. The social and economic rewards of French education for many Corsican have implicitly validated dominant models of cultural and linguistic identity and value. On the other hand, as Corsican discourse about the diaspora shows, it is impossible to be Corsican in France without having been reminded of one's otherness. These limits to belonging can create detachment, moments of critical distance from the dominant system and its categories of value. Both are part of Corsicans' lived experience, both can be found in language planning strategies and in reactions to them. They are, perhaps, two sides of the same coin. But while language domination produces complex and blended/multilayered identities, it also produces a discourse of identity that denies or denigrates this complexity.

2. Applying dominant models of language to minority contexts

This point–that dominant ideologies reduce complex identities–has been one of the major themes in this book. Over and over again, we have seen the extraordinary definitional power of a view of language as a closed, autonomous formal system that has a direct and unproblematic relationship with equally bounded cultural identities. This ideology of language is a cornerstone of the nationalist project; it is, in effect, the only discourse of legitimate identity that has political currency. All minority activists (linguistic, cultural, political) are highly constrained by this dominant discourse. Its definitional power reaches well beyond the purely political realm: it is both sustained and reproduced in metalinguistic discourse (particularly in the schools and other social institutions) and given a material reality through everyday enactments. At a very basic level, dominant language ideology defines the axes on which claims for language legitimacy can be made (in the Corsican case, this amounts to being either "like French" or "not-French"). A vast array of language planning strategies pursue a strategy of similarity–they seek the "same" symbolic resources as the dominant language. This is the kind of action I have glossed as the *resistance of reversal*. As previous chapters have made clear, many language planning strategies of "elaboration" (standardization and normalization) widely used by minority language activists in many places, including Corsica, are generated out of a diglossic model, and in that sense, leave its criteria of value intact. I have argued that this kind of resistance has a number of unintended consequences. These include the alienation of minority language speakers from new, authoritative models of the minority language (the whole issue of Corsican language standards), and the de-legitimation of the hybrid communicative practices (and by extension, cultural identities) that are a defining feature of the Corsican sociolinguistic landscape and, I would argue, of all situations of language contact, domination and shift. I have also argued that because the resistance of reversal fails to challenge dominant models of language value, it is also the catalyst for what I have called a resistance of separation, which restricts the value of the minority language to a negative (the definition of Corsican as "not-French"). The popular and academic language purism that inheres in both these forms of resistance defines as inauthentic *both* normal consequences of language contact (the use of French words in Corsican speech), *and* the efforts by language planners and public practitioners (like teachers and radio personnel) to create a new minority language lexicon that would make it possible to avoid recourse to the dominant language.

Both the resistance of reversal and the resistance of separation amount to "a closing of the limits of two languages [which] is a closing of the speaker's identity categories" (Wald 1986: 425). Similarly, Shapiro writes that forms of linguistic legitimation that emphasize the autonomy of minority language boundaries "move in the direction of narrowing legitimate forms of meaning and thereby declaring out-of-bounds certain dimensions of 'otherness'" (1989: 28). The problem is, that otherness is also part of the minority culture; Corsicans are both French and "not French". That is, in the oppositional division of linguistic labor and value, Corsican is restricted to everything French is not (and vice versa) but Corsicans continue to live and use language in lives that transcend these boundaries, lives that are both Corsican and French in varying and inconsistent proportions. From this perspective, Corsican adherence to an ideology of mutually exclusive linguistic and cultural identities is as damaging as it is empowering.

In the Corsican case, we can see several specific sociolinguistic consequences of this damage. First of all, minority language purism can create new forms of linguistic alienation (Joseph 1985; see also Jernudd and Shapiro 1989; Coulmas 1991; Eckert 1983; Hill 1985). That is, when purism works, and creates a prestige form of the minority language, the "authoritative becomes authoritarian" (Pratt, in Grillo 1989: 222). Examples from preceding chapters show that because language shift automatically involves dominant language influence on the minority language, when "ordinary" Corsicans become aware of and accept academic language purism, they can become linguistically insecure in Corsican, and may avoid speaking it out of fear of error and inauthenticity. This phenomenon can be seen in the Basque country, where Batua (standard) is institutionalized and official to a far greater degree than in Corsica (Urla 1987; Mahlau 1991: 90). It is also evident in Galicia, where "standard" Galician is on roughly the same, shaky social ground as "standard" Corsican, but where the recently-acquired social consciousness of the possibility of a standard leads many speakers to denigrate the quality of their own speech (Roseman 1995). A formalist, purist (and French) model of language also leads Corsicans to view standardization and normalization as enemies of linguistic variety. This has the potential to alienate people from the language planning process, as we have seen in discourses about regional pronunciations in the Spelling Contest. Within this framework of value, the presence of both regional dialectal variation and mixed codes also impute Corsican's status as a language. This illustrates another danger of the minority language adopting the dominant language's criteria of formal value: the minority language is bound, by definition, not to measure up. This comes out clearly in Eckert's observations of Occitanie; she writes that any variability in the minority language "is invoked as evidence of a process of decay, and the comparative homogeneity of French is taken as proof of that language's superiority" (1983: 294).

There are also many Corsican speakers, however, who are not particularly influenced by academic models of "standard" or "pure" Corsican. While not alienated from their own use of language, these people are alienated from the process of language planning, which they perceive as an activity of elites that has little connection with the meaning or value of the Corsican they speak (see Edwards 1985: 64). This is the thrust of Mascone's and the MCs' comments in the Spelling Contest broadcast. Overall, the focus on language as a formal system deflects attention from communicative *practice*; from the shared language habits that are distinctly Corsican. These language habits include shared repertoires of literature, oral literature and other verbal routines, knowledge of genre, manipulation of style and other norms of linguistic socialization and interaction in both Corsican and French as well as in hybrid forms which include codeswitching and other mixtures and varieties of the two languages. In other words, the symbolic value of language as a formal system in the articulation of identity has little to do with those heterogenous linguistic practices which are invested with affective, collective significance for what it means to speak and be Corsican.

What I have sketched above is a critique of forms of resistance (reversal and separation) that remain anchored in dominant criteria of value and identity. It is tempting to view more plural models of language and identity as an antidote, for such models acknowledge the mixed and complex nature of Corsican linguistic and cultural identity. Yet I would like to complicate this picture, by returning to the theme of the many faces of the experience of domination.

3. Lived experience and the persuasive power of dominant discourses

It is a fact that language domination produces a discourse of identity that denies or denigrates the heterogenous nature of minority identity. But this does not mean that this heterogeneity is "truer" to the Corsican experience than a discourse that emphasizes closed boundaries. Corsican metalinguistic discourse about language boundaries is not a form of "false consciousness" that covers up a different existential reality. It is a reality in its own right. The experience of language shift, and of life in a diglossic sociolinguistic context creates powerful experiences of value through opposition that are not easily discarded. Plural ideologies like polynomy tend to underestimate the force of these experiences. Moreover, the experience of domination also shapes how mixed codes and identities are evaluated. Because these mixed codes and competencies are results of language domination, they come inevitably to symbolize language domination. It is very difficult, therefore, to reverse the meaning of linguistic heterogeneity.

A dominant idiom of language value remains extraordinarily persuasive, particularly given the boundary-marking role ascribed to language in the politics of minority identity. Not only is this the only idiom acknowledged by the dominant society, whose cooperation is required for institutional reforms, but it is also part and parcel of the way that the general public defines and evaluates language. In short, essentialist views of language and identity are strategic, despite their unintended consequences, because it is very difficult to make an argument for identity on any other grounds (see Field 1999). It is this perspective that has led me to reevaluate some of my initial impressions of literacy-oriented language activism. In the early phases of my research, I was preoccupied with the disjuncture between such strategies and the kinds of communicative practices used and valued by ordinary Corsicans. This disjuncture is real. But over the course of almost fifteen years of observation of language planning on Corsica, I have come to appreciate the slow accretion of status and value to Corsica as a result of literacy-based corpus planning. This can take place at the same time as people resist language hierarchy. Let me illustrate this with respect to people I know well from Riventosa. Germaine and Santa, both in their seventies, have told me the following story many times with some pleasure: once, over ten years ago, they attended a debate on language at the University. Two University professors got up to speak. Germaine and Santa acknowledged that they "spoke beautifully," they also told me that they "couldn't understand anything they said". The University discourse, they concluded was "not really Corsican". They also reported feeling out of place, and said they would never go back to such an event. In this story, speakers of Corsican express their alienation from a new academic standard, which they implicitly contrast with the "real" Corsican they speak. Yet Germaine and Santa's story was also a little bit about a brush with celebrity; they had met professors who were also authors whose names everybody knew. While they were unlikely to read any Corsican language text, they had certainly read and heard *about* a Corsican literary corpus. The presence of that corpus served a significant legitimating function and was invoked in conversation with me as proof of Corsican legitimacy. The teaching of Corsican in the school has a similar function, also in spite of lukewarm popular support for language legislation that would make it mandatory. Germaine, for example, was quick to dismiss neologisms developed for use in the village's bilingual elementary school as inauthentic: she found them laughable. Yet I can remember the great pleasure she took in helping two girls in the village with the Corsican homework they brought home from the *lycée*.

4. Problems of legitimation

In short, Germaine's responses show that in contexts like the Corsican one, there is no single, simple recipe for language legitimation, since multiple models of legitimacy and authenticity and value circulate simultaneously in social life. The problems of social legitimation for Corsican are multiple; it is fair to say that there is not one single source of linguistic authority that is not problematic or contested. Below, I list some of the key institutional, cultural, economic and ideological obstacles to language legitimation on Corsica. These are the kinds of factors that I see as key axes for an important (as yet unrealized) project of systematic, ethnographically based comparison and contrast of minority language planning contexts.

4.1. The absence of an Academy

One of the reasons that Corsican society is hostile to and divided by efforts to standardize Corsican is the difference between the minority and the dominant languages' access to social power that Mascone (in the Spelling Contest) identifies so succinctly: "They [the French] have an Academy" (and we don't). I do not think that Mascone is advocating creating an actual language academy; rather, I think that he is commenting on Corsicans' historical lack of linguistic institutions. Historical depth, and its potential to legitimate certain forms of language, cannot, by definition, be created from scratch. In effect, this is what Corsican language planners have been involved in doing: creating Corsican–as a recognized, authoritative code–from scratch. I do not want to suggest that institutionalized linguistic authority is ever complete, or ever stifles ideological debate. But structures like language academies have the potential to render the authority of at least some linguistic forms "natural" and uncontested. As Chapters 4 and 5 show, this is not the case in Corsica. Without institutional history, even those language planners occupying positions of authority in contemporary institutions (educational and governmental) did not enjoy unquestioned linguistic authority. Another result of this absence of an academy (and the knowledge of the extremely conservative, purist role played by the French one) is that the debate over standards on Corsica is always polarized, always viewed in extreme terms. In public discourse, any standardization is viewed as puristic and/or hegemonic, and the only alternative an extreme laissez-faire approach.

4.2. A short literary history

Connected to the absence of an Academy is the fact that Corsican does not have a long literary tradition. This creates a deficit of both symbolism and practice. Not having a long historical tradition of writing can be used (both by Corsicans and non-Corsicans) to discredit Corsican's status as a language. It also leaves a void in the popular Corsican imagination of the language: there is no body of written work, familiar to all (even if read by only a few) that has existed so long that it has acquired an unquestioned cultural status as a linguistic model. Again, this is not to say that issues of language standardization are not contentious for those minority language communities with a deeper literary tradition than Corsican (see, for example, Gardy and Lafont 1983 on Occitan and Urla 1993on the Basque Country). But the nature of debate in such contexts may be less divisive. For example, in Wales, people who take part in the musical and linguistic contests of the Welsh *Eisteddfods* (where both the event, texts and performance criteria have a long history) seldom question the criteria of accomplishment used by the judges, even though they might disagree with the outcome of a particular contest (Trosset, personal communication).

4.3. Linguistic value and identity as local and oppositional

Kulick makes the point that macrosocial features (such as education, out-migration and so forth) are not sufficient explanations for language shift; that shift takes place when those features are interpreted within the framework of the local culture in ways that have a direct bearing on language (1992: 17). One of those interpretive frameworks is "how locally-grounded conceptions of self generate understandings of difference, and how those understandings of difference in turn influence a community's interpretation of the social world and the type of verbal behavior that speakers feel presents them in the most positive light..." (1992: 263). In the Corsican case, the understandings of linguistic difference Corsicans acquired as a result of their exposure to French language ideology and their personal social and economic trajectories are consistent with notions of difference embedded in traditional Corsican social organization. That is, embodied in the clan system is a view of identities as inherently polarized, antagonistic, divisive and hierarchical. Social life is a zero-sum game. It is "us against them" at every level, from intravillage politics to Corsican–French relations. On Corsica, we have seen that any "solutions" to the problem of linguistic variation–selection of one variety as the standard, or selection of a "homogenized" standard–risk being rejected as bids for social power or as inauthentic. Rather than uniting Corsicans around a shared code, standardization divides Corsicans into competing linguistic camps.

This view of identity contributes to Corsican linguistic campanilism, and short-circuits popular consciousness of a pan-Corsican linguistic identity (we have also discussed the role of Corsican geography in this respect). Finally, as Eckert points out, the process of language shift itself contributes to the loss of pan-dialectical minority language identity and consciousness, since the dominant language takes the place that was (or could be) occupied by a minority lingua franca or standard (Eckert 1983: 294). The result of Corsican social dynamics coupled with the localization of linguistic identity and authority is the following : since "authentic" Corsican must be a distinct, microregional variety of Corsican, there are no authentic varieties of Corsican that are not "from" somewhere. Since every locality also defines a social group, the selection as a standard of any variety that is viewed as "authentic" will automatically be read as an act of political dominance by, or on behalf of that group. There are thus no language decisions that are seen to emanate from a disembodied, unseen "they"; all language policies are attributed to individuals and groups and are always read in terms of their implications for the status or interests of the social actors involved. We can see this principle at work very clearly in a recent issue of the *Journal de la Corse* (a weekly paper). In a regular feature called *"Les Notes de la Semaine"* [Grades of the Week], the editors gave a "zero out of ten" to: *"certains prétendus linguistes qui inventent des mots corses et essaient ensuite de nous les faire avaler au prétexte qu'ils sont tout à fait authentiques alors qu'en réalité ils ne relèvent que de l'imagination de leurs auteurs"* [certain so-called linguists who invent Corsican words and then try to make us swallow them on the pretext that they are completely authentic, where in reality their only source is the imagination of their authors] (*Notes de la semaine* 1999).

4.4. Lack of a strong base of oral practice

One of Fishman's theses in *Reversing Language Shift* (1990) is that legal and institutional language planning measures can only be successful after a certain level of social practice of the minority language has been reached. This may ignore the fact that some forms of language planning can provide strong pragmatic incentives for people to learn the language and build up that very practice.

But in Corsica, there has been no language legislation that has had this sort of coercive or instrumental effect, and the success of Corsican language planning depends to a large extent on collective acceptance of Corsican language standardization and normalization. In this sort of situation, Fishman's thesis has its application. In Corsica, the absence of a strong base of public practice of Corsican amounts to an absence of a de facto source of community language standards. That is, the fact that Corsican is not spoken by all Corsicans has prevented the linguistic marketplace from settling the issue of competing models of language intervention in the way that the Italian neologisms launched by Mussolini (in his attempt to "purify" the language) survived or perished in the mill of massive, everyday use. I have suggested that Corsican bilingual radio is an emerging domain of practice that will act as such a mill; that the sheer volume and popularity of the broadcasts has the potential to create tacit acceptance of neologisms and other "new" forms of Corsican.

4.5. The politicization of language and language choices

On Corsica, the political/symbolic value of the language far outstrips its level of practice in everyday life; there is more talk *about* Corsican than there is talk *in* Corsican. Everything to do with language on Corsica is politicized. This applies at the most general level (to language policies), as well as to the dynamics of individual choices in interpersonal communication. This is the inevitable result of the tight association of the promotion of Corsican with Corsican nationalism, in which language has played a central role for all of the reasons cited at the beginning of this chapter. In the early to mid-eighties, there was a lot of evidence of people taking politically motivated stances towards the promotion of Corsican. If you were nationalist, you were "for," if you were not a nationalist, you had to be "against". In these years, people told me of parents who refused to come forward in favor of Corsican language instruction in their children's schools "for fear of being labeled nationalists". Sampiero Sanguinetti, former director of the regional television station, reported the same rationale being used by people who refused to be interviewed in Corsican on camera (Sanguinetti 1987: 12–28).

By the end of the eighties, expressing support for Corsican no longer immediately branded a person as a nationalist. But the Corsican nationalist movement did leave an indelible mark on the social life of the language, because it had successfully pushed language to the forefront of the public debate about identity and power. It created a cultural context in which both individual language choices and public policy would be interpreted within the matrix of this general politics of identity. In some cases, this has led Corsicans who do speak Corsican to refrain from doing so to avoid the interactional burden of making language an issue. In other words, when language choice is interpreted as a political or cultural statement, it puts a strain on "normal" communicative uses of that language. Chapter 5 illustrated how, in other cases, the politicization of Corsican has loaded the act of acquiring Corsican with so much ideological baggage that Corsican learners have become discouraged.

This politicization takes place, to a degree, in all minority language planning contexts. But it is also intimately connected with questions of minority language practice, and in this respect, is likely to be manifested in rather different ways in different places. The politicization of language choices is intensified in Corsica because the language is not practiced widely by a majority of speakers in a wide variety of contexts. As we have seen, this increases the number of interactions and contexts in which speaking Corsican can be marked and, potentially, "overloaded" with political or ideological meanings. In other minority contexts, a more "even" kind of bilingualism may attenuate these effects. This suggests a focus for a comparative study of minority language planning on the way that language as symbolic and political action articulates with language use in its more mundane communicative functions.

4.6. No social or economic coercion

At the same time that Corsican carries a surfeit of political and cultural value, the language has a serious deficit of any other sources of socioeconomic power. As we have seen, popular Corsican resistance to any compulsory use of Corsican in the schools or in government has prevented the Regional Assembly from passing aggressive and coercive language legislation. This contrasts sharply with the actions of parallel Regional Assemblies in Catalonia, the Basque country and Wales, which have taken much stronger legislative steps towards the teaching and institutionalization of their languages, creating situations in which it is legally-required and often economically and socially desirable for all non-speakers ("natives" and outsiders) to learn the language. Woolard's analysis of language use and ideology in Catalonia underscores the way in which the economic power of the region (and hence, since the end of the Franco era, of the language) has acted as an effective counterbalance to the institutional hegemony of Castilian (1989a).

These new speakers, and the requirement to teach them, can form a critical mass of practitioners which can play a critical role in the standardization and normalization of the language. First, the need to educate large numbers creates a pressing practical need to establish standards, since (particularly in France) most educational systems demand uniformity in publications and testing. In the Corsican case, universal education in Corsican could result in one of two things: the enforcement of a single standard (on the model of French) or the adoption of some sort of polynomic approach to judging students' mastery of Corsican. There is no doubt that Corsicans would be divided on how linguistic standards should be set if there were obligatory Corsican language instruction, but because school is taken so seriously on Corsica, the public debate might encourage people to come to some sort of consensus. Given the strong role played by parents' associations and teachers unions, most of the partners to the debate would be likely to feel that they had a suitable and democratic voice in the issue, and therefore, more likely to actually accept the consensus position. "School" Corsican might still carry some of its present stigma, but if Corsican language instruction were generalized, and people who learned it at school gained access to desired jobs, "school" Corsican would also become the tool of a significant body of interactions. This would have the potential of lending it greater legitimacy over time.

5. The production of authoritative discourses

The problems of legitimation for Corsican posed by its weak base of practice and even weaker sources of extra-linguistic sources of power can be linked to some general principles in the social construction of authoritative discourses. In order for authoritative discourses to work, they must mask their social origins, become part of the "habitus" which is so "powerful and hard to resist" precisely because it is "silent and insidious" (Bourdieu 1991: 51). According to Bourdieu, "one cannot save the value of competence unless one saves the market, in other words, the whole set of political and social conditions of the production of producers/consumers" (1991: 57). As we have seen, authoritative discourses about Corsican never pass unnoticed and uncontested in Corsica because there is no domain of social or economic practice of Corsican and no group of speakers of Corsican that exerts an unquestioned, invisible power that spills over into the linguistic arena.

Edwards believes that "It is simply not possible to bring about widespread language shift when the appeal is made on the basis of abstractions like culture, heritage or tradition" (1985: 64). On Corsica, we can see that the only marketplace in which the value of Corsican is taken as uncontested is a purely cultural one which is defined as nonauthoritative by most Corsicans. The success or failure of language planning on Corsica rests, as its proponents are coming to understand with increasing clarity,[98] on the sole force of Corsicans' commitment to the preservation of their culture. This kind of commitment is rare, and it is difficult to maintain on behalf of a language stripped of its pragmatic functions. In my observations, few people (even if they are generally supportive of Corsican) are inclined to make ideologically-motivated language choices the guiding force in their day to day interactions–even if they consistently interpret their own and others' communicative behavior in political and cultural terms. And, as some of my descriptions of highly dedicated linguistic militants shows, dedicated use of Corsican has a social price. This is because it violates politeness codes that require accommodation to the speaker, and generally gives precedence to the speaker's political/ideological agenda rather than to the congeniality of interpersonal interactions.

I mentioned above that the minority experience includes moments of critical distance from dominant ideologies. In a curious way, this facet of Corsican experience of linguistic and cultural domination comes into conflict with plural models of language value. Let me return to the popular resistance to mandatory Corsican classes and to homogenized orthographic norms described in Chapters 5 and 7. This popular voice insists on ascribing social authorship to linguistic action, and denies the possibility of a disinterested, value-neutral, politically neutral policy with regard to Corsican. The notion of "interest" maps on to Corsican views of social action and identity, and in some ways, it can be a very parochial sort of argument. But at some larger level, it is a theory of inequality that is grounded in Corsicans' experience of linguistic and cultural domination under France. It amounts to a recognition that in the process of standardization, some ways of speaking get valued (and institutionalized) over others. Situated action takes place in institutions like schools where (as the discussion in Chapter 5 shows) even the most deliberately social-constructionist perspective does not eliminate hierarchies of value. The power to define those hierarchies, moreover, is seldom democratic, because some people in those institutions simply have more legitimacy and authority than others. From this perspective, the polynomic ideal can be experienced as disingenuous–a refusal to admit to power relations embedded in contexts of linguistic action.

To summarize, the experience of language domination has multiple, and sometimes contradictory effects. On the one hand, it makes dominant language ideologies a part of minority language speakers' structures of feeling and identity. On the other hand, it provides these speakers with an acute sensitivity to the mechanisms of domination and sets the scene for strategies of resistance to those mechanisms. In this respect, we can say that the hegemony of dominant language ideologies is never complete. Yet that hegemony is even more tenuous and partial in the minority language market.

French language ideologies are not powerful because they are elegant, but because they are embedded in very powerful social institutions and economic fields in which French has instrumental value. By becoming part of the "habitus," authoritative discourses about French masquerade as "natural" rather than social and artificial. The habitus, Bourdieu reminds us, is "powerful and hard to resist" precisely because it is "silent and insidious" (1991: 51). As we have seen, this is not the case for Corsican. Authoritative discourses about Corsican never pass unnoticed and uncontested in Corsica because there is no domain of social or economic practice in which speaking Corsican has an unquestioned pragmatic value.

In this respect, the question of whether that market should revolve around similar or different material or symbolic resources can be rephrased, for what we have seen is that the context of minority language planning fundamentally transforms the meaning of dominant material and symbolic resources. Corsican language planners cannot bank on acceptance of a monolingual norm; they are forced to negotiate the meanings of every last spelling standard. Nor can they shake off a monolingual ideal in favor of a plural vision of language and identity with impunity.

6. The role of ethnography in the comparative project

What I have sketched in this chapter is my assessment of the kinds of legitimation with the potential to persuade on Corsica. I have argued that some of these forms of legitimation are rooted in dominant ideologies of language and identity that are influential in any number of minority language contexts across the globe. There are some authoritative discourses about language that are hard to avoid.

At the same time, the Corsican case in and of itself illustrates that there is still a considerable range of variation in how people respond to linguistic, cultural and ideological domination. This nature of these responses can only be discovered ethnographically, which is why I think ethnographic research must be the foundation of a comparative study of minority language revitalization. The meaning, and the consequences of any future language legislation or policy in Corsica will be linked to culturally-embedded notions about human motivation, agency and autonomy as well as influenced by ambient ideological formations. In another minority language context, there will be a different cultural matrix affecting the potential for and outcomes of language planning.

Ultimately, ethnography is also crucial for understanding the very thing we are talking about: the minority language. As we have seen, a good deal of the public struggle over language revolves around the very definition of what counts as Corsican. Even as we (researchers on minority language contexts) watch and record these struggles with a certain critical distance, we are all too often tempted to adopt an essentialist discourse about language identity–to simply take for granted that the boundaries around Corsican (or Basque, or Navajo or any other language) are given and unproblematic to identify. We may assume, for example, that we know what "reversing language shift" would mean. Yet this case study and others show that "successful" minority language policy–like enforcing mandatory Corsican language teaching from Kindergarten through University–creates new contexts of practice that have the potential to modify existing understandings of cultural and linguistic identity. The approach I have tried to take, and the one that I am advocating for future comparative research, examines, through the study of language practice, the social and ideological processes by which language identity and legitimacy are accomplished and (potentially) modified.

The dilemmas of contemporary Corsican language planning are, as I have suggested at the beginning of the chapter, the pivotal dilemmas of Corsican society, torn between competing visions of what it means to be Corsican, and, as a consequence, what language practices should be invested with cultural value. It is difficult to say whether Corsican language planners' efforts will ever "reverse language shift" in Fishman's (1991) terms. Perhaps not, if we define such a reversal as bringing Corsican back into social play in with its past structure and social vitality intact and unchanged. But perhaps so, if reversing language shift is defined more broadly as the revitalization of those indigenous ways of speaking that are defined by the community as being key elements of its cultural identity. What those ways of speaking–and being–will be still remains open for definition.

Notes

1. *Association pour la défense de l'étude de la langue corse de l'est et du centre* (Eastern/Central association for the defense of the study of Corsican)
2. See for example Rampton (1995); Heller (1994); Urla (1987); Trosset (1986).
3. See McDonald (1989), for a parallel case in Brittany.
4. See Quéré (1987: 75) and Rumsey, cited in Woolard (1992: 241).
5. See also Friedrich (1989: 29); Gal (1989a: 352–353).
6. See Gal (1989a: 349); Grillo (1989: 16); Heller (1994); Rampton (1995); Urciuoli (1996).
7. See Gal (1989a: 355; 360–361) and Heller (1994: 16). As Street (1993: 8) puts it, "ideology is the site of tension between authority and power on the one hand and resistance and creativity on the other."
8. See Bowie (1993), O'Brien (1993), Heller (1985) and Gal (1995: 412) for other examples of the range of meanings particular language choices can have in diglossic contexts.
9. Matras and Reershemius document Romani resistance to language standardization. This resistance is based on the that it might "facilitate access to the community on the part of non-Roma" (1990: 108). While the role of the minority language in cultural boundary maintenance is certainly an issue on Corsica, the Corsican case is not in other ways comparable to the Romani one.
10. See also Bourdieu 1977a and Woolard's 1985 critique of his notions of covert prestige.
11. This theme is elaborated by Hill (1989) and Gal (1989a) in reference to contemporary speakers of Mexicano and Hungarian, who avoid honorifics and other linguistic markers of status or formality in the minority language that are inconsistent with the values of solidarity and egalitarianism they associate with these languages and contrast with the languages of power. See also Woolard (1985: 744); Gal (1987); Urciuoli (1996: 103); Rampton (1996: 130).
12. Rampton (1996) makes the same point about "crossing".
13. Statistics in this section taken from Pomponi et. al. 1982, *Le Mémorial des Corses*, pp. 225–398.
14. Culioli (1990: 245) uses the same image of parentheses that I first employed in my 1990 dissertation.
15. We can see this played out in Corsican public discourse, in which France's Overseas Departments (Départements-Outre-Mer, or DOMs) are frequently used as an image of exotic otherness against which Corsicans measure their inclusion in French society. So while Corsicans of all political parties have argued that Corsica should be allowed to maintain its special jural status regarding taxes and inheritance laws, there has been resistance to the idea of treating Corsica as a DOM. During a three-month strike in 1989, a Corsican journalist responded to the suggestion that the situation resembled that of New Caledonia by writing that

"This image of Corsica as the exotic dancing girls of France is simply unacceptable" (Santarelli 1989: 15).

16. Codaccione (1988: 114); see also Messenger (1983), Parman (1990) and Wylie (1974) for parallel cases in small communities.

17. Fern and brush are symbols of Corsica. The idiom used to say that someone has not forgotten his or her cultural roots is, "*ùn si n'hè scurdatu(a) di a filetta*" [literally, 'has not forgotten the fern'].

18. Figures drawn from the *Tableaux d'Economie Corse*, 1986, Institut National Statistique et Economique (INSEE) Ajaccio.

19. Repatriated former Algerian colonial: after Algerian independence, the French government resettled many *pieds noir* on underpopulated Corsica, facilitating their acquisition of fertile land on the Eastern plain by offering them large loans. Some of these people were Corsicans who had settled in Algeria. Nevertheless, it was felt that these practices had been at the unfair expense of Corsican farmers living on the island.

20. In 1971 there were 9 bombings; in 1972 there were 18; in 1975, there were 226 bombings (Simonpoli 1981: 75).

21. This same logic is used in the contemporary U.S. by supporters of English Only. It is echoed in Canada, where Heller quotes an Ontario City Council's defense of their 1983 English Only motion: "social equality among ethnolinguistic groups can only be achieved through the use of one language." That one language is English, which is presented as neutral, and as providing equal opportunities for all (1994: 83).

22. Cameron describes a very similar equation of correct usage and moral/civic order in the "grammar panic" in England that began in the 1980s (1995: 95).

23. The logic of the rule of agreement of the participle with the auxiliary "avoir" is patently artificial: it is only required when the object of the verb precedes the participle, as in the phrase "*les fleurs que j'ai données*" [the flowers I gave], in which -*es* is added on the participle because flowers are feminine and plural. When the object comes after the verb, there is no agreement, as in the sentence: "*J'ai donné les fleurs à Marie*" [I gave the flowers to Marie].

24. See, for example, Hélias 1980; McDonald 1990; Bonn 1985; Prost 1968; Maynes 1985.

25. Although some Corsican teachers used to give a child an object (a *symbole*) to hold in shame until it could be passed on to the next transgressor–a practice reported in Brittany, Occitanie, Scotland and elsewhere (see Kuter 1989, McDonald 1989, Dorian 1981: 24), there were also Corsican teachers who were relatively tolerant of the use of the language.

26. Guidicelli's comments are echoed by Paul Simon, a French sociologist cited in Kuter (1989: 79) who wrote of the Bretons: "*On s'affirme deux fois français tant qu'on craint de ne pas l'être assez*" [Being so fearful not to be French enough, one defines oneself as French twice over].

27. Heller (1994: 146) reports on the same poor self-assessment of French skills by Francophone high school students in Ontario.

28. The converse case is reported in Kulick's study of Gapun parents in Papua New Guinea, whose frequent codeswitching masked, for them, the extent to which they chose to use Tok Pisin instead of Taiap with their children (1992: 257).
29. See Kulick (1992) for evidence of similar patterns of address to children in a situation of language shift in Papua New Guinea.
30. I have a vivid personal memory of the same sort of shock. After living in Corsica for nine months, I took a trip to Sardinia. The first time I heard a child speaking Italian, my head whipped around to look. Hearing italianate sounds coming out of a child's mouth had become marked for me, since the use of Corsican was so strongly correlated with age.
31. This question was obviously not well-phrased, since the person who evaluated their use of Corsican at about 50% could have checked any one of the three answers.
32. This is probably because questions like this one do not measure or define what "average" is, or reveal who the respondents were comparing themselves to. It would be quite possible for two people with vastly different speaking ability to rate themselves as "average".
33. Heller (1994: 165) provides some interesting examples of this kind of resistant use of English by students in a high school where there were strong social sanctions against speaking English, and where speaking French was heavily charged with social and political meaning.
34. Most French people over the age of fifty still refer to money in "old francs"; one hundred new francs is equal to one thousand old ones. One Corsican language book, *Assimil*, claims that old francs are still current in Corsican usage. In effect, this reflects the fact that those who practice Corsican the most lived through the currency change and cling to the old system.
35. See Rampton 1995 for similar social uses of a small repertoire of conventionalized forms of language crossing.
36. In contrast to this situation, in which linguistic practice was based on the social definition of my husband as an insider, Woolard reports a woman failing to register (or even acknowledge) that she had been speaking Catalan, since it was her identity as a foreigner that prevailed in the interaction between strangers (1989a: 75).
37. Philippe, the shopkeeper mentioned above, interpreted some of his older customers' refusals to speak Corsican back to him within this framework.
38. Sometimes, speaking Corsican can generate intimacy; three people I knew addressed me in Corsican as *tu* before they did so in French.
39. See, among others, Gysels 1992: 46–47; Gal 1987: 644; Hill 1989: 157 for examples of the power–solidarity dynamic in codeswitching.
40. Crowley (1996: 180) gives an interesting example of the stigma of "talking posh" recorded in an 1885 grammar of Dorset dialect. A little boy wept at corrections of his dialect saying "there now, if you do meake [sic] me talk so fine as that, they'll laef [sic] at me at hwome zoo [sic], that I can't bide there."

41. Like French speaking Ontarians, Corsicans focused on nationhood rather than "ethnic group," for, as Heller writes, "the term has come to signify powerlessness: nations may lay claim to the control of states, but ethnic groups are necessarily a minority who can never claim exclusive control of any political unit" (1994: 102).

42. This is in evidence in a citation in Crowley (1996: 178) which describes working class language in this way: "In imitating the one code, unsuccessfully, they lose hold on the other. Their very speech–a mixture of dialect and Standard English with false intonations–betrays them. *They are like a man living abroad who has lost grip on his native customs, and has acquired ill the customs of his adopted country*(emphasis added)."

43. Heller (1994: 59) shows how evidence of Francophone assimilation to English outside Quebec was a rallying point for collective mobilization around the cause of French.

44. See Crowley 1996: 134 on the invention of Irish Ireland by the Gaelic League.

45. In this debate, the Corsican case was seen as a slippery slope: if they were recognized as a people, the Basques, the Bretons–every minority–would clamor for the same title. This was viewed as undermining national unity.

46. See also Urla 1987: 10–13; Mc Donald 1989: 14–22 and Di Giacomo 1991.

47. Wald and Manessy (in Quéré 1987: 61) and Poche (1987: 101) also underscore that the struggle over the representation of identity conducted through language revolves around linguistic difference.

48. As Wald and Manessy write, varieties of a language are not concrete, linguistically discrete essences but *"effets linguistiques des représentations sociolinguistiques propres à la communauté"*[linguistic effects of the community's sociolinguistic representations] (in Quéré 1987: 61).

49. Dalbera-Stefanaggi makes a similar point, writing that "If the romanness and italianness of Corsican parlers has never been in real question, a relatively educated discourse has [occasionally] emerged which tends to obscure the linguistic relationship to Italy and thus to exaggerate the originality of Corsican" (1989: 126) [my translation].

50. In one conversation with my mechanic, I was asking questions about the recent increase in numbers of Italian tourists. I had heard, I told him, that in comparison to the German tourists, Italians were seen as better and more sympathetic clients. He did not overtly disagree with me, but his response was meant to discourage me from waxing too enthusiastic: *"Oui, nous aimons les Italiens...mais pas trop"* ['Yes, we like Italians...but not too much'].

51. There is also a social bias against Italians on Corsica that stems from the days in which impoverished migrant workers from Lucca came to Corsica to find work.

52. The orthography used in this letter is highly personal; it relies most heavily on Italian orthographic norms rather than on any of the orthographic systems used and advocated by Corsican language planners. This is hardly surprising, given the fact that the letter was sent to a pro-Italian publication.

53. A linguistic evaluation of the Basque case–a non Indo-European language–would have revealed the inconsistencies in both the French government's and the Council of Regional Languages and Cultures' system of classification, but the Corsicans were in no position to quibble.

54. This articulates with a purist position in which Italian as a point of reference allows gallicisms to be cleansed from Corsican. For example, Peretti, another *Viva Voce* editor, writes that "*Il còrso è una maniera di parlare consacrata da un uso familiare e conviviale. Anche come tale potrà meglio esser parlato se sbarazzato da ogni espression spuria e forestiera e se grammaticalmente purificato*" [Corsican is a way of speaking that is limited to familiar and convivial use. As such, it could become better spoken if it were stripped of all spurious and foreign terms and if it were purified grammatically] (1995: 2).

55. Although, ideologically, Comiti writes in Marcellesi's framework of "langues polynomiques," described below, in which languages are defined by the collective will rather than on any predefined linguistic criteria.

56. Because Marchetti did not make explicit reference to the origin of words and phrases, I ended up using bits and pieces from different lessons indiscriminately. This caused some amusement in the early stages of my language learning, since I would utter a markedly "southern" word in my village (in the northern dialect region). People laughed, but it was clear that this mixing was unacceptable.

57. Ghjuvan Natale Colonna wrote an article called "*Un dite micca...ma dite*" [Don't say...but say] which offered a familiar laundry list of gallicized Corsican and "authentic" replacements but poked gentle fun at the whole issue by ending his article with advice to the reader how to say 'I don't give a hoot about your advice' in an authentic Corsican way (1998: 1).

58. This is a criticism that he levels at popular and academic discourse alike.

59. This brand of purism contrasts with that reported by Hill and Hill (1980), where Nahuatl language purism deemphasized linguistic forms linked with social hierarchy in the service of Nahuatl's increasingly restricted use as a language of solidarity vs. a language of power (Spanish).

60. I asked a wide range of teachers and administrators in charge of Corsican language education how many parents had exercised their existing right to decline Corsican language teaching for their children. Only one case was ever reported to me, in which the child in question was put in the back of the room with drawing materials during a Corsican lesson which he obviously overheard.

61. With 43% men and 57% women, there was an 8% over-representation of women. There were 13% fewer "inactive" (nonemployed) respondents in the survey than in the general population, and the "inactive" portion of my sample was over-represented by students. My sample also under-represented (by 20%) the number of people over 45 in Corsica, a category that is disproportionately swelled (in relation to the national average) by the large number of Corsican retirees. White or blue collar semiskilled workers) were also under-represented by about 13%, and managers and academics were over-represented by 7%.

62. This citation follows, insofar as it is possible, the original orthography of the text provided to the Assembly by Santoni. He, however, typed the whole text in uppercase letters, which means that there are no accents. It is therefore impossible to determine where he would have put accents, so I have refrained from imposing current conventions on a text written at a time when there was no consensus on spelling norms.

63. These and other quotes from the 1997 session are taken from the proceedings of the Assembly session of 5 July 1983.

64. This sentiment was shared by another Assembly member, who responded to Chiarelli by saying "so you're for optional French and maths, then?"

65. See McDonald (1989: 94) for a similar reaction to the first Breton to pass the Baccalauréat in that language

66. There is an interesting parallel with the Roma case scribed by Matras and Reershemius (1991: 108) who write that "Many Romani communities fear language standardization as it might facilitate access to the community on the part of non-Roma."

67. During one of the planning meetings I attended, the committee had expressed interest in an English version, and I agreed to do the translation.

68. Some of his specific recommendations include not mixing different grammatical and phonemic systems. For example, he advises against mixing feminine plurals (*i* in the South; *e* in the North) or those pronunciations ([d] vs. [l]) which differentiate the two major Corsican dialectal areas.

69. The image of Corsican as a code impenetrable to foreigners has even influenced some Corsicans' interactions with Italian tourists, despite widespread experience of mutual comprehension. I have heard several stories in which Corsicans have been extremely embarrassed after saying something rude about an Italian in Corsican and being understood and confronted.

70. Woolard, (1989: 78) reports a similar incident in her fieldwork on Catalan. In Catalonia, the expectation is that foreigners will speak Castilian. When she went into a store and spoke Catalan, the shopkeeper responded to her in Castilian. Woolard kept up her side of the exchange in Catalan. At a certain moment, the woman asked her why she had used the Catalan word for "dog". Woolard pointed out that she had been speaking completely in Catalan, to the shopkeeper's great surprise.

71. There was also an old guard of linguistic militants, who, in the last 20 years, had seen outsiders come and go, not always serving their particular cause. For them, my interest was not enough, nor was the display of amateur competence. In a few cases, I had the distinct feeling that I was judged quite critically and that I was only accepted as serious after I reached a certain level of competence. Here my evaluators made a realistic assessment of the effort involved and recognized that I had to work hard, and seek out opportunities to learn. They reserved their confidence in me until they had proof that I had paid my dues.

72. In her study of French–Swahili codeswitching, Gysels (1992) identifies *"enfin"* and *"bon"* as pragmatic particles that act as floor-holders or turn-takers. We can

see this sort of usage in the following chapter, in Mascone's comments. Here, it is my interpretation of the students' overall performances and all the nonverbal and paralinguistic cues that signaled their insecurity, that leads me to associate these particles with problems in fluency. 73. See Gal (1989), and Mougeon and Beniak (1989) for a discussion of these phenomena in Hungarian and Welland French.

74. See also McKechnie (1993: 129–30).

75. See Urla (1988: 389); McClancy (1993) and McDonald (1989: 87) for parallels in Basque and Breton activist circles.

76. McDonald (1989: 87–88) reports on a similar environment in Breton militant student circles in Brittany.

77. On minority language purism see Hill and Hill (1980); Trosset (1986: 175); McDonald (1989: 113); Dorian (1994); Annamalai (1989: 227); Thomas (1991: 201).

78. For this reason, as Preston (1985), Edwards (1992) and others have pointed out, the use of orthographic distance to draw boundaries between "standard" and nonstandard" linguistic codes runs the risk of de-legitimizing the "nonstandard" code's claim to be a language (to be "like" the "standard").

79. Woolard, (1989a: 11) writes of a similar "problematic relation between public ideology and cultural practice" in regard to Catalan.

80. I use the word "relatively" because, as Cameron points out, the potential for linguistic alienation is built into the commonplace view that "language using is a normative practice, properly subject to judgments of correctness and value" (1995: 114).

81. The first prize was about $3000.

82. Thiers' comment is made in reference to a very similar example of language mixing he documented in an interview of a middle-aged Corsican speaker asked to talk about a topic which overflows the boundaries of his Corsican vocabulary and experience. "*A Corsica,*" he said, "*ùn hà micca cunnisciuta...cumu si pò dì...enfin!...u 'boom' ecunomicu.*" [Corsica has not known...how can one say...*well!*... an economic 'boom..'].

83. This phenomenon has been reported by Urla (1988) and McDonald (1989) in militant linguistic circles.

84. This question is a surprisingly hostile one to be asked of a broadcast sponsor and I am not exactly sure why Leca was hostile.

85. Southern speakers of Corsican pronounce the word for 'horse' with a medial /d/ instead of /l/.

86. This has been the case in creole contexts, in which linguistic differences mark class, rather than regional distinctions (Winer 1990: 251; Schieffelin and Doucet 1992: 251).

87. For example, I observed that in primary school classes that Corsican children tended to pronounce written Corsican as it was pronounced in their region even when the spelling reflected a "foreign" dialect. This translation mechanism worked even among children who were far from fluent Corsican speakers.

88. The childrens' surface compliance with school structures was part of a strategy of resourcefulness whose goal was "subtly to exploit the outside world while keeping oneself and one's group (family, peers, community) guarded" (Reed-Danahay 1987: 87).
89. As Thiers remarked in a 1993 roundtable on language, in public discourse speaking Corsican was always referred to as an onerous responsibility, thus occluding the pleasure and social rewards it brought (see "U Corsu in Scola" published in *Arritti* 1387: 10).
90. As Thiers writes, "*la parole médiatique consacre définitivement dans la pratique communicative l'évidence du continuum interdialectale, prélude indispensable à l'acceptation de la diversité*" [media language is a communicative practice that provides definitive evidence of the interdialectal continuum, which is an indispensable precondition for the acceptance of diversity] (1989a: 104).
91. I believe he was the person who had been crushed by the corrections to his entry in the first Spelling Contest.
92. Achard contrasts this method with the *dictée* 'dictation' based pedagogy of the 20th Century, where the language as system was "given" to students who were not presumed to know it.
93. *Toussainte* is the French version of the Corsican name *Santa*.
94. As Auer (1984: 47) writes, "bilingual conversationalists seem to monitor their partner's speech production very carefully for 'mistakes' or insecurities...and adapt their own language choice to the assessed bilingual abilities of the other."
95. In Corsican, *alivu* 'olive' is masculine; in French it is feminine. For this reason it is hard to assign a masculine or feminine ending to the adjective in the text, since it is a malapropism.
96. All of these options were suggested to me by interviewees who listened to this segment.
97. RCI (*Radio Corse International*) and *A Viva Voce* of the ADECEC had both broadcast in Corsican, but both of these stations' broadcast area was quite limited geographically.
98. In one case, when several old ladies arrived and joined in an interview I was conducting with one of their friends, the two skits above prompted a whole series of (mostly risque) stories about mangled French. In one of these, a pharmacist is supposed to have reported that he had corrected a mistake in the spelling of a patient's name in his official notebook "*en grattant le cul de Monsieur X*," in which the error in pronunciation of the letter –*q* transforms the sentence from 'I scratched out the "q" from Monsieur X with a pen' to 'I scratched Monsieur X's butt (*cul*) with a pen.'

References

Auer, Peter
    1984   *Bilingual Conversation*. Philadelphia: John Benjamins.

Abu-Lughod, Lila
    1990   The Romance of resistance: tracing transformations of power through Bedouin women. *American Ethnologist* 17(1): 41–55.

Achard, Pierre
    1980   History and the politics of language in France: a review essay. *Historical Workshop Journal* 10: 175–183.
    1987   Un idéal monolingue. In Geneviève Vermes and Josiane Boutet (eds.), *France, pays multilingue*, 2: 38–58. Paris: L'Harmattan.

Acquaviva, Jean-Étienne and Paul Canarelli
    1984   Retour à mer. In Sébastien Giudicelli (ed.), *La Corse: Une Affaire de Famille*, 39–45. Marseilles: Éditions du Quai.

ADECEC
    1986   *A scrittura di a lingua corsa: Intricciate è Cambiarine quindeci anni dopu*. Cervione: Publications de l'ADECEC.

Albertini, Marie
    1984   La passion d'être Corse ou le risque d'en mourir. In Sébastien Giudicelli (ed.), *La Corse: une affaire de famille*, 137–178. Marseilles: Éditions du Quai-Jeanne Laffitte.

Anderson, Benedict
    1983   *Imagined Communities: Reflections on the Origin and Spread of Nationalism*. London: Verso.

Annamalai, E.
    1989   The linguistic and social dimensions of purism. In Bjorn Jernudd and Michael Shapiro (eds.), *The Politics of Language Purism*, 225–131. New York: Mouton de Gruyter.

Anonymous
    1989   Letter to the Editor. *Kyrn* 193: 4.

Arrighi, Jean-Marie
    1992   Quelle(s) norme(s) pour l'enseignement d'une langue polynomique? Le cas du corse. *PULA* (3/4): 41–45.

Argumentaire à ras de terre.
    1991   *Paese*, May: 4.

Arritti   Weekly newspaper.

Assemblée de Corse
    1984   Rapport du Président de l'Assemblée sur la promotion et le développement de la langue corse. Ajaccio, 23 November.
    1996   Délibération 96/43 de l'Assemblée de Corse relative à la promotion de l'enseignement de la langue corse. Ajaccio, 3 May.

1997   Délibération 97103 de l'Assemblée de Corse portant adoption de dispositions relatives à la langue corse. Ajaccio, 20 November.

A. V-P.
1991   Lingua è cultura. *A Fiara* July 13: 15.

Balibar, Etienne
1991   The nation form: history and ideology. In Immanuel Wallerstein and Etienne Balibar (eds.), *Race, Nation, Class: Ambiguous Identities*, 86–106. New York: Routledge, Chapman and Hall.

Balibar, René
1987   La langue de la France exercée au pluriel. In Geneviève Vermes and Josiane Boutet (eds.), *France, Pays Multilingue*, 9–20. Paris: L'Harmattan.

Bassani, Lisandru
1989   Chinamaghjina: a china in maghjine. *Arritti* 5 January: 11.
1991   La coofficialité: pourquoi?   In Scola Corsa (ed.), *Concept de Coofficialità l'Edea di a Cuufficialità*, 11–16. Bastia: Edizioni Scola Corsa.

Beriss, David
1990   Scarves, schools and segregation: the foulard affair. *French Politics and Society* 8(1): 1–13.

Berruto, Gaetano
1989   On the typology of linguistic repertoires. In Ulrich Ammon (ed.), *Status and Function of Languages and Language Varieties*, 552–569. Berlin: Walter de Gruyter.

Biggi, Michel
1989   Présentations des îles invitées et de la problématique du colloque. Actes du colloque sur le développement économique et l'identité culturelle des îles de l'Europe. *Cahiers de l'IDIM* 1: 12–19.

Blok, Anton
1974   *The Mafia of a Sicilian Village 1860-1960.* Prospect Heights, IL: Waveland Press.
1981   Rams and Billy-Goats: A Key to the Mediterranean Code of Honor. *Man* 16: 427–440.

Blom, Jan-Petter and John Gumperz
1972   Social meaning in linguistic structures: code-switching in Norway. In John Gumperz and Dell Hymes (eds.), *Directions in Sociolinguistics*, 407–434. New York: Holt, Rinehart, Winston.

Blommaert, Jan and Jef Verscheuren
1992   The role of language in European nationalist ideologies. *Pragmatics* 2(3): 355–376.

Bonn, Charles
1985   Entre ville et lieu, centre et périphérie: la difficile localisation du roman algérien de langue française. *Peuples Méditerranéens* 30: 185–195.

296   *References*

Boswell, James
  1768   *An Account of Corsica: the Journal of a Tour to That Island; and Memoirs of Pascal Paoli*. London: Edward and Charles Dilly.
Brown, Becky
  1993   The social consequences of writing Louisiana French. *Language in Society* 22 (1): 67–102.
Bourdieu, Pierre
  1977a   *Outline of a Theory of Practice*. Translated by Richard Nice. New York: Cambridge University Press.
  1977b   Cultural Reproduction and Social Reproduction. In Jerome Karabel and A.H. Halsey (eds.), *Power and Ideology in Education*, 487–511. New York: Oxford University Press.
  1982   *Ce que parler veut dire*. Paris: Fayard.
  1991   *Language and Symbolic Power*. John B. Thompson (ed.), Translated by G. Raymond and M. Adamson. Cambridge: Polity Press.
Boutet, Josiane
  1987   La diversité sociale du français. In Geneviève Vermes and Josiane Boutet (eds.), *France, pays multilingue*, Vol. 2., 9–28. Paris: L'Harmattan.
Bowie, Fiona
  1993   Wales from within: conflicting interpretations of Welsh identity. In Sharon MacDonald (ed.), *Inside European Identities*, 167–193. Providence: Berg.
Boyer, Henri
  1991   *Langues en conflit: Études sociolinguistiques*. Paris: L'Harmattan.
Bucholz, Mary
  1996   Marking Black: the construction of White identities through African-American Vernacular English. Paper presented at the Annual Meeting of the Georgetown Linguistics Society, Washington, DC.
Cadiot, Pierre
  1989   On language mixtures. In Ulrich Ammon (ed.), *The Status and Function of Languages and Language Varieties*, 570–580. Berlin: Walter de Gruyter.
Caisson, Max
  1974   L'hospitalité comme relation d'ambivalence. *Études Corses* 2: 115–127.
Calvet, Louis-Jean
  1974   *Linguistique et colonialisme*. Paris: Payot.
Cameron, Deborah
  1995   *Verbal Hygiene*. New York: Routledge.
Carbuccia, Anghjulamaria
  1988   Letter to the Editor. *Corse-Matin*. March 23: 9.

Casale, Beatrice and Ghjacumu Luciani
   1980   A lingua. In Ghjermana de Zerbi (ed.), *Cantu Nustrale*, Corbara: Accademia d'i Vagabondi.
Casanova, Jean-Charles
   1996   Letter to the Editor. *A Viva Voce* 14: 10.
Castelli, Michèle
   1986   *Rue Chateau Payan*. Paris: Editions Universitaires.
Charnet, C.
   1992   Rapport: Textes et Polynomie. *PULA* (3/4): 29–31.
Chiorboli, Jean
   1993   Conférence de Presse 28/6/93.
   1994   *La langue des Corses: notes linguistiques et glottopolitiques.* Bastia: JPC Infograffia.
Choury, Maurice
   1958   *Tous bandits honneur: résistance et libération de la Corse.* Paris: Éditons Sociales.
Codaccione-Meistersheim, Anne
   1987   La Corse: L'en-vie, la mort. *Peuples Méditerranéens* 38: 105–122.
   1988   Insularité insularism, îléité, quelques concepts opératoires. *Cahiers de l'IDIM* 1: 96–120.
   1989   Images d'iléité. *Cahiers de l'IDIM* 1: 30–36.
Colombani, Jean-Marie
   1990   Interview. *La Corse-Le Provençal,* 9 July: 17.
Colonna, Ghjuvan Natale
   1998   Un dite micca...ma dite. *Journal de la Corse* 34: 1.
Comiti, Jean-Marie
   1992   *Les Corses Face à Leur Langue.* Ajaccio: Edizione Squadra di u Finisellu.
Conseil de la Culture, de l'Éducation et du Cadre de Vie (CCECV)
   1986   *Cungressu internaziunale nantu à u bislinguismu: Atti. Actes du Congres International sur le Bilinguisme*, Bastia, 12–15 April 1984. Bastia: Scola Corsa.
   1989a   *Rapport du groupe de travail: Lingua Corsa.* Assemblée de Corse.
   1989b   *Cultura: essai sur l'approche d'une politique culturelle.* Assemblée de Corse
Corse: éviter l'ultra-purisme.
   1988   *Corse Matin,* 19 July: 24.
Corse-Matin   Weekly newspaper
Corsu in Scola, U
   1993   U Corsu in Scola: Spechju di u corsu in sucietB. Compte-rendu des débats sur la langue du 5.11.93. *Arritti* 1387: 8–10.

Couderc, Yves
1974   D'après Ninyoles, idioma i prejudici: le problème linguistique en
              Occitanie. *Cahier no. 1 du Groupe de Recherche sur la Diglossie*
              (Montpellier): 3–10.
Crowley, Tony
1994   *Language and History: Theory and Texts*. New York: Routledge.
Culioli, Gabriel Xavier
1986   *La terre des seigneurs*. Paris: Lieu Commun.
1990   *Le Complexe Corse*. Paris: Gallimard.
Culioli, Jean Dominique, Antoine Lous, Gabriel Xavier and Vannina Sandra
1997   *Dictionnaire Français-Corse, Corsu-Francese*. Ajaccio: Éditions
              DCL.
Dalbera-Stefanaggi, Marie-José
1978   *Langue Corse: une approche linguistique*. Paris: Editions
              Klingsieck.
1989   Corse: réalité dialectale et imaginaire linguistique: du coeur de
              l'Italie aux marges de la France. In Georges Ravis-Giordani (ed.),
              L'Île miroir, 121–131. Ajaccio: La Marge.
De Certeau, Michel, Dominique Julia and Jacques Revel
1975   *Une politique de la langue: la Révolution et les patois*. Paris:
              Gallimard.
Decrosse, Anne
1987   Un mythe historique: la langue maternelle. In Geneviève Vermes
              and Josiane Boutet (eds.), *France, pays multilingue*, Volume 2,
              29–37. Paris: L'Harmattan.
Desanti, Jean-Toussaint
1984   Effacer la mer. In Sébastien Giudicelli (ed.), *La Corse: une affaire
              de famille*, 15–24. Marseilles: Editions du Quai-Jeanne Laffitte.
Désideri, Lucie
1991   Tradition et modernité–manières de revenir. *Kyrn* 362: 30.
Di Giacomo, Susan
1991   "The Catalan we wpeak now": language and memory in Catalan
              nationalist politics. Paper presented at the 1991 Spring Meeting of
              the American Ethnological Society.
De Zerbi, Ghermana
1987   Appiu di ghjumentu un tomba cavallu. *Peuples Méditerranéens*
              38/39: 219–226.
1980   *Cantu Nustrale*. Corbara: Accademia d'i Vagabondi.
1997   U dragu cù i setti capi. *A Messagera* 18: 32.
DiMeglio, Alain
1992a   Polynomie et enseignement de la langue corse. *PULA* (3/4):
              127–130.
1992b   Rapport: Glottopolitique et Glottodidactiques. *PULA* (3/4): 33–35.

Dorian, Nancy
1981   *Language Death.* Philadelphia: University of Pennsylvania Press.
1994   Purism vs. xompromise in language revitalization and language
            revival. *Language in Society* 23(4): 479–494.
Dottelonde, Pierre
1989   Regard sur le nationalisme corse contemporain dans le miroir de la
            réalité insulaire. In Georges Ravis-Giordani (ed.), *L'île miroir*,
            107–113. Ajaccio: La Marge.
Eastman, Carol
1992   Codeswitching as an Urban Language-Contact Phenomenon.
            Journal of Multilingual and Multicultural Development 13(1/2):
            1–17.
Eckert, Penelope
1983   The Paradox of National Language Movements. *Journal of
            Multilingual and   Multicultural Development* 4(4): 289–300.
Eckert, Penelope and Sally McConnell-Ginet
1992   Think practically, look locally: language and gender as community-
            based practice. *Annual Review of Anthropology* (21): 461–477.
Edwards, Jane
1992   Transcription of discourse. In William Bright (ed.), *International
            Encyclopedia of Linguistics* Vol. 1, 367–370. New York: Oxford
            University Press.
Edwards, John
1985   *Language, Society and Identity.* New York: Basil Blackwell.
Entre nostalgie et modernité
1991   *Corse-Matin*, 16 June.
Ettori, Fernand and Jacques Fusina
1980   *Langue corse: incertitudes et paris.* Ajaccio: A Stampa.
Fairclough, Norman
1989   *Language and Power.* New York: Longman.

Falce, A
1988   Campiunatu d'Ortograffia. *Arritti*, 1 September: 3.
Fanon, Frantz
1967   *Black Skin, White Masks.* Translated by Charles Markmann. New
            York: Grove Press.
Ferguson, Charles
1950   Diglossia. *Word* 15: 325-340.
Ferguson, J.
1991   Diglossia revisited. In Allan Hudson (ed.), Studies in Diglossia.
            Southwest Journal of Linguistics 10(1): 14–34.
Ferrandi, Ghjilorma
1987   Lingua è cultura, corpu è anima di un populu. *A Gravona* 1: 3.

Ferrandi, M.J.
1991   Intervista bislingua: Théâtre Point. *A Fiara* March: 7.

Field, Les W.
1999   Complicities and collaborations: anthropologists and the "unacknowledged tribes" of California. *Current Anthropology* 40 (2): 123-135.

Filippi, Paul
1992   Le français régionale de Corse. Ph.D. dissertation University of Corsica.

Fishman, Joshua
1991   *Reversing Language Shift*. Philadephia, PA: Multilingual Matters.

Franceschi, Danièle
1991   Editorial. *Corsica Infurmazione* 13: 1–3

Franceschi, Danièle and Vitale Geronomi
1991   La corse entre nationalisme et clanisme–illogique ou fatalité? *Corsica Infurmazione* 13: 24–27.

Franchi, Jean-Joseph
1984   De la sociolinguistique à la langue. Unpublished Ms.
1988   Cuntrastu: A Sociolinguistica: una bona o una mala. *Rigiru* 24: 14–27.

Franzini, Antoine
1991   Une île dans la tête. *Kyrn* 362: 35.

Friedrich, Paul
1989   Language ideology and political economy. *American Anthropologist* 91: 295–312.

Front Regionaliste Corse (F.R.C.)
1971   *Main basse sur une île*. Corbara: Accademia d'i Vagabondi.

Furet, François and Jacques Ozouf
1977   *Lire et écrire: l'alphabétisation des Français de Calvin à Jules Ferry*. Paris: Éditions de Minuit.

Fusina, Jacques
1994   *L'enseignement du corse*. Ajaccio: Editions A Squadra di u Finusellu.

Gal, Susan
1978   "Peasant men can't get wives": language change and sex roles in a bilingual community. *Language in Society* 7: 1–17.
1979   *Language Shift*. New York: Academic Press.
1987   Codeswitching and consciousness in the European periphery. *American Ethnologist* 14(4): 637–653.
1989   Language and political economy. *Annual Review of Anthropology* 18: 345–367.
1989   Language ideology and political economy. *American Anthropologist* 91: 295–312.

1992   Multiplicity and contention among ideologies: a commentary. *Pragmatics* 2(3): 445-450.
1993   Diversity and contestation in linguistic ideologies: German speakers in Hungary. *Language in Society* 22(3): 337–360.
1995   Language and the "arts of resistance". *Cultural Anthropology* 10(3): 445–450.

Gardner-Chloros, Penelope
1991   *Language Selection and Switching in Strasbourg*. Oxford: Clarendon Press.

Gardy, Philippe and Robert Lafont
1981   La diglossie comme conflit: l'exemple occitan. *Langages* 61, 75–91.

Geronimi, D. and P. Marchetti
1971   *Intricciate è cambiarini: manuel pratique d'orthographe corse.* Nogent-sur-Marne: Éditions Beaulieu.

Geronimi, Dumenicantone
1997   L'italien a joué le rôle de langue dominante. *A Messagera* 18, 33–36.

Giard, Jean and Jacques Schiebling
1981   *L'enjeu régional.* Paris: Editions Sociales.

Gil, Jose
1984   *La Corse: entre la liberté et la terreur.* Paris: Éditions de la Difference.

Gilmore, David, ed.
1987   *Honor and Shame and the Unity of the Mediterranean.* Washington, D.C.: American Anthropological Association.

Giordan, Henri
1982   *Democratie culturelle et droit à la différence.* Paris: La Documentation Française.

Giudicelli, Sébastien
1984   Les Corses entre l'insularité et l'exil. In Sébastien Giudicelli (ed.), *La Corse: une affaire de famille,* 179–216. Marseilles: Éditions du Quai-Jeanne Laffitte.

Graff, Harvey J.
1987   *The Legacies of Literacy.* Bloomington: Indiana University Press.

Granarolo, Philippe
1984   La thèse de Malikha: une nouvelle vision du colonialisme en Corse.In Sébastien Giudicelli (ed.), *La Corse: une affaire de famille,* 55–87. Marseilles: Éditions du Quai-Jeanne Laffitte.

Graves, William
1991   Conflicting Ideologies of Language, Identity and Authority in an American Indian Community. Paper presented at the 113th Annual Meeting of the Americal Ethnological Society, Charleston, NC.

Graziani, Ghjuvan Petru
    1986   *Un ciel de fer.* Nucario: Cismonte è Pumonti.
Grice, H.P.
    1975   Logic and Conversation. In Peter Cole and J.L. Morgan (eds.),
                Speech Acts, 41–58. New York: Academic Press.
Grillo, Ralph
    1989   *Dominant Languages: Language and Hierarchy in Britain and
                France.* Cambridge: Cambridge University Press.
Grimaldi, Rigòlu
    1995   Letter to the Editor. *A Viva Voce* 10: 12.
Gysels, Marjolein
    1992   French in Urban Lubumbashi Swahili: Codeswitching, Borrowing
                or Both? *Journal of Multilingual and Multi-Cultural Development*
                12(1/2): 41–55.
Handler, Richard
    1988   *Nationalism and the Politics of Culture in Quebec.* Madison:
                University of Wisconsin Press.
Hanks, William
    1996   *Language and Communicative Practices.* Boulder CO: Westview
                Press.
Hélias, Pierre Jakez
    1978   *The Horse of Pride.* New Haven: Yale University Press.
Heller, Monica
    1985   Ethnic relations and language use in Montreal. In Nessa Wolfson
                and Joan Manes (eds.), *Language of Inequality*, 75–90. New York:
                Mouton.
    1994   *Crosswords.* New York: Mouton de Gruyter.
    1996   Legitimate language in a multilingual school. *Linguistics and
                Education* 8: 139–157.
Herzfeld, Michael
    1985   *The Poetics of Manhood.* Princeton: Princeton University Press.
    1987   *Anthropology Through the Looking Glass.* New York: Cambridge
                University Press.
    1996   National spirit or the breath of nature? The expropriation of folk
                positivism in the discourse of Greek nationalism. In Michael
                Silverstein and Greg Urban (eds.), *Natural Histories of Discourse*,
                277–300. Chicago: University of Chicago Press.
Higonnet, Patrice
    1980   The politics of linguistic terrorism and grammatical hegemony
                during the French Revolution. *Social History* 5(1): 41–69.
Hill, Jane
    1985   The grammar of consciousness and the consciousness of grammar.
                American Ethnologist 12 (4): 725–737.

1989 The social functions of relativization. In Nancy Dorian (ed.), *Investigating Obsolescence*, 149–164. New York: Cambridge University Press.

1992 "Today there is no respect": nostalgia, "respect" and oppositional discourse in Mexicano (Nahuatl) language ideology. *Pragmatics* 2 (3): 263–280.

Hill, Jane and Kenneth Hill

1980 Mixed grammar, purist grammar and language attitudes in modern Nahuatl. *Language in Society*(9): 321–348.

Hobsbawm, E.J.

1990 *Nations and Nationalism since 1780*. New York: Cambridge University Press.

Holmes, Douglas

1989 *Cultural Disenchantments*. Princeton: Princeton University Press.

Holmquist, J.C.

1985 Social correlates of a linguistic variable: a study in a Spanish village. *Language in Society* 16: 179–204.

Hudson, Alan

1992 Diglossia: a bibliographic review. *Language in Society* 21(4): 611–655.

Hymes, Dell

1996 *Ethnography, Linguistics and Narrative Inequality*. Bristol, PA: Taylor and Francis.

Institut National Statistique et Economique (INSEE)

1986 *Tableaux d'Economie Corse*.

Irvine, Judith

1989 When talk isn't cheap: language and political economy. *American Ethnologist* 16: 249–278.

Jacob, James E. and David C. Gordon

1985 Language policy in France. In William R. Beer and James E. Jacob (eds.), *Language Policy and National Unity*, 107–129. Totowa, NJ: Rowman and Allanheld.

Jaffe, Alexandra

1989 L'angoisse de l'être et l'enjeu du Corse. *PULA* 1: 17–29.

1990 Corsica on strike: the power and the limits of ethnicity. *Ethnic Groups* 8: 91–111.

1991 La femme, le mot et le pouvoir en Corse. *Meridies* 13/14: 131–146.

1993a Obligation, error and authenticity: competing cultural principles in the teaching of Corsican. *Journal of Linguistic Anthropology* 3(1): 99–114.

1993b Corsican identity and a Europe of peoples and regions. In Thomas Wilson and Estellie Smith (eds.), *Cultural Change and the New Europe: Perspectives on the European Community*, 61–80. Boulder, CO: Westview Press.

1993c   Involvement, detachment and representation on Corsica. In
               Caroline Brettell (ed.), *When They Read What We Write: the
               Politics of Ethnography*, 52–66. Westport CT: Bergin and Garvey.
1996   The second annual Corsican spelling contest: orthography and
               ideology. *American Ethnologist* 23 (4): 816–835.

Joseph, John Earl
1985   "Superposed" languages and standardization. *Studi italiani di
               linguistica teorica e applicata* 1-3: 39–51.

Kloss, H. and G. Mc Connel
1984   *Composition linguistique des nations du monde/Linguistic Compo-
               sition of the Nations of the World*, Vol. 5: Europe and the U.S.S.R.
               Québec: Presses de l'Universite Laval.

Kristol, Andres
1996   Sondages d'opinion thématique sociolinguistique: problèmes de
               fiabilité. *Lengas* 40: 123–137.

Kuter, Lois
1989   Breton vs. French: Language and the Opposition of Political,
               Economic, Social and Cultural Values. In Nancy Dorian (ed.),
               Investigation Obsolescence. New York: Cambridge University
               Press, 75–89.

Kyrn   Weekly magazine published in Ajaccio.

Labov, William
1998   The Intersection of Sex and Social Class in the Course of Linguistic
               Change. In Jenny Cheshire, (ed.), *The Sociolinguistics Reader vol
               2: Gender and Discourse*, 7–53. New York: Arnold.

Laponce, Jean
1984   *Langue et térritoire*. Québec: Les Presses de L'Université Laval.

Le Corse   Daily Newspaper

Luedi, Georges
1992   French as a Pluricentric Language. In Michael Clyne (ed.),
               Pluricentric Languages,149–177. New York: Mouton de Gruyter.

Mahlau, Axel
1991   Some aspects of the standard of the Basque language. In Utta Von
               Gleich and Ekkehard Wolff (eds.), *Standardization of National
               Languages*, 79–94.. Hamburg, Germany: UNESCO Institute for
               Education.

Marcellesi, Jean-Baptiste
1989   Corse et théorie sociolinguistique: reflets croisés. In Georges
               Ravis-Giordani (ed.), *L'île miroir*, 165–174. Ajaccio: La Marge.

Marcellesi, Jean-Baptiste and Bernard Gardin
1974   *Introduction à la sociolinguistique*. Paris: Larousse.

Marchetti, Pascal
1974   *Le corse sans peine*. Paris: Assimil.
1989a   *La corsophonie*. Paris: Editions Albatros.

1989b   Les Corses ne sont pas les Basques de la Méditerranée. *Corse-Matin* 19 December: 5.

1991   Baptême à la tronçonneuse. *Corse-Matin* 27 May: 27.

1997   L'italien est notre langue historique. *A Messagera* 18: 33–36.

Martin-Jones, Marilyn and Monica Heller

1996   Introduction to the special issues on education in multilingual settings: discourse, identities and power. Part II: contesting legitimacy. *Linguistics and Education* 8: 127–137.

Martin-Gistucci, Marie-Gracieuse

1987   *L'île intérieure.* Ajaccio: La Marge.

Marty-Balzagues, Jacqueline

1996   Compliments et monologues pour mariage en situation de diglossie. *Lengas* 40: 89–121.

Matras, Yaron and Gertrud Reershemius

1991   Standardization beyond the state: the cases of Yiddish, Kurdish and Romani. In Utta Von Gleich and Ekkehard Wolff (eds.), *Standardization of National Languages*, 103–123. Hamburg, Germany: UNESCO Institute for Education.

Maynes, Mary Jo

1985   *Schooling in Western Europe: a Social History.* Albany, New York: SUNY Press.

MacClancy, Jeremy

1993   At play with identity in the Basque arena. In MacDonald, Sharon (ed.), *Inside European Identities*, 84–97 Providence: Berg.

Ma u corsu, si pò amparalla?

1991   *A Fiara*, September: 12.

McClure, J. Derrick

1985   The debate on scots orthography. In Gorlach, Manfrend (ed.), *Focus on Scotland*, 203–209. Amsterdam: Benjamins.

McDonald, Maryon

1989   *We Are Not French.* New York: Cambridge University Press.

1994   Women and linguistic innovation in Brittany. In Burton, Pauline, Ketaki Dyson and Shirley Ardener (eds.), *Bilingual Women: Anthropological Approaches to Second Language Use*, 85–109. Providence: Berg.

McKechnie, Rosemary

1993   Becoming celtic in Corsica. In MacDonald, Sharon (ed.), *Inside European Identities*, 118–145. Providence: Berg.

Merler, Alberto

1987   Evolution de la classe politique dépendante en situation de complexité sociale accrue. *Peuples Méditerranéens* 38: 269–280.

1988   Note su alcuni precondizionamenti allo sviluppo endogeno in Corsica e in Sardegna. *Cahiers de l'IDIM* 1: 75–89.

Mertz, Elizabeth
    1989   Sociolinguistic creativity: Cape Breton Gaelic's linguistic "tip." In
                Nancy Dorian (ed.), *Investigating Obsolescence*, 103–115. London:
                Cambridge University.

Messenger, John
    1983   *Inis Beag: Isle of Ireland*. Prospect Heights: Waveland Press.

Mewett, Peter G.
    1986   Boundaries and discourse in a Lewis crofting community. In
                Anthony Cohen (ed.), *Symbolizing Boundaries: Identity and
                Diversity in British Culture*, 71–87. Wolfeboro NH: Manchester
                University Press.

Mezzadri, Mathieu
    1991   Tous ne sont pas ministres. *Kyrn* 375: 57.

Mollard, Pascale
    1982   *Ici, on parle Corse*. Supplément à CFJ (Centre de la Formation des
                Journalistes) Informations. Paris.

Mondoloni, Pierre
    1998   Comment halez-vous? *Corse-Matin* 28 July.

Moore, Sally Falk
    1977   Uncertainty in Situations: Indeterminacies in Culture. In Sally Falk
                Moore and Barbara Myerhoff (eds.), *Secular Ritual*, 33–53.
                Amsterdam: Van Gorcum.

Moore, Sally Falk and Myerhoff, Barbara
    1977   Introduction: Forms and Meanings. In Sally Falk Moore and
                Barbara Myerhoff (eds.), *Secular Ritual*, 1–29. Amsterdam: Van
                Gorcum.

Moracchini, Georges
    1992   Rapport: Glottopolitique et Polynomie Corses. *PULA* (3/4): 21–22.
    1998   De la polynomie à la polynomité. In Robert Lafont (ed), *Quarante
                ans de sociolinguistique à la périphérie*,149–155. Paris:
                L'Harmattan.

Mougeon, Raymond and Édouard Beniak
    1989   Language Contraction and Linguistic Change: the Case of Welland
                French. In Nancy Dorian (ed), *Investigating Obsolescence*,
                287–311. New York: Cambridge University Press.

Multedo, Roccu
    1996   Tra il còrso ed il francese, l' italiano. *A Viva Voce* 14: 5–6.

Murati, Antoine
    1983   Culture corse ancestrale, culture française importante: la vie des
                Corses durant le XXième siècle. *Cuntrasti* 1: 47–73.

Myerhoff, Barbara
    1978   *Number Our Days*. New York: Simon and Schuster.

Notes de la semaine, Les
  1999   *Journal de la Corse*, 2 April: 2.
Nichols, Patricia
  1983   Linguistic options and choices for black women in the rural south.
                In Barrie Thorne, Cheris Cramarae, and Nancy Henley (eds.),
                Language, Gender and Society, 54–58. Rowley, MA: Newbury
                House.
O'Brien, Oonagh
  1993   Good to be French? conflicts of identity in North Catalonia. In
                Mcdonald, Sharon (ed.), *Inside European Identities*, 98–118.
                Providence: Berg Publishers.
Olivesi, Claude
  1983   Le système politique corse: le clan. *Cuntrasti* 1: 13–24.
  1991   Concept de coofficialité. In Scola Corsa (ed.), *Concept de
                Coofficialità/l'Edea di a Cuufficialità*, 23–30. Bastia: Edizioni
                Scola Corsa.
Orsoni, Claude
  1990   Clanisme et racisme: hypothèse sur les relations inter-communaires
                en Corse *Peuples Méditerranéens* 51: 191–201.
Ottavi, Antoine
  1979   *Des Corses à part entière*. Paris: Editions du Seuil.
Parman, Susan
  1990   *Scottish Crofters*. Philadelphia: Holt, Rinehart and Winston.
Perfettini, Francescu
  1994   Comprendre ce qu'on écrit. *Arritti* 6 June: 4.
Perfettini, Francescu and Paul-Marie Agostini
  1987   *Corsi di Corsu*. Bastia: Centre Régionale de Documentation
                Pédagogique.
Peretti, Philippe
  1995   La scelta alsaziana. A *Viva Voce* 12: 1–2.
Piroddi, J.
  1994   Lingua corsa, lingua materna. *Arritti* May 4: 14.
Poche, Bernard
  1987   La construction sociale de la langue. In Geneviève Vermes and
                Josiane Boutet (eds.), *France: pays multilingue*, 79–105. Paris:
                L'Harmattan.
Poli, Gisèle
  1991   Vive la pollution, le béton et l'exploitation. *Corse- Matin*, 24
                March: 20.
Poli, Moune.
  1991   *La Corse au Point*. Paris: L'Harmattan.
Polidori, Ghjacumu
  1988   Pulemica nant'à lingua corsa. *U Ribombu* 15 June: 15.

Pomponi, Francis et. al. (eds)
    1982   *Le Mémorial des Corses*. 6 Vols. Ajaccio: SARL Le Mémorial des Corses.

Préfecture de la Région de Corse
    1990   *Livre Blanc Préparatoire au Schéma d'Aménagement de la Corse*. Ajaccio: Éditions Cyrnos et Méditerranée.

Preston, Dennis
    1985   The L'il Abner syndrome: written representations of speech. *American Speech* 60: 328–336.

Prost, Antoine
    1968   *Histoire de l'enseignement en France 1800-1967*. Paris: Armand Colin.

Quéré Louis
    1987   Le statut duel de la langue dans l'Etat-Nation. In Geneviève Vermes and Josiane Boutet (eds.), *France: pays multilingue*. Paris: L'Harmattan, 59–78.

Rampton, Ben
    1995   *Crossing: Language and Ethnicity Among Adolescents*. London: Longman.

Ravis-Giordani, Georges
    1979   Ethnologie. In Charles Bonneton (ed.), *Corse*, Paris: Bonneton, 59–167.
    1983   *Bergers corses*. Aix-en-Provence: Edisud.
    1984   Affari di casa. In Sébastien Giudicelli (ed.), *La Corse: une affaire de famille*, 33–38. Marseilles: Éditions du Quai-Jeanne Laffitte.
    1989   Jeux de miroir et autres spéculations. In Georges Ravis-Giordani (ed.), *L'Île miroir*, 7–13. Ajaccio: La Marge.

Raymond, Alain
    1991   Poème. *Kyrn* 378: 23.

Reed-Danahay, Deborah
    1987   Farm children at school: educational strategies in Rural France. *Anthropological Quarterly* 60: 83–88.
    1993   Talking About resistance: ethnography and theory in rural France. *Anthropological Quarterly* 66: 221–229.

Renucci, Janine
    1974   *Corse traditionelle et Corse nouvelle*. Lyon: Audin.

Rogers, Susan Carol
    1991   L'ethnologie nord-américaine de la France: entreprise ethnologique "près de chez soi". *Ethnologie Française* 1: 5–12.

Romaine, Suzanne
    1995   Hawai'i Creole English as a literary language. *Language in Society* 23: 527–554.

Roseman, Sharon
1995 "*Falamos como falamos*": linguistic revitalization and the maintenance of local vernaculars in Galicia. *Journal of Linguistic Anthropology* 5(1): 3–32.
Roselli-Cecconi, Carlu
1995a Una sosta per riflettere. *A Viva Voce* 10: 1–2.
1995b Detti e Fatti. *A Viva Voce* 11: 11.
Rotily-Forcioli, Marie-Madeleine
1988 U Corsu Schiettu. *A Spannata* 18: 7.
Salvi, Salvatore
1975 *Le Lingue Tagliate*. Milan: Rizzoli.
Sanguinetti, Sampiero
1987 L'information télévisée en Corse. *Cuntrasti* 2: 12–28.
Santarelli, Paule
1989 Miroir, méchante miroir. *Kyrn* 248: 15–17.
Sasse, Hans-Juergen
1992 Language decay and contact-induced change: similarities and differences. In Matthias Brenzinger (ed.), *Language Death: Factual and Theoretical Explorations With Special Reference to East Africa*, 59–79.. New York: Mouton de Gruyter.
Schieffelin, Bambi and Rachelle Charlier Doucet
1992 The "real" Haitian Creole: metalinguistics, and orthographic choice. *Pragmatics* 2(3): 427–444.
Sebba, Mark
1996 How do you spell Patwa? *Critical Quarterly* 38(4): 50–63
in press Phonology meets ideology: the meaning of orthographic practices in British Creole. To appear in *Language Problems and Language Planning*.
Scola Corsa
1991 *Concept de Coofficialità/l'Edea di a Cuufficialità*. Bastia: Edizioni Scola Corsa.
Scott, James C.
1990 *Domination and the Arts of Resistance*. New Haven CT: Yale University Press.
Scotton, Carol Myers
1986 Diglossia and codeswitching. In Fishman, Joshua, A. Tabouret-Keller, M. Clyne, Bh. Krishnamurti, M. Abdulaziz (eds.), *The Fergusonian Impact*, 403–415.. New York: Mouton de Gruyter.
Shapiro, Michael
1989 A political approach to language purism. In Bjorn Jernudd and Michael Shapiro (eds.), *The Politics of Language Purism*, 22–29. New York: Mouton de Gruyter.

Shuman, Amy
    1993   Collaborative writing: appropriating power or reproducing author-
                 ity? In Brian Street (ed.), *Cross-Cultural Approaches to Literacy*,
                 247–271. New York: Cambridge University Press.

Silverstein, Michael
    1987   Monoglot "standard" in America: Standardization and Metaphors
                 of Linguistic Hegemony. *Working Papers and Proceedings of the
                 Center for Psychosocial Studies* 13, Chicago.

Simonpoli, Paul
    1981   Corse: pour une approche du phénomène national. Ph.D.
                 dissertation, Université de Provence.

Stafford, Susan Buchanan
    1987   Language and identity: Haitians in New York. In Constance R.
                 Sutton and Elsa M. Chaney (eds.), *Caribbean Life in New York
                 City: Sociocultural Dimensions,* 202–215. New York: Center For
                 Migration Studies.

Street, Brian
    1993   Introduction: the new literacy studies. In Brian Street (ed.), *Cross-
                 Cultural Approaches to Literacy*, 1–22. New York: Cambridge
                 University Press.

Susini, Marie
    1981   *La renfermée, la corse.* Paris: Editions du Seuil.

Terdiman, Richard
    1985   *Discourse/Counter-Discourse.* Ithaca, NY: Cornell University
                 Press.

Thiers, Jacques
    1984   Diglossie corse et dysfonctionnement du langage. In Sébastien
                 Giudicelli (ed.), *La Corse et la folie.* Marseilles: Éditions du Quai,
                 Jeanne Laffitte, 37–40.

    1986a   Elaboration linguistique et individuation sociolinguistique. In J. B.
                 Marcellesi and G. Thiers (eds.), *L'individuation sociolinguistique
                 corse*, 19–25. Mont-Saint-Aignan: GRESCO-IRED.

    1986b   Enquête sur la situation linguistique des collèges de Corse. In J. B.
                 Marcellesi and G. Thiers (eds.), *L'individuation sociolinguistique
                 corse*, 25–55. Mont-Saint-Aignan: GRESCO-IRED.

    1987a   Idéologie diglossique et production de sens.*Peuples
                 Méditerranéens* 38: 139–154.

    1987b   L'enquête épilinguistique. *Études Corses* 28: 39–75.

    1988a   Epilinguisme et langue polynomique: L'exemple Corse. Ph.D.
                 dissertation, Université de Rouen.

    1988b   Cuntrastu: A Sociolinguistica: una bona o una mala? *Rigiru* 25:
                 14–27.

    1989a   *Papiers d'identité(s).* Levie: Albiana.

    1989b   Le temps d'un drâme. *Kyrn* 285: 41–42.

Thomas, George
1991   *Linguistic Purism*. London: Longman.
Thompson, Ian
1971   *Corsica*. Newton Abbott: David and Charles.
Thompson, John B.
1984   *Studies in the Theory of Ideology*. Berkeley: University of California Press.
Tollefson, James W.
1983   Language policy and the meanings of diglossia. *Word* 34: 1–9.
Trosset, Carol
1986   The Social Identity of Welsh Learners. *Language In Society* 15: 165–192.
Tsitsipis, Lukas
1991   Terminal-fluent speaker interaction and the contextualization of deviant speech. *Journal of Pragmatics* 14(2): 153–173.
Urban, Greg
1991   *A Discourse-Centered Approach to Culture*. Austin: University of Texas Press.
Urciuoli, Bonnie
1996   *Exposing Prejudice*. Boulder CO: Westview Press.
Urla, Jacqueline
1987   Being Basque, speaking Basque: the politics of language and identity in the Basque country. Ph.D. dissertation, University of California, Berkeley.
1988   Ethnic protest and social planning: a look at Basque language revival. *Cultural Anthropology* 3: 379–394.
1993   Contesting modernities: language standardization and the production of an Ancient/Modern Basque Culture. *Critique of Anthropology* 13(2): 101–118.
Vermes, Geneviève and Josiane Boutet
1987   Introduction. In Geneviève Vermes and Josiane Boutet (eds.), *France, Pays Multilingue*, 21–37. Paris: L'Harmattan.
Wald, Paul
1986   Diglossia applied: vernacular mixing and functional switching. In Joshua Fishman, A. Tabouret-Keller, M. Clyne, Bh. Krishnamurti, M. Abdulaziz (eds.), *The Fergusonian Impact*. 417–429. New York: Mouton de Gruyter.
Weber, Eugen
1976   *Peasants Into Frenchmen*. Stanford: Stanford University Press.
Weinstein
1989   Francophonie: purism at the international level. In Bjorn Jernudd, and Michael Shapiro (eds.), *The Politics of Language Purism*, 53–80.. New York: Mouton de Gruyter.

Winer, Lise
  1990   Orthographic standardization for Trinidad and Tobago: linguistic
              and sociopolitical considerations in English Creole community.
              Language Problems and Language Planning 14(3): 237–259.

Woelck, Wolfgang
  1991   The standardization of Quechua: some problems and suggestions.
              In Utta Von Gleich and Ekkehard Wolff (eds.), *Standardization of
              National Languages*, 43–54. Hamburg, Germany: UNESCO
              Institute for Education.

Woolard, Kathryn
  1985   Language variation and cultural hegemony: toward an integration
              of sociolinguistic theory and social theory. *American Ethnologist*
              12: 738–748.
  1989a   *Double Talk: Bilingualism and the Politics of Ethnicity in
              Catalonia*. Stanford: Stanford University Press.
  1989b   Language convergence and language death as social processes. In
              Nancy Dorian (ed.), *Investigating Obsolescence: Studies in
              Language Contraction and Death*, 355–365. London: Cambridge
              University Press.
  1990   Codeswitching as practice and consciousness: codeswitching and
              comedy in Catalonia, revisited. Paper presented to the International
              Pragmatics Conference, Barcelona.
  1992   Language ideology: issues and approaches. *Pragmatics* 2(3):
              235–250.

Wylie, Laurence
  1974   *Village in the Vaucluse*. Cambridge: Harvard University Press.

Name index

A Falce 218, 225, 227, 228, 297
A. V-P., 298
Abu-Lughod, L., 25, 297
Achard, P., 82-84, 88, 136, 223, 256, 296, 297
Acquaviva, J., 40, 64, 71, 297
ADECEC, 12, 131, 134, 152, 223, 232, 245, 254, 270, 296, 297
Agostini, P., 204, 309
Albertini, M., 59, 69, 297
Anderson, B., 297
Annamalai, E., 209, 219, 295, 297
Ariosto, 76
Arrighi, J., 145, 146, 191, 192, 265, 297

Baggioni, J., 185
Balibar, E., 22, 84, 89, 124, 126, 127, 129, 298
Balibar, R., 78, 79
Barre, R. 84
Bassani, L., 51, 52, 187, 254, 255, 298
Beniak, E., 207, 295, 308
Beriss, D., 89, 298
Berruto, G., 23, 298
Biggi, M., 52, 298
Biron, 86
Blok, A., 50, 53, 298
Blom, J., 113, 298
Blommaert, J., 126, 298
Bonn, C., 85, 291, 298
Boswell, 76, 265, 298
Bourdieu, P., 32, 87, 89, 249, 286, 287, 290, 299
Boutet, J., 88, 297-299, 301, 309, 310, 313
Bowie, F., 290, 299
Boyer, H., 22, 23, 299
Brown, B., 216, 219, 221, 299
Bucholz, M., 299
Bungelmi, 174, 179

Cadiot, P., 271, 299
Caisson, M., 299
Calvet, L., 299
Cameron, D., 6, 18, 32, 84, 151, 238, 291, 295, 299
Canarelli, P., 40, 64, 71, 297
Carbuccia, A., 158, 299
Casale, B., 272, 299
Casanova, J., 136, 144, 300
Castellani, 133, 166, 169, 177, 230, 243, , 247
Castelli, M., 60, 242, 243, 244, 300
Charles-le-Chauve, 82
Charnet, C., 300
Chiarelli, 175, 185, 294
Chiorboli, J., 160-162, 300
Choury, M., 300
Colombani, J., 59, 300
Comiti, J., 146, 147, 149, 182, 293, 300
Couderc, Y., 22, 300
Crowley, T., 32, 33, 82, 86, 114, 128-130, 292, 300
Culioli, G., 49, 62, 63, 85, 111, 149, 290, 300

Dalbera-Stefanaggi, M., 300, 301
De Certeau, M., 87, 89, 301
Decrosse, A., 82, 88, 220, 301
Desanti , J., 39, 40, 301
Di Giacomo, S., 135, 293, 301
DiMeglio, A., 301
Désideri, L., 301
Dorian, N., 31, 85, 91, 92, 115, 151, 194, 209, 291, 295, 301, 305-308, 313
Dottelonde, P., 39, 301
Doucet, R., 206, 220, 245, 296, 311

Eastman, C., 114, 301
Eckert, P., 24, 278, 282, 301
Edwards, Jane, 291

Edwards, John , 302
Ettori, F., 76, 302

Fairclough, N., 6, 302
Falce, A., 218, 225-228, 297, 302
Fanon, F., 87, 302
Fazi, A., 97, 98
Ferguson, J., 302
Ferrandi, 127, 169, 266, 302
Fichte, 126
Filippi, P., 90, 116, 189-191, 302
Fishman , J., 22, 302, 311, 313
Fontana, 229, 229, 231, 248
Franceschi, D., 48, 302
Franchi, J., 16, 78, 153-157, 192, 220,
           266, 276, 302
Franzini, A., 39, 68, 302
FRC, 72, 116-120, 215, 237, 273
Furet, F., 89, 303
Fusina, J., 76, 85, 86, 224, 302, 303

Gaffori, 48
Gal, S., 24, 27, 110, 113-115, 135, 207,
          290, 292, 295, 303
Gardin, B., 22, 307
Gardner-Chloros, P., 114, 303
Gardy , P., 22, 303
Garoby-Colonna, 142, 143
Geronimi, D., 48, 130, 131, 145-147,
           227, 303
Geronomi, V., 44
Giard, J., 70, 72, 303
Gil, J., 50, 53, 56, 303
Gilmore, D., 50, 303
Giordan, H., 22, 303
Giudicelli, S., 39, 55, 88, 297, 301,
           304, 310, 312
Gordon, D., 82, 305
Graff, H., 83, 89, 304
Granarolo, P., 46, 304
Graves, W., 219, 304
Graziani, G., 60, 147, 304
Grice, H., 227, 304
Grillo, R., 20, 32, 278, 290, 304

Grimaldi, R., 139, 304
Gumperz, J., 298
Gysels, M., 113-115, 206, 292, 295,
          304

Handler R., 27, 135, 304
Hanks, T., 26, 304
Heller, M., 20, 31, 84, 86, 87, 90, 102,
           123, 126, 129, 181,
           205, 206, 213, 262,
           275, 290-292, 304,
           307
Herder, J., 126
Herzfeld, M., 30, 50, 126, 304
Higonnet, P., 83, 84, 126, 305
Hill, J., 28, 32, 112, 113, 151, 155,
           209, 241, 278, 290,
           292, 294, 295, 305
Hill, K., 32, 151, 155, 209, 294, 295
Hélias, P., 304
Hobsbawm, E., 27, 126, 305
Holmes, D., 53, 305
Hudson, A., 302, 305
Humboldt, 126, 128, 129
Hymes , D., 6, 298, 305

Irvine, J., 19, 25, 305

Jacob, J., 82, 305
Jaffe, A., 9, 112, 141, 305
Johnson, S., 76
Joseph, J., 32, 153, 278, 302, 306
Julia, D., 87, 301

King of Aragon 48
Kloss, H., 149, 306
Kristol, A., 91, 306
Kuter, L., 84, 85, 88, 91, 110, 291, 306

Labov, W., 306
Lafont, R., 22, 72, 298, 303, 308
Laponce, J., 102, 306
Leca, P., 233-235, 237-239,241, 244,
           247, 295

Louis-le-Germanique, 82
Luciani, 170, 272, 299
Luedi, G., 32, 82, 84, 306

MacClancy, J., 128, 307
Mahlau, A., 278, 306
Maistrale, 77
Mallory , M., 43, 44
Marcellesi, J., 22, 189, 190, 192, 306,
          307, 312
Marchetti, P., 75-77, 86, 130, 140, 142,
          144-146, 149, 151,
          152, 192, 223, 224,
          293, 303, 307
Mari, P., 180, 229, 0, 230, 231, 233,
          248, 253, 254, 256,
          258, 273
Martin-Gistucci, M., 307
Martin-Jones, M., 206, 307
Marty-Balzagues, J., 110, 307
Mascone, Teatru, 51, 233, 236-238,
          240, 241, 281
Matras, Y., 177, 290, 294, 307
Mauroy, 133, 166
Maynes, J., 85, 291, 307
Mc Connel, G., 306
McClure, J., 220, 245, 307
McConnell-Ginet, S., 24, 301
McDonald, M., 30, 85, 128, 176, 181,
          207-210, 213, 241,
          290, 291, 294, 295,
          307, 309
McKechnie, R., 207, 295, 307
Merler, A., 53-55, 307
Mertz, E., 24, 307
Messenger, J., 51, 291, 308
Mewett, P., 308
Mezzadri, A., 49, 64, 66, 308
Mollard, P., 72, 308
Mondoloni, P., 221, 308
Moore, S., 32, 226, 308
Moracchini, G., 191, 192, 308
Mougeon, E., 207, 295, 308
Multedo, R., 143, 308

Murati, A., 71, 308
Mussolini, B., 138, 283
Myerhoff, B., 226, 308

Napoleon , 75
Nichols, P., 110, 308

Olivesi, P., 53, 55, 64, 187, 309
Ornano, C., 140
Orsoni, C., 53-55, 59, 309
Ottavi, P., 138, 309
Ozouf, F., 89, 303
O'Brien, R., 290, 308

Paoli, P., 48, 76, 83, 131, 265, 299
Parman, S., 51, 291, 309
Peretti, P., 144, 293, 309
Perfettini, F., 155, 192, 193, 204, 220,
          224, 309
Piroddi, J., 181, 309
Poche, B., 6, 84, 136, 245, 248, 293,
          309
Poli, G., 141, 309
Poli, M., 309
Polidori, G., 221, 222, 309
Pomponi, F., 71, 290, 309
Pope Boniface VIII, 48
Preston, D., 222, 223, 295, 309
Prost, A., 85, 291, 309

Quéré, L., 18, 20, 35, 82, 87, 136, 214,
          290, 293, 310

Raffaelli, J., 98
Rampton, B., 20, 24, 25, 103, 114,
          213, 262, 272, 273,
          290, 292, 310
Rancelli, G., 265, 266
Ravis-Giordani, G., 300, 301, 307,
          310
Raymond, A., 58, 84, 299, 308, 310
Reed-Danahay, D., 24, 249, 310
Reershemius, G., 177, 290, 294, 307
Renucci, J., 310

Revel, J., 87, 301
Rocchi, C., 72
Rogers, S., 9, 310
Romaine, S., 97, 310
Roselli-Cecconi , C., 141-144, 310
Roseman, S., 28, 278, 310
Rotily-Forcioli, M., 152, 310

Salvi, S., 80, 81, 310
Sambuccio d'Alando, 48
Sanguinetti, S., 284, 310
Santarelli, P., 290, 310
Santoni, D., 60, 167, 186, 294
Sasse, H., 24, 311
Schiebling, J., 70, 72, 303
Schieffelin, B., 206, 220, 245, 296, 311
Sciacci., R., 66, 264, 267
Scott, J., 311
Scotton, C., 101, 112, 114, 311
Sebba, M., 220, 311
Shapiro, M., 152, 277, 278, 297, 311, 313
Shuman, A., 25, 311
Silverstein, M., 305, 311
Simonpoli, P., 66, 291, 311
Stafford, S., 311
Stefani, 171
Street, B., 14, 101, 240, 290, 311, 312
Susini, M., 312

Tasso, 76
Terdiman, R., 24, 27, 312
Thiers, J., 10, 22, 59, 91, 100, 112, 149, 154-158, 161, 162, 205, 211-213, 215, 216, 240, 251, 252, 254, 256, 265, 276, 296, 312

Thomas, G., 209, 295, 306, 312
Thompson, I., 124, 151, 153, 299, 312
Thompson, J., 312
Tollefson, J., 22, 312
Tommaseo, 76

Trosset, C., 196, 199, 200, 202, 209, 216, 238, 282, 290, 295, 312
Tsitsipis, L., 103, 312

Ungaretti, 76
Urban, G., 17-19, 76, 260, 301, 304, 305, 312
Urciuoli, B., 32, 96, 107, 114, 290, 312
Urla, J., 28, 56, 128, 135, 149, 207, 241, 278, 290, 293, 295, 313

Vermes, G., 88, 112, 297-299, 301, 309, 310, 313
Verscheuren, J., 126, 298
Veuvet, A., 223, 224
Viale, S., 76
Vuillier, 76

Wald, P., 114, 136, 181, 260, 277, 293, 313
Weber, E., 82, 83, 87-89, 313
Weinstein, B., 82, 313
Winer, A., 220, 245, 296, 313
Woelck, W., 313
Woolard, K., 20, 30, 35, 91, 102, 106, 200, 226, 262, 290, 292, 294, 295, 313
Wylie, L., 51, 85, 291, 314

Subject index

Academy, Corsican language, 229, 230, 233, 234, 277
Accademia della Crusca, 72
Accademia di i Stralampati, 249, 253
ADECEC *(see* language planning)
accommodation, linguistic, 102, 265, 272, 282
Aleria, 69
alienation, linguistic, 41, 68, 125, 188, 233, 234, 242, 246, 247, 274, 291 *(see also* insecurity, linguistic)
Annu Corsu, 132
Arritti, 127, 138, 261
attitudes, cultural *(see also* authority, diaspora, identity, kinship and resistance)
- self-interest and motivation, 175, 283
    zero-sum game, 70, 135, 175, 278
attitudes, language, 103, 108, 119, 125, 144, 148, 162, 167–170, 173 *(see also* diglossia, language practice)
- in debate on mandatory Corsican, 172–177, 186, 188
ausbau (see language planning: elaboration)
authenticity *(see also* mandatory Corsican education)
- cultural, 8, 39, 57, 67, 93, 97, 121, 124, 179, 183, 247, 266
- education and, 192, 202–204, 206–9, 213, 275
- linguistic, 121, 124, 143, 148, 149, 152, 153
- local definition of, 177, 187–188, 206, 244
- media/performance and, 237, 252, 262, 266
- problems of, 9, 30, 32, 152, 173–174, 187–189, 208
    front vs. back-region, 204

    inauthenticating error, 8, 201–203, 208
    outer-sphere use, 201–202
- "school"/academic language, 208, 226, 229, 276
authority
- rejection of, 174–176, 246
- sources of linguistic, 208, 229, 282, 283
- school curriculum and, 168–169

Basque, 126, 135, 274, 282, 284, 291
bon usage, 80, 83, 86, 144
Breton, 79, 87, 135, 177, 203, 207, 209, 241, 286, 288–290

Canta u Populu Corsu, 127
Cape Breton Gaelic, 20, 111
Catalan , 27, 141, 278, 288, 290, 291
Chjami è Rispondi, 73
codeswitching, 108–111 *(see also* media practice)
- Corsican–English, 259–261
- Corsican–French, 93, 99, 100, 110, 111, 260, 261
- Corsican–Italian , 73–74
- evaluation, sociolinguistic, 257, 258
- intrasentential, 111, 257
- metaphorical, 26, 109
- sequential unmarked choices, 108
- unmotivated, 110, 111, 256
Conversational Maxims, 223, 227
coofficiality, 18, 29, 130, 161, 189, 270
- CCECV resolution on, 179–185
communities of practice, 18, 32
corpus planning *(see* language planning)
Corsican Regional Assembly, 9–11, 25, 29, 38, 47, 69, 93–95, 101, 128–130, 289 *(see also Lingua Matria* and coofficiality)

- *Cunsigliu Culturale, Suciale è Ecunomicu* 136
- language legislation, 18, 29, 160, 281 (*see also* mandatory Corsican)
  1983 resolution/deliberations, 129, 161, 162, 182, 183
  1985 Castellani motion, 129, 162, 181
  1997 resolution/deliberations, 93, 161, 167, 168, 171
- *Motion du Peuple Corse,* 128
Corsicanness, 8, 12, 29, 38, 43, 51, 70, 181, 202, 212 (*see also* diaspora)
Corsican Studies Institute (*see* University of Corsica)
critical grammar, 156–158
culturels, 4, 6

Detti è Scritti (*see* media practice)
Deixonne law, 8, 126, 128, 129, 136, 144, 159, 166
diaspora, Corsican, 33, 52–66
- *amicales,* 53, 57, 59
- "*U mo figliolu*", 61
- "*O Signora cosa ci hè?*", 64
- *Décalage Horaire,* 56, 265
- departure and return, 55
- exile, discourse of, 56, 57, 60
- identity, 53, 54, 58, 59,
- voting patterns and rights, 63
diglossia, 18–20, 26, 27, 30, 145, 159, 174, 185, 186
- compartmentalization of domains of practice and value, 20, 27, 92, 96
- French–Corsican , 76–78
- intimacy/solidarity 11, 26, 208, 233, 244, 246
- Italian–Corsican, 71–76
- oppositional identity and, 26, 27, 30, 245, 246
- power/distance, 22, 26, 109, 110

economy, Corsican, 50, 51, 67, 106
education

- Corsican language (*see also* language planning, Corsican Regional Assembly, mandatory Corsican education and Deixonne law)
- 1982 Ministry of Education Circular, 129
- 1990 and 1994 contracts with the state, 130
- 1996 survey of, 131
- CAPES, 130
- Corsican Studies classroom (*see* language acquisition and University of Corsica)
- Mediterranean classes, 130
- French
  Corsican language as a handicap in 80–82
  French citizenship and 80, 84, 85
  reconnaissance 85
  grammaire générale 80
  Jules Ferry Law 71
  success and, 81, 82
  language ideologies in (*see* language ideology and nationalism)
  elaboration (*see* language planning)
  ethnography, 284, 285
European Community, Corsican identity and, 137, 183

Falce, A, 215, 221–224
fieldwork, 2–6
Francophone Ontario, 82, 177, 201, 209, 233, 286
francophonie, la, 83, 214
Francorse (*see* mixed forms of language)
Français Régional de Corse (*see* mixed forms of language)
Frenchness, 12, 29, 55, 57, 65, 70, 84, 211
FRC (*see* mixed forms of language)

gallicized Corsican (*see* mixed forms of language)
Galician, 275

Haitian Creole, 202
Hawaii Creole English, 93
hierarchy, linguistic, 13, 28, 30, 157, 158, 202, 209, 248, 272, 276 (see also language ideology; insecurity, linguistic mixed forms of language)
- diglossia and, 23, 72
- French–Corsican, 17–19
- Italian–Corsican, 72
- language legislation and, 172
- performance and, 261, 268
history, Corsican, 43–44
hybridity, 14, 19, 25, 31, 118, 178, 207, 273 (*see also* mixed forms of language)

identity
- Corsican language and (*see* language acquisition, language ideology, language practices, mandatory Corsican education and nationalism)
- cultural (*see* Corsicanness, diaspora, kinship, authenticity, authority)
- French (*see* education, Frenchness and nationalism)
- monolingual/monocultural norms, 2, 24, 78, 117, 190
- mixed, blended, hybrid, plural, 17, 29, 32, 179, 189, 210, 247, 270
- oppositional, 13, 19, 30, 159, 173, 270, 278
internal colonialism (*see* nationalism)
insecurity, linguistic, 24, 63, 84, 86, 109, 155, 187, 198, 224, 234, 237, 247, 274, 291 (*see also* alienation, linguistic; language competence)
- language classes, in, 7, 201, 202, 210, 248
islandness, 17, 33, 35, 36, 57

Italian
- anti-Italianist position, 141–144
- closeness to, 73, 141, 199
- diglossic relationship with, 71–76
- differentiation from (*see* language ideology)
- linguistic comparison, 74–76
- metalinguistic judgments, 134, 135, 199, 288
- promotion of, 29, 135, 137–140
- speaking it defined, 73, 76, 134
- as a literary register, 72–73
Italians, perceptions of, 133–135, 288
Italy
- boundaries with, 134, 139
- cultural partnership, 71
- "natural" connections with, 32, 137, 138
- RCFM and, 26, 263, 264

kinship, 17, 44, 46–48
- clan, the, 49-52
Kyrn, 127, 261

language activism (*see also* language ideology, linguistic diversity, nationalism)
- corpus planning, 23, 215, 276
- eighties, in the, 128–130
- elaboration, 19, 144–146, 273
- language legislation (*see* Corsican Regional Assembly and education)
- linguistic associations
    Lingua Corsa, 126
    Scola Corsa, 8, 107, 126, 127, 151, 177, 200, 249
    ADECEC, 8, 127, 130, 148, 219, 228, 242, 250, 291
- officialization, 18, 33, 120, 129, 173, 184, 233, 247
- nineties, in the, 130–131
- normalization, 23, 24, 28, 126, 145, 185, 214, 218, 240, 247, 274,

280, 282 *(see also* standardization literacy, orthography)
- seventies, in the, 126–128
- standardization, 7, 25, 136, 210, 215, 222, 273, 277–281, 286 *(see also* normalization)

language acquisition, Corsican *(see also* education)
- Corsicans', 200-213, 191, 200, 206 *(see also* authenticity)
- ethnographer's, 41, 191-200, 204
- learners as performers, 196, 204
- non-Corsican speakers', 192, 260

language competence, in Corsican *(see also* language acquisition; language practices; insecurity, linguistic; media practice) 18, 117, 147, 170, 227, 237, 238, 244, 248, 282
- education and, 204–206, 208, 210, 212 *(see also* authenticity)
- evaluation of others, 100, 102, 181, 187, 194–199, 202, 290
- self-evaluation, 91, 97–106 *(see also* language practices)

language ideology *(see also* diglossia, language activism, legitimacy, monolingual norm, nationalism, polynomy)
- autonomous codes, 24, 32, 150, 154, 219, 246
    boundary-marking, 9, 146, 158, 179, 187, 189, 193, 198, 258, 275, 285
- differentiation from Italian, 132–136, 140, 142–144
- dominant, 9, 16, 23, 29, 31, 119, 120, 157, 158, 189, 247, 273, 275
- essentialism, 70, 117, 137, 140, 144, 158, 160, 173, 200, 275 *(see also* coofficiality, mother tongue, nationalism and purism)
    biological, 120, 121, 122, 125, 143, 159, 190
    strategic, 121, 122, 126, 142, 143, 160, 161

- form, linguistic, 29, 31, 80, 117, 131, 137, 139, 151, 153   *(see also bon usage,* political economy, resistance)
    French, 17, 18, 23, 85, 117, 278
    legitimation and, 277, 289
    pedagogy and, 9, 10, 204, 209, 212
    orthography and, 215, 216
- linguistic unity, role of, 17, 23, 25, 78, 79, 122, 131, 136, 144–146, 185
- plural *(see* polynomy)
- social position and, 120

language practices, 87–93, 101, 103–108, 279
- language choice, 7, 11, 12, 22, 46, 49 *(see also* codeswitching)
    markedness, 97, 98, 102, 203
    politeness norms, 86, 87, 102, 103, 255, 282
    political identity and, 14, 21, 23, 30, 93, 97, 98, 124, 241, 280, 288
- outer sphere, 93, 94, 100, 101
- political nature of, 6, 7, 9, 25, 30, 93, 202–204, 209, 280, 281, 288

language shift, 1, 18, 20, 23, 71, 118, 199, 206, 256 *(see also* diglossia, education)
- from above, 106–108
- language legislation, 166, 173, 174
- language practice, effect on, 87, 88, 90
- legitimation and, 274, 275, 278, 282, 284
- nationalism and, 125, 145

langue du mot, 98, 99, 100
langue du pain, 97
legitimacy, cultural, 51, 213
legitimacy, linguistic, 141, 146, 152, 154, 168, 170, 171, 272, 276, 282 *(see also* authenticity, form and language ideology)

– education, in, 9, 201, 202, 210, 213
  (see also language acquisition)
– orthography and, 215, 216, 238, 246
– polynomic, 184, 187, 188
– problems of , 277–283
Lingua Corsa (*see* language activism)
Lingua Matria, 18, 29, 161, 177–179,
  181, 183, 189, 272
linguistic diversity, 8, 17, 25, 121, 143,
  145, 146, 161, 188, 208, 241, 246,
  251 (*see also* education, language
  planning, mandatory language education, orthography, polynomy)
linguistic marketplace (*see* political
economy of language)
linguistic terrorism, 79, 237
literacy (*see also* orthography)
– French, 79
– Corsican, 186, 215, 222–224, 227,
  233, 247, 249, 266, 270, 277
Louisiana French, 212, 217

mandatory Corsican language education,
  161–179
– opposition to, 170–178 (*see also*
  mother tongue)
– support for, 163–167
Main Basse sur Une Île, 68, 125, 144,
  158
media practice (*see also* Italian)
– blurring of linguistic boundaries and,
  247, 268
– codeswitching in, 253–258, 260
– competence and politeness in,
254–256, 264
– dedramatization of dominance, 3,
  247, 252
– ludic quality, 249–253
– mixed forms of language in, 248,
  252, 253, 267–269
– newspaper, 262
– television, 130, 214, 260
– theater, 261–262
– radio

audience evaluations of, 256,
  258, 266–269
A Viva Voce, 127, 130
RCFM, 130, 214, 248–269
RCI, 130
purism and, 266–268, 270
metadiscourse, 14, 15, 31, 43, 92, 174,
  273
Mexicano, 211, 212, 186
military and French language acquisition, 72, 84, 118
mixed forms of language, 15, 30 (*see
  also* codeswitching, hybridity and
  media practice)
– Francorse, 86, 112–115, 154, 158,
  187, 269
– French calques, 149, 153, 203,
  208, 209
– FRC, 111–114, 211
– gallicisms, in Corsican, 8, 9, 125,
  205, 147, 252, 288, 114–116
– "interference", 1 25, 153, 209, 211,
  257, 258
– malapropisms, 211, 258, 268, 291
– stigma and, 15, 31, 187, 212, 268,
  274
monocultural norm, 2, 189
monolingual norm, 2, 25, 78, 117, 161,
  180, 202, 212, 237, 269, 283 (*see
  also* authenticity, language ideology, legitimacy)
– challenges to, 18, 161, 176, 183,
  189
mother tongue, 8, 80, 95, 143, 161,
  173, 183, 189, 191, 202, 212, 237,
  269, 284
– language learning and, 205, 207,
  247
– Lingua Matria, vs., 176–178
– national identity and, 84, 85
– orthography and, 216
– blaming women for language shift,
  107, 108
Motion du Peuple Corse 128

nationalism, Corsican, 1, 11. 12. 66–69
- internal colonialism , 57, 68
- language ideology, 15, 16, 23, 24, 84–85, 125, 131, 132
- *Main Basse Sur une Île,* 68
nationalism, French language, 78–80, 128
neologisms, 148, 266
normalization (*see* language planning)

officialization (*see* language planning)
orthodoxies, linguistic, 175, 272
orthography, 9, 10, 11, 216(*see also* authenticity, authority, language ideology, literacy)
- *A Falce,* 214, 221, 223, 224
- ADECEC roundtable on, 219, 242
- Corsican Spelling Contest, 222, 227, 229, 232, 233, 222–225, 230, 233 (*see also* authenticity, linguistic diversity)
- esthetics of , 220, 242, 243
- *Ghjustra Paesana,* 250
- *Intricciate è Cambiarini,* 126, 218, 219, 220, 223, 243
- linguistic differentiation, 216–218
- legitimacy, 216, 217, 222
- regional variation and ,237–245
- social control, 216, 217
- Spelling Championship, International Francophone, 214, 233
- unity of language and, 239–241
otherness, 17, 33, 45, 58, 59, 272, 273, 285

paghjella, 127
partitu (*see* clan)
performance, 31, 47, 112, 153, 196, 209, 236, 256, 259–263, 278
- linguistic performance variables, 73, 204
pied-noir, 69
political economy of language, 12, 16, 25, 26, 29, 77, 78, 86, 110, 158, 280

polynomy, 18, 29, 161, 184–190, 234, 270, 275, 281, 282, 288 (*see also* mixed forms of language)
polyphony (see *paghjella*)
pronunciation, 75, 76, 89, 99, 113, 116, 117, 134, 151, 153, 173, 208, 211, 237, 290 (*see also* purism)
- orthography and, 219, 220, 24, 243, 251, 252
purism, minority language , 25, 146–152, 204, 205, 247, 267, 273, 274 (*see also* mixed forms of language, pronunciation, sociolinguistics, stress patterns)

reconnaissance, 14, 86 (*see also* education)
resistance, 16, 20, 21, 32, 158, 172, 202, 221, 247, 274, 283, 286
- popular resistance/counter resistance, 1, 25, 26, 161, 281
- of reversal, 2, 23, 24, 173, 244, 275
- of separation, 2, 25–27, 51, 119, 160, 161, 190, 245, 273
- radical, 29, 38, 271
- to authority/imposition, 24, 28, 45, 46, 48, 246
Resistance, World War II, 44, 59
Revolution, French, 78, 79, 122
Rigiru, 8
Scola Corsa (*see* language planning)
semispeakers, 101, 194, 197, 206
Serment de Strasbourg, 78
seventies generation, 6
slim texts, 99, 100
social relations, Corsican, 3, 15, 16, 20, 26, 39, 43, 46, 49, 65 (*see also* attitudes, kinship, village)
sociolinguists (vs. purists), 1, 18, 146, 152–156
standardization (*see* language activism)
stereotypes of Corsicans, negative, 45
storytelling, bilingual, 260, 262

stress, syllabic, 116, 148, 166, 203, 210, 237

strikes, 36, 45

Stylized Asian English, 21, 258, 268

Teatru Mascone, 47, 229–234, 237, 246, 274, 277, 297

terre-mère, 35

Tuscan (*see* Italian)

University of Corsica, 2, 105, 127, 174

– Corsican Studies Institute 4, 7, 9, 130, 185

– Corsican language classes 7, 9, 200–216

village life, 2–4, 17, 37–43, 65, 101–103, 198

Villers-Cotterets, edict of, 79

verbal hygiene (see puristm)

voting patterns, 46

Welsh, 192, 195, 196, 234, 278, 282

Language, Power and Social Process

Edited by Monica Heller and Richard J. Watts

Mouton de Gruyter · Berlin · New York

Srikant Sarangi and Celia Roberts
(Editors)

Talk, Work and Institutional Order
Discourse in Medical, Mediation and
Management Settings
Cloth. ISBN 3-11-015723-3
Paperback. ISBN 3-11-015722-5
(Language, Power and Social Process 1)

This book takes an interdisciplinary approach to talk and its role in creating workplace practice and relationships. Analytic tools drawn from ethnography, conversation analysis, interactional sociolinguistics and discourse analysis illuminate a range of workplace discourses from medical, mediation and management settings (e.g., hospital rounds, divorce mediation, enterprise bargaining).

The book consists of fourteen specially commissioned contributions to address the thematic focus of how professional knowledge and identities are constituted in discourse vis-à-vis a given institutional order. These discourse practices shed light on what it is to be a member of a profession and how the lives of both clients and professions are affected by institutional processes. In addition to both, clients and professions are affected by institutional processes. In addition to the theoretical insights into workplace discourse and an extended editorial introduction, the final section of the book debates methodological issues and the need to combine disciplinary rigour with diversity.

This book will be a key text for graduate students as well as for lecturers and researchers across a range of disciplines: sociolinguistics, sociology, culture and communication studies, applied linguistics.

Language, Power and Social Process

Edited by Monica Heller and Richard J. Watts

Mouton de Gruyter · Berlin · New York

Jan Blommaert
(Editor)

Language Ideological Debates

Cloth. ISBN 3-11-016350-0
Paperback. ISBN 3-11-016349-7
(Language, Power and Social Process 2)

Language Ideological Debates presents analyses of historically situated discursive events – debates – during which ideas about language are formed, articulated, and authoritatively entextualized. The studies cover cases as diverse as Corsica, the US, Singapore and Congo. Based on detailed empirical analyses, the book intends to fuel the theoretical discussion on language, history, and society.
The studies aim at offering insights in the concrete human-agentive and sociopolitical dimensions of language history, thus enriching the historiography of language with more mature insights in the dynamics of power and politics.